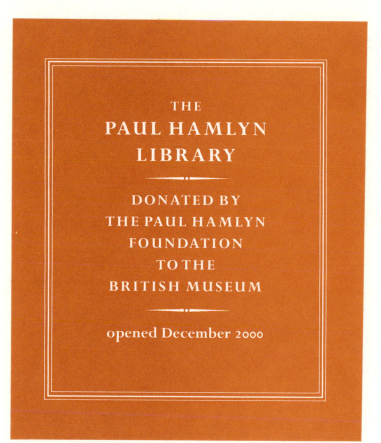

REFUSE AND DISPOSAL
AT AREA 16 EAST, RUNNYMEDE

REFUSE AND DISPOSAL AT AREA 16 EAST RUNNYMEDE

Runnymede Bridge
Research Excavations, Volume 2

STUART NEEDHAM AND TONY SPENCE

with major contributions by
Dale Serjeantson and Marie-Louise Stig Sørensen

and further contributions by
Janet Ambers, Caroline Cartwright, Mike Cowell, Rowena Gale,
Lorrain Higbee, Sylvia Humphrey,
Morven Leese, Ian Longworth,
Gillian Varndell and Sue Wales

and line drawings by
Stephen Crummy, Phil Dean, Karen Hughes
and Meredydd Moores

Published for the Trustees of the British Museum
by British Museum Press

© 1996 The Trustees of the British Museum

First published in 1996 by British Museum Press
A division of The British Museum Company Ltd
46 Bloomsbury Street, London WC1B 3QQ

A catalogue record for this book is available from the British Library

ISBN 0 7141 2307 2

Designed by John Hawkins
Typeset in Ehrhardt
Printed in Great Britain by Henry Lings

Contents

Contents

List of Plates

List of Figures

List of Tables

Acknowledgements

As the first full publication to appear in the Research Excavations series, this volume offers us an ideal opportunity to thank key individuals and organisations who facilitated the British Museum campaign. First and foremost we should acknowledge the support received from various people at the Museum, in particular Dr Ian Longworth as Keeper of Prehistoric and Romano-British Antiquities. Equally essential was permission to excavate from the Department of the Environment and Transport (South-East Regional Office), as landowners, and scheduled monument consent from English Heritage. We are indebted to both bodies and personnel involved, especially Mrs R. Lambourne and Mr G. Cocksedge (DOT) and Roger Thomas (EH). We had a number of occasions to be grateful for the enduring interest of Michael O'Dwyer at the adjacent Runnymede Hotel.

Of special note for this volume was a financial contribution made by Associated Leisure Hotels Ltd (owners of the Runnymede Hotel) in 1985 which funded much of Sørensen's detailed pottery study. Further vital financial support came from a Leverhulme grant won to allow Serjeantson's detailed taphonomic study of the Area 16 animal bones.

As always, the relative success of a large excavation project hangs on the capabilities and dedication of the excavation team. I wish to seize this opportunity to express my warmest thanks to all who excavated at Runnymede and most especially to the staff, who helped tread the difficult path between maintaining research standards and covering significant ground. On this occasion, in the context of Area 16, I wish to single out the sterling contributions of Dr Marie-Louise Stig Sørensen as area supervisor, Dr Phil Mason as her assistant (1986) and Cath Price and Julie Carr for their masterly control of the finds hut under all pressures.

Amongst the many individuals who played a part in the post-excavation process we would like to mention Dr Peter Main for his help with computerisation of the levels data, Nick Ashton and John McNabb for advice on the flintwork, Robin Sanderson for helping Sylvia Humphrey with certain petrographic identifications, and Marie-Louise Stig Sørensen would like to thank Steve Trout for advice and Chris Evans for discussion. Tim Clark and Usha Woochit are to be thanked for their help in producing the volume, as are the team of illustrators in Prehistoric and Romano-British Antiquities for the splendid series of line drawings. Tony Spence would like to thank Stuart Needham for his help and guidance on the many facets of Runnymede post-ex.

Dale Serjeantson is greatly indebted to A. J. Legge, Centre for Extra-Mural Studies, Birkbeck College, University of London, for his interest and encouragement and for providing facilities for the work. She also warmly thanks M. A. L. Bracegirdle, Centre for Extra-Mural Studies, and Virginia Smithson, Medieval and Later Antiquities, British Museum, who assisted with bone recording. The Department of Archaeology at Southampton University is thanked for its support.

Abbreviations

The Contributors

Janet Ambers, Department of Scientific Research, British Museum.

Caroline Cartwright, Department of Scientific Research, British Museum.

Mike Cowell, Department of Scientific Research, British Museum.

Rowena Gale, Chute Cadley, Hampshire.

Lorrain Higbee, *ex* Department of Geography, University College, London.

Sylvia Humphrey, Department of Scientific Research, British Museum.

Morven Leese, *ex* Department of Scientific Research, British Museum.

Ian Longworth, *ex* Department of Prehistoric and Romano-British Antiquities, British Museum.

Stuart Needham, Department of Prehistoric and Romano-British Antiquities, British Museum.

Dale Serjeantson, Faunal Remains Unit, Department of Archaeology, University of Southampton.

Marie-Louise Stig Sørensen, Faculty of Archaeology and Anthropology, University of Cambridge.

Tony Spence, Department of Prehistoric and Romano-British Antiquities, British Museum.

Gillian Varndell, Department of Prehistoric and Romano-British Antiquities, British Museum.

Sue Wales, Institute of Archaeology, University College, London.

Prefixes for catalogued artefacts

AM	Amber
B	Bone/antler
C	Clay artefacts (including refractories)
FL	Flint
M	Metalwork
NP	Neolithic pottery
P	LBA pottery
S	Stone

Abbreviations for dimensions in artefact catalogues

B	Breadth
D	Depth
d	Diameter
E	Extant
L	Length
M	Maximum
T	Thickness
W	Width
wt	Weight

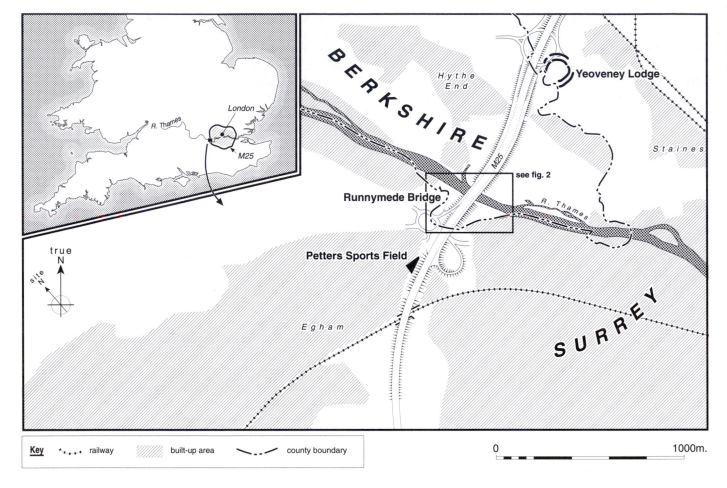

Key: ∙∙∙∙∙ railway   ▨ built-up area   ⌐·⌐·⌐ county boundary

0   1000m.

Fig. 1 *Location map of Runnymede Bridge, Berkshire.*

Summary

British Museum research excavations in the small zone of Area 16 East yielded an astonishingly rich assemblage of Neolithic and Late Bronze Age material, even by the standards of the Runnymede Bridge site (see fig. 2). For the later period a thick body of dark earth was found to contain an unusual density of artefact clusters and small structures such as burnt clay beds. Lower down many of the Neolithic finds were concentrated in a thinner deposit regarded as an undisturbed soil profile. Similar but more abraded Neolithic material was recovered from overlying alluvial deposits of gravel and silt. Generally artefact remains were diverse with particularly good representation of pottery, animal bones, fired clay, burnt flint and foreign stone. Less frequent finds include flintwork, portable clay objects, copper and lead alloy objects, amber beads, worked bone and antler, charred remains, charcoal and coprolites. All but charred plant remains are described in this volume.

The methods employed during the research excavation campaign of 1984–89 are outlined, as are the definitions of context types. These will remain applicable to future volumes concerned with the cultural deposits at Runnymede.

The main thrust of the research reported here has been to identify variation in formation processes through the detailed study of taphonomy and gross assemblage composition. This had the further objective of modelling refuse cycles and drawing conclusions on the changing activity status of the zone. It is recognised that these are necessary preliminaries to the proper evaluation of temporal changes in the formal characteristics of finds, notably style/fabric changes in pottery, or species representation amongst the animal bones. The taphonomic aspects of the dominant categories (pottery, animal bone, fired clay, worked stone) were considered. The pottery in particular was susceptible to a range of attribute analyses involving abrasion, sherd size, intra- and inter-context joins at various scales, which in combination yield much information on the refuse cycles experienced prior to incorporation in these deposits.

A number of theoretical and methodological points are developed in order to conceptualise better the relationship of recovered material to refuse cycles. It was found necessary to define a series of terms to aid articulation of the complex processes (both systemic and transformational) involved. The utility of the term *midden* is given particular attention; the conclusion drawn is that this should be retained for deposits exhibiting particular characteristics rather than being applied loosely to all relatively refuse-rich contexts. It is argued in conclusion that part of the dark earth sequence in Area 16 East can be regarded as *midden* deposits, but that other in situ deposits featuring high refuse densities were formed through processes of *undirected refuse aggregation*. These deliberations lead on to a consideration of the cause and meaning of 'midden sites' dating to the early part of the first millennium BC.

Specific conclusions for the Neolithic material in Area 16 East are reserved for future consideration owing to the relatively limited evidence. However, much interpretation was possible for the Late Bronze Age sequence despite the small size of the excavation trench. Early activity is attended by post holes and relatively sparse finds in a buried soil profile (unit G), on which dark earth began to accumulate around 800 cal BC on the evidence of radiocarbon. The ceramic sequence argues for a duration of several decades at least for the ensuing deposits.

A series of concentrated dumps of refuse quickly led to midden formation with the repeated accumulation of material. Yet specialised activity was taking place amongst this accumulating refuse in the preparation of materials for pottery manufacture and probably even its firing. Pottery production is attested not only by tools, but also by in situ clusters and structures. Higher in the midden (unit J) there was a distinctive horizon rich in pot groups for which an interpretation as *provisional refuse* is advanced. Subsequent accumulation (unit K) was of a different character and is regarded as *undirected refuse aggregation* and this deposit was truncated by flood action and partially infiltrated by redeposited LBA material (units L & M).

As with previously studied assemblages, pig bones continue to be well represented and this gives an opportunity for a thorough consideration of the possible backgrounds to pig-keeping in economic and social terms.

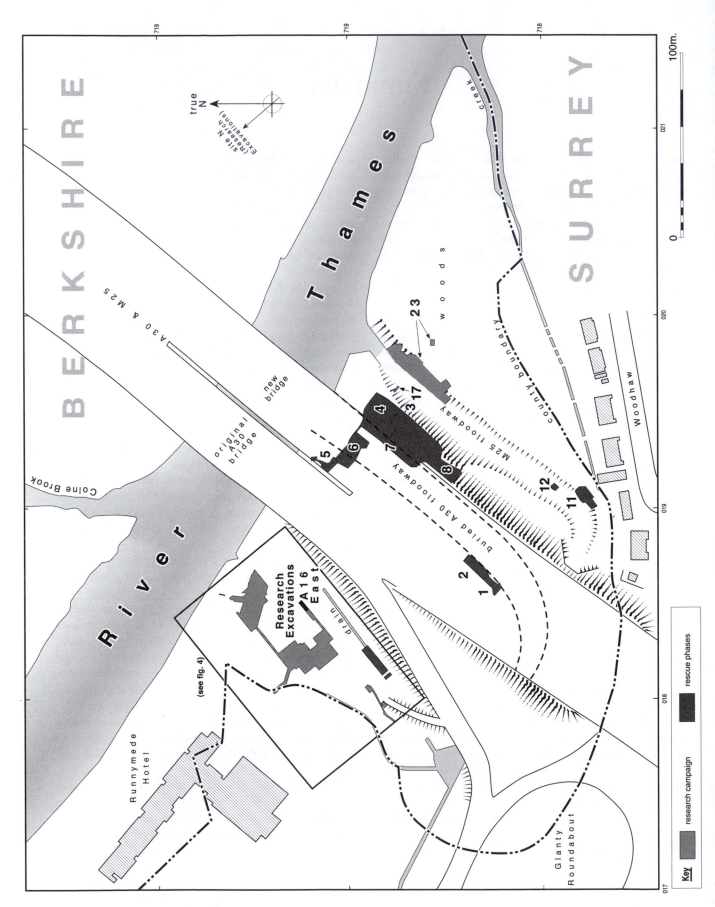

Fig. 2 *Runnymede Bridge: site plan (1:2000). Showing Areas 1–2 (1975/6), Areas 4–8 (1978), Areas 9–12 (1980) and the research excavations, Areas 13–32 (1984–89) with Area 16 East highlighted.*

CHAPTER 1

The study of occupation refuse and deposits

STUART NEEDHAM

In recent years there has been a growing appreciation that occupation refuse, as one of the major archaeological sources, is worthy of study in its own right. This has demanded a change in approach in order to view the objects as categories of refuse rather than as simply the intrinsic materials and forms that they represent. In settlement sites, amongst others, this avenue of enquiry is now widely understood to be integral to the proper understanding of formation processes; its earlier neglect has certainly led to an over-simplified conception of the way objects and deposits relate to the living world of the settlement. This volume is ostensibly an excavation report, but we offer it also as a contribution towards the deepening enquiry into the nature of archaeological evidence and, therefore, towards the development of necessary methodologies to enable a better construction of the past living system. We are working primarily from the archaeological residues specific to the particular site, and this empirical side will inevitably not be easily married with ethnoarchaeologically derived data or purely theoretical frameworks. We are not, however, working in a theoretical vacuum, indeed we have attempted where it seemed relevant and necessary to inject some fresh theoretical constructs into the analytical process. Some elements of this volume may thus have wider ramifications.

The key at Runnymede that has undeniably opened up rich interpretative possibilities is the single fact of the extensive preservation of in situ deposits. This may seem a very basic point of characterisation, but we should not underestimate its fundamental importance. It is our view that without such extensive survival many essential lines of enquiry about the workings of settlements in general and this one in particular would be ruled out. The constraints imposed as soon as occupation deposits are more than minimally transformed by cultural and natural processes are considerable. Indeed it is only through the study of in situ assemblages that we can begin to see the extent to which we are being misled by apparent interrelationships on less well-preserved sites. It may be depressing to acknowledge great limitations on the interpretative scope of some sites, but it is nevertheless necessary that archaeology should face up to potentially serious consequences. We are not of course saying that sites well endowed with in situ deposits can somehow act as archetypes, but they may offer some salutary points which can be legitimately used for the process of studying other sites. It is equally vital to pose the question, is the very existence of a site such as Runnymede actually a product of a set of formation processes which were not commonplace, even in the particular period setting? If this notion proved to have any substance, then it would deny further the validity of extrapolating site-specific *interpretations* from the Runnymede evidence for the purposes of explaining less well-preserved sites.

Having stressed the paramount importance of in situ evidence, it is incumbent upon us to state what perhaps is self-evident. We have arrived at the conclusion that certain deposits at Runnymede are in situ (in our terms – see definition below); this is of course an interpretation, albeit based on many branches of evidence and in-depth study. It is for each archaeologist to see how we have constructed the argument and decide whether he/she finds agreement with that broad, but essential, classification.

Terminology

Most of this chapter is concerned with terms relating to settlements and their refuse. It is worth clarifying initially one or two broader terms which are relevant to the state of preservation of the archaeological deposits at Runnymede. At a general level the site can be described as a *sealed site*. This means little more than that the archaeological materials are engulfed in a sediment matrix, thus geologically in situ (Butzer 1982, 104). There is a danger that a sealed site is treated automatically as having archaeologically in situ deposits but this does not necessarily follow. This problem has been noted in the specific context of alluvial sites elsewhere (Macklin and Needham 1992, 12–13).

The use of the term in situ does in fact vary even in archaeological parlance (e.g. Schiffer 1987, 17). Sometimes it is used to connote that material is in the locus of its production or use, a relationship which is otherwise described by terms such as 'primary'. Alternatively the term in situ is used merely to indicate that deposits, which may be of variable character, are free of significant disturbance from later transformations, whether cultural or natural. This is the sense in which we employ in situ in the Runnymede project for the artefacts and deposits at large. In situ needs to have a different sense, however, in the case of structural elements. Here in situ means specifically that the structure or component thereof is believed to be situated at the place where constructed and used in antiquity: for example, in situ burnt post base, in situ hearth or oven, or in situ wall footings of clay or stone. It will be appreciated that these definitions can lead to situations where structural components not in situ may nevertheless occur within in situ deposits along with an in situ finds assemblage.

At Runnymede we can demonstrate that the process of sealing has given rise to the survival of extensive in situ material, as well as much transformed material. The one remarkable feature of the site which explains much else that appears to place it apart is the sheer extent of survival of in situ deposits. In this respect it is matched by very few prehistoric sites in Britain, e.g. Potterne (Gingell and Lawson 1985; Lawson 1994) and East Chisenbury (Brown *et al* 1994). Virtually every investigated part of the site at Runnymede (projected to be 1.5 or more hectares) has yielded a continuous bed of in situ deposits, although obviously variable in thickness and detailed character. Thus the site is marked by extensive old land surfaces covered by in situ deposits. This stands in contrast to the more typical situation on other sites with the survival of pockets of in situ deposits in ditches and pits, in the lee of ramparts, under earthworks or in hut platforms cut into slopes.

The basic aim of the combined analyses presented in Chapters 4–6, 10 and 12 is to understand the nature of the formation processes responsible along with something of the earlier history of the finds. The broad composition of unit assemblages in terms of material categories is one important and often neglected area of characterisation (Chapter 6). In addition, three materials – bone, pottery and fired clay – were studied separately in much greater depth because they are both prolific in quantity and sensitive to the identification of progressive degradation when under attrition of various kinds. The distribution and condition of other materials will be drawn in to the overall interpretation as relevant. It is worth stressing at this point that the interpretative potential of all in situ deposits should be regarded as essentially similar, regardless of differences in the quantity, quality and disposition of the material inclusions.

Analysis of occupation material, especially when prodigious as at Runnymede, is becoming more complex with several possible lines of enquiry. As yet, however, little standardised terminology has been generated and we find it essential to start by defining a series of terms. Their formulation obviously owes much to the Runnymede experience, but the intention is that most could be employed for a variety of site analyses; these add to as well as qualify terms defined previously, notably by Schiffer (1987). The terms are a mixture of 'descriptive' labels based primarily on observation in the field and 'interpretative' labels referring to the status of refuse, the context or the activity represented. Methods used to arrive at these interpretations are described individually for relevant materials (Chapters 4, 8, 10, and 12). In reality every term introduced in this section is interpretative. The point of providing definitions is not to lend credence to an 'objective' system, but instead to allow the reader to know exactly what we mean when we employ a particular term.

Figure 3 shows the relationships between the various terms employed, which divide loosely into those that deal primarily with soil matrix and those that deal primarily with contained finds. Although sedimentary particles and artefacts are clearly distinct elements whose association need not imply contemporaneous arrival at the locus (e.g. Matthews 1993), they are both integral parts of an 'archaeological deposit' which can be regarded as the appropriate analytical unit for identifying formation processes (Schiffer 1987, 265–7).

Settlement/occupation

We regard these as essentially synonymous terms, one referring to the physical substance of a settlement, the other to the act of living there. Obviously occupation takes place at many scales and firm distinctions will not be easily drawn. We would not however consider desultory use of a site, or stopping over on it, to constitute occupation (in this respect we prefer not to follow Schiffer (1987, 100)), whereas a short-stay seasonal site is a particular kind of settlement. Evidence for food consumption is not on its own sufficient to identify occupation, since this will often take place at other activity areas, in the fields or down mines for example. Evidence for food preparation is a useful further indicator, although we must allow that certain aspects of food preparation occur at places of procurement, away from a settlement.

In essence a settlement is seen to provide living and sleeping quarters for a significant portion of the day, season and year. We expect thus to recognise structures (appropriate to the socio-economic context) which were primarily for dwelling, with the optional addition of others for storage, cooking, penning of livestock and specialised activities. It is clear that no simple definition of settlement would be wisely ventured, but that the conjunction of various aspects referred to above will give added confidence to the recognition of a settlement and

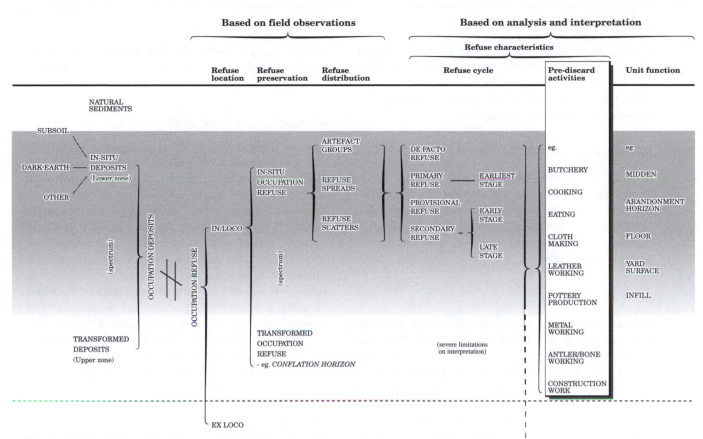

Fig. 3 *The interrelationship of terms relating to occupation deposits and refuse.*

its occupation. This does then mean that the sites capable of yielding a variety of well-preserved evidence are those that will best allow distinctions to be drawn. Surface sites yielding, for example, only a spread of flintwork will not readily lend themselves to the discrimination of occupation (long- or short-term) from a specialised activity area, e.g. a butchery site or knapping zone.

Occupation deposits

A general term for soil, sediment or surface contexts associated directly with evidence (structural/artefactual) for occupation. The deposits may be effectively un-altered, thus retaining the contemporary stratigraphy of formation, or be transformed to varying degrees by subsequent natural or cultural agencies. The sequence in which 'associated' artefact and sediment components come to form a deposit is a matter of great importance in interpretation, but does not affect the application of this general label. We note Matthews' reservations about the term occupation deposit (1993), but see no difficulty in accepting it as useful, once adequately defined.

In situ occupation deposits

In situ deposits are left as formed by human activity. Deposits may have been subjected to micro-turbation,

but disturbance must be limited thus leaving the tang-ible evidence of internal structure relating to episodes of accumulation. In situ deposits may be defined regardless of their spatial extent; on many sites they might survive just in pockets. Care must be taken not to mistake patterning created by post-depositional agencies for original structure of formation (Schiffer 1987,131, 234).

Transformed occupation deposits

Deposits still include occupation refuse, but reworking (by any agency) is sufficient to have severely distorted or removed stratigraphic markers and potentially re-sorted material components into a 'false' stratigraphy. Essen-tially this is to do with later reworking, after occupation. How distinct this material is from in situ occupation deposits will inevitably depend on the particular assemblage and site and the transformations that acted on it. At Runnymede there tends to be a relatively abrupt transition, but gradational change might be more general.

It is of course accepted that natural agencies, as well as cultural ones, may be at work on deposits during a period of occupation and may result in some modific-ation. We have to work on the basis that the balance and character of inputs (natural and anthropogenic) will allow some boundary to be drawn between those relevant to contemporary formation and those relevant to subsequent transformations. Transformed deposits have often been described in the past as reworked deposits. We avoid this term here because 'reworking' of refuse and matrix is a dominant feature in contemporary formation and would thus invite confusion.

Lower/upper zone

Because of a fairly clear twofold division in the Runnymede Late Bronze Age deposits the terms *lower zone* and *upper zone* have been coined in the past (e.g. Needham and Sørensen 1988); these are effectively synonymous with in situ deposits and transformed deposits respectively.

Dark earth

Dark earth is a term which has mainly been associated with deposits in late Roman to Medieval urban sites characterised by their dark colour and apparent homogeneity (Courty *et al* 1989, 261). Such deposits can be thick (e.g. up to 2 m) and extensive; 7 hectares of migration period dark earth survives on the island of Birka, Sweden (Ambrosiani and Clarke 1992). Much of the Runnymede lower zone has at least a superficial similarity, but whether of similar origin remains to be seen. Some variation may exist in terms of artefact quantities; Runnymede dark earth, for example, contains much greater densities than reported for London deposits. Such differences may have more to do with the superimposed level and type of cultural activity than with the origin of the soil 'type'. It may be worthwhile ultimately to seek a distinction between dark earth formed after the abandonment of sites, largely from the collapse of structures and the collection of wind- and water-carried detritus, and that originating during occupation from the continued dumping of organic matter and a cycle of building demolition, decay and reconstruction. This could, for example, provide one possible cause of significant differences in artefact quantitites.

Courty *et al* felt that the mechanisms responsible for dark earth were likely to be 'ubiquitous', deriving partly from repeated decay of insubstantial building materials mixed with debris from burning and organic matter, partly from refuse (1989, 268). A degree of homogeneity was created through intensive faunal reworking, but Farrington and Bateman (1992, 190) have suggested that a range of less obvious differences may still survive to reflect a real stratigraphic sequence.

The rich artefactual evidence from the Runnymede dark earth (typified in the studies presented here) gives weight to the partial retention of stratigraphy, but there is a danger that sites with a lower artefact yield may not easily allow that to be recognised. There is the further question as to whether the fine material (i.e. mainly sediment) will quite independently be re-sorted to varying degrees according to site environment.

Sub-soil/buried land surfaces

This is difficult to define unequivocally because of potential infiltration of material into any original land surface. At Runnymede there is generally a rather rapid change seen in a marked diminution of finds and a lightening of soil colour at the base of dark earth deposits. This underlying lighter soil/silt tends to contain a scatter of finds which peters out downwards very quickly. For convenience it is termed sub-soil, although it is accepted that it may only approximate to an original sub-soil beneath the land surface on which the cultural activity took place or cultural material first accumulated. Neither is the term intended to be specific in terms of the former A and B horizons of the buried soil profile. Validation of a 'sub-soil' appellation will depend on a variety of factors including the penetrability of the soil matrix (Schiffer 1987, 126 ff), the rates of refuse accumulation at the locus and the processes to which it was subjected, e.g. worm incorporation or trampling. (A detailed micromorphological study of several soil profiles at Runnymede is to be presented by Limbrey in Volume 1).

Occupation refuse

This is a generic term for the assemblage associated with occupation deposits. It is the material fall-out of human occupation activities, viz artefacts, structural remnants, charcoal, food and related organic detritus. As always, context is crucial and the simple presence of one or more such materials is not in itself sufficient to determine an 'occupation deposit'.

Occupation refuse should *derive* from settlement activities, but need not always mark the settlement locus. The case will be clear-cut when, as at Runnymede, there is abundant evidence for everyday human activities, dwellings and other structures. Where such evidence is lacking, for example domestic-like refuse in a barrow mound or chamber-fill, interpretation becomes more tentative, but obviously there is a strong chance that such material is *ex loco*.

The term has no bearing on the extent to which activities are seen to serve purely subsistence ends or to have ritual components; nor is the scale or pattern of residence considered relevant (e.g. seasonal versus permanent). The term merely follows from interpretation that at least part of the given site served as a living area, including sleeping quarters. Occupation refuse, both *in loco* and *ex loco*, may be present in a wide range of soil/sediment matrices.

Refuse comprises three main categories:

1. artefacts and materials that have been lost, discarded or abandoned;
2. waste from artefact production or food preparation;
3. components of buildings and other structures that have decayed or collapsed.

These are all products or by-products of human artifice. Their initial discard, abandonment or collapse does not mean that such refuse was ineligible for secondary use, but it does mark the beginning of the refuse cycle within the overall life cycle (see Chapter 14 – Fig. 106).

Ritually deposited or deliberately concealed material is not considered to be refuse, although isolating such categories when physically associated with refuse, may be difficult (Schiffer 1987, 76–80).

In situ occupation refuse

Concentrating now on material still present at the settlement locus, in situ occupation refuse follows from in situ occupation deposits. In other words, much evidence of the internal structure (e.g. stratigraphy) and therefore also of the original spatial relationships of objects at abandonment will have survived. Perhaps only in a minority of situations, notably sub-surface features, would artefacts be absolutely unmoved since the end of an occupation phase. Hence there is a need to identify potential non-cultural transformations in deposits even when the refuse is considered to be in situ. In the particular case of organic-rich deposits, for instance, there is the likelihood of perceptible deflation during decay.

At Runnymede it is probable that even the best-preserved deposits have been modified since abandonment by turbation associated with micro-fauna. This has almost certainly resulted in minor movements of objects, particularly in their angle of rest and vertical position. The soil particles themselves are thereby reworked and precise associations between object and engulfing matrix are far from guaranteed as reflecting those at the point of incorporation of the objects. However, various analyses on the Runnymede material convince us that such movements in a horizontal plane are very minor indeed and can be treated as largely insignificant with respect to the inter-relationship of objects. Such effects lie at the finer end of the range of effects which Butzer labels 'disturbance', a term to cover the rearrangement of sealed sites in place (1982, 104).

Immaterial to the definition of in situ occupation refuse are the cultural agencies acting during the site's life since these are an integral part of the pattern of cultural activity we wish to document; the circumstances by which material became re-used or reworked are of equal importance to those pertaining to primary use or primary discard (Schiffer 1987).

Transformed occupation refuse

Again this is intertwined with 'transformed occupation deposits' and the artefacts themselves might often present important information pointing to this classification. In practice, difficulty can arise in distinguishing later-transformed material from that culturally reworked during the occupation phase. It may also be difficult to determine the particular agencies responsible for reworking, but the key point is that the artefact components will have different spatial patterns from in situ refuse and may also show distinctive marks of the transformation in their condition. These changes result in serious limitations in the interpretation of the activity origins and refuse histories of assemblages.

Conflation horizon

This describes a particular product of transformation such that processes of differential retention and sorting lead to a naturally formed concentration of artefacts, notably relatively heavy ones, at a given horizon. When such a horizon occurred just above in situ deposits, subsequent natural processes (e.g. worm-sorting) could lead to the conflated material wholly or partly infiltrating those in situ deposits; this is thought to have happened at Runnymede, as argued below for unit 16.L (Chapters 2 and 14).

Discard

We mean discard to cover conscious human acts of rejecting objects, fragments or material as being of no perceived imminent value or use. There is thus both a human intention and a physical action upon the object. An object may be discarded any number of times, these events constituting certain critical parts of the full refuse cycle experienced by that object. *Initial discard* refers to the first act of rejection after the original period of use. Subsequent discards may occur after any period of re-use or may result from a decision to reject provisional refuse.

Abandonment (*of objects/materials*)

Abandonment is complementary to discard. It may be conscious or unconscious. *Conscious abandonment* involves a decision not to retrieve the object/material. As with discarding no further value or use is perceived, but in contrast the mental process is not attended by a physical action upon the object. *Unconscious abandonment* is a more gradual process by which objects/materials left ready for use never in fact find further use (for whatever reason). They gradually become 'lost' from the systemic inventory but there is no point of decision. This is likely to account for a lot of material in archaeological deposits stemming from communities which regard a significant proportion of their refuse as 'provisional refuse', since normally much of this would never actually be put to use. Unconscious abandonment may also be a frequent cause of activity-specific sets of equipment surviving in deposits at their place of last use (a form of *de facto* refuse).

Deposition

Best treated as a general collective term for all processes in the systemic sphere which lead towards incorporation.

Incorporation

Incorporation in a soil or refuse body takes the object/material out of visibility and easy retrieval, although this does not preclude later retrieval.

Ultimate incorporation refers to the process of incorporation which led to the object's position as archaeologically recorded.

Artefact groups

The in situ deposits are understandably of much interest and contain aspects requiring further definition. At Runnymede concentrations of material that stood out against the quantity and/or character of surrounding artefacts were contexted separately (see Chapter 2). The distinction between concentrations and more general refuse spreads is taken *a priori* to be significant in terms of formation process, and to have specific episodic and/or functional connotations. Nevertheless there can be a degree of subjectivity in placing a line between the two categories. The concentrations are referred to as *artefact groups*.

In situ structures

Concentrated materials of a structural nature regarded as remaining in the place of construction. Even small-scale structures should normally be self-evident when well preserved (hearths, ovens etc), but degraded remnants may not be distinguishable from, say, dumps of clay or stone. For our purposes in situ structures must be *in loco*, whether degraded or not. In this way we would consider a concentration of daub clearly deriving from a structure to be refuse, even if it lay alongside the original wall position, and it would thus be treated as an artefact group. A collapsed wall, which preserved its structural integrity, would be a rare intermediate situation.

Refuse spreads and refuse scatters

The more general background of in situ occupation refuse beyond specific concentrations can be usefully described by such terms as 'refuse spread' or 'refuse scatter' according to the relative density of the artefact components. We do not propose to define these more closely. The presumption here, however, is that the distribution of the material (spread/scatter etc) when part of in situ deposits is still primarily a result of activities during occupation and should be explicable in these terms.

Refuse characteristics

A general term to cover various attributes of a context assemblage, ranging from finds-type composition to condition patterns. These lead to interpretations of pre-discard activities, refuse cycles and post-deposition transformations. Although the terms considered so far have covered various matters ranging from specific contexts to generic deposits, definition has not required specific identification of the types or life cycles of the artefacts present. Obviously any context assemblage can bring together material of diverse origins or histories. Although such analysis works on a premise of many individual life cycles, in practice this has to be dealt with aggregately, both to aid comprehension and to allow for variable effects on individual objects and their multiple possible functions.

Refuse cycle

The chain of movements and processes to which refuse was subjected from its initial discard, loss or abandonment through to its ultimate incorporation in a deposit which remained essentially undisturbed until excavation. Such chains are infinitely variable. They must be deduced from the condition of material refuse and the character of the particular context, such as soil type. The refuse cycle is only one component of the full life cycle, as for example outlined by Lambrick for pottery (1984, 162). Schiffer (1976) broadly placed refuse found on archaeological sites into three categories: *de facto*, primary and secondary. He accepted that additional varieties of refuse could be defined based on other dimensions of variation in discard processes (Schiffer 1976, 30). Lambrick, for example, recognised Schiffer's neglect of redeposition as a cause of great variation within secondary refuse (Lambrick 1984, 162). Schiffer's subsequent treatise (Schiffer 1987) retained the basic threefold refuse classification, but investigated sequences in more detail, adopting Hayden and Cannon's term 'waste stream' to cover the history of refuse. The concept of a refuse cycle was arrived at independently allowing for the recognition of stages from *early-stage* to *late-stage*. Refuse cycle is to be preferred because of its clear relationship to the use cycle and overall life cycle of objects (Needham and Sørensen 1988, 125). Schiffer's primary refuse (discards at the location of use) can only occupy a position at the very beginning of our refuse cycle ('earliest stage') since it becomes secondary refuse by default the moment it is transported or its sedimentary body is disturbed. In fact the nature of refuse cycles needs to be considered independently for each material category, since different conditions apply (cf. Chapter 14).

The refuse cycle can include a stage during which material removed from its original sphere of use (usually because of damage or replacement) is intentionally stored with the prospect of some future re-use. Deal described this phenomenon as 'provisional discard' (1985, 253) and showed, using his case-study on pottery disposal in the Maya Highlands, that it could occur in quite different modes. One strategy involved the isolated storage of artefact fragments, another was storage of damaged vessels in discrete clusters. Schiffer preferred instead to talk of 'provisional refuse' (1987, 64–72) and documented ethnoarchaeologically its widespread occurrence. It is clearly a phenomenon deserving of consideration when interpreting refuse cycles, but it is important to recognise that even in the systemic sphere its definition might be blurred by an imperceptible slide in status from provisional refuse to abandoned refuse. This slide and the need to recognise human intentions make it especially difficult to categorise archaeological material as provisional refuse with any confidence.

De facto refuse, Schiffer's term for the potentially distinctive refuse assemblages that resulted from site abandonment, is usefully separated from the 'standard' refuse cycle. It can itself be regarded as a cycle or chain, since there may have been a period of preparation for abandonment which resulted in sequences of actions on material stockpiles and refuse. For the most part *de facto* refuse is likely to involve some material with similar characteristics to early-stage refuse. The crucial difference is that a different set of rules is likely to have governed the discard, dispersal, accumulation and utility of artefacts than had applied prior to the decision to abandon settlement. The degree of difference in behaviour and thus in assemblages will have depended on many factors, as discussed by Schiffer (1976, 33ff). The new practices associated with abandonment preparations are likely to replace some of the traditional 'occupation' activities, but may run in parallel with others which continued unchanged through to the point of abandonment.

Added complications arise from the need to consider abandonment at different scales, from individual building, to zone, to whole site (Schiffer 1987, 89ff).

Pre-discard activity

An obvious direction in the interpretation of occupation refuse and one widely considered. Some examples of specific activities relevant to Runnymede are given in Fig. 3. These interpretations obviously depend on good identification of artefact functions. Where functions are ambiguous (as often) then association between activity-related types may become of paramount importance in confidently interpreting the activity in question. (The Area 16 East pottery production equipment is a case in point – Chapter 8). This in turn depends on the recognition of very early stages of the refuse cycle where such associations may be retained (but see also Schiffer's cautionary – 1987, 19–21).

Some human activities, such as floor sweeping, ground clearance or hole digging, do not habitually generate their own artefact refuse, but may redistribute pre-existing refuse. These are not considered under this heading, but instead as actions within the refuse cycle.

Unit function

Interpretation of unit function will generally need to be composite depending on the evidence for contemporary structures, refuse characteristics and sediment type. Terms such as *midden, floor, yard surface or abandonment horizon* belong here. Although those of 'surface' character might give the impression of being stratigraphic interfaces, therefore having no soil or artefact constituent, in practice they always have some associated matter – otherwise they would not be interpretable as anything other than erosion or stasis surfaces!

Unit function cuts across all the modes of classification described so far. For example, a midden may tend to be dense in inorganic refuse and incorporate specific dumps which show as artefact groups, but this need not be invariable (e.g. a green midden – manure). Floors may typically be characterised by a thin scatter of well-broken (trampled) material, whereas, on abandonment or change of function, *de facto* refuse might well be featured on a floor surface, showing as artefact groups or a refuse spread.

Midden

The term midden needs careful definition in the context of this report. A midden can be regarded as a particular type of occupation deposit which must be relatively rich in occupation refuse, although this may include archaeologically less tangible elements (e.g. decayed organics). Analysis should indicate that there was deliberate and sequential accumulation of refuse at one location and there should normally be a noteworthy component of refuse at early stages of the refuse cycle. If the last condition is not met, then it is inherently likely that the refuse accumulation is 'incidental' in the course of other activities (Needham and Sørensen 1988, 125). A single-phase dump, however large, is better termed simply a dump and not a midden, even though it may derive directly from a pre-existing midden.

In situ deposits are essential for confident interpretation of middens. Evidence of episodic dumping needs to be capable of observation or firm deduction. Episodes may or may not be of similar character. The diversity or otherwise of sources contributing to the midden would help clarify the type of midden involved. By way of example, for limited materials we might identify pot dumps or green middens; for mixed materials, house-hold waste or workshop waste. Middens should not be held synonymous with manure and manuring; their interrelationship is a matter for discussion given the particular period/geographic context (Needham and Sørensen 1988, 125). Neither do they necessarily need to be located on a settlement site; a midden could be formed off-site by regular transportation of material.

It follows from the above that deposits suitable for labelling as 'middens' are likely to have some vertical depth, since a shallow deposit could equally be an abandonment horizon. This is not, however, to deny the possibility of a lateral dimension in midden accumulation.

CHAPTER 2

Area 16 East and the excavation methods of the Research Campaign

STUART NEEDHAM

The excavation of Area 16, 1985–86

The overall strategy and history of the research campaign at Runnymede Bridge, 1984–89, is described in Research Volume 1 (Needham *et al* forthcoming). Area 16 was initially laid out in 1985 as a long trench 2 m, or in part 1 m, wide with the aim of giving relatively rapid information on lateral changes in the topography and associated archaeological deposits (Fig. 4). It was hoped to complete excavation of the Late Bronze Age levels during 1985 and perhaps have a chance to sample the underlying stratigraphy. However progress was unavoidably slow, in part owing to the unexpectedly deep and complex LBA deposits towards the eastern end. Partway through the season, having excavated a few spits into the upper silts bearing LBA material, it was clear that the objectives were not going to be met. Consequently a decision was taken to halt excavation over a large central part of the trench (part of it only 1 m wide) and concentrate on establishing the sequences at the two ends. An intermediate profile was provided by a deep modern pit (16.802) which intruded into the northern edge of the trench at *c*.49E (Fig. 4).

In the westernmost 8 m², designated Area 16 West, Late Bronze Age layer deposits were relatively thin. These and a few cut features were fully excavated in 1985. Thereafter Area 16 West was subsumed within Area 19 and Neolithic finds and contexts were labelled accordingly (i.e. Area 19.xxx). The evidence from these 8 m² is part of the interior zone and will be published thus.

In Area 16 Centre excavated spits were largely through flood-reworked layers, perhaps just entering the in situ LBA deposits. No features were revealed and nothing significant can be made of stratification. The evidence from this zone is thus to remain in archive without comprehensive publication.

This volume attempts to publish comprehensively Area 16 East. At the eastern end of the trench there were indications that the dark soil representing in situ deposits might be relatively thick. It was desirable to excavate a reasonable sample of this potentially rich

store of evidence. Initially an area of 12 m², east of 54.00E was defined, and a thirteenth grid square was soon added (53/12) to embrace a pot group (16.848/867). By the end of the 1985 season a thick deposit of dark earth had been gradually removed from these 13 m². However, the lower deposits became more and more complex. Many in situ clusters of artefacts and structural debris required detailed recording and some rich basal deposits had to be left for excavation the following season. These remaining concentrations lay in the eastern part of Area 16 East where the deposits had survived thickest overall. Anything fragile was removed from the surface reached which was then carefully covered with builders' polythene and a cushion of soft soil before machine backfilling.

In the 1986 season the remaining dark earth deposits were lifted, followed by the excavation of LBA cut features as they became identifiable in the underlying clean silt. Next the silt body was removed in spits by careful spade excavation until the exposed surface showed a patchy mixture of pure and gravelly silts. At this point (after contexts 16.922–930) the active trench was narrowed to 1 m (grid squares 53/12–59/12) and trowel excavation resumed. Beneath a complex of gravels and silts containing some Neolithic finds was revealed a reasonably dense spread of similar material in what was taken to be an old soil profile sealed under the gravel. The artefact-rich layer quickly gave way to sterile silt, into which no obvious features were cut. This point was reached at the very end of the 1986 season and no deeper exploration was possible. However, a modern pit several metres to the west (16.802) did provide a deeper profile which will be published in Volume 1.

Various sample columns were taken from the baulk sections of Area 16 East for phosphates, soil micromorphology and snails. These are detailed in Volume 1, but some of the broader conclusions are drawn into relevant parts of this volume, notably Chapters 3 and 14.

The Late Bronze Age deposits in Area 16 East were stunning not simply for their depth, but primarily because of the density of material finds with a significant proportion in discrete clusters, which isolate a succession of short-lived events or episodes. This rich sequence was

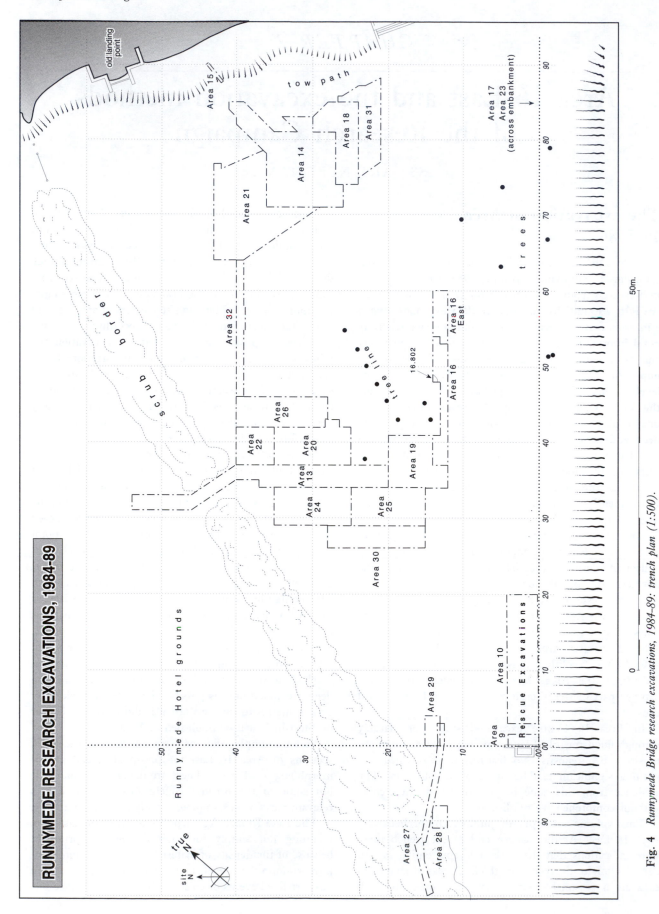

Fig. 4 *Runnymede Bridge research excavations, 1984–89: trench plan (1:500).*

both a bonus and an impediment. Its excavation was labour-consuming and temporarily detracted from other major objectives of the research campaign (see Volume 1). For this reason it was decided not to explore further the area surrounding Area 16 East in subsequent seasons. Nevertheless, despite the small area opened (13 m^2), the Area 16 East deposits were seen to have considerable potential for characterising one part of the Runnymede settlement, as well as having broader ramifications, perhaps beyond the site itself. It has been possible to undertake detailed analysis of many aspects of the material evidence and we hope that the results published here justify their wider importance and separate publication.

Excavation methods, recording and processing

Excavation and recording methodology during the research campaign evolved from that employed in the previous rescue excavations, drawing on accumulated experience of the nature of the Runnymede deposits. The system was essentially one of single-context recording, similar to that commonly adopted during the 1980s. The procedures outlined here relate to the research campaign at large and they will not necessarily all be relevant to Area 16 East.

Excavation methods were those generally employed: machine clearance above cultural layers of overlying modern rubble, topsoil and largely sterile sediments and occasionally also of large modern pits (late 20th century AD); trowelling of all definite or suspected cultural or artefact-bearing sediments and, whenever necessary, use of more delicate (e.g. dental) tools; occasional spade excavation of sediment bodies which seemed to be bereft of artefacts and archaeological features. In early seasons machining was halted high in the overlying sediments once finds began to be noticed. Later, however, with greater confidence in identifying flood-reworked deposits machining was taken lower, to levels closer to in situ LBA occupation.

To supplement the material recovered by hand excavation, numerous soil samples were collected by individual trowellers for flotation and sieving. This had the joint purpose of recovering both environmental/economic evidence and artefacts overlooked by the excavator. The strategy is to be fully set out in Research Volume 1, but it is important to draw attention here to a series of *sieve control columns* taken across the site. These are designated metre squares, usually one or two per trench, from which all excavated soil was kept for sieving throughout the sequence. The soil was sieved on a mesh of 4 mm, so that the procedure should thus give full recovery (by adding in the hand-excavated finds) of all artefactual material down to 4 mm for a column of 1 m^2 through the hand-excavated deposits. These control columns offer a research tool for investigating changes in assemblage character without significant bias from individual excavators, supervisors, weather or seasons.

Context definition

Each trench or Area had a single sequence of three-digit numbers covering contexts of all types. Area sequences were started at different points (e.g. 001, 301, 801) for administrative reasons, but whenever they reached 999, they returned to 001 thus remaining as three digits. However, in no Area is the same three digit number repeated. Since many Area sequences overlap, unique numbering requires the Area number prefix, thus 16.854 or 21.854. Whenever there is a danger of ambiguity five-digit numbers of this kind will be used in publication reports. They are consistently used in the computerised archive.

In broad terms contexts fall into four types, each with a single number, although three types were generally sub-divided into component parts. The four basic types are:

1. Layer-type contexts
2. Artefact groups
3. In situ structures
4. Sub-surface contexts.

LAYER-TYPE CONTEXTS

Layer-type contexts may be true layers in the sense that definable boundaries marked their upper and lower interfaces. More often, however, one or both interfaces were ill-defined, arbitrary, or marked only intermittently by spatially dispersed 'markers' such as distinct clusters of material. These are strictly speaking 'spits', but they were rarely totally arbitrary slices of soil, since their excavation always took account of tangible evidence relating to soil type, colour and visible finds characteristics (e.g. density, condition, range). There was rarely any attempt to make these spits uniform in depth, but rather to respond to whatever subtle changes could be discerned in the deposits. In this way we hope to have defined deposits which were internally coherent in most tangible respects.

Surfaces were almost invariably recorded by photography (colour slides and monochrome prints) and 1:20 plans with differentiation of major artefact materials (by colour coding) and any soil variation.

ARTEFACT GROUPS

These were normally, but not invariably, dense clusters of artefacts which stood out against the surrounding finds distribution. Definition was variable in accordance with perceived spatial relationships and a degree of pragmatism in whether it was useful to distinguish a particular set of finds from others at the same 'level'. There is thus a measure of subjectivity in what constituted an artefact group, but in most cases they were distinguished by their relative concentration, noteworthy interrelationships (e.g. alignments), or relationships to other features. The underlying tenet was that groups so defined (and hence uniquely contexted) had a specific connotation in terms of a unitary deposition event, or a short-lived sequence from a particular activity.

Normally if 'scatters' of finds were defined as artefact groups they had a very limited spatial extent, rarely above 2 m maximum spread. Occasionally, however, a much wider spread of finds of very homogeneous character and appearing at a distinct horizon was treated effectively as an 'artefact group'. In these situations finds were appropriately labelled, but no soil excavated (for otherwise they would be undifferentiable from layer-type contexts). In a sense then these can be regarded as a form of 'interface' context lying between layers. None occur in Area 16 East.

Even clusters of very limited extent could theoretically be regarded merely as specialised cases of layers, i.e. very localised lenses trapped within a broader layer system. Many artefact groups were excavated in association with a body of soil, however thin that may have been, but again this varied according to specific circumstance. For example, a single layer of potsherds in a group exposed by the removal of the previous layer context could easily be lifted as a new context without further soil removal. There is no essential difference conceptually between those groups accompanied by soil removal and those without.

In the analysis of finds distributions, artefact groups can be viewed in different ways. On the one hand they obviously reflect one or more of the activities contributing to the deposits at the particular stratigraphic horizon and in this respect they are inseparable constituents of the group assemblage, even if they show a different pattern. Following this thesis, the Area 16 East groups have been assigned to augmented layer contexts, or 'amalgamated contexts' (Table 1). For certain questions, however, they might be regarded as discrete entities to be excluded from the background level of finds in surrounding contexts.

The artefact types embraced in such artefact groups were usually determined purely by spatial considerations so that composition was not skewed towards a perceived 'type' of deposit. For example, a few pieces of pottery might be admitted with a cluster of butchered bone. In some circumstances, however, there was a deliberate decision to restrict the context to the material type, thus leaving any proximate objects of a different material to the more general layer context. There is no clear distinction between these alternative approaches to contexting groups, although certain situations would almost invariably lead to one solution; for example, groups of articulated bones would be contexted to exclude other 'associated' objects.

These choices can be difficult, not least because of the real possibility of random pieces coming into contact with clusters by separate mechanism, although this is probably a feature that should be sought in analysis rather than prejudged. Further imprecision in defining clusters inevitably arises from the likelihood that some finds would have already been lifted before the excavator realised that a noteworthy cluster was present. It needs to be remembered that virtually all the dark earth deposits at Runnymede were constantly yielding finds during excavation.

Artefact groups, once defined, were almost invariably photographed in situ and planned at 1:5. Overlays to the plans were then used to number uniquely all or most of the contained artefacts; however, burnt flint pieces in particular were excluded from this unique numbering. The unique numbers are suffixed as 'point-numbers' to the main context, thus 16.857.1, 16.857.2 etc. Sometimes a remainder of less diagnostic material, e.g. tiny potsherds, was merely attributed to the artefact group context without unique numbering, hence 16.857.

IN SITU STRUCTURES

Given that the cultural levels excavated during the research campaign were all above the water table, and that timber and clay building traditions are involved, structural evidence takes the form of either cut features (see below) or remnant parts of walls and other structures, such as hearths or ovens. When such features were thought certainly or possibly to be in situ they were separately contexted. Distinct components, such as pebble foundations, different clay bodies or associated soils, would then be identified by point-numbers.

E.g. hypothetical hearth:

16.371.1   reddened clay bed
16.371.2   yellower clay
16.371.3   burnt pebble foundation
16.371.4   'halo' of burnt soil around.

As for all contexts, any finds made would be labelled accordingly. However, with this kind of context there may be a higher chance of fortuitous associations between finds and the structure being contexted.

SUB-SURFACE CONTEXTS

Mostly these are 'cut' features, i.e. humanly dug or driven, but features which turned out to be root holes and natural depressions were initially treated as potential cut features and thus recorded in the same way. Subsequently, after interpretation the last category (depressions) would normally be re-absorbed into an appropriate layer-type context or group.

Although it is acknowledged that the different fills of a single feature can have very different origins, being separated in time, it was felt desirable for administrative reasons amongst others to retain all components of a definable sub-surface feature under a single context number. A point-number system was again used to identify the individual components.

E.g. hypothetical post hole:

16.426.1   upper fill, after compaction
16.426.2   *post pipe*
16.426.3   packing
16.426   post hole cut (i.e. the interface).

Occasionally sub-contexts were defined as .0 (thus 16.426.0); this system was usually employed when a cut feature was suspected but far from certainly present. In these situations the .0 sub-context would be attached to material excavated off the surface in the hope of clarifying the soil plan of the feature. Needless to say some soil contexts treated in this way were, after further excavation, no longer regarded as part of clear-cut features. Consequently the existence of a point-number context for a context which is neither artefact group nor structure does not invariably imply a feature fill.

Even those contexts which may be confidently regarded as cut features present problems of definition, most notably at the top, a problem that has been outlined previously (Longley 1980, 7; Needham and Sørensen 1988, 113). It stems from the usually close similarity between the soil filling upper parts of features and that in surrounding surface contexts. This means that there is a possibility that feature fills, which did not become visible until they were seen against lighter coloured sub-soil, had in reality extended higher into the dark earth of the layer-type deposits. Such reconstruction would put the position of cuts at a higher, but perhaps undefinable, stratigraphic level. During one season (1987) there was an attempt to identify post holes at an earlier stage using close-range remote sensing, but this was not successful. Subsequently infra-red photography was used to record spit surfaces in case it enhanced soil differences caused by, for example, moisture retention or texture. This overall problem has potentially serious consequences for understanding the true relationship between cut feature and layer-type contexts, and therefore our ability faithfully to reconstruct site sequence.

In order to mitigate the inherent dangers, we have adopted the following principles and practices:

1. The spit plans of overlying layers/spits need to be consulted systematically to search for possible indications (largely from finds disposition) that a cut feature, or its contained structural member, left evidence at a higher level. In practice this is unlikely to be helpful for small features such as stake holes when looked at individually. For larger features, however, this approach has already been employed usefully in Area 6 (Needham 1991, 111–2) and Area 16 East (Chapter 3) and suggests strongly that the level at which a feature became visible cannot be regarded as a secure stratigraphic marker (with rare exceptions, such as 16.900 below).

2. Consequently, we take those levels only as an initial indication of *possible* stratigraphic position and do not use them too literally in interpretation.

3. In some cases relative differences between, say, a set of features found at the top of the sub-soil and another set seen only after further trowelling *might* be evidence of a sequence. However, even this is fraught with difficulties relating to the vagaries of fill formation and is unlikely to be more than a rough equation.

4. Ironically, it may be that the best evidence for the stratigraphic position of features may derive from interpretation. This can only really work when sets of features can be linked together as coherent structures, this process itself being interpretative. Structural layouts can then be compared with the differential character of the surface deposits in the hope of identifying correlations explicable in terms of standing walls etc. When such relationships are shown they can be used to correlate features and layers temporally. There is obviously a danger of circular argument here with observed relationships of this kind being used to 'justify' the coherence of given feature sets. We acknowledge this difficulty. However, given the limitations of the evidence at Runnymede all we can do is make explicit the fact that most structures and their constituent features will only be positioned in the stratigraphic matrix of surface deposits at an interpretative stage, whereas other context types will generally be placed in the matrix more directly from the excavation record.

Overall then a fairly flexible approach to context recording was taken at Runnymede to suit the nature of the archaeological deposits: in essence the deposits can be regarded as a three-dimensional continuum with very rare hard boundaries, yet constantly changing characteristics. This kind of formation is rarely encountered in British prehistory where, more normally, severe truncation has separated pockets of surviving evidence.

Site grid and surveying

A metre grid based on a site base-line was used as the basis for all horizontal spatial recording. The base-line ran along the foot of the slip road embankment on a near SW-NE alignment. Site North was determined as the axis 40 degrees west of true North. Each 1 m grid intersection was marked and positions periodically checked as the trench surfaces were lowered. In addition to providing reference marks for planning frames and for establishing the locations of special finds and features, the metre squares were used as units for recording the spatial location of virtually all remaining finds. Individual excavators were thus usually working within one m² at a time. Rare exceptions were 'cleaning' spits, taken across a trench as a single unit when there was a risk of mixing or contamination from above due to adverse conditions during excavation.

The metre grid was also used for regular grid-levelling, after virtually every spit was removed. This had a twofold purpose: to allow reconstruction of the topography of each surface and to enable approximate soil volumes to be calculated for stratigraphic units. These estimates can be used to evaluate relative finds densities (see Chapter 6).

Most cut features were of small or modest size and their fills attributed to a single metre square even when impinging partly on one or more other squares. Only a few larger features were sub-divided according to the metre grid.

Surveying was largely confined to horizontal levelling to establish vertical heights in relation to a permanent site bench mark which was in turn tied in to the Ordnance Datum. In use throughout the campaign were dumpy levels and a more sophisticated instrument used in a similar mode. Only in the final season was an EDM introduced to the site; this was used in tandem with the conventional surveying instruments.

Finds recording

The position of finds was generally recorded at two levels of precision, but in three modes. The great majority of finds, known as the bulk finds, were located only to their smallest context unit; in the case of a layer-type deposit, that is the particular metre square concerned. Vertical position is known only within the thickness of the excavated context, the thickness being recorded in section drawings for cut features and through the grid levels data for layers.

Two kinds of more precise location recording stem from the above described procedures. Special finds recognised at the time of excavation were pinpointed three-dimensionally in the usual manner, the vertical position being established by survey levelling (Table 12). Orientation in the ground was also noted. Objects deemed to be 'special finds' had of practical necessity to be kept to a minor proportion of the large assemblage and were restricted to artefact types thought to be particularly instructive on matters of chronology or specific activity (they are listed in Table 12). Where such finds were only recognised later during finds processing, they were nevertheless still defined as special finds on the grounds that they offer more intrinsic information than other finds. It is also desirable for museological reasons to have them treated in a consistent manner. Some special finds thus lack precise three-dimensional coordinates and can, like their associated bulk finds, only be attributed to a context/metre square or a feature fill.

The third mode of finds recording stems from the artefact group and in situ structure contexts. Most finds in such contexts were uniquely identified (as described above) and marked on the detailed plans giving a precise horizontal location. Vertical levels were only established for the context as a whole, although this was normally of small range. In this mode bulk finds were thus given fairly accurate three-dimensional coordinates on the grounds that their spatial interrelationships were of unusual significance, rather than the objects themselves having great intrinsic importance.

Special finds numbering and unique object identification

Special finds numbers start at 1 for each Area and in each season. Unique identification thus requires, for example, ERB89 A20 sf23. For the 1984 season it is also essential to cite the context since the special finds number was reset at 1 for each new context (thus: ERB84 A14 335 sf2). Fully published finds can be readily referred to by their catalogue numbers (e.g. M23) which will form a single series throughout the BM publication series, starting with the existing report on the 1978 campaign. Both these and selected other finds (see next section) can also be uniquely identified by the published BM registration number.

British Museum registration sequence

Publication of successive Runnymede assemblages will include BM registration numbers. These will uniquely identify objects in the following categories:

1. Fully published special finds (illustrated and catalogued).
2. Remaining special finds (summary details in tabular form as Table 12).
3. Bulk finds selected for detailed publication (illustration and description) – primarily catalogued pottery. Individual numbers are here applied to a 'reconstructed' vessel, whose constituent parts may come from more than one context.

4. Further featured pottery that has contributed towards a study, but is not catalogued in the publication.
5. Pottery sherds bearing potential food residues, regardless of whether sampled or published, but not included in 3 or 4 above.

All remaining bulk finds are grouped according to their material (pottery, fired/burnt clay, struck flint, stone, bone etc.) and specific context, each group then being assigned a single registration number above 10,000. Thus, all unpublished fired clay from ERB89 A26 502 42/39 might hypothetically be registration P1989 10–1 12820.

Finds processing

The prodigious flow of finds yielded during the excavation seasons required a dedicated finds team. The aim was to process fully as much as possible of the season's assemblage in the field, but in practice much always remained for processing at the BM's post-excavation centre between seasons. Treatment of the assemblage was essentially the same in both locations.

With rare exceptions from special groups, burnt (unworked) flint was systematically separated from the other finds prior to reaching the finds centre; it was weighed and logged by the excavation teams. The remaining bulk finds were initially scanned whilst dirty to prevent certain materials – notably fired clay – being washed. An eye was also kept open for special finds which had escaped notice in the trench, since many of these were fragile and required special treatment. Washers were also asked to look out for food residues on pottery and to desist from washing as soon as any was suspected. The success rate in preserving such remains is of course impossible to assess. A British Museum conservator was present on-site during every season to give urgent treatment to important and fragile finds. This work was normally undertaken in the finds hut, but in-trench consolidation was necessary on occasion.

Washing was conducted, one context group at a time, in plain water with brushes which were not hard, so as to avoid additional abrasion of the softer materials. Air-drying was followed by initial study and then recording on a proforma with quantification of number and weight in each material category, some of which were sub-divided. The different materials were then stored separately.

CHAPTER 3

The stratigraphic sequence

STUART NEEDHAM

In broad terms the profile excavated in Area 16 East presents five obvious deposits beneath modern make-up, from top downwards (Fig. 5):

- pale grey-brown silt   [reworked LBA].
- dark grey silt   [in situ LBA].
- light yellowish-grey silt
- dense gravel in a light   [reworked MN, with in situ grey-brown silt   MN towards base].
- light yellow-brown   [in situ MN in surface]. silt.

The silts are generally of a clay-loam character, but can occasionally be more sticky due to a higher clay fraction. All but the middle one of these five units were hand-excavated in spits, as described above. These spit/layer-type contexts have been grouped in various ways to form *stratigraphic units*. There is no single criterion for the grouping, with both soil and finds characteristics contributing in variable balance to the definitions. The overriding intention was to produce groupings which are thought to be most useful to aid interpretation, rather than necessarily to be empirical.

Inevitably this has led to the sub-division of most of the broad definitions above, most notably at the horizons containing in situ cultural material. In consequence fourteen stratigraphic units, 16.A-N, have been defined (starting from the base of the sequence). Fig. 8 presents the stratigraphic matrix and the grouping of contexts into units. It should be emphasised that, while the basis for stratigraphic relationships was observation in the field, there is also an element of 'reconstructed' relationships based on careful evaluation of plans and context records during post-excavation analysis. This sort of stratigraphic 'hindsight' is normally made possible by specific features such as artefact groups believed to mark a temporary surface. In the case of spit 16.836, for example, post-excavation analysis suggested that the eastern part was broadly later than the western part, although any time lapse is thought to have been small and both parts are placed in a single stratigraphic unit. 16.930, on the other hand, is seen to be an amalgam of two components relating to distinct units, 16.E and 16.C.

The Neolithic – MBA sequence

As already mentioned, below unit 16.E the 2 m wide trench was narrowed to 1 m in order to ensure that as full a profile as possible of the pre-LBA deposits was obtained in what remained of the 1986 season. This enabled a horizon rich in Neolithic debris to be excavated down to a clean silt surface.

Many of the contexts are very localised, reflecting detailed variations in matrix, particularly the gravel constituent, or mineral (iron, manganese) enrichment zones. The stratigraphic units regroup contexts where such variation is thought to be post-depositional or to reflect natural variation as part of a simultaneous deposition process. The resulting sequence is relatively straightforward with marked changes from the bottom upwards: sterile silt, cultural horizon, gravel incursion, re-erosion, silt alluviation.

Stratigraphic unit 16.A (16.939,958,959,960)

A thin spit of sticky clay silt with occasional small stones mottled red-brown/yellow/greyish, in part due to iron-staining (particularly heavy in 16.958). There was some charcoal present at the eastern end (16.960), presumably relating to the overlying cultural debris, but otherwise the spit was effectively barren of finds. It is thought likely that this was the top of a deepish body of sterile alluvial silt similar to that seen just to the west in modern pit 16.802 (Research Volume 1).

Stratigraphic unit 16.B (16.934, 937, 938, 950, 952, 953, 954, 955, 956, 957; in part 930 west).

This is the main cultural-bearing layer. A fairly stiff and grainy clay silt, mainly greyish light brown with variable reddish (iron) mottling. Occasional small stones and a general dispersed constituent of charcoal (Plate 1). Limbrey's soil study (Research Volume 1) suggests that this is the gleyed 'B' horizon of a truncated soil profile, whilst the snail evidence (Evans – Research Volume 1) points to perennially damp conditions in the depression.

Most of this material (contexts 16.937, 950, 952–956)

can be regarded as well sealed and barely, if at all, disturbed by later fluvial action. However, 16.934 and its contained bone group 16.938 were first revealed at the base of the presumed erosion gully of unit E (16.925/932). Excavation proceeded on the basis that the top at least might have been a basal deposit in that gully, or might have been earlier material disturbed by the gully erosion. Subsequent exposure of the horizon (unit B) underlying the gravel banks suggested that the bulk of 16.934/938 represented a continuation of that unit, and there is little to suggest any later disturbance. 16.934/938 was actually relatively thick and was excavated as three mini-spits, each planned. It is proposed that only the uppermost spit (including bones 16.938.1–19) is at risk of including material reworked during unit E. The bones shown in Fig.10 are from the next spit down (16.938.20–40).

Context 16.957 was a cleaning spit after heavy rain. The great majority of the finds can be attributed to unit B (mainly its upper surface, but beneath B at the west end), but there is a risk of some contamination. The western part of 16.930 (grid square 53/12) includes a scatter of gravel and some large bone finds and it almost certainly belongs to unit B, C or to both.

The combined plan of finds in the top of unit B (Fig. 10) shows a dense concentration of bones and, to a lesser extent, potsherds. Medium to large fragments are present in both categories. The density of finds, however, falls off a little towards the west end of Area 16 East. This may be due to a rise in the topography leading to preferential scouring, and consequently the survival of less material in situ.

Stratigraphic unit 16.C (16.944, 945, 946, 947, 948, 949, 951; in part 930 west).

This embraces a suite of contexts having the main characteristics of units B and D combined: still rather dense refuse, but here mixed in with a significant quantity of gravel. The first impression is of flood-reworked cultural material representing the erosion preceding the big gravel inwash. However, the inclusion of two articulated bones (cattle radius/ulna from 16.951) within this unit (a relationship encountered at this stratigraphic horizon elsewhere on the site) questions the contemporaneity of deposition of the gravel and contained artefacts. It is now strongly suspected that the lowest part of the gravel-rich bed infiltrated essentially intact soil deposits after its initial deposition. One cannot, however, rule out some disturbance and reworking of the infiltrated soil profile during earlier erosion phases, and this unit is therefore kept separate from B.

Finds density is significantly reduced from that in the underlying B contexts and this in itself may reflect earlier processes of downward migration following the occupation.

Interpretation of the concentration of finds in units B-C needs to take account of the topography. The main trend is a fall of 25 cm from the west end (c.13.90 m OD) to 58E (c.13.65 m OD). There is then a slight rise to the east end (c.10 cm) along the south baulk, but this appears to have been much more pronounced (over 20 cm) on a diagonal towards grid 60/13 (Figs 5 and 6). This suggests that Area 16 East may contain a localised hollow rather than simply being part of a general slope from the high bank to the south-west down towards a contemporary river channel to the north-east. The concentration of finds in this hollow could be due to either discard patterns or later erosion. The surface condition of the bones is mainly in Serjeantson's 'good' category; this is not as good as the general condition of bone low in the LBA deposits, but the difference is possibly just a function of total age, the Neolithic material being twice as old. Weathering of the Neolithic bones is not clearly of a degree to indicate any lengthy exposure or re-deposition under flood conditions. Furthermore, the in situ articulation (16.951) in unit C argues against anything more than minimal post-discard movement.

Stratigraphic unit 16.D (16.929, 931, 933, 935, 936, 940, 941, 942, 943).

This unit covers a range of contexts dominated by dense gravel in a light grey-brown clay silt with variable iron-mottling (Plates 2 and 3). Although covering most of the trench, this deposit was interrupted by pockets of silt (attributed to unit E – Fig. 12). The gravel component was estimated generally to be 70–90%, or 60% on some flanks of the mounds (contexts 16.935, 936). Most stones were less than 2 cm across. Inspection of the south section (Fig. 5) suggested the possibility of some tip lines within the main body (16.931, 943 etc), but these cannot be correlated with the excavated divisions. This gravel bed defines alluvial parcel 2F (Volume 1 – Needham *et al* forthcoming).

There were very few finds within this unit, and they are presumed to have been reworked from eroded land surfaces. The bone was more fragmentary and eroded than that in the underlying units.

Stratigraphic unit 16.E (16.922, 923, 924, 925, 926, 927, 928, 930 east, 932).

While this unit also includes a lot of gravel in the matrix (16.922, 924, 926, 927 – gravel 40–60%), there is evidence that it represents a reworking of the underlying gravel beds with near-simultaneous deposition of more silty pockets (16.923, 925/932, 928 – gravel less than 20%). It is possible, though by no means certain, that the large silt-filled hollow (16.925, 932) lying between unit D gravel deposits (Plate 2) is actually a later cut-

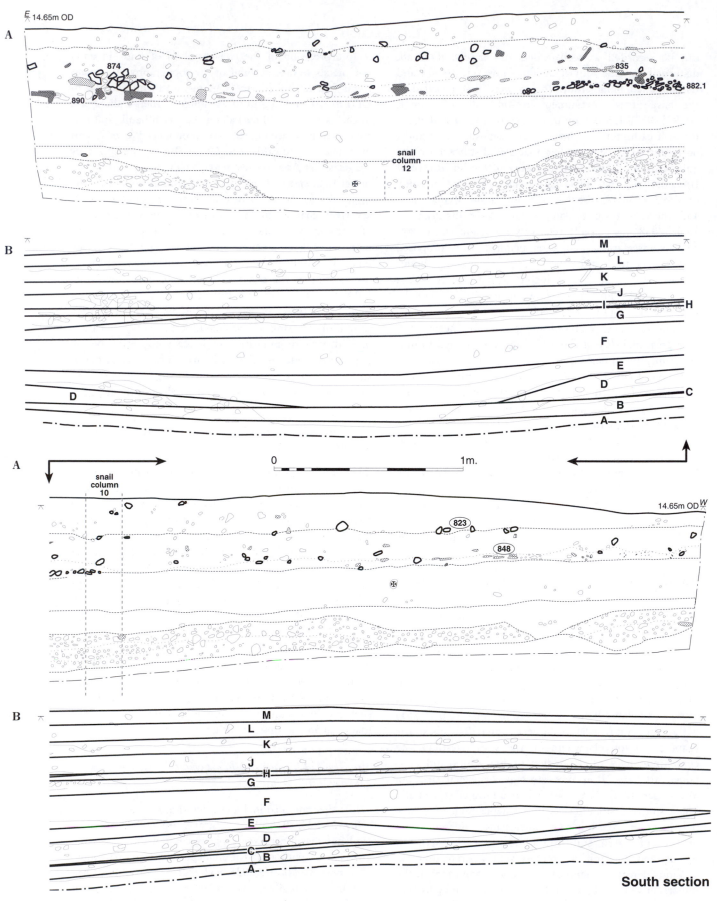

Fig. 5 *The south section of Area 16 East: A. as recorded in the field; B. stratigraphic units presented schematically using the levels data.*

West section

East section

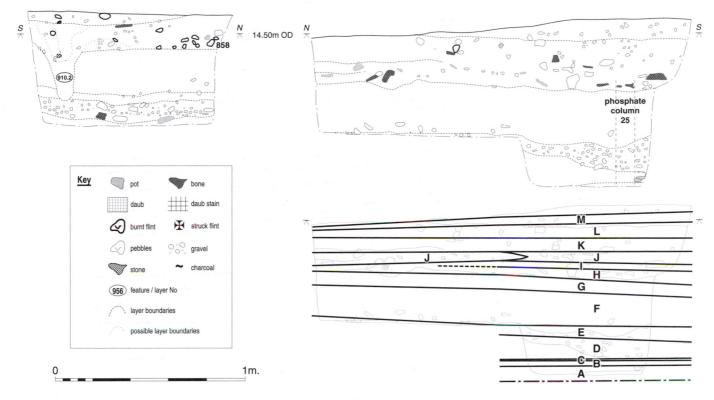

14.50m OD

phosphate
column
25

Key

pot		bone	
daub		daub stain	
burnt flint		struck flint	
pebbles		gravel	
stone		charcoal	
956	feature / layer No		
	layer boundaries		
	possible layer boundaries		

0   1m.

Fig. 6 *The west and east sections of Area 16 East: presentation as for Fig. 5.*

South section - *(see page opposite)*

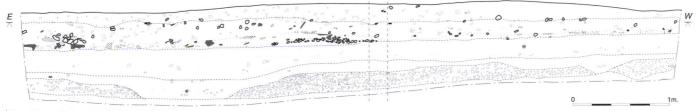

Fig. 5 (continued) *Whole section*

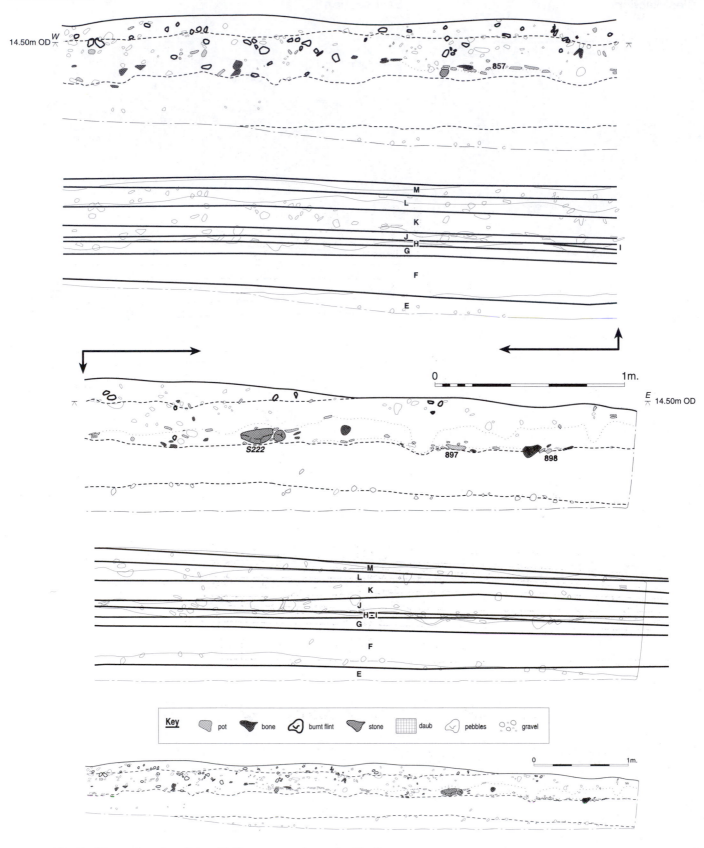

14.50m OD *W*

857

M
L
K
J
H
G
F
E

0   1m.

E 14.50m OD

S222   897   898

M
L
K
J
H
G
F
E

Key pot   bone   burnt flint   stone   daub   pebbles   gravel

0   1m.

Fig. 7 *The north section of Area 16 East: presentation as for Fig. 5.*

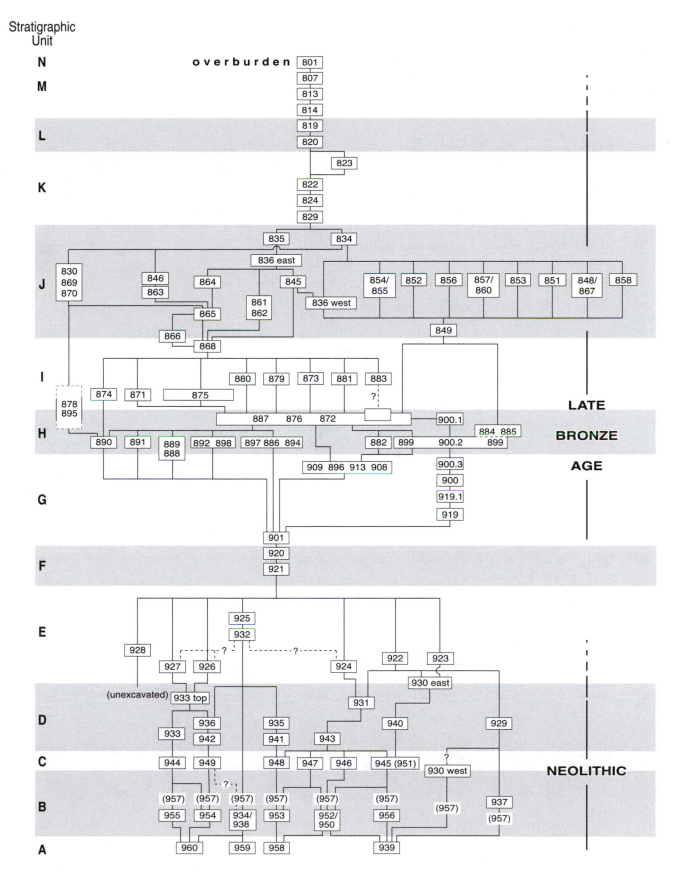

Fig. 8 *Area 16 East stratigraphic matrix. NB. A minority of contexts are excluded, notably those poorly phased.*

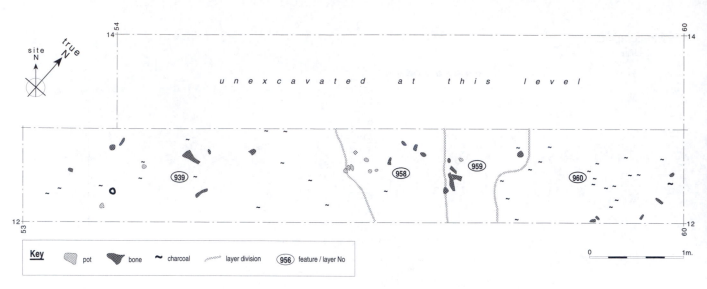

Fig. 9 *Refuse at the interface of stratigraphic units A and B.*

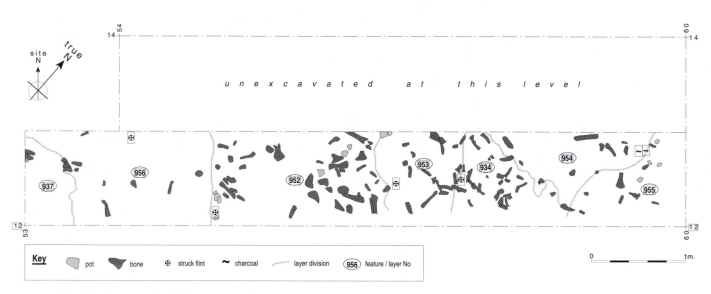

Fig. 10 *In situ refuse high in stratigraphic unit B.*

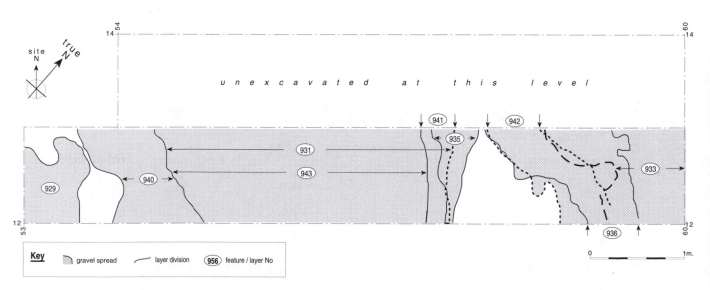

Fig. 11 *The distribution of the gravel contexts through the full depth of stratigraphic unit D; see the matrix (Fig. 8) for stratigraphic relationships of overlapping contexts.*

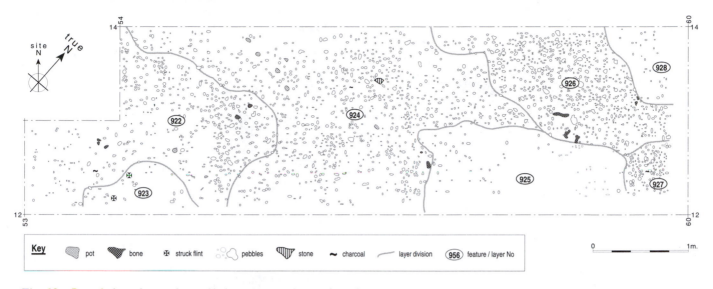

Key   pot   bone   struck flint   pebbles   stone   charcoal   layer division   (956) feature / layer No

Fig. 12   *Reworked artefacts and gravel/silt contexts at the interface of stratigraphic units E and F.*

and-fill than the surrounding unit E contexts (16.924, 926, 927). However, the diffuse and wandering nature of gravel/silt boundaries makes it difficult to argue for clear cut-lines. Another silty pocket showing at the surface in the west (as 16.923) continued lower (16.930 east), possibly spreading laterally under gravelly deposit 16.922, but it overlapped the tail of the main gravel bank (16.940). These deposits are part of alluvial parcel 2B.

The matrix is a stiff to sticky grey-brown, clay silt. Cultural material was again rather sparse.

Stratigraphic unit 16.F (*16.920, 921*).

A fairly homogenous body of yellowish-grey clayey silt with a sparse small-gravel component increasing towards the bottom. The deposit varies between 12 and 22 cm thick. This also is attributed to alluvial parcel 2B . Finds were sparse in this deposit.

The Late Bronze Age sequence

Stratigraphic unit 16.G: early occupation evidence (*16.896, 900, 900.3, 901, 906, 908, 909, 913, 919, 919.1*).

The unit F/G interface dips from the west (*c.*14.29 m OD; Fig. 13) to the SE corner (14.10 m OD). The depression at the eastern end may in part be due to underlying deposits, in particular the silt-filled gully or hollow (unit E) 16.932 between thick gravel banks (units C-D). It is possible, however, that there was differential truncation of the LBA ground surface prior to dark earth accumulation (unit H). Unit G comprises a fairly shallow 'soil' containing limited cultural debris, and a few cut features. Although all the features in this small trench were first visible at, or close to, the 16.896/901 interface, which suggested provisionally that they belong to unit G, only two or three have subsequently been

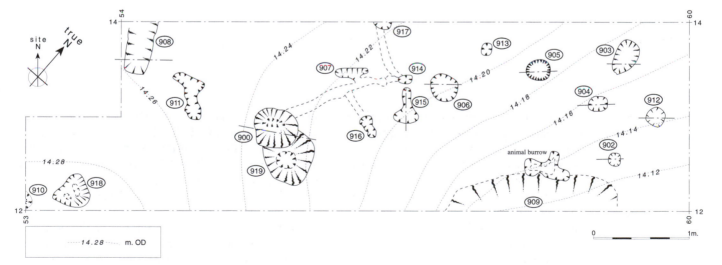

Fig. 13   *Contour plan of the surface of stratigraphic unit F, beneath LBA deposits, with cut features of various LBA phases superimposed.*

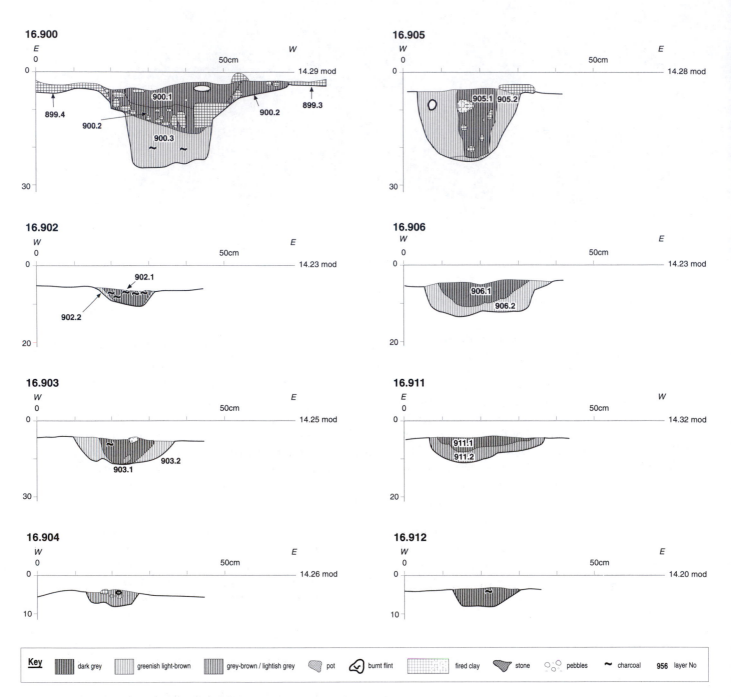

Key dark grey   greenish light-brown   grey-brown / lightish grey   pot   burnt flint   fired clay   stone   pebbles   ~ charcoal   **956** layer No

Fig. 14 *Section drawings of LBA cut features (all phases).*

attributed to unit G with any confidence (Fig. 15). Since any higher continuation of a cut and its dark fill would probably be rendered invisible by the dark 'occupation' earth of units H upwards, confirmation of stratigraphic horizon depends on whether filled post holes were covered by later refuse. Most features are tentatively placed in later units (Table 1) on the evidence of planned soil marks, or relationships of conjectured post positions to debris spreads.

Two intercutting post holes clearly preceded unit H. Post hole 16.900, the later of the two, was covered by the bed of burnt clay 16.899, but evidently before

consolidation of the lowest fill (16.900.3) during decay and/or compaction. Consolidation caused the subsidence of the part of the clay bed immediately overlying the post hole into its fill (16.900.2). In this process the clay bed fragmented, but nevertheless the resulting lumps still formed a near-continuous layer linking up with the undisturbed clay layer surrounding the feature (Fig. 14). The dark earth lens sitting in the top of the post hole (16.900.1) was therefore in this instance clearly unrelated to initial backfilling and can be regarded as a slumped part of 16.872 and/or 16.865.

Post hole 16.919 is cut by 16.900 and suggests at least

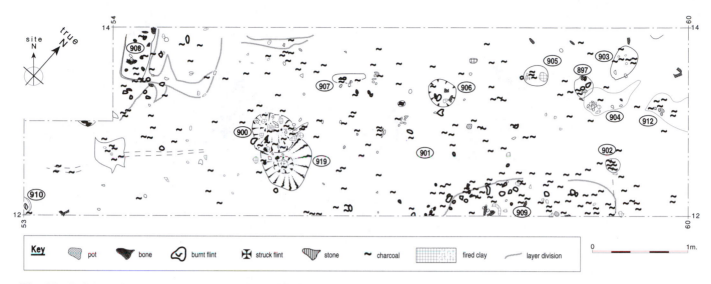

Fig. 15 *Refuse in the surface of 16.901 (unit 16.G) and occupying the top of feature fills of various LBA phases. Features shown hachured belong to unit 16.G.*

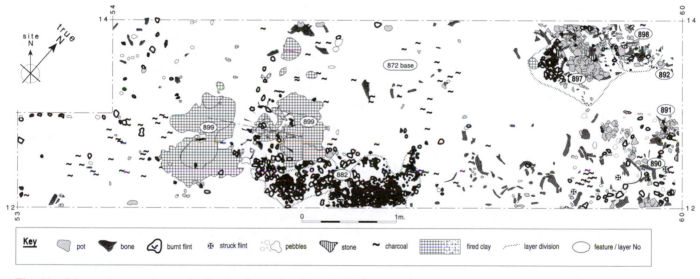

Fig. 16 *Primary dumps and general refuse low in stratigraphic unit 16.H.*

some repair of structures prior to unit 16.H. A fairly shallow feature, 16.906, could have belonged either to 16.G or 16.H.

The soil layers (16.901, 896) were of a somewhat mottled, greenish-light brown colour and of variable consistency, being more friable in patches. Finds from the lower member, 16.901, are very sparse (total weight: *c*.200g). Finds density increases significantly in overlying soil 16.896 (>4000g). Some pockets of finds in the surface after 16.896 had been removed can be regarded as parts of 16.896 sitting in localised undulations – 908, 909, 913.

Stratigraphic unit 16.H: primary dumps, spreads and dark earth (16.872, 876, 882, 884, 885, 886, 887, 888, 889, 890, 891, 892, 894, 897, 898, 899, 900.1, 900.2, 904, 906, 911, 912).

This unit comprises the lowest soil layers of full dark earth character – 16.872/876/887/890. At the extreme east end, where the deposit is thicker beneath burnt clay 16.875, soil was labelled as two main contexts: 16.876/887 around the upper levels of primary dumps and 16.890 surrounding their bases. These soil layers were themselves rich in finds quite apart from the dense dumps they contained. 16.872 covered western and central parts of the trench and was generally a lighter colour than the dark grey of 16.876/890, probably due to fewer charcoal inclusions. 16.872 was also taken in two passes and the lower finds distinguished (872 base). There is not thought to be any stratigraphic significance to any of these differences and collectively these four contexts represent the lowest soil member containing high-density finds (Fig. 16).

43

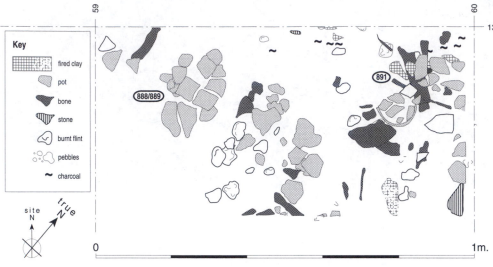

THE MAIN DUMPS AT THE EAST END

1. 16.888/889/890/891 in grid 59/12 (Fig. 17; Plates 4 and 5).

16.888/889 and 891 are more specific clusters (of primarily pot) within a more general concentration. Group 16.891, situated against the east baulk, included a near intact cup (Cat. No. P651).

Against the south baulk, the large bone and pot debris within context 16.890 is immediately covered by a dump of burnt flint, 16.874 (Plate 12; Fig. 5). It could be part of the same episode, but it does not cover much of this refuse scatter in 59/12 and thus is not clearly related functionally (i.e. sealing organic refuse). 16.874 has instead therefore been correlated laterally with the burnt clay 16.875 of unit 16.I.

2. 16.886/892/894/897/898 in grid 59/13 (Fig. 18; Plates 4 and 6).

This is the densest concentration of finds in the trench. Various component parts may be isolated within it. The major division into 16.897 and 16.898 may not be significant.

At the eastern end the dump was fairly thin (16.898); it included another small cup on its edge, 16.892 (P652). The main dump, 16.897, was however relatively thick and was excavated as three 'spits' of diminishing size downwards. The dump was primarily composed of pottery (343 sherds weighing 1.12 kg), but two groups of other materials were identified:

(a) a stretch of articulated vertebrae, 16.886, and
(b) a group of burnt/flint nodules forming a crescent on the western edge of 16.897.

These two groups lay together and could be regarded as being associated with an underlying slab of coarse

pottery 16.897.110, which is somewhat distorted, perhaps burnt (too featureless for cataloguing).

Although these sub-groups were in direct contact with the main body of 16.897, it is possible that they were later additions to it, for example contemporary with 16.875 alongside (see below).

BURNT SPREAD (*Fig. 19; Plates 7, 9 and 10*)

One of two fairly extensive spreads of burnt material low in the dark earth is attributed to unit H, 16.899. Burnt clay and clusters of burnt flint seem to be intimately related. On the strength of various kinds of evidence it is thought that these deposits relate to pottery production (Chapter 8).

The Unit H burnt clay (16.884/885/899/900.2) was an amorphous spread between 54.5 and 57 east, with a large adjacent spread of burnt flint (16.882). The clay was apparently split by a circular area of dark soil (16.900.1). At first it was thought that this represented a void created by a standing post contemporary with or later than the clay. As excavation proceeded a post hole was indeed found to lie beneath this void. However, within its fill was discovered a depressed layer of burnt clay (16.900.2) which formed a link between 16.899.1 and .3 on the west and 16.899.2 and .4 on the east (Fig. 14; Plate 10). It is clear that a continuous bed of clay was laid across a backfilled, but unconsolidated post hole. Subsequent compaction of the lower fill (16.900.3) led to slumping and fragmentation of the immediately overlying clay (16.900.2) and, in turn, the downward movement of dark soil above into the upper hollow (16.900.1). There was clearly no great time interval between the backfilling of the post hole and the formation of the burnt clay.

The western area of 16.899 rose to form peaks (contexted 16.884 and 885) around grid 55 east (Plate 9).

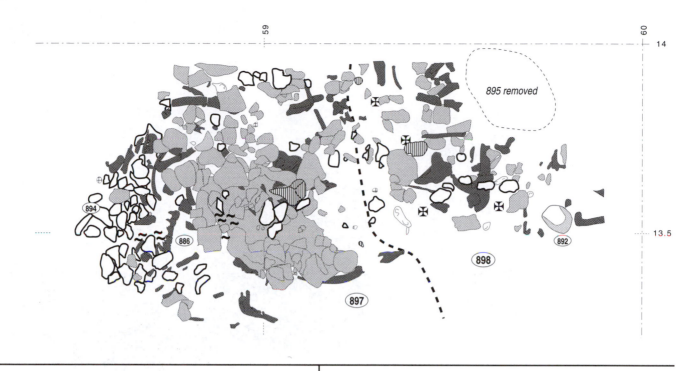

a

895 removed

894

886

898

897

892

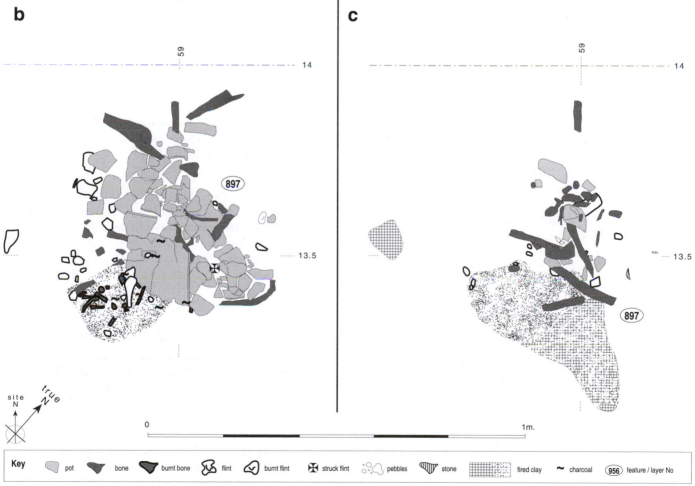

b

897

c

897

site N

true N

0   1m.

Key   pot   bone   burnt bone   flint   burnt flint   struck flint   pebbles   stone   fired clay   charcoal   956 feature / layer No

Fig. 18 *Details of three planned levels within refuse dump 16.897/898 including 16.886, 892, 894, unit 16.H.*

Key: pot, bone, flint, burnt flint, struck flint, pebbles, stone, charcoal, fired clay, layer division, (956) feature / layer No

Fig. 19 *Detail of burnt clay 16.899 and burnt flint 16.882 spreads, unit 16.H.*

They can be regarded as integral parts of the main context and rose to a greatest height of 14.37 m OD, showing as a restricted weathered concentration at the 16.834/836 interface. Where it flanked post hole 16.900, the surface of the burnt clay lay at around 14.26–14.28 m OD.

The burnt flint spreads, 16.882.1 and 882.2, were absolutely contiguous with the burnt clay on its southeast side, and they extended into the baulk, showing clearly in the south section (Fig. 5). Although the two materials had mainly exclusive distributions, some burnt flint cobbles on the edge of 882.2 did impinge on 16.899.4 and also featured as part of 'fill' 16.900.2, notably as a lining behind the burnt clay on the southeastern lip of the cut of 16.900.

The division of 16.882 is significant in terms of both ground plan and the character of the material. Although they touched, two discrete clusters were evident, 16.882.2 being dominated by fairly large lumps, whilst 16.882.1 had a high proportion of medium to fine grit sizes but still with some large lumps present. Over 6 kg of burnt flint was recorded from each context, whilst other finds within were few.

The burnt flint spreads were effectively a lens one cobble thick which only appeared high in 16.872 after the removal of 16.868. A concentration of charcoal flecks in the top of 16.872/876 around grid 57/12 occurred close to a lobe of 16.882.1 (Fig. 19).

CUT FEATURES

A few shallow features could be contemporary with unit H (Table 1). The clearest association is that of 16.904, the fill of which was directly covered by burnt clay 16.875. Feature 16.912, also shallow, may similarly underlie a pot group (unnumbered) and the edge of 16.875.

A soil mark visible low within soil 16.872 may be a higher extension of feature fill 16.906. If so, it was clearly sealed by the edge of a spread of bone and pot (16.873/881) and a post cannot therefore have stood after unit H. A soil mark for 16.911 also showed low in 16.872; it is conceivable that the burnt clay portion 16.884 butted up against the standing post, but insufficient evidence exists for a stratigraphic relationship.

Stratigraphic unit 16.I: continued dumping
(*16.866, 868, 871, 873, 874, 875, 879, 880, 881, 883, 905*).

The dumps of material attributed to this unit are essentially similar in density and character to those of unit

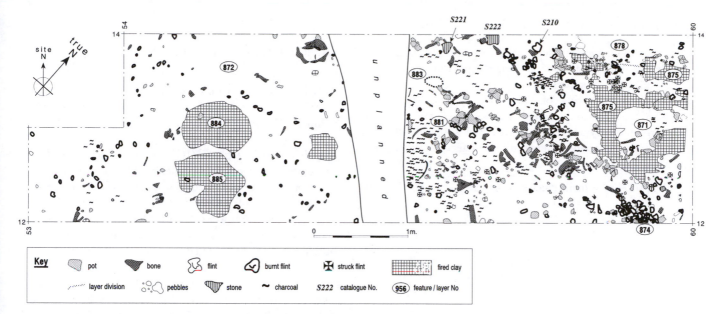

Fig. 20 *Dump deposits and refuse scatter towards the base of unit 16.I in the eastern half and on the surface of unit 16.H in the western half.*

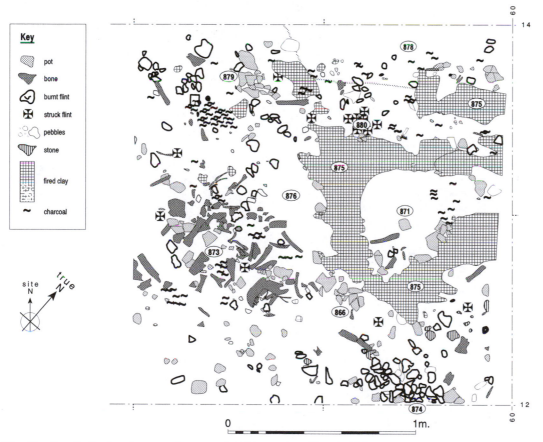

Fig. 21 *Detail of refuse dumps at the east end within stratigraphic unit 16.I.*

16.H and there may have been no hiatus in the build up (Fig. 20; Plate 13). Soil deposit 16.868, also rich in finds, enveloped the dumps and is included here. Context 16.868 was excavated as a wedge of soil tapering out between 56 and 57 east, and unit I as defined is thus confined to the eastern half of the trench.

BURNT CLAY (*16.875; Fig. 21*).

This ragged spread, with a basically annular plan and various additional lobes, seals certain primary dumps (parts or all of 16.890, 891, 889, 892, 897, 898). It is not inconceivable that 16.875 represents an in situ structure

47

foundation, but if so its rather ragged shape suggests a degree of disruption of the original plan during or after levelling of its superstructure.

Within the ring of clay was a charcoal-rich soil, 16.871, which could be either strictly contemporary or a part of overlying 16.868 which had slumped into the central depression. Burnt flint clusters occur on two sides:

1. 16.874, the main cluster is detached from 16.875, but a trail of cobbles bridges the gap;
2. a thin scatter of burnt flint cobbles on the northern side, grid 59/13 (not uniquely numbered).

As mentioned above, it is possible that the crescentic cluster within 16.894 also belongs to this horizon, since it lies on the edge of 16.897 and was not sealed by 16.875.

OTHER REFUSE GROUPS (*Fig. 21*)

Another cluster of burnt flint, this time a small cache of finely crushed material (16.883) occurs at this horizon at grid 57.4/13.5. This would appear to have been dumped within 16.872, or to have been inserted from around the 16.872/868 interface.

A rich spread of refuse (16.873), dominated by little-fragmented bone material, lay alongside the burnt clay zone 16.875 in grid squares 58/12 and 58/13 and was set in the top of 16.876/872 (i.e. at the unit H/I interface). Although a notable concentration, it was not wholly discrete and it is possible that some of the surrounding material contexted 16.876 and 872 represents the same dumping event. The bones appeared to be somewhat jumbled with an admixture of other cultural debris and none were recognised on site to be articulated. Study of the group, however, reveals that a fair proportion of a lamb's carcass can be reconstructed from

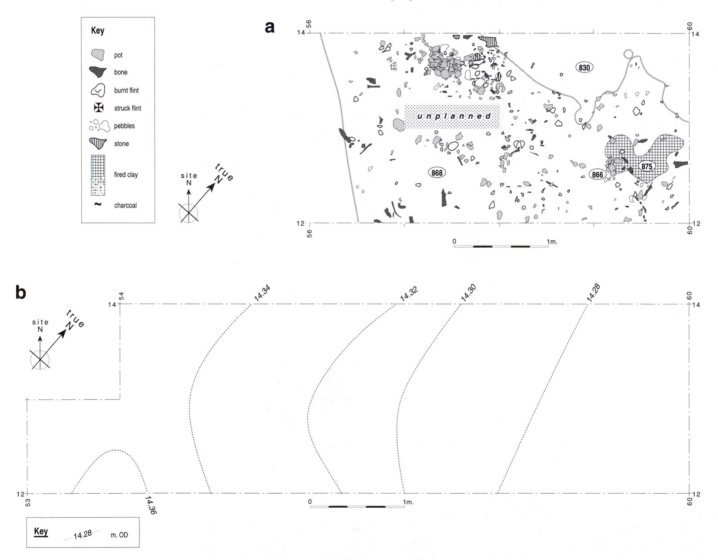

Fig. 22 (a) *Refuse on the surface of 16.868, the unit 16.I/J interface, in the eastern half; 16.830 overlies the interface zone.* (b) *Interpolated contour plan of the same surface after the removal of 16.830, with the unit 16.H/J interface at the western end.*

amongst them and the 1:5 plan shows that limited elements were articulated in the ground (Chapter 12).

POT GROUPS (*Fig. 21*)

Around the peripheries of dump 16.873 were a few small pot groups:

1. 16.881 on the west at 57.6/13.1
2. an unnumbered group on the north-west at 58.0/13.3
3. 16.879 on the north-east at 58.6/13.7
4. 16.866 on the south-east at 59.10/12.6. This last group can be placed in either unit 16.I or 16.J depending on its exact relationship to surrounding deposits. Some sherds were already showing on the surface of 16.865, viz 866.1–.8. An immediately adjacent group (unnumbered) appeared after 16.865 was cleared and overlapped the edge of burnt clay 16.875. Yet more, 16.866.9–.20, lay below on the surface of 16.876, these being vertically below 16.866.1–.8.

The soil thickness involved (i.e. from 16.876/868 to 16.865/836) is 6 cm at 59/12 and 1 cm at 59/13). The three planned levels therefore could easily belong to one stacked pot group, perhaps forming a small heap. Alternatively, the group could have occupied a feature fill, indeed a shallow feature, 16.902, was found immediately beneath. Such a feature would have been cut from the top of 16.865, if not higher. In fact many of the sherds from 16.866, from both its 'spits', were found to belong to a single vessel, P659. Sherds from

16.868 and 16.875 in the same grid, as well as others more dispersed, also joined this vessel.

Other large sherds were scattered throughout this zone. The distribution of the pot groups may be fortuitous, but deliberate positioning around the bone dump 16.873 seems possible.

A small cluster of unburnt struck flint (16.880) occurred at 59.2/13.5 alongside burnt clay 16.875 and between layers 16.868 and 16.876.

CUT FEATURE

The fill of post hole 16.905 can be attributed to this unit with fair confidence. It showed as a charcoal-rich patch at the surface of 16.876 but, more critically, its pipe fill contained a number of burnt clay lumps almost certainly derived from the adjacent spread, 16.875. On these grounds the post would have been withdrawn, or rotted after the burnt clay went down and probably while it was still exposed on the surface. The fill was totally sealed by the clean clay lens (16.830 etc.).

Stratigraphic units 16.H – early 16.J: poorly phased early dark earth deposits (16.878, 895, 903).

The early refuse deposits in the north-eastern corner of the trench, beneath 16.830 etc, were not excavated in sequence with adjacent deposits. A thin soil body, comprising contexts 16.878 and 895, was a grey-green friable silt containing 'pockets' of potsherds, as well as a knife blade (M20). This deposit was stratified between

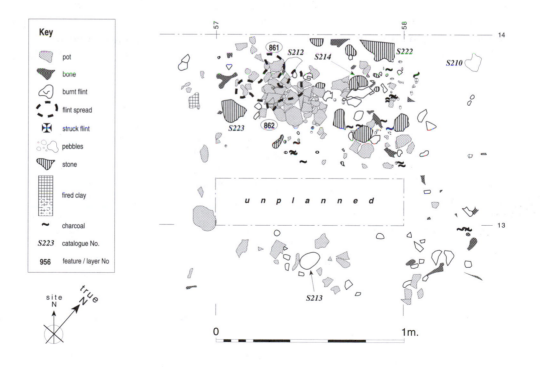

Fig. 23 *Detail of pot group 16.862, overlying burnt flint 16.861, and adjacent stone equipment, close to the unit 16.I/J interface.*

Key

- pot
- bone
- burnt flint
- flint spread
- struck flint
- pebbles
- stone
- fired clay
- charcoal
- *S223* catalogue No.
- 956 feature / layer No

site N   true N

0   1m.

the subsoil of unit G and the sterile clay lens of mid–unit J. It could thus be coeval with unit H, I or conceivably the earliest part of unit J.

Post hole 16.903 was partly overlapped by dump 16.898 of unit H, but there is scope from the finds distributions for a post pipe to have continued up between 16.898 and 897. At a higher level, 16.875 skirts around this position and 16.903 is only certainly sealed by the clean clay deposit (16.869) somewhat later.

Stratigraphic unit 16.J: dark earth rich in pot groups (16.830, 834, 835, 836, 845, 846, 848, 849, 851, 852, 853, 854, 855, 856, 857, 858, 860, 861, 862, 863, 864, 865, 867, 869, 870, 902, 910, 917).

The dark earth layers (16.865, 849, 836, 834) which cover the concentrations described so far do not contain quite such dense clusters of refuse, but nevertheless contain a good number of discrete in situ groups as well as a strong background of more dispersed debris (Figs 24 and 25; Plates 14–17).

A surface planned part way through these pot-group rich soils (Fig. 24) showed two slightly different soils, 16.865 and 16.849, the difference mainly being of colour: 16.865 was a typical dark grey, loamy soil whilst 16.849 had brown-grey/greeny-grey hues. The boundary between them was effectively marked by the fired clay humps already poking through from beneath (16.884/885, 845) and the pot/burnt flint group, 16.862/861 (Plate 16). The two soils may not be strictly coeval, but are broadly so. Context 16.849 was a thin spit (max. 2 cm thick), yet contained good quantities of finds. Many were in the upper planned surface and therefore difficult to divorce from the lower elements of the various pot groups of unit J.

The division between soil 16.849 and overlying

16.836 west was effectively defined by the base of the various pot groups. It is possible that 16.849 also over-laps 16.868 (unit 16.I) temporally. Both 16.849 and 865 came away from the protruding fired clay 16.884/885 (unit H) to reveal a greater spread, but while the full limit was effectively revealed on the west by removal of 16.849, some of the fired clay (16.899.2 and .4) was still concealed in the east. These were only revealed after the upper part of 16.872 was lifted.

Owing to the frequency of eastward-dipping pot groups in and around 16.836 in the middle of the trench, it seems likely that spit 16.836 ran slightly skew to any true stratigraphic lines. In broad terms it is possible to suggest that the eastern half of 16.836 (east of 57E) is later than the western (Fig. 8), although variation may well have been more local. There is unlikely to be any great time difference and both are attributed to unit J. It is possible that the same applies to 16.834, but only one dipping pot group was contained and this is considered insufficient grounds for any subdivision.

POT GROUPS

There is a string of good pot groups running through from 16.863 and 16.864 in grid 58/12 (immediately overlying bone group 16.873) to 16.860 at *c*.56/14 (Figs 23–7). These seem to spread vertically through depths ranging locally from *c*.2 cm to *c*.10 cm or in terms of the excavated spits from the 16.865/868 or 16.836/849 interfaces up to the 16.836/834 interface (an exception is the peak of group 16.835 rising to the surface of 16.834). Other pot groups at a similar level occur further west (Figs 24 and 28). A specific activity 'horizon' can be interpreted here, characterised by a particular kind of refuse dumping. Whether it is basically one episode or a repetition of smaller-scale dumping of uniform

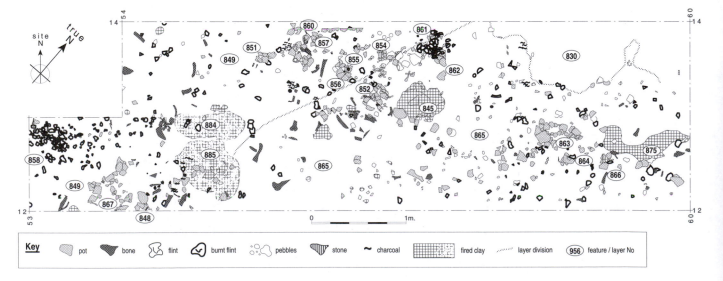

Fig. 24 *The main pot groups and clay spreads in unit 16.J; surface of 16.865/849 and within 16.836 west.*

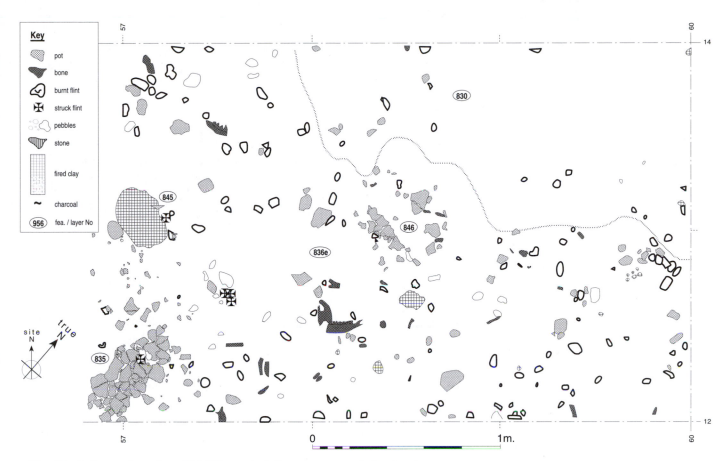

Fig. 25 *Refuse at the surface of 16.836 east, including pot groups and clay deposit.*

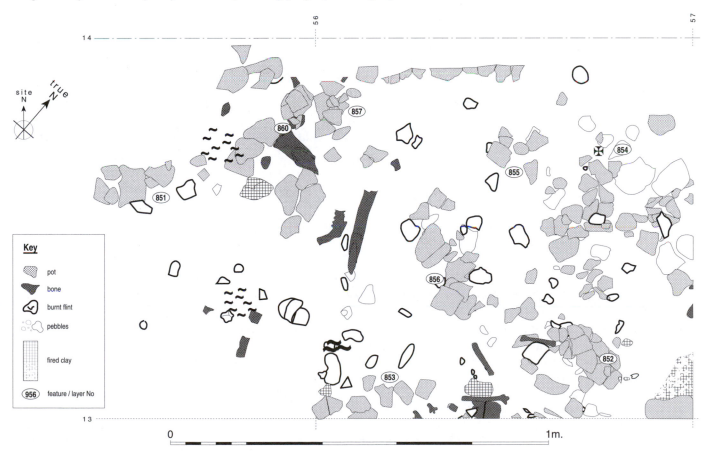

Fig. 26 *Detail of pot groups and surrounding refuse in 16.836 west around grid 56/13, unit 16.J.*

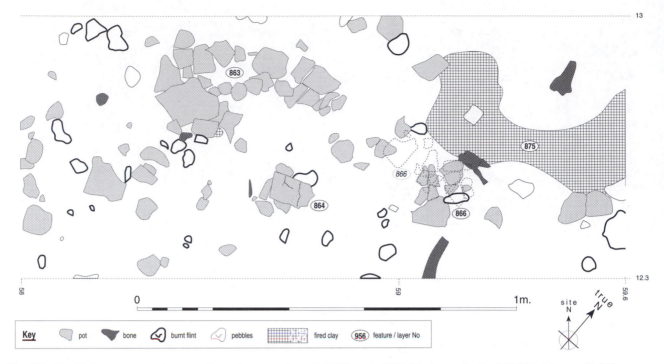

Fig. 27 *Detail of pot groups and surrounding refuse on surface of 16.865, unit 16.J. The lower sherds of 16.866, lying on 16.876, are shown in dashed outline.*

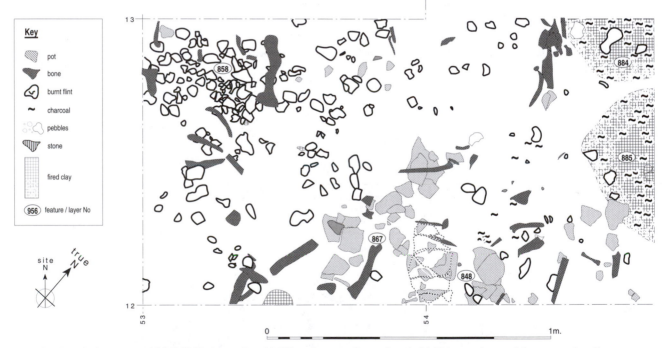

Fig. 28 *Detail of pot group 16.848/867, burnt flint 16.858 and surrounding refuse in 16.836 west (top and bottom conflated), upper part of 16.848 shown in dashed outline, unit 16.J.*

character, is more difficult to evaluate. Certainly a number of individual pot groups seem to span at least one spit thickness due to either an overall dip or the 'stacking' of sherds:

1. dipping groups – 16.857/860, 856, 852, 835, and perhaps 855/854;
2. stacked groups – 16.848/867, 854, 862 with burnt flint 861, and 866.

The dip trend is generally east to north-east, a declination repeated in the burnt clay dump 16.845 and its associated pot base; there is, however, one exception which instead dips westwards, 16.857/860 (assuming these separately numbered groups were co-lateral). There must be doubt then as to how much time depth can necessarily be inferred from the purely vertical dimension of the enclosing soil matrix represented by layers 16.865, 849 and 836. Indeed an element of lateral

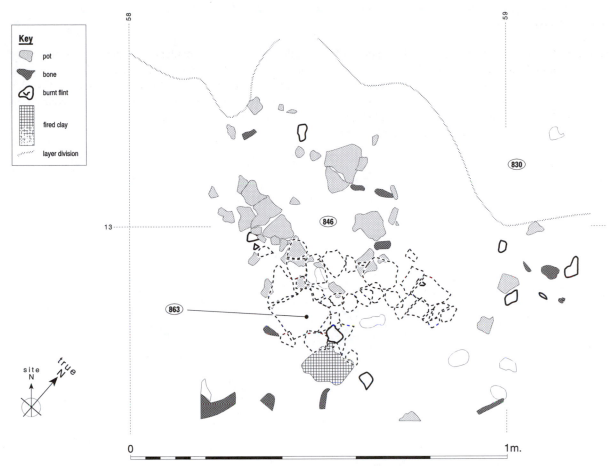

Fig. 29 *Detail of pot group 16.846 in surface of 16.836 east, with underlying group 16.863 (on 16.865) in dashed outline.*

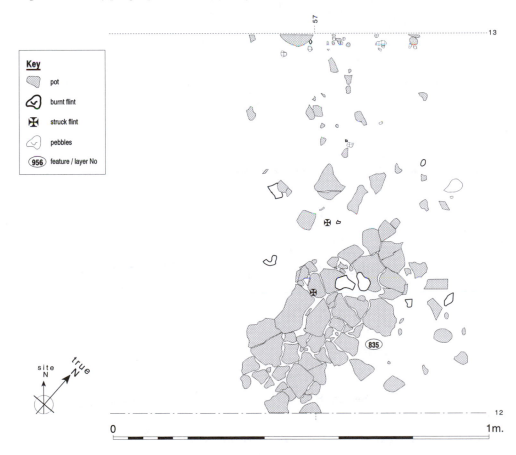

Fig. 30 *Detail of pot group 16.835 in 16.834 and on 16.836 east.*

53

accretion can be suggested by the predominance of dipping pot groups locally around 56/13.

At the east end, where the deposits are thickest, four pot groups were recorded. A 'deep' one, 16.866, has already been discussed (unit I). Groups 16.863 and 16.864 lie vertically above bone group 16.873. This would seem to be coincidence as there was intervening soil 6–8 cm thick after the decay of any organic component. Pot group 16.846 partly overlapped the plan of 16.863 (Fig. 29), but did not appear to be contiguous with it and is thus regarded as a separate dump.

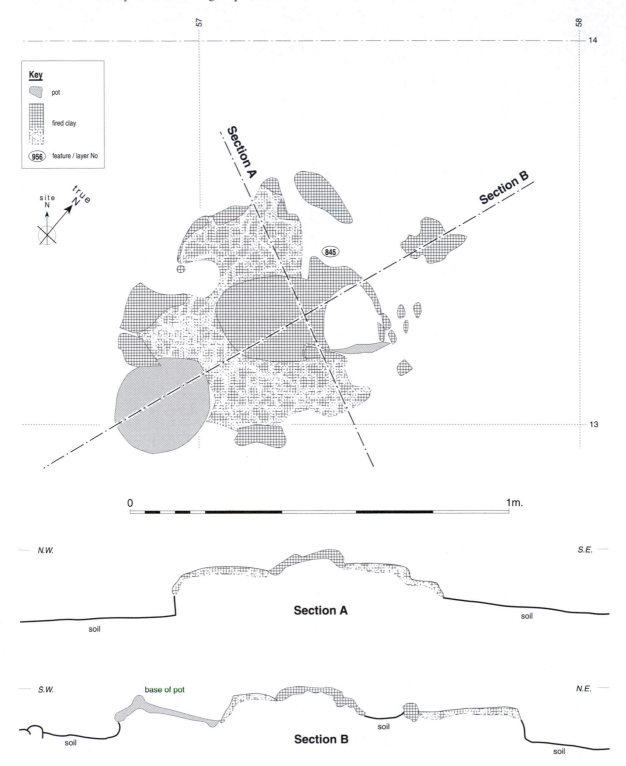

Fig. 31 *Detail of fired clay dump 16.845 and accompanying pot base in plan and surface profile.*

BURNT CLAY DUMP (*16.845*)

At grid 57/13 was found a compact lump of burnt clay. Although somewhat disjointed with an irregular surface (Fig. 31; Plate 17), this was so concentrated and continuous that it gave the appearance of an in situ structure. Closer inspection of the component parts, however, shows more of a jumble, with the juxtaposition of distinct lumps of clay and it should therefore be treated as a dump of redeposited or at least rather disturbed material (Chapter 10). It is conceivable that it came originally from walling, although there are no wattle impressions surviving. It is thought more likely that the dump derived from a hearth scooped up from nearby.

The fabric is generally silty and poorly fired, varying in colour from light yellow to buff and pale orange (fabric 3 – Chapter 10). Much is crumbly, but many surfaces are smooth and more compact, though it is not clear whether this is due to working or weathering.

The full roundel of a pot base (P747) was associated and dipped under the edge of the clay dump at an angle of around 30°. Another associated sherd was pitched vertically.

CUT FEATURES

Two or three features seem likely to belong roughly to unit 16.J. Context 16.917 was a shallow bowl-like cut seen to be penetrating the pot groups around 56/13 – 16.854, 860/857 etc. (Fig. 7). It was probably therefore dug from high in unit 16.J. Similarly, on the strength of the main section recording (Fig. 6), a deep post hole (16.910), seems also to have been cut from at least the upper part of unit 16.J. If feature 16.902 contained pot group 16.866, it too would have been cut from a level not lower than within unit 16.J deposits.

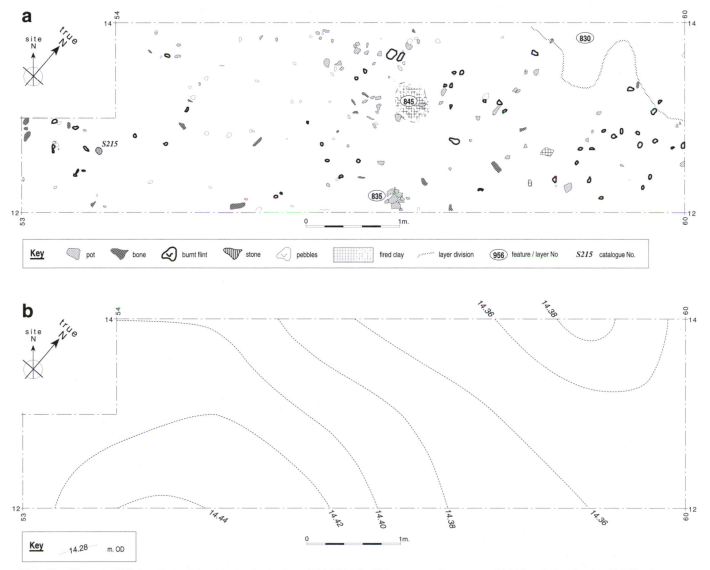

Fig. 32 *The unit J/K interface: (a) refuse in the surface of 16.834; the highest parts of pot group 16.835 and clay humps 16.845, 830 are exposed; (b) interpolated contour plan.*

55

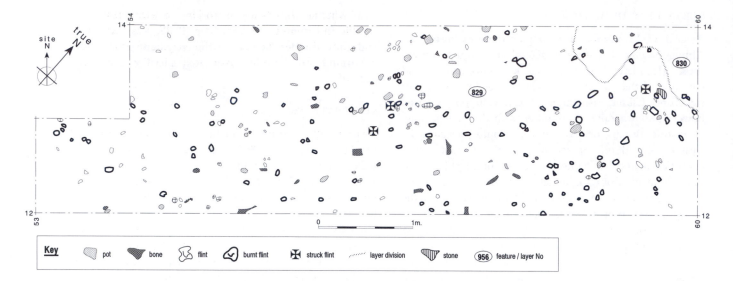

Key ◆ pot ▼ bone ◇ flint ◇ burnt flint ✚ struck flint ······ layer division ◒ stone 956 feature / layer No

Fig. 33 *Refuse in the surface of 16.829, low in unit 16.K. 16.830 was first exposed at this level.*

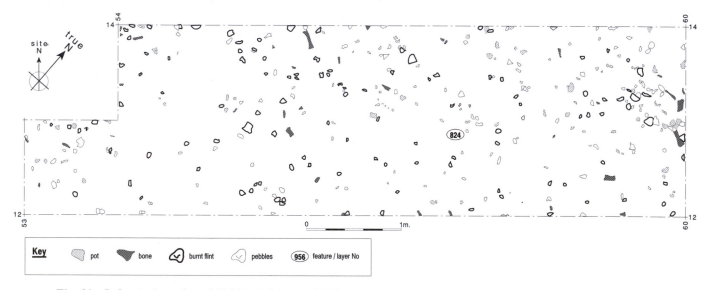

Key ◆ pot ▼ bone ◇ burnt flint ◇ pebbles 956 feature / layer No

Fig. 34 *Refuse in the surface of 16.824, high in unit 16.K.*

CLEAN CLAY LENS (*16.830, 869, 870*)

The final major component of unit 16.J is a lens of clean clay with sandy patches, mottled light yellow/grey (Plates 13 and 14). This was remarkable for the virtual absence of finds, in marked contrast with all juxtaposed contexts. It first became visible in the north-eastern corner of Area 16 East after the removal of spit 16.824 (Fig. 33). However, its full plan was not evident until the level of 16.836 was reached, below which it contracted in plan (Fig. 25). It appeared to be a unitary deposit and is therefore bracketed stratigraphically between 16.865 and 16.834, both of unit 16.J. The lens had a maximum thickness of about 11 cm at the northern baulk (Figs 6 and 7).

The possibility that this was a flood deposit has been considered, but dismissed on the grounds that it had relatively abrupt boundaries, both laterally and vertically. There was no sign of flood disturbance to cultural debris flanking it or to the dense groups sealed immediately underneath (e.g. 16.875, 897, 898). It is therefore considered most probable that this was a man-made dump. Its basal level fluctuated around 14.27–14.30 m OD, which is essentially the same as the surface of 16.865 at this end of the trench and it would appear, therefore, to have been deposited on a more or less level surface. The top was more convex with heights varying between 14.32 and 14.39 m OD.

The presence of evidence for pottery production in the lower dark earth deposits might give an explanation for this clay as raw material for potting (Chapter 8).

Stratigraphic unit 16.K: later stage refuse accumulation (*16.822, 823, 824, 829*).

Above unit 16.J there is a marked decline in the occurrence of in situ groups (Figs 33–5). However, large pieces of cultural debris – bone, pot and occasional fired clay lumps – occur throughout the deposits attributed to unit 16.K (Plate 18). It is judged that the lack of in situ groups is not due to later natural alteration of the deposits.

This would find support, locally at least, in the occurrence of an in situ cluster of burnt flint (16.823) at the top of the unit, between contexts 16.822 and 16.820, grid 53/12–54/12, (Fig. 35). There was also a degree of clustering seen in some large debris at the eastern end on the surface of 16.824. Explanation of the generally dispersed nature of the material is therefore thought to

lie in the original formation process. The area was no longer an immediate dumping ground or a specific or intensive activity area, but was instead subject to more undirected rubbish accumulation, probably a palimpsest of material from a range of intra-settlement sources and arriving after very variable lengths of refuse cycle. The presence of large material within these contexts suggests that if there was an element of trampling during accumulation, it was not comprehensive.

Stratigraphic unit 16.L: conflation horizon (*16.819, 820*).

Unit 16.L can probably be regarded as a conflation horizon resulting from the preferential settling out of heavier items during flood reworking of the soils above (defined in Chapter 1; see also Fig. 36). Burnt flint

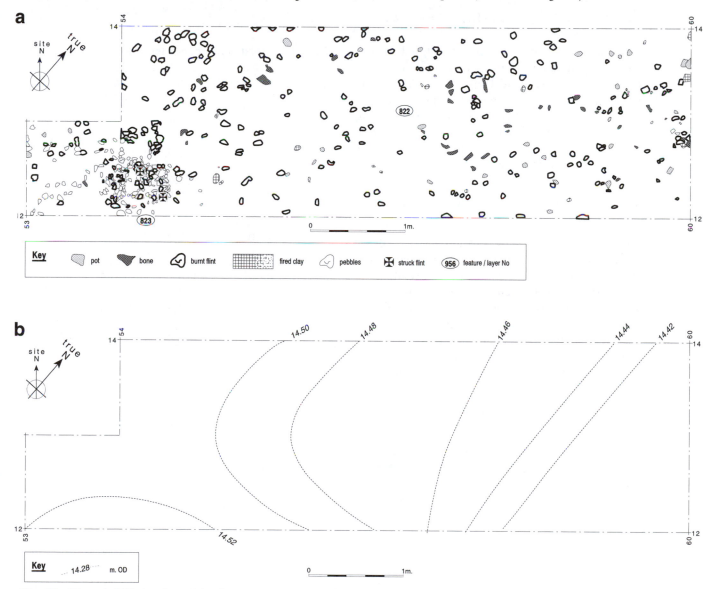

Fig. 35 *The unit K/L interface: (a) refuse in the surface of 16.822, including burnt flint cluster 16.823; (b) interpolated contour plan.*

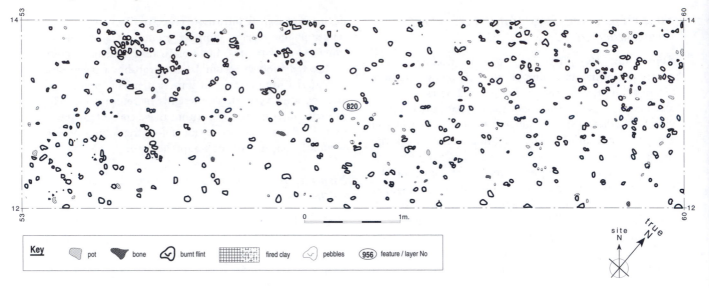

Fig. 36 *Refuse in the surface of 16.820, within unit 16.L.*

densities are high between spits 16.819 and 16.822, whereas pot and bone densities drop from 16.822 to 16.819 suggesting preferential loss by weathering and being swept away. Another possible explanation for a concentrated band of finds would be a worm-sorted horizon; however, the different density changes observed between the various materials suggest that some erosive agency was the primary means of alteration.

Stratigraphic unit 16.M: reworked deposits (16.807, 813, 814).

There is a decline in the density of all the major cultural materials from unit 16.L and the density continues to fall from bottom to top of unit 16.M. The condition of pot and bone indicates severe attrition, almost certainly from natural agencies, whereas burnt flint survives in moderate quantities. The soil is a rather pale grey-brown colour. It is proposed that most degradation is due to flood-reworking, though other natural causes of weathering might also have made a contribution.

Stratigraphic Unit 16.N: modern and disturbed contexts (16.801).

Overlying layers disturbed by machine excavation in the 1985 season include modern rubble layer and some silt/soil beneath.

Table 1: Context concordance for Area 16 East

Unit	Amalgamated Contexts	Layer Type	Artefact Groups, etc	Cut Features
16.N		16.801		16.802
		.803		.804
		.806		.805
16.M	16.807*	16.807		
	.813*	.813		
	.814*	.814		
16.L	16.819*	16.819		
	.820*	.820		
16.K	16.822*	16.822	16.823.1>	
	.824*	.824		
	.829*	.829		
16.J	16.830*	16.830		16.(902)
		.869		.(910)
		.870		.917
	16.834*	16.834	16.835.1>	
	16.836(e)*	16.836(e)	16.846.1>	
	16.836(w)*	16.836(w)	16.845.1>	
			.848.1>	
			.851.1>	
			.852.1>	
			.853.1>	
			.854.1>	
			.855.1>	
			.856.1>	
			.857.1>	
			.858.1	
			.860.1>	
			.867.1>	

Table 1: Context concordance for Area 16 East (continued)

Unit	Amalgamated Contexts	Layer Type	Artefact Groups, etc	Cut Features
16.J cont'd	16.849*	16.849		
	16.865*	16.865	16.861.1>	
			.862.1>	
			.863.1>	
			.864.1>	
			.(866.1>)	
16.I	16.868*	16.868	16.866.1>[1]	16.905
		.871	.873	
			.874	
			.875.1–5	
			.879.1>	
			.880.1>	
			.881.1	
			.883	
16.H–early J	16.878*	16.878		16.903
		.895		
16.H	16.872*	16.872	16.882.1–2	16.904
		.872 base	.884	.(906)
		.900.1	.885	.(911)
			.899.1–4	.(912)
			.900.2	
	16.876*	16.876	16.886	
		.887	.892	
			.894	
			.897	
			.898	
	16.890*	16.890	16.888.1>	
			.889.1>	
			.891.1>	
16.G	16.896*	16.896		16.900
		.908		.900.3
		.909		.(906)
		.913		
	16.901*	16.901		16.919
				.919.1
16.F		16.920		
		.921		
16.E		16.922		
		.923		
		.924		
		.925		
		.926		
		.927		
		.928		
		.930(e)[2]		
		.932		
16.D		16.929		
		.931		
		.933		
		.935		
		.936		
		.940		
		.941		
		.942		
		.943		
16.C		16.930(w)[3]	16.951	
		.944		
		.945		
		.946		
		.947		
		.948		
		.949		
16.B		16.934	16.950	
		.937		
		.938[4]		
		.952		
		.953		
		.954		
		.955		
		.956		
		.957		
16.A		16.939		
		.958		
		.959		
		.960		

N.B. Correlation of cut features with stratigraphic units is rarely precise. When in parentheses they cannot be attributed unequivocally to one stratigraphic unit (16.906 is duplicated), whilst others are attributed only at unit level and not to individual layers or amalgamated contexts.

Notes

1. 16.866.1> is in both units J and I.
2. 16.930(e) may partly belong to unit D.
3. 16.930(w) may partly belong to unit B.
4. Finds in some 'layer-type' contexts were uniquely numbered (e.g. 938.1>) when constituting important refuse spreads.
> point-numbers run upwards from .1.

Summary of the phosphate levels

MIKE COWELL

The soil phosphate sampling strategy and analytical method are detailed in Volume 1, where consideration is also given to the evidence for the stability or otherwise of phosphate within the soil profile (Cowell in Needham *et al* forthcoming). Samples from Area 16 East form two series:

1. Two sets of horizontal transects taken at 1 m intervals from the south section; the sets were taken from the LBA dark earth deposit, notionally an upper and lower series (Plates 1–3); they cannot be correlated specifically with excavated contexts but together broadly equate with unit I-K deposits.
2. Two columns through all the excavated deposits. One was at the eastern end (grid 60/12), sampled at 3 and 2 cm intervals; the column was taken in two parts in successive seasons separated horizontally by 30 cm, but overlapping vertically. The second was at grid point 55/12 and only covered the LBA profile, at 3 cm intervals. Again individual sample positions cannot be linked precisely to excavated contexts.

The horizontal transects present a fairly uniform set of phosphate measurements, with thirteen of fourteen results in the range 230–350 mg/100g and a probable 'outlier' of 450 mg/100g (Table 2). There was no systematic difference between the 'upper' and 'lower' series. The range might be taken to typify the bulk of the Late Bronze Age in situ deposits in this area. The columns, however, included some higher concentrations, peaking at around 700 mg/100g. Looking at the results collectively the sequence through the LBA deposits is as follows. The underlying sterile deposits (units D,E,F) have relatively constant concentrations of around 150–200 mg/100g which then steadily rise through unit G-H deposits to over 400 mg/100g. Four samples roughly equatable with unit I are notably high, *c*.500–700 mg/100g. In the overlying units J and K the measurements fall back closer to the range seen in the horizontal series: J has six samples between 250 and 500 mg/100g, and a further two within 500–630; whilst 5 samples in K fall in the range 270–440. Although the 6 samples from L generally fall low in these ranges, 220–310 mg/100g, only one value is significantly lower at 120 mg/100g, being a sample from a high stratigraphic position. A single sample from unit M, measured as 40 mg/100g, suggests a rapid decline in phosphate values upwards from unit L.

The Neolithic occupation horizon was also marked by a substantial rise in phosphate values, peaking at around 700 mg/100g at a level approximating to the unit A/B interface. Values for the deposits above this fell rapidly to the D/E/F range noted above.

Whilst individual sample measurements may fluctuate as a result of very localised irregularities in phosphate concentrations, in addition to possible measurement errors, the broad trends described above for the unit groups appear to be significant. At a very general level the Area 16 East in situ deposits seem mostly to contain between 230 and 450 mg/100g phosphates. Unit I, however, has higher values which suggest a richer organic input relative to the matrix at large. Occasional values in unit J are again in this higher range (>450 mg/100g), but these show no stratigraphic clustering – they are not, for example, close to the unit I/J interface. The unit L results may be instructive; although they fall at the low end of the in situ range, significant depletion of phosphates seems only to have taken place from a point higher in the unit. This would seem to argue against any wholesale flood-reworking of the L deposits.

Table 2: Phosphate results from horizontal transects through LBA in situ deposits in the south section. Values in mg/100g.

Grid	53/12	54/12	55/12	56/12	57/12	58/12	59/12	mean
Upper	290	260	340	240	230	450	300	290±41*
Lower	260	340	300	280	280	310	280	300±26

*excluding possible outlier at 58/12

CHAPTER 4

Pottery evidence for formation process in the Late Bronze Age deposits

All major categories of finds need to be considered in the assessment of formation processes. At Runnymede the following should make significant contributions: pottery, bone, fired clay and stone. In theory at least the taphonomic aspects of their study can be treated separately from the more traditional lines of enquiry regarding morphology, material or species. In practice, however, separation is not always straightforward and the branches seem especially intertwined for animal bone. Evidence relating to formation should be understood before attempting to interpret the sequences of the various materials in terms of cultural activity or consumption changes (e.g. Schiffer 1987).

We found it relatively easy to deal with the LBA pottery in discrete ways – hence this chapter which is an essential prelude to Chapter 6 and others. The taphonomic aspects of two other major studies are to be found in the relevant chapters (10 and 12) and the synthesis (Chapter 14) attempts to draw together all the significant points on formation process.

In recent years there has been a growing realisation of the potential of pottery assemblages for understanding formation process (e.g. Schiffer 1987, 285; Sullivan 1989; Kobyliński and Moszczyński 1992; Bullong 1994). The approach taken has generally been to look at the gross trends in assemblages and sub-assemblages with respect to sherd size and abrasion. In the Area 16 East study we have found it necessary to supplement this approach with more detailed studies of the constituents of pot groups and the comparative condition of cross-context joins, as well as the total distribution of all joins.

Sherds and pot groups as keys to site formation process

MARIE-LOUISE STIG SØRENSEN

The information contained in pottery relates to many human activities, such as production, procurement of raw material, style and design systems, use and consumption, as well as to depositional mechanisms. It is therefore important from the outset to make it clear that some of these potential factors were given primacy. Due to the importance of understanding the nature of the site and its constituent activities, emphasis is given to those variables that may help in elucidating the formation processes of the site. This means that aspects of the pottery which relate to specific activities (e.g. the speed of accumulation, the type of in situ activities) were given priority in the analysis, while variables relating to the production of pottery and choices of style were seen as less crucial in this particular study and are dealt with in Chapter 8. In short, the sherds were studied in terms of the events and behaviour that created the deposit.

The following analysis is therefore aimed at distinguishing pre- and post-depositional disturbances and characterising the sherd material deposited.

The important question about Runnymede is clearly, what is the nature of the site? At the most basic level we need to comprehend what kind of site this is, what kind of activities constituted it, and what were their temporal and spatial order. Despite the abundance of material from Area 16 East, understanding its deposits is inhibited by the fact that no clear view of structures is possible. Hence, the residual materials, the rubbish, become the key to what happened on the site, and therefore what kind of place it was.

In the final analysis the contribution from pottery should be compared with that of other materials since each finds category is biased because of factors unique to its logic of production, use, consumption and post-depositional disturbance. In fact, one could say that each category produces a slightly skewed picture of what was going on, and their contribution must be set against that of all the others. Usually, the larger site structures (walls, eaves-drip gullies, pits, ditches) aid the interpretation of artefact distributions, but not so in Area 16 East. The logic referred to is, therefore, particularly important as it implies unique inherent characteristics within different finds categories which cause them to behave differently. Ceramic material, as often pointed out, has a lasting quality compared to many other materials in that it relates to stress by breaking rather than dissolving and it is relatively resistant to environ-

61

mental decay. This means that the ceramics originally present in a deposit can generally be expected to survive; their alteration is in terms of size and abrasion, and possibly colour, but only rarely is the stable state of the material altered. Recovered pottery can therefore be highly representative of the original pottery assemblage incorporated. It is furthermore possible to reconstruct the activities altering the pottery prior to, during and after its final incorporation, e.g. trampling causing breakage or sweeping resulting in abrasion.

In effect this study analyses the deposits in terms of their micro-stratigraphy. It aims to separate out the discrete events that made up the mass of finds and created superficially homogeneous deposits.

One critical issue is the extent and type of secondary usage of sherds and their general transformation from primary to secondary refuse (Schiffer 1987). As stated above, pottery behaves distinctively when affected in certain ways but the processes of transformation are nonetheless so complex that it is extremely difficult to decode the traces left on the individual sherd (cf. Schiffer and Skibo 1989). Various attempts have been made to establish correlates. Bradley and Fulford (1980), for instance, in a study of the pottery from Aldermaston Wharf, investigated whether sherd size can be used as an indication of the distance the sherd has moved from its area of primary use. This may be the case for a clearly limited site with structured activities and well-defined activity areas. It is not, however, so easy to apply to midden-like sites which are composed of material with different 'biographies' in complex combinations. As a consequence this analysis explores variables such as size with regard only to their final stage. Certain observations indicate various types of retrieval and re-use, but it was felt that quantification of this would not be informative at this stage. For instance, the number of vessels represented by base sherds is far too low compared to rim sherds. This suggests that the lower parts of broken vessels were regularly re-used in such ways that it affected their rate and context of deposition. The consequences of such a simple observation may be far-reaching and complex. It suggests among other things that even some durable fragments may be missing from the site assemblage unless, of course, the base sherds were dumped in areas not yet excavated. It is often the case that such issues cannot be pursued in any constructive manner beyond mere observation, but they provide important warnings about the cultural mechanisms which have given rise to the excavated assemblage.

Methodology

As outlined above, the methodology was designed to maximise the effectiveness of using pottery to understand the nature of the area excavated. Emphasis was given to variables that relate to the conditions of deposition, involving the act of deposition, the character of the land surfaces created and factors affecting the formation of the deposits. Characteristics which relate to production stages, such as fabric, type, shape and decoration, were always considered to be of secondary importance in this particular study and are only mentioned briefly below.

The potsherds were analysed on the following broad assumptions:

1. many characteristics of an object (e.g. its size or abrasion) depend on what happened to it prior to its incorporation, on the manner in which it was deposited and on the various post-depositional influences to which it was subjected;
2. certain activities (sweeping, trampling) will often leave specific traces on an object;
3. size, weight, and abrasion are meaningful variables illuminating certain aspects of the formation/depositional processes.

The pottery found ranges from deposits of complete vessels and deliberately placed large vessel fragments, to small heavily abraded sherds. All the sherds (a total of 9505) were analysed with respect to weight, size and abrasion. All pot groups from this area were studied separately with respect to these variables. In addition re-fit analysis was done for the following sub-sets of the large assemblage:

1. all sherds within each context-square;
2. within each pot group;
3. between all pot groups;
4. between each pot group and the layer-type contexts immediately around it both horizontally and vertically;
5. between all pot groups and sherds of similar fabric from contexts 16.829–894;
6. amongst all feature sherds.

This set of analyses was directed explicitly towards the questions set out above; a later section of this chapter uses re-fits for a related, but rather different purpose.

The variables analysed will be discussed in order of their importance for the objectives of this study.

Pot groups

The study of the formation of the deposits is greatly enhanced by the definition and separation of pot groups. These are contexts where a substantial part of one or several vessels is believed to have been deposited together in one act. The pot groups stand out as a distinct component of the Area 16 East assemblage, i.e. they generally do not merge into an amorphous category

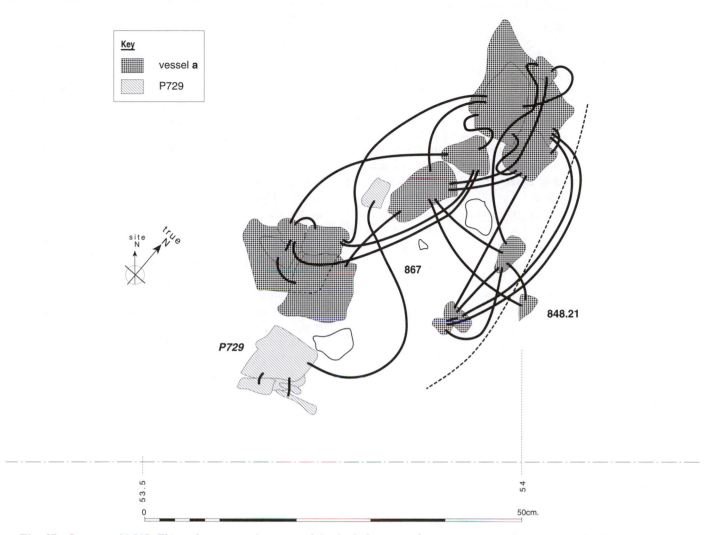

Fig. 37 *Pot group 16.867. This re-fit pattern, where some of the sherds from a pot fragment were pressed almost vertically down, demonstrates that the surface beneath must have been very soft.*

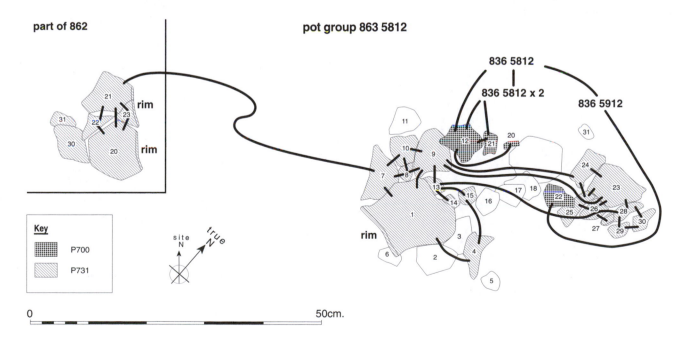

Fig. 38 *Pot group 16.863: re-fits within and beyond the group, illustrating the apparent discrete dumping of originally joining portions of a single vessel.*

with the bulk finds (see Chapter 2 for definition). They therefore pose the question of how their formation relates to other activities, for they would seem to be caused by a different disposal regime. This could bear on the issue of distinction between rubbish formation and ritual or deliberate depositions (e.g. Hill 1993). Obvious special deposits are present at Runnymede in the form of pits located at the periphery of the site and clearly holding deliberately placed and selected objects (Needham 1991, 382).

The analysis of the pot groups was primarily aimed at reconstructing the ways in which groups of sherds have been deposited and the extent to which they have subsequently been disturbed. The pot groups, which are discussed individually in archive, were recorded by 1:5 plans with each sherd separately numbered (e.g. Figs 37–41). During post-excavation analysis the single sherds were laid out according to their original spatial configuration, and it was then possible during re-fitting to attempt three-dimensional reconstructions of the manner in which the pot portion had broken up. These exercises made it apparent that additional information could be extracted about the characteristics of the surface on which the groups had been deposited, such as whether it was sloping or soft; in other words how a pot is broken both reflects the manner of its deposition/

incorporation and the nature of the surface it rests upon, see for example Fig. 37.

Within the pot groups the individual sherds are generally positioned in close proximity to each other (in the order of 0.03 m apart), and joining sherds were often found immediately adjacent to each other. Joining sherds were at times extracted from different spits and/or different squares, but the patterns of their dispersal and joining usually suggest that this was due to the manner of their deposition as opposed to later disturbances. This is, for example, demonstrated by re-fitting sherds frequently lying immediately adjacent to each other or alternatively in discrete clusters at some distance from each other (Fig. 38). Such displacement of different parts of a vessel can be caused either by modest post-depositional disturbance (probably caused by a single event) or by the separate deposition of single fragments broken prior to the deposition. In the cases where displacement may be argued to have happened after deposition, the positions of the sherds usually suggest that this was caused by the flattening effect of the overburden. With the mounting pressure from above pot fragments with a good curvature would break and the different parts become relocated, while the material accumulated around the fragment would preserve the relative positions of joining sherds as illustrated in Fig.

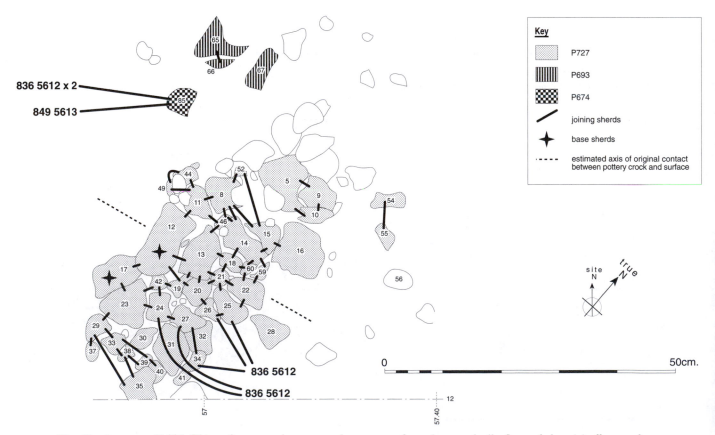

Fig. 39 *Pot group 16.835. This re-fit pattern demonstrates how pressure from above gradually flattened the originally curved pot fragment.*

39. If the curvature is strong so that only a small part of the fragment originally rested on the surface, individual sherds might even become superimposed one on top of the other as opposed to being pushed apart.

The lack of disturbance must mean that this area was either not trampled or dug over after the deposits formed, or that the deposits were quickly covered thus protecting against trampling and eroding mechanisms. Considering the variables it seems most likely that little regular movement of humans or animals took place here while the deposit developed and it is unlikely that it was left open for any substantial length of time.

The pot groups also show that the area at the time of deposition had an uneven surface, and this provides interesting clues as to the nature of the site. The impression gained is that the deposit rich in pot groups was made up of a series of small overlapping dumps which, due to speed of accumulation (and the apparent absence of major eroding factors), were only gradually flattened (see Fig. 40).

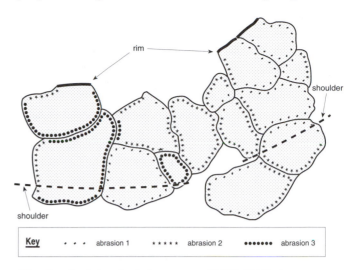

Fig. 41 *Re-fitting sherds from context 16.890 59/12 (not recorded in situ). Detailed mapping of the degree of abrasion along sherd edges shows that one side of the part-vessel is generally less abraded than the other. High abrasion occurred after the portion broke up further into the sherds recovered.*

Most pot groups consist of large fragments of one or more pots. Their abrasion usually suggests that they had been moved around or re-used prior to their inclusion in the deposit. During and after deposition impacts and pressure caused them to break further, as demonstrated by some fresh unabraded breaks and the varied abrasion along the edges of joining sherds (e.g. Fig. 41). Eroding influences were minimal since large sherds are present and, even more importantly, strongly curved sherds have often remained unbroken. The latter situation could arise when the sherds are protected by soft midden material. This again all points to limited post-depositional disturbance.

The majority of specific pot groups (i.e. not mixed dumps including pottery) were found within three layers/spits (contexts 16.834/836/849; unit J) with a few located in lower contexts, see Table 6 and Figs 24–30. Most of the vessels found in pot groups are large- to medium-size coarse-ware jars, such as P727 (context 16.835). An interesting factor is the lack of whole bases (as noted above) and the observation that many vessels had broken along the often fragile line of contact between base and side. This indicates that the pot groups, despite their differentiation from the bulk finds, are likely also to be rejected domestic ware rather than objects withdrawn from use for symbolic or ritual purposes. In this light it is significant to mention that two small undecorated semi-fine-ware cups, one whole (P651) and the other almost so (P652), were found standing upright but slightly tilted in a dense cluster of materials at the base of the dark earth below the general level of specific pot groups (Plates 5 and 19). These small vessels do not constitute pot groups as defined here and it may be significant that they occur at the

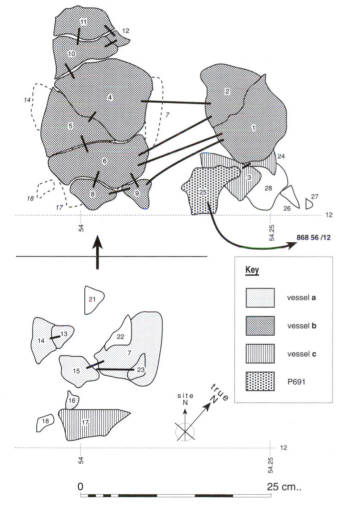

Fig. 40 *Pot group 16.848, showing the layering that sometimes develops in pot groups.*

earliest stage of this sequence (base of unit H). The complete vessels incidentally further demonstrate that these deposits were protected from disturbance. It is noteworthy, in this context, that earlier excavations of the river channel (Area 6; Longley 1991) resulted in several reconstructible fine-ware vessels. The type of vessels deposited, the character of their deposition and the subsequent history of their immediate depositional environment may therefore in the future provide quite detailed insight into variations across the site.

In Area 16 East the pot groups illustrate two different types of activities throughout units H-J and a third is represented at the very base of the LBA dark earth deposit. The first type involves substantial parts of individual vessels (up to almost half a vessel) deposited either alone or simultaneously with a few single, possibly incidental sherds from other vessels. This is similar to activities proposed, but only informally analysed on other sites such as Down Farm (Barrett, Bradley and Green 1991, 206). The second type is represented by dumps of large fragments from numerous pots including several non-joining fragments from the same pots, thus having the characteristics commonly associated with material from the cleaning of living surfaces. The small number of sherds outside the pot groups which re-fitted with pot groups (56 joins) suggests strongly that whole pots were not deposited in these spits. This implies an earlier refuse history for these sherds, even if one of short duration. Whole pots, as mentioned above, potentially represent a third type of activity confined to the lowest level.

The pot groups were concentrated in one particular stratigraphic unit in the matrix and will thus have special implications for this phase of the deposit. Primarily, they imply that unit J is likely to have been deposited over a relatively short time period and at some distance from major areas of activity, both of which would have protected the material against disturbances. The interrelationship between some of the pot groups is interestingly illustrated by the re-fitting of sherds from the pot groups themselves. For instance, the portions reconstructed as vessel P674 include sherds from several different pot groups as well as a few layer-type contexts, mainly at a similar horizon. Similarly, the re-fit pattern of pot group 16.863 (Fig. 38) is complex with some joining sherds in close proximity to each other, some isolated joins from different contexts and squares, and the two major fragments located a short distance apart.

The overall implications from the study of the pot groups are:

1. there was only limited post-depositional disturbance in units H-J;
2. there are two different depositional regimes involved

in the inclusion of pottery in the refuse deposit, and one type of activity (whole pots) limited to the lowest level;
3. the fragments were in several instances placed on a soft, soggy surface sloping slightly towards the east and containing localised troughs and peaks;
4. trampling or other post-depositional disturbances seem generally negligible, while breakage due to pressure was common.

On this basis we must conclude that most of these groups are composed of pots that were broken away from their excavated location, and then incorporated into the deposit while still in relatively large fragments.

Analysis of re-fit patterns

The aim of this re-fit analysis (for which only actual joins were included) was to investigate the spread of sherds originally joined, and to study the processes, including post-depositional activities, which caused their relative positions (for other aspect of re-fit patterns see the last part of this chapter).

From this analysis it appears that amongst the bulk finds re-fits are rare in the highest levels, are most common at the levels around the pot groups (unit J), and then decline towards the lowest level (unit G). In addition there are more fits towards the east end of the trench particularly in the lower contexts. The latter is important as it corresponds with an increase in low-abraded sherds at this end. It is quite likely that this re-fit pattern reflects original heap-like concentrations. The pattern in the highest levels is most likely due to a combination of an originally wider dispersal of sherds and the narrow limits of the trench.

In broad terms one can define two types of re-fit pattern. One consists of joining sherds in close proximity, often contiguous, a pattern most clearly reflected by pot groups. The other shows the joining of sherds more than 1 m apart or from spits which are not in contact. Given the total sherd assemblage from Area 16 East and the extensive join searches, surprisingly few sherds outside the pot groups were found to join (340 sherds). This is most clearly demonstrated by feature sherds (rim, base and decorated sherds) not included in pot groups, which should generally provide very good re-fit prospects, but nonetheless yielded relatively few joins (28 out of 311 sherds, approx. 9%). No spatial pattern was discerned in the re-fitting (beyond the pot groups) that could be interpreted as constituting original surfaces or slope-lines, as both horizontal and vertical joins can exist within the same context. This confirms the impression of small dumps and much secondary deposition.

Analysis of abrasion

Abrasion is one of the most important indicators of what happened to individual sherds during the refuse cycle; it is, however, also a characteristic which is very difficult to interpret. The degree of abrasion is obviously dependent on the characteristics of the individual sherd as well as on the abrasion agencies. Some investigations have been made into this relationship (e.g. Schiffer and Skibo 1989), but as yet this has not resulted in a generally applicable methodology for the study of this variable. In the case of Area 16 East, the mixed nature of the assemblage in terms of fabric and degrees of fragmentation as well as the relatively low pottery quality meant that the specific character of sherd and abrader were considered not to be significant at a coarse level of relative differences in the degree of abrasion. These variables do, however, become more relevant if the material from Runnymede is compared with that of other sites.

The large size of the sample studied and the small average size of individual sherds meant that it was only realistic to consider abrasion according to a coarse division. Three stages were thus defined:

1 = low   Very low or no abrasion. The sherd has fresh breaks as indicated by the 'freshness' of the colour of the core, by the unaltered surface, sharp corners and edges, and by the presence of pieces of temper which constituted obvious obtrusions. Abrasion and breakage seen to be caused by excavation and post-excavation work was of course ignored.

2 = medium   Some abrasion indicated by the absence of fresh breaks and patinated core colour, but sharp corners are still present.

3 = high   High abrasion is indicated by rounded corners and edges, the outline of the sherd is rounded, and its surface may be eroded.

It is not obvious how abrasion should be assessed as different stages of activity can affect the final appearance of a sherd. For example, a sherd may have medium-abraded sides along half of its periphery while the remaining part shows low abrasion. Minor differences in the position of the sherd in the ground and the nature of the abrading activities might have caused such differences. It might, however, also be the case that a medium-abraded sherd broke during its final deposition and was not further altered after this activity. This would mean that the less abraded side relates most directly to the final locus, since it demonstrates the absence of abrading factors there. This study aims to relate the degree of abrasion to the formation of the excavated deposits, which means that the focus was on the extent to which sherds were abraded during this ultimate process, theoretically disregarding abrasion prior to the final deposition. In practice, however, abrasion from different stages is only likely to be separated on sherds which have wide ranging states of abrasion.

The sherds with low abrasion demonstrate that they were deposited without their state becoming further altered. Sherds with medium and in particular high abrasion, on the other hand, can only be used to show that at sometime during their life they underwent activities which caused abrasion.

Because of this association between events and abrasion the sherds are here analysed in terms of their lowest degree of abrasion, as this would provide the best signature of the *formation* of the deposits as opposed to the life histories of the constituent materials. The following assumption was used as a starting point: if the abrasion observed had been caused entirely by post-depositional processes one would expect both horizontal and vertical uniformity or gradual changes. The analysis shows a far more complex picture (Fig. 42).

The general trend is an uneven increase downwards (until unit H) of low- and medium-abraded sherds and a corresponding decrease in highly-abraded ones. Against this trend, however, peaks and falls in the distribution of the three degrees of abrasion throughout the deposit demand further consideration. These irregularities are primarily found from context 16.834 downwards. Before offering any explanation, these irregularities must be assessed in terms of the dispersion within each context in order to evaluate the degree to which the pattern represents the composition across all grid squares.

To obtain this information the standard deviation of the degree of abrasion was established across Area 16 East for each layer-type context (Fig. 42). This showed the greatest 'trench-uniformity' (i.e. the contexts with less deviation in sherd abrasion pattern across the trench) in contexts 16.819 to 16.829 (units K-L) with the highest uniformity in contexts 16.820 to 16.824. Hence, variation is limited within these contexts, which means they are likely to have accumulated in a comparable manner, to consist of sherds affected by a similar range of mechanisms and influenced by post-depositional abrading factors to a comparable extent. Such uniformity is absent from contexts 16.834 to 16.849 and decreases even further in the lowest contexts (16.865 to 16.872). This seems to suggest that the early (lower) stages of the deposit were due to a different range of activities than the rest and, furthermore, that it was little affected by any homogenising transformations (post-depositional mechanisms).

The degree of uniformity of contexts across the trench corresponds generally with increased abrasion in the sense that a high percentage of low-abraded sherds

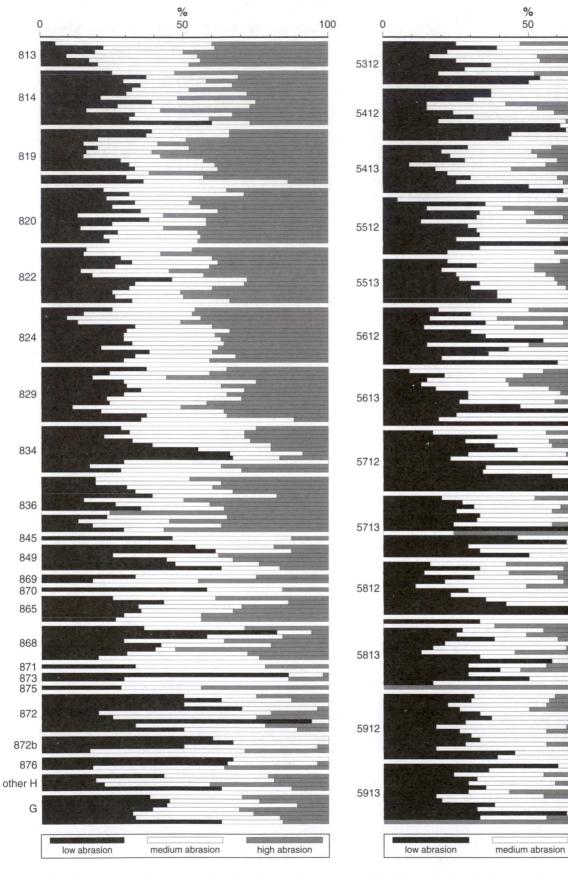

Fig. 42 *Percentage distribution of the three degrees of abrasion within each context-square.*

Fig. 43 *Percentage distribution of the three degrees of abrasion organised according to grid squares, and then contexts.*

within an overall context tends to correspond with a high level of deviation within that context. This means that in contexts where some squares have a substantial number of low-abraded sherds there will be other squares with many highly-abraded ones. This may suggest that low-abraded sherds did not come into the deposits in the same ways as the other sherds, and that when deposited they were either accompanied by incidentally included medium- and high-abraded sherds or deposited next to such sherds. The more abraded sherds may thus constitute a kind of 'noise' which is commonly present and which arrives at the deposit already heavily or moderately abraded. This association between low abrasion and a high degree of deviation furthermore suggests that the units underneath context 16.829 (units J–H) do not consist of uniformly built-up deposits composed of sherds with similar past histories. Rather, we see the accumulation of distinct deposits covering a limited area of the trench resulting in heaps whose central peaks and sloping peripheries are marked by high percentages of low-abraded sherds and other materials. This suggests that separate depositional events were either superimposed on or juxtaposed against the rubbish heaps created by previous depositions. Single heaps might at one time have been separated from one another by differentially composed materials from the surfaces of previous deposits or superimposed on a 'background' not unlike that seen in relatively 'pure' form in unit K (contexts 16.822 to 16.829). There seems furthermore to be a higher percentage of low-abraded sherds in certain contexts in the middle of the trench (around grid 56–58E), which may indicate differences in refuse contributions at a very localised scale (Fig. 43).

There are of course various possible correlations between size and abrasion, although they are not exclusively caused by the same activities. Their correlation may in fact in some cases indicate whether abrasion happened contemporaneously with or subsequently to fragmentation. We cannot isolate a single reason for what caused sherds to be both very fragmented *and* very abraded; but some light can be shed on the mechanisms behind, for example, big *and* abraded sherds. The latter correlation cannot be caused by typical fragmenting activities such as digging, trampling or throwing. It is more likely that the abrasion would be due to processes such as weather, flood reworking and secondary use. Similarly, if sherds are unabraded then their fragmentation must be due to activities which do not in themselves cause substantial abrasion – for example digging, throwing and smashing – and it can furthermore be concluded that they were not additionally affected by natural or cultural transformations. To check on the nature of this correlation the degrees of abrasion of sherds in different size groups were analysed for the whole assemblage except context 16.807 (a total

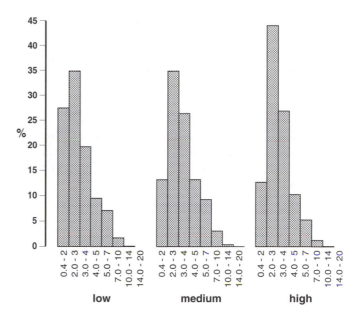

Fig. 44 *The distribution of the three degrees of abrasion in relation to size groups (measurements in centimetres).*

of 9007 sherds; Fig. 44), and two size groups (2.0–3.0 cm and 5.0–7.0 cm) were compared with regard to the abrasion within each context-square (results in archive).

This analysis showed firstly and somewhat surprisingly that low-abraded sherds are relatively most common amongst small sherd sizes. Secondly, that different size groups are unlikely to diverge significantly from the general pattern. This suggests, amongst other things, that large sherds were not generally freshly broken on their deposition. The high frequency of small, low-abraded sherds may be interpreted in different ways. (It is not thought that any significant number are due to damage on excavation.) Clearly these are not continuously eroding objects finally being swept away, which might have been assumed to be the norm. Rather one can suggest that these sherds were either broken during or after final deposition and were not thereafter affected by eroding mechanisms, or alternatively that these are in fact early-stage refuse which suffered no erosion after discard. In this connection it should be emphasised that a pot or pot fragment when breaking falls into pieces of different size and that big sherds therefore are not automatically more primary in terms of refuse history than small sherds. Of the two explanations proposed for small, low-abraded sherds the latter may in this particular case be supported by the relatively low frequency of re-fits amongst the sherds, which contradicts expectations of the results of breakage at the locus of final deposition.

Overall these analyses of abrasion show a far more complex picture than expected. There is considerable variation in the degrees of abrasion from context to context. The most obvious patterns emerging are:

1. The deposits are neither uniformly composed with respect to the degree of abrasion nor are there any simple gradual horizontal or vertical changes.
2. There is high variability between the individual squares of each context/layer-type with respect to the proportion of the three degrees of abrasion.
3. Low-abraded sherds are mainly small and large, as opposed to middle-sized, and these are best explained as part of refuse which comes to the deposits straight from their primary discard zones.

This analysis shows that the effects of post-depositional disturbances were certainly not identical throughout the deposits and may even have been limited in much of it. It also suggests that sherds arrived at the area already differentially abraded and broken. At the same time there are no concentrations of consistently low or high abrasion to distinguish particular contexts as separate features or activity areas. This does not rule out the recognition of activity areas using other criteria.

Analysis of weight and size

The analysis of the average weight and average size of the sherds (not including pot groups) supplements the patterns produced by the pot groups and the analysis of abrasion. Size was established as the maximum diameter of each individual sherd, which was then located in one of the following size-groups: 0.4–2.0 cm, 2.0–3.0 cm, 3.0–4.0 cm, 4.0–5.0 cm, 5.0–7.0 cm, 7.0–10.0 cm, 10.0–14.0 cm, and 14.0–20.0 cm. The sherds from each size group were counted and weighed for all context-squares (Fig. 45). Both measurements were actual

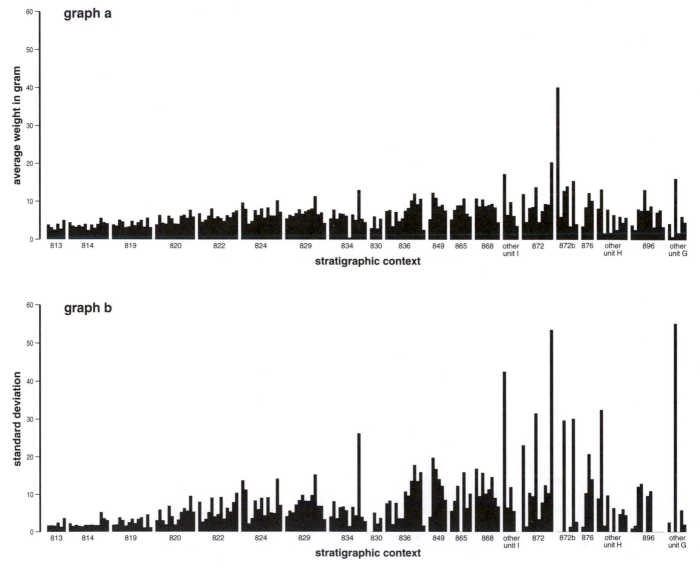

Fig. 45 *(a) Average weight of sherds and (b) standard deviation in sherd weights within each context-square shown stratigraphically from left (top) to right (base).*

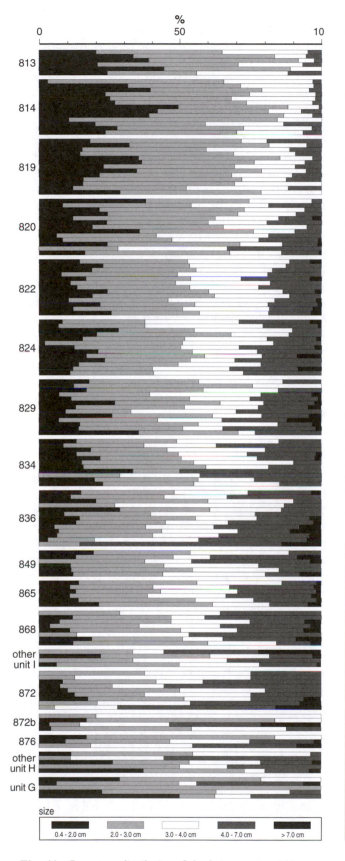

Fig. 46 *Percentage distribution of sherd size groups within individual context-squares.*

measurements and no attempts to adjust for sherd thickness or other variables were made, since the differences were considered not to be substantial (see also Millett 1979, 78).

The most important results are that there is neither uniformity in average weight within particular contexts, nor gradual horizontal or vertical changes. The highest values came from contexts 16.836 to 16.901, which are also contexts with generally less abraded sherds and, more obviously, a higher proportion of large pieces (Figs 42 and 46). The degree of uniformity, measured in terms of deviation (Fig. 45b) for single layer/spits also changes at about this point, suggesting a significant difference between the lower units (contexts 16.834 to 16.901) and the upper ones (16.814 to 16.829) in terms of homogeneity. It is worth noting that this change occurs above the main level of pot groups.

Analysis of average size (Fig. 46) produces very similar patterns to those of abrasion, despite the detailed abrasion:size relationships noted above. There is, however, a tendency towards larger sherds in lower contexts. Meanwhile, it is worth investigating the details behind such averaged patterns. For this purpose the modality of the size distribution within each context was investigated. Counting the number of peaks in the size distribution within each context-square is a simple way of assessing this variability (no statistical test has been applied). This shows that a number of contexts have bimodal size distributions (Fig. 47). This might well be within the expected variability of broken pots (cf. Shennan 1988, 39), but it is interesting to note that, although never dominant, such bi-modality is particu-

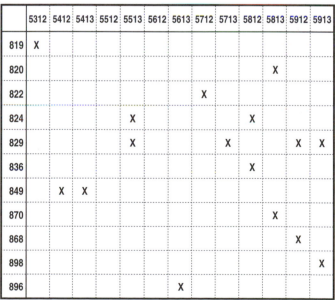

	5312	5412	5413	5512	5513	5612	5613	5712	5713	5812	5813	5912	5913
819	X												
820											X		
822								X					
824				X					X				
829				X				X				X	X
836								X					
849		X	X										
870									X				
868											X		
898													X
896							X						

Fig. 47 *The spatial distribution of context-squares showing bi-modality in sherd size distributions.*

71

larly frequent in units I-K (contexts 16.868 to 16.822). These are contexts which other variables show to be the less uniform, and the bi-modality may therefore suggest that at these levels different activities were involved in terms of what refuse was collected, how it was introduced to the deposit and their (limited) post-depositional transformation.

Both high average weight and large sizes appear to cluster at certain levels and in particular at various locations within the trench. There are, furthermore, instances of marked change from one spit to the next, and the highest readings shift around within the trench. This patchy distribution is particularly characteristic from context 16.824 downwards. It supports the interpretation that we are studying the accumulation of discrete dumps rather than homogeneous horizontal layers. The sharp but localised differences in average weight and the presence/absence of bi-modal size distribution furthermore suggest that the material did not come from identical sources or alternatively that it has been sorted in some way. It also shows that post-depositional mechanisms were not of a kind to have totally homogenised these original differences.

Fabric, colour and decoration

It is often the case that different types of vessels/fabrics are incorporated preferentially in certain types of deposits. Analysis of the Early Iron Age site at Winnall Down shows, for example, that the less common fabrics are deposited in specific parts of the site and Hill argues that pottery deposition was associated with a range of values constructed around the settlement boundaries and mediating between different areas (Hill 1993, 183). Within the limits of Area 16 East this kind of evaluation would not be meaningful and has no contribution to our understanding of the formation processes.

It is, however, worth pointing out a number of variables which in subtle ways may have influenced the rates at which eroding processes operated and therefore have differentially skewed representation. The quality of the pottery can, for example, have affected the overall composition and characteristics of the deposit. Poorly fired and very coarse pottery may break more easily, whilst coarse sandy ware seems to be particularly susceptible to erosion. Colour differences, like those consistently observed between so-called fine- and coarse-ware, can suggest different production practices for the two groups with regard to firing techniques and possibly also variations in the raw material. This does of course have various implications for the pottery not only in terms of breakage and abrasion but possibly also in terms of status.

The status of the pottery potentially has substantial ramifications for the refuse pattern as it would have determined where on the site different types of pots were used (and broken) and what happened to their sherds thereafter. Such status differences were, however, not clearly perceived in the sherd assemblage and no attempt was made to group the material accordingly. Variations in fabric and decoration might be indicators of such differences. These two variables neither show significant correlations nor do they seem to indicate obvious spatial patterns. Coarse-ware sherds are the most common and decorated sherds only make up 1.8% of the total assemblage. This may lead us to conclude that the sherds were mainly from low status or domestic pottery, and that the differences within the assemblage are more likely due to chronological changes than to changing strategies with regard to the status of the pottery incorporated (possibly with the exception of the lowest level with the whole pots). This would suggest that in general cultural terms, the material taken to this part of the site and the reasons for doing so remained similar throughout the formation of the deposit. Consideration of all the zones at Runnymede will, however, show that there are differences between this material and that recovered from other parts of the site such as the Area 6 river deposit, these having more bowls and decorated sherds and apparently a more diverse assemblage.

Maximum vessel count

A vessel count was made on the basis of rim sherds only (excluding those in pot groups). This selection was made because an assessment of the total number of vessels would be both extremely time-consuming and very inaccurate due to the size of the assemblage, the coarse and indistinct nature of most sherds, and the high degree of fragmentation (see also Millett 1979, 78). Rim sherds provide more features for comparison than body sherds and they can give a reliable impression of vessels represented by a particular sample. 651 rim sherds (7% of all sherds) were included in the Area 16 East material, and they represent an estimated maximum of 454 single vessels. [Needham's quite separate evaluation (below) gave a total of 363 vessels represented by rims, this being closer to a minimum vessel count]. In terms of formation processes the important implications are:

1. that in most cases only a few sherds from any individual vessel were found within the limited area and thus we must assume they were spread over a larger part of the site;
2. that Area 16 East for the most part acted as a locus of final deposition for much late-stage refuse with only limited trapping of primary refuse.

The same pattern is suggested by the re-fitting of decorated sherds, and since they provide very good opportunities for recognising sherds from the same vessel this gives us a reliable impression of the extent to which given vessels are represented in the deposits. Out of a total of 173 decorated sherds only seventeen joined or were clearly from the same vessels. These patterns collectively stress the difference noted already between the bulk of the ceramics and the pot groups with their high join rate.

Summary interpretation

With respect to the formation of middens or similar deposits one can suggest that various dumpings of refuse would 'naturally' have been placed next to each other, perhaps being conditioned by structures and activity areas. With time this would result in an extremely mixed deposit with respect to its constituent units, but one which at the same time might superficially appear even and homogeneous. Area 16 East has these characteristics, and the analysis of its formation processes suggests that this is a midden-like deposit.

The analysis has established that the activities causing the deposit varied through time; the distance to contemporary use zones varied, as did the rapidity with which contexts accumulated and became sealed. The status of the pottery deposited and the general characteristics of the sherds (such as the small number of joins, the general presence of some abrasion and small size sherds) at the same time suggest that such changes were not due to the area gaining a different rank status within the site but rather result from a change in the distance from refuse creating activities or, alternatively, from a change in attitudes towards refuse and the maintenance of space. Post-depositional disturbance is surprisingly limited in the deposits below unit M, and one must assume that the single deposits were usually quickly sealed and generally not subjected to radically distorting mechanisms such as digging. The disturbance of some pot groups was clearly caused by pressure upon them, such as would result from further deposits over them or light walking. These groups also demonstrate that the surfaces, upon which the deposits were placed, in many instances would have been soft and soggy so that parts of joining fragments were pressed down into a soft matrix or old cavities without becoming further abraded or fractured in this process. The pot groups furthermore demonstrate that although various types of disposal activities contributed to the deposit, the material dumped in any one act would often only consist of what a single person could carry. We might therefore expect that varied dumping would often have happened in quick succession; and these repeated dumpings would mean that the surface continuously changed nature, appearance and configuration. The surprisingly high amount of low abrasion confirms such rapid accumul-ation in at least some parts of the sequence and the number and patterns of joins, together with the existence of pot groups, support the notion of heaps or single acts of refuse deposition.

The possibility of phasing and characterising these superficially homogeneous deposits of Late Bronze Age material has emerged from analysis. Although the original duration and intervals between the different phases cannot be reconstructed, it is possible to argue for 'passive' and 'active' stages in the accumulation of the deposit. This has ramifications for our understanding of the relationship between this area and the site at large since it implies change either in the use of the areas adjacent to the study area or changes in parts of the site that used this area for deposition, and therefore in the cycles involved in moving sherds (and other refuse) to Area 16 East.

The study has focused on documenting differences at a fine level, that is within and between excavated layer/spits. Changes at this level in certain variables such as density, degrees of clustering and size, as well as the overall composition of the bulk finds (Chapter 6), provide a more detailed insight into the formation of the deposit than that produced by stratigraphic unit analysis alone. The detailed analysis of these activities provides insight into mundane events, while the changes between units allow synthesis of broader alterations – however slight – in the nature and location of these activities. In short this detailed study represents some of the single events and variability which create the broad trends discussed in Chapters 8 and 14.

Success in applying the more traditional archaeological divisions of the material is dependent upon an understanding of the site formation processes. The question of how this deposit was formed must be solved before the pottery can be used as typological, chronological and cultural historical evidence. Characterisation of the type of activities responsible for the pottery in these deposits should facilitate more valid comparison with deposits elsewhere at Runnymede and on other sites. The two types of activities responsible for the pot groups do, for example, seem to correspond with the variations represented in the midden deposits in the enclosure ditch of Down Farm, Dorset (Barrett, Bradley and Green 1991, 200). This kind of analysis will gradually make it possible to trace differences and similarities between a range of contemporary sites not only in terms of site functions, structures and scale but also in terms of behaviour and specifically in terms of attitudes to the maintenance of space.

Pottery joins for understanding refuse cycles and redeposition

STUART NEEDHAM

Relatively few attempts have made use of cross-context to joins to understand formation processes (e.g. Kobyliński and Moszczyński 1992; Bullong 1994). Earlier work has more often been undertaken following the naïve assumption that joins will establish the contemporaneity of separate deposits. Bullong makes no such assumption but he does suggest that such studies can '... generate stratigraphic information from sites that lack visible stratification' (1994, 15). Having established in the current study the occurrence of much redeposition in Area 16 East, it is clear that one should be very wary of deducing stratigraphic relationships from cross-context joins in isolation. On the other hand, when compared against other data, in particular independently established stratigraphic information, such studies can clearly contribute substantially to our understanding of material cycles on the site.

This section is thus complementary to that on re-fits by Sørensen (above). Whereas the latter was concerned essentially with the implications for the conditions and inputs at the time of the given deposit's formation, here we investigate instead the temporal and redepositional relationships between different stratigraphic units and thereby attempt to document something of pottery refuse cycles prior to final incorporation.

A theoretical consideration of abrasion sequences

In order to grasp the potential significance of pottery joins it is necessary to give some thought to the circumstances by which re-fitting sherds might have ended up in different relationships in terms of their respective conditions and stratigraphic positions. This section does no more than outline a range of theoretical circumstances to illustrate the possibility that diverse pathways led to the relationships found.

When dealing with material linkages within an isolated trench, where the surrounding areas are effectively *terra incognita*, it is easy for thinking to become narrowly focused, as if the confines of the trench should provide all explanations for its contained material. Such a blinkered view would be particularly inhibiting to the interpretation of a small trench, as Area 16 East. It may be postulated that the zones beyond will have been the prevalent source of all kinds of material, at whatever refuse stage. It is thus essential to bear in mind the unknown lateral extension of the deposits and their contained finds beyond the excavated area.

On occasion a link between two specific contexts in the excavated area may be direct and simple in that the fragment at one location has been displaced directly from the locus of its conjoin to become rapidly incorporated in the new context, whence it was retrieved archaeologically. It seems inherently likely, however, that in the great majority of cases conjoining sherds would be linked via at least one unknown locus. Locus here can be read as either a point locus – e.g. buried or undisturbed – or an active context such as a surface over which objects might move.

The hypothetical cases shown schematically in Fig. 48 are largely self-explanatory. For the sake of clarity the diagrams illustrate the pathways of only two joining sherds; obviously multiple joins could introduce much greater complexity. The vertical axis of each diagram represents stratigraphic sequence, thereby corresponding with the stratigraphic matrix. As a starting point we take a case of minimal refuse history for both sherds (Fig. 48A); discard (normally following directly on vessel breakage) and possible horizontal dispersal leads to rapid incorporation in the same stratigraphic horizon; no further significant movement takes place.

The further sequence of diagrams falls into two main groups (Fig. 48B and C); those processes which tend to result in *upwards abraded sequences*, that is, differential abrasion is in the expected relationship to stratigraphy; and those where the reverse is true, processes leading to *downwards abraded sequences*. The latter deserves more attention because it results in unexpected or 'inverted' relationships and can have various causes. The group is thus further divided to show how these could result from either the particular combination of object refuse cycles, or the differential action of subsequent in-deposit transformations, involving weathering or migration. A final possibility is entered in Fig. 48D. In this case the inverted relationship is merely 'apparent' owing to a failure to perceive a discrete context (normally a cut feature) and therefore a failure to register the true positions of the contained objects in the stratigraphic matrix.

In reality there is doubtless a similar degree of variability in the pathway patterns leading to upwards abraded sequences, but because the excavated material lies in the 'expected' relationship there is a temptation to look for the most straightforward explanations. It is feasible, for example, for certain combinations of circumstances normally leading to downwards abraded sequences to cancel each other out, thereby creating a final upwards abraded sequence in the excavated record.

The model presented here has only taken account of different histories during the refuse cycle. A further range of possibilities is introduced when one considers the re-use of part-pots after the initial breakage of the vessel. The retention of part of a pot in the systemic sphere (a well-documented practice in many cultural settings for a variety of reasons, e.g. Sullivan 1989;

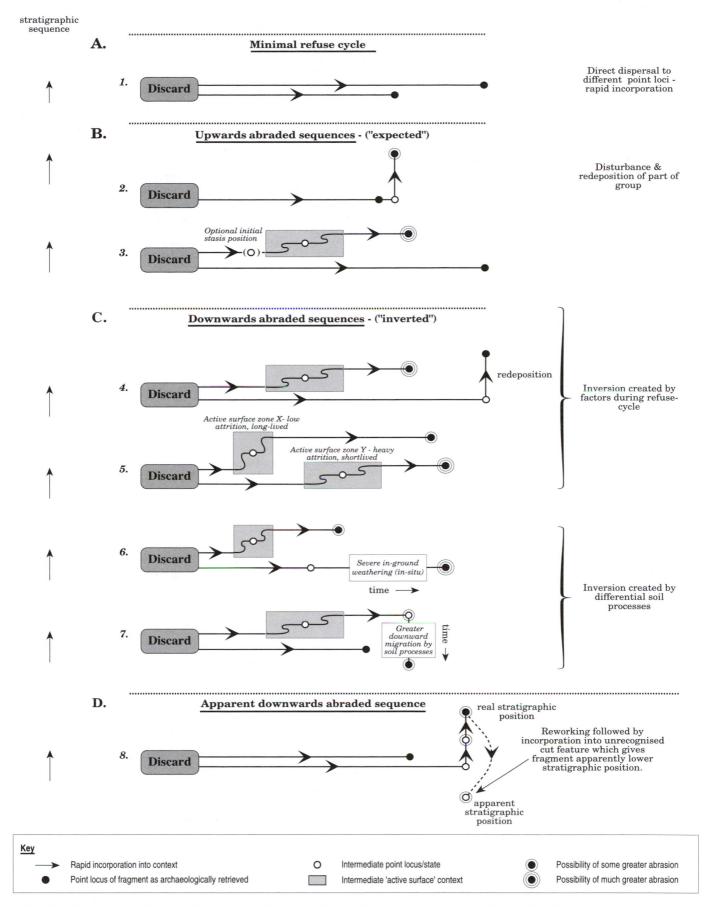

stratigraphic sequence

A. ....

Minimal refuse cycle

1. **Discard**

Direct dispersal to different point loci - rapid incorporation

B. ....

Upwards abraded sequences - ("expected")

2. **Discard**

Disturbance & redeposition of part of group

3. **Discard**

Optional initial stasis position

(O)

C. ....

Downwards abraded sequences - ("inverted")

4. **Discard**

redeposition

Inversion created by factors during refuse-cycle

5. **Discard**

Active surface zone X - low attrition, long-lived

Active surface zone Y - heavy attrition, shortlived

6. **Discard**

Severe in-ground weathering (in-situ)

time →

7. **Discard**

Greater downward migration by soil processes

time →

Inversion created by differential soil processes

D. ....

Apparent downwards abraded sequence

8. **Discard**

real stratigraphic position

Reworking followed by incorporation into unrecognised cut feature which gives fragment apparently lower stratigraphic position.

apparent stratigraphic position

Key

→ Rapid incorporation into context

● Point locus of fragment as archaeologically retrieved

○ Intermediate point locus/state

▨ Intermediate 'active surface' context

◉ Possibility of some greater abrasion

◎ Possibility of much greater abrasion

Fig. 48 *Hypothetical pathway combinations to explain the condition of 'joining' sherds relative to their stratigraphic positions.*

75

Schiffer 1987, 30, 49) while belonging fragments are instantly discarded, thus entering a refuse cycle, would give an obvious tendency for time lag between their respective incorporations. However, even when incorporation sequence immediately followed the sequence of discard, it would not consistently lead to upwards abraded sequences for much would depend on the use to which the part-pot was put. If its re-use involved heavy attrition of its edges subsequent breakage could result in a mixture of sherds, some with little abrasion and others with some edges highly abraded.

Offering these hypothetical pathway combinations is intended primarily to increase awareness of the likely complexities of dispersal, redeposition and incorporation, rather than necessarily to relate particular conjoins at Runnymede to a specific pathway combination.

The Area 16 East pottery joins

In addition to those found by Sørenson (above), this analysis made use of linkages that were established during the study of morphology and decoration, and the selection for cataloguing.

Linkages were classified into three categories, as in the previous study (Needham 1991, 209):

(i) joining sherds;
(ii) non-joining sherds thought almost certainly to belong to the same vessel;
(iii) non-joining sherds thought likely to belong to the same vessel.

Category (iii) has not been included in the figures presented in Table 3. However, it was thought to be important to retain category (ii) given that these linkages are treated as good for the formulation of 'vessels' in Chapter 8. This means that interpretation in these respects rests on a consistent base. The more extensive categorisation used in some recent studies (e.g. Bullong 1994) allows greater scope in interpretation but is difficult to apply to large, relatively uniform assemblages such as Runnymede.

Cross-stratigraphic unit linkages amongst the pottery (categories i and ii) are summarised in Table 3. Where a given vessel contains more than one linkage between two units (e.g. 16.868(I) with 897(H) and 876(H) such duplicates have been suppressed in the diagram. In other words, an individual vessel is only counted once in each cell representing an association between two stratigraphic units. On the other hand an individual vessel may be included in the totals of two or more cells.

For a variety of reasons it is difficult to normalise the values in this table. Consequently, formal statistics have not been attempted. However, to give some idea of relative frequencies, the total weight of pottery for each stratigraphic unit is given alongside.

Table 3: Minimum LBA pottery linkages (Nos. of vessels) between stratigraphic units, and between different excavated contexts within each unit (bold)

	G	H	H-J*	I	J	K	L	M
M	-	1	-	-	-	1	2	-
L	-	1	-	-	2	11	**2**	
K	-	3	-	1	16	**7**		
J	-	8	-	8	**21**			
I	-	11	3	**2**				
H-J*	-	5	-					
H	-	**7**						
G	-							
Total pottery weight (g)	356	7901	626	6162	20303	20550	9824	3914

*Contexts attributable just to H-early J.

The main elements presented by the table are as follows:

1. No joins/belongs involving unit G have been found;
2. Units H and I show a reasonable number of linkages, both between the groups (11) and between different contexts within unit H (7). The number of linkages within unit I (2) seems small by comparison. H and I show similar patterns of association with upper strata: moderate linkage with unit J (8, 8) then rather few linkages with K and higher units. All cases of differential abrasion fall in the expected direction, that is the greater abrasion being higher stratified (Table 4). This is even true of the one such case associating H and I. It is noteworthy that of the 16 H and I associations with J (involving twelve different vessels), five associations (or four vessels) show some greater abrasion on the J contexted material. (It should be borne in mind that this does not mean that all sibling sherds in the higher context are more abraded than all those in the lower one);
3. Two contexts phaseable just to H-early J (16.878, 895) provide a surprising number of links to both H and I (5 and 3 respectively) amongst which seven vessels are distinct from those contributing to the HI association of 11 links. No links were found with unit J and upwards;
4. Unit J, while showing reasonable linkage with lower stratified units, differs from them in having a strong association with unit K (16 links). There is a marked fall-off with higher units. Unit J also features a large number of vessels (21) having cross-context joins/belongs within the unit (as established above in Sørensen's study). This absolute value may reflect the

quantity of pottery material embraced within unit J and the fact that it contains many separately contexted pot groups. This has the effect of increasing cross-context joins within the unit purely on account of the way in which context numbers were assigned within the overall soil volume. A similar high value for within-unit linkages would, for example, be created by combining units H and I.

Most differential abrasion connected with unit J conforms to the upwards abraded norm. Two vessels, however, show less abraded sherds in higher contexts *within* the unit (P687, P693); in one case the contexts were contiguous in the ground and the relative stratigraphy of individual sherds may not be reliable.

5. As we have seen, unit K shows strong linkage with unit J, presumably partly due to contact between some of the respective contexts, and partly due to redeposition and different lengths of life cycle. Three vessels (P703, P725, P726) have more abraded sherds in K than J, whilst a further two (P674, P750) show the reverse. This might suggest either some difficulty in defining the interface between these two units, or that material deposited during this period was subject to a range of processes leading to mixed assemblages in terms of the abrasion sequence (as outlined in the previous section – Fig. 48, C4½–5).

Unit K also shows strong linkage with unit L having eleven vessels represented of which only two show signs of increased abrasion in upper contexts. This might point not only to a close affinity between K and L material, but also to sherds in L experiencing relatively little additional degradation despite the processes causing conflation. This evidence needs to be compared with that for an overall decline in sherd size and bone fragment size (Chapter 6).

6. Outside the LK associations, units L and M only show a few linkages scattered through the stratigraphy down to unit H. The instances of differential abrasion are all in the expected direction (upwards abraded).

In summary, there would appear to be a strong material linkage between the low stratigraphic units H and I (including the H-early J group) and, furthermore, little sign of any significant time lapse whenever redeposition was suspected. Although belonging fragments also came to be incorporated at a significant rate in unit J deposits, here there is increased incidence of attrition (still light), suggesting a perceptible though not necessarily long time lapse.

The strong association between J and K combined with the occurrence of occasional inverted abrasion relationships (downwards abraded) suggests at least some common elements in the history of incorporated rubbish. However, to set against this are some basic differences in the disposition of the finds in the two units (Chapters 3 and 4) and a range of changes in pottery fabric and form (Chapter 8).

Unit K seems to have largely sealed J and all previous deposits (presumably including their extensions and equivalents beyond the trench) since belonging sherds in unit L above are predominantly linked to K rather than any lower contexts. Linkages here span the full depth of these two units and may suggest a degree of persistent reworking of lateral equivalents, although only two of eleven vessels represented show upper sherds any more abraded than their lower-stratified siblings.

The fact that a small number of joins/belongs could be found between unit L and various lower units, added to the fact that many such had suffered no greater abrasion, suggests that a component of unit L material was only minimally disturbed by the flooding thought to have affected this horizon. One possibility is that these elements are in situ and have been infiltrated by burnt flint and more abraded finds due to post-flood worm-sorting. Well-abraded pottery does not of course lend itself to finding matches and joins, as may be illustrated by the unit M group. Only four associations have been made, represented by just two vessels, one of which (P661) shows a little more abrasion in the unit M context.

Table 4: Numbers of vessels showing differential abrasion of sherds between LBA stratigraphic units, and between different contexts within each unit (bold). Upwards abraded relationships are shown in the upper left segment, downwards abraded in the lower right.

	G	H	H-J*	I	J	K	L	M
M	-	1	N/A	-	-	1	1	/
L	-	-	N/A	-	1	2	/	-
K	-	1	N/A	-	3	/	-	-
J	-	3	N/A	2	**5**/**2**	2	-	-
I	-	1	N/A	/	-	-	-	-
H-J*	N/A	N/A	N/A	N/A	N/A	N/A	N/A	N/A
H	-	/	N/A	-	-	-	-	-
G	/	-	N/A	-	-	-	-	-

* The poorly phased contexts (H-early J) could not easily be used for this analysis. The group has, however, been retained in this diagram to facilitate comparison with the cells in Table 3 .

CHAPTER 5

The radiocarbon results and their interpretation

JANET AMBERS AND MORVEN LEESE

Sample selection and measurement

Samples of bone from a sequence of Late Bronze Age contexts in Area 16 East (Table 5) were analysed for ^{14}C content at the British Museum laboratory, using liquid scintillation counting and the methods described in Ambers and Bowman (1994). More details of the radiocarbon process are given in Bowman (1990). The laboratory maintains a programme of continual quality assurance procedures, with additional participation in international intercomparisons. These checks serve to justify the precision claimed and indicate no laboratory offsets, as further demonstrated by the results of the recent IAEA organised inter-laboratory comparison (Rozanski *et al* 1992) and the third international radiocarbon intercomparison (pers. comm. from the organising committee).

For all of the samples only well-preserved protein extracts were used for dating, thus avoiding any of the potential contamination problems discussed in Gillespie (1989). In each case only sample material showing no visible erosion or wear was selected and all the pieces were large, thus minimising the possibility of residuality or of post-depositional movement. Since only bone was dated there are none of the potential problems of initial age associated with wood or charcoal.

The results are given below in Table 5, quoted in the form recommended by Stuiver and Polach (1977) in uncalibrated years BP (before 1950), corrected for isotopic variation (measured or estimated) and set out in stratigraphic order. Calibrations listed were generated from the curve of Pearson *et al* (1986) as calculated using CALIBM, an in-house British Museum adaptation of revision 2.0 of the University of Washington Quaternary Laboratory Radiocarbon Calibration Program (CALIB, published in Stuiver and Reimer 1987) and the probabilistic method of calibration. Calibrated date ranges are quoted in the form recommended by Mook (1986) with the end points rounded outwards to five years. One effect of this is slightly to overestimate the date range for the stated confidence level.

Calibrated ranges for the results are also shown diagrammatically in Figs 49 and 50. Fig. 49 shows the one and two sigma age ranges as lines, while Fig. 50 shows the full probability distribution of possible calendar age. For a fuller explanation of this method of display see Kinnes *et al* 1991.

While all of the samples come from sealed contexts, the bones used to produce BM-2771 and -2651 come from adjacent areas of deposition in the sequence, and are felt on archaeological grounds to be contemporary. Since the two uncalibrated results are statistically indistinguishable (x^2 value of <1), it is therefore justified to combine the figures before calibration, producing a weighted mean figure with greater overall precision. This is also listed, with calibrated age ranges, in Table 5, and shown in Figs 49 and 50.

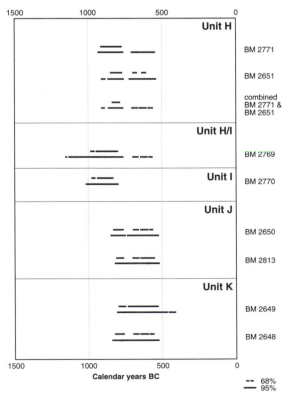

Fig. 49 *Calibrated age ranges for the radiocarbon results shown as simple lines for summed 68% and 95% confidence*

In order to have a large enough sample to obtain a usable error term for BM-2769 it was necessary to combine material from contexts 16.876 and 16.873, deposits which were in contact with one another and were probably separated by a very short time interval on archaeological evidence. Unfortunately, final phasing assigned these to units H and I respectively, although the division is somewhat arbitrary.

It was initially hoped that it would be possible to carry out a similar dating exercise for the Neolithic material in this area, but testing of a range of bone samples from these contexts proved them to have very poor collagen preservation, presumably as a result of environmental conditions. In the absence of other suitable dating materials no such programme was possible.

Additional radiocarbon dates for Area 6 to those published in Needham 1991, 346 are listed in Chapter 14 (Table 63).

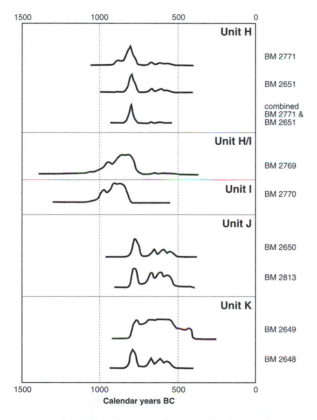

Fig. 50 *Calibrated age ranges for the radiocarbon results given as probability distributions.*

Simulation of calibrated date spans

Calibration is essential prior to any realistic attempt at understanding radiocarbon chronologies, but the interpretation of calibrated radiocarbon results is notoriously complicated. The main aims in analysing the Area 16 East data were to attempt to estimate the overall time-span of the sequence, and to assess the apparent reversal of the phase H and I samples. These problems would ideally be treated using a Bayesian analysis (see for example Buck *et al* 1991) which allows for any number of dates to be considered simultaneously and also takes account of stratigraphic information; however, software for this is not yet available. (See note on p. 82.)

The most practical solution, short of a full Bayesian analysis, is simulation, the end result of which is a simulated frequency distribution for the *differences* between dates (as opposed to that for the dates themselves). The main drawback of the approach is that it involves substituting a simulated frequency distribution for the full probability distribution as produced by the calibration program CALIBM. This inevitably introduces a degree of approximation, as discussed below.

Two pairs of dates were compared. The first was BM-2648 and BM-2771, representing the top and bottom of the sequence, and hence the overall time-span. The second was chosen to investigate the possible reversal of H and I. In this comparison the two figures for BM-2771 and BM-2651 were combined prior to calibration to represent H, and BM-2770 was used to represent phase I.

Steps in the simulation of dates and date differences

The simulation involved the following series of steps:

Step 1: Simulate, for each sample, a set of calendar dates having roughly the same relative frequencies as found by CALIBM, the probability-based calibration program. CALIBM produces, for each radiocarbon result, a list of calendar dates, usually spaced at yearly intervals, with their associated probabilities. The simulation proceeds by generating repeats of each date, the number of repeats of a given date being proportional to the CALIBM probability associated with that date. Note that the CALIBM probabilities are only relative measures of probability density and do not sum to unity; this means that the number of values produced by the simulation for different dates will vary.

Step 2: Take the two samples whose date-difference is to be considered. Since the number of simulated dates available for each of these samples is initially different they must be equalised. This is done by 'throwing away' the least probable dates for the sample with more simulated dates, until the number of simulated dates is the same for each sample.

Table 5: Radiocarbon dates for Late Bronze Age contexts in Area 16 East

BM number	Context	Unit	Material	Radiocarbon result (BP)	Possible calibrated age range (Calendar years BC)	
					68% probability	95% probability
BM-2771	A16 897 5813, 5913 and 898 5913	H	cow, cow/horse, pig and sheep/goat bone frags	2620±60	895 to 870 or 855 to 765	920 to 755 or 695 to 540
BM-2651	A16 872 5813	H	tibia (cow) scapula (?cow)	2590±50	835 to 760 or 680 to 660 or 620 to 600	895 to 875 or 850 to 750 or 705 to 535
BM-2771 BM-2651	weighted mean of two results	H		2600±40	825 to 780	895 to 885 or 850 to 760 or 685 to 655 or 635 to 595 or 580 to 560
BM-2769	A16 873 5812 and 876 5812, 5712	H & I	patella, mandible, ulna, vertebra, rib (cow) sacrum (cow/horse)	2710±90	985 to 955 or 940 to 800	1155 to 1145 or 1135 to 760 or 685 to 660 or 635 to 595 or 575 to 565
BM-2770	A16 868 5612, 5613	I	scapula, tibia, rib, vertebra (cow)	2740±60	980 to 960 or 935 to 825	1020 to 805
BM-2650	A16 865 5512	J	femur (cow)	2570±50	820 to 760 or 685 to 655 or 635 to 595 or 580 to 560	840 to 750 or 725 to 525
BM-2813	A16 836 5312	J	tibia (cow-sized) rib (5 pieces)	2530±45	800 to 755 or 685 to 655 or 640 to 550	810 to 520
BM-2649	A16 829 5512	K	radius, ulna, rib (cow)	2490±60	785 to 750 or 720 to 525	795 to 460 or 450 to 415
BM-2648	A16 824 5512	K	animal bone frags (various species)	2560±50	810 to 760 or 685 to 655 or 635 to 590 or 580 to 555	830 to 525

Step 3: Take pairs of simulated dates from the two samples at random. This can be achieved by numerically 'shuffling' one of the sets of dates: this involves assigning a random number to each date and re-ordering the dates according to the magnitude of the random number. Associating the two sets of dates together then allows differences in dates to be calculated.

Step 4: Display the sets of individual simulated dates and date differences as histograms using bin-sizes of 10–20 years (Fig. 51). The date difference histograms reflect the relative likelihoods of different time-spans, given the calibrated date distributions.

Approximation introduced by simulation

The procedure involves three sources of approximation. First the number of repeats must be whole; for example, if the probability is, say 73%, then seven repeats would be generated. Secondly, dates with low probability are omitted at step 2. This leads to distributions being

Dates

Date differences

BM2648

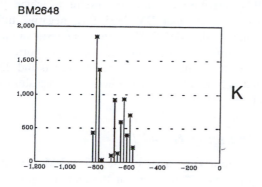

K

Time-span

BM2648 - BM2771

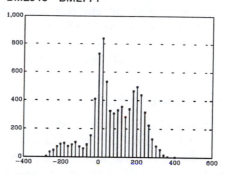

BM2771

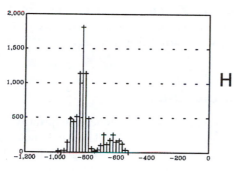

H

BM2770

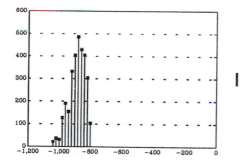

I

Reversal H-I

BM2771,BM2651 - BM2770

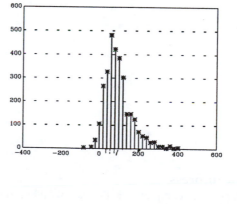

BM2771,BM2651 combined

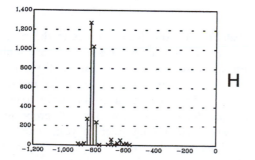

H

```
AXES
Vertical: simulated frequency
Horizontal: calendar years BC
```

Fig. 51 *Results of simulating distributions of dates (left) and date differences (right) as discussed in the text.*

81

truncated on either side rather than tailing off gradually. Thirdly, different ways of shuffling will give rise to different pairings of the dates.

It is impossible to assess the consequent errors on the results but they are likely to be at least twenty years for any given time-span. However, despite the inaccuracies, the histograms of date differences should at least indicate major effects such as reversals of expected sequences. Repeat simulations of one particular date, using slightly different values and different random numbers in step 2, confirmed that the method is sufficiently stable for this level of interpretation.

Results of simulation

Fig. 50 shows the smoothed probability distributions for the dates in Table 5, as produced by CALIBM. The simulation of all the dates used in the comparisons is shown on the left in Fig. 51. Comparison with the smoothed probabilities in Fig. 50 for these samples shows that the peaks are in the correct places and roughly of the correct magnitudes, although dates with very low probabilities have been truncated. Two sets of date differences, representing time-spans H-K and H-I, are now discussed.

Overall time-span

The result of simulating the difference between BM-2648 and BM-2771 is shown in the top right of Fig. 51.

The distribution shows the extent to which BM-2648 (K) is later than BM-2771 (H), negative differences implying that BM-2771 is later. The results indicate that the time-span between the top and bottom of the sequence could be anywhere between 0 and 250 years, but is most likely to have been of rather short duration (0–40 years).

Reversal of H and I

The difference between BM-2771/BM-2651 combined and BM-2770 is shown at the bottom right of Fig. 51. Here positive differences imply that H is later than I. The distribution implies that there is evidence for a 'reversal' of the H and I samples, with a difference of about 40–100 years, though contemporaneity is also a possibility. There is very little evidence that the unit H samples are earlier than that in I.

Conclusions

The overall time-span is difficult to quantify on the basis of the radiocarbon results alone, and could range from zero up to *c*.250 years, although it is unlikely to be longer than that. There is evidence for a reversal of the expected dates of phases H and I.

Note added in press

Since this paper was completed a PC-based calibration program including Bayesian analysis has become available (OxCal; Bronk Ramsey 1995). Complete analysis of the data given here, using OxCal, confirms the suggestion made above that there is a high probability of an inversion in the sequence for the unit H and I samples. Looking at the difference in age between BM-2771 and BM-2648 again shows a very similar pattern to that predicted above, with a 68% probability that the difference lies in the range of 0 to 250 years. However OxCal allows a more sophisticated approach to be taken, incorporating all the radiocarbon results and their stratigraphic relationship in the analysis. This suggests a considerably longer overall time span for the group, with a 68% probability that it is between 250 and 430 calendar years if the apparently anomalous unit I samples are included, and a 68% probability that the time span is between 210 and 400 calendar years if these are excluded.

CHAPTER 6

Characterisation of the Late Bronze Age artefact assemblage

Bulk finds spatial analysis

TONY SPENCE

Introduction

The bulk finds archive for the whole Runnymede Research assemblage consists of records of the number and weight in dry, clean condition of potsherds, imported stone, struck flint, animal bone and antler, and the weight of fired clay, burnt flint and recoverable charcoal. All weights are to the nearest gram, with the exception of the burnt flint which was weighed on site to the nearest 25 g and then generally discarded. A few samples from clusters of burnt flint deemed to be important were retained.

The 'bulk finds', being those excavated and recognised during trowelling, are augmented for many contexts by sieve-retrieved finds. All soil from selected metre squares was washed through a 4 mm mesh, giving control columns through the layer sequence. In addition the majority of feature fills and additional buckets of soil taken fairly randomly from layer contexts were also thus processed. These sieved assemblages give an invaluable check on the state of the recovered bulk find assemblage relative to the in-ground assemblage. However, the sieve-find weights are not included in this study as they would be liable to enhance the minority of metre squares selected for sieving relative to all others.

Thus the statistical data represented here are based on all non-special finds recovered in the course of normal excavation and subject to the usual biases of excavation method, excavator skill and soil conditions. These are assumed to vary in a similar fashion throughout the excavation and no attempt has been made to adjust figures to take them into account (cf. Clarke 1978). There is a case for adding the special finds weights into the relevant material totals, but that has not been done here as they represent a tiny minority of the total finds and would not significantly alter the results presented below. The special finds are studied in a separate section at the end of this chapter.

Given the recording system, gross finds characteristics within the deposits at Runnymede can be considered at various scales. Seven fundamental 'scales' may be defined (for the site at large):

1. a single layer/spit over one metre square; such units exclude any associated artefact groups;
2. a single artefact group, as defined on excavation; in some cases these may be divided according to the metre grid, but normally they are more sensibly regarded as an integral unit;
3. individual cut feature assemblages; these can be treated in entirety or sub-divided by different fills;
4. a single layer/spit over its full distribution, as excavated; associated artefact groups still excluded;
5. an amalgamated context; either a single layer-type context, or two or more contiguous contexts which are regarded as very close in their formation; any artefact groups physically contained within the defined soil body are also amalgamated (amalgamated contexts are labelled using one of the major layer-type contexts involved, distinguished by a suffixed asterisk – Table 6);
6. stratigraphic unit assemblages; the amalgamation of finds from all contexts assigned confidently (on stratigraphic grounds) to a defined stratigraphic unit;
7. feature group assemblage; amalgamation based on the interpretation of features as belonging to a coherent structure or alignment.

For inter- and intra-site analysis there may be a need for coarser amalgamations of stratigraphic units, although the use of the 'trench' as a unit is not anticipated.

These seven scales provide a framework within which to work; they need not inhibit a flexible approach allowing for the particular analysis being undertaken. Ultimately in the large area zones of excavation there will be a need for the definition of finds groups on the basis of the combinations and intersections of some of these scales. These will revolve around the interpretation of coherent structures (scale 7) or specific activity zones, the horizontal spread of which may be used to define a sub-area within one or more of the associated surface deposits, at whichever scale of analysis is deemed

Table 6: Distribution of excavated artefact groups

Context	Amalgamated Context	Unit	Material	Notes
16.823.1>	16.822*	16.K	Burnt Flint	
16.835.1>	16.834*	16.J	Pottery	
16.845.1>	16.836(w)*	16.J	Fired Clay	
16.846.1>	16.836(e)*	16.J	Pottery	
16.848.1>	16.836(w)*	16.J	Pottery	Contiguous with 16.867.1>
16.851.1>	16.836(w)*	16.J	Pottery	
16.852.1>	16.836(w)*	16.J	Pottery	
16.853.1>	16.836(w)*	16.J	Pottery	
16.854.1>	16.836(w)*	16.J	Pottery	Contiguous with 16.855.1>
16.855.1>	16.836(w)*	16.J	Pottery	Contiguous with 16.854.1>
16.856.1>	16.836(w)*	16.J	Pottery, Burnt Flint	
16.857.1>	16.836(w)*	16.J	Pottery	Contiguous with 16.860.1>
16.858.1	16.836(w)*	16.J	Burnt Flint	
16.860.1>	16.836(w)*	16.J	Pottery, Animal Bone	Contiguous with 16.857.1>
16.861.1>	16.865*	16.J	Burnt Flint	Directly above 16.862.1>
16.862.1>	16.865*	16.J	Pottery	Directly beneath 16.861.1>
16.863.1>	16.865*	16.J	Pottery, Burnt Flint	
16.864.1>	16.865*	16.J	Pottery	
16.866.1>	16.868*	16.I	Pottery	
16.867.1>	16.836(w)*	16.J	Pottery	Contiguous with 16.848.1>
16.873	16.868*	16.I	Animal Bone	Including disarticulated lamb
16.874	16.868*	16.I	Burnt Flint	
16.875	16.868*	16.I	Fired Clay	?in situ structure
16.879.1>	16.868*	16.I	Pottery	
16.880.1>	16.868*	16.I	Struck Flint	
16.881	16.868*	16.I	Pottery	
16.882.1	16.872*	16.H	Burnt Flint	
16.882.2	16.872*	16.H	Burnt Flint	
16.883	16.868*	16.I	Burnt Flint	Well crushed
16.884	16.872*	16.H	Fired Clay	Peak of 16.899
16.885	16.872*	16.H	Fired Clay	Peak of 16.899
16.886	16.876*	16.H	Animal Bone	Articulated vertebrae in 16.897
16.888.1>	16.890*	16.H	Pottery	
16.889.1>	16.890*	16.H	Pottery	
16.891.1>	16.890*	16.H	Pottery, Burnt Flint and Bone	
16.892	16.876*	16.H	Pottery Cup	Part of 16.898
16.894	16.876*	16.H	Burnt Bone, Burnt Flint	Part of 16.897.1
16.897.1>	16.876*	16.H	Pottery, Animal Bone	
16.898	16.876*	16.H	Pottery, Animal Bone	
16.899	16.872*	16.H	Burnt Clay	
16.900.2	16.872*	16.H	Burnt Clay	Subsided part of 16.899

Note: > point-numbers run upwards from .1

most appropriate. Again, in the interests of simplifying site history, it might be desirable at times to combine feature group assemblages with the relevant surface assemblage(s) on the basis of argued contemporaneity.

In the Area 16 East stratigraphic units under study here, it is apparent that there are considerable variations in the bulk finds assemblage both horizontally and vertically. Although such spatial studies are hampered by the limited size of the trench, it is still possible to draw some meaningful conclusions. Cut features were only identified in the subsoil beneath the Late Bronze Age dark earth deposits. It is suspected that some features were cut from a higher level (Chapter 3), but it is not thought that such intrusions will have significantly interfered with the finds density values obtained for the layers. Since Area 16 East has rather few cut features their finds densities are not considered here; however, future analysis for other zones of the site will involve evaluation of finds in features as well as those in layers.

Theoretically, finds in any defined group can be quantified by number, weight or volume. Any of these variables can be standardised as 'densities' by taking them as percentages of the volume of soil excavated. This volume is calculated as the average spit depth at the four corners (given by the differences in the relevant grid levels at the top and bottom surfaces of the spit) multiplied by the surface area (effectively 1m²). The grid square volumes are summed to give the layer total, and these in turn summed for the stratigraphic unit. To produce a more manageable scale the bulk find weights are expressed in kilograms, and hence the overall densities as kg/m³.

Densities of finds at the scale 1 level generally show considerable variation which may obscure broader trends. Consequently in this summary it has been found more useful for interpretation to concentrate on the pan-trench view by taking layers/spits as a whole with the addition of relevant artefact groups to form a new group of 'amalgamated contexts' (scale 5 outlined above). For a broader grouping these are further combined into the stratigraphic units – scale 6. For the Late Bronze Age deposits discussed here these are labelled G-M in ascending order of deposition. The assessment of these changes through time is the primary aim of these analyses and is presented below under the heading 'vertical distribution'. Thereafter briefer consideration is given to variability in finds densities within layers under the heading 'horizontal distribution'.

A better indication of the importance of a particular finds category in a particular unit might be to determine the actual volume occupied. This is, after all, what the archaeologist notes when describing any particular soil layer, yet such quantification is absent from the standard analyses of finds assemblages. This is probably due to the fact that volume is not an easy quantity to calculate,

particularly given the varying specific densities of apparently similar materials, whereas number or weight is more readily available. Number can be susceptible to alteration due to damage during excavation and processing, and in certain cases such as fired clay, it is meaningless. For the most part, therefore, this analysis of bulk finds is based on weight. This leads to an under-representation of certain categories of finds with low material densities, notably bone and antler (charcoal has been excluded as insignificant). Unfortunately under-representation may not always be by a constant factor; in particular degradation of bone might well lead to diminishing material density, i.e. with greater loss of weight than volume, whereas for pottery these variables would decline *pro rata*. Such differentials need to be sought in analysis.

The most basic derived quantification is the total weight of bulk finds for any unit – a simple sum of all the categories of bulk find. To show variability between layers and units three materials were chosen as key measures – pottery, bone and burnt flint. In the trench these were found in sufficient quantities to be statistically reliable. They can also be argued to represent different, albeit interrelated, functions in 'use' and to have been subjected to different life cycles; they may thus fluctuate independently of one another. They have been evaluated as percentages of two totals for the given context group:

1. the sum of the pot, bone and burnt flint weight;
2. the bulk finds total.

For the purposes of this study other recurrent finds (imported stone, struck flint and fired clay) were considered only as a group ('other').

A further type of variable also considered to be fundamental to our investigations is the average weight of particular finds categories. For the Late Bronze Age assemblage the most significant indicators are those for bone and pottery. The result gives one method of establishing in broad terms something of the depositional history of the constituent material – in general, the higher the average, the less fragmentation has been caused by human or natural agencies such as trampling and flood reworking. While average weight is a generalised indicator for unit or layer, square by square it is susceptible to influence from pottery or bone artefact groups. More detailed analysis of fragment size distributions for pottery and bone may be found in Chapters 4 and 12.

In studying refuse-rich deposits there is the problem of survival being governed by the nature of the raw materials. As with all but the best preserved sites there is a loss of most of the organic material associated with all functions of the site. In such deep deposit as Area 16 East, where rubbish accumulated from a number of sources, it is the loss of this organic component that potentially inhibits interpretation of many aspects of the site. Even in the most artefact-rich units in Area 16 East the weight of the finds did not exceed 25% of the calculated weight of soil (based on a crude equation that $1m^3$ of soil weighs 1000 kg). It seems unlikely that this upper limit would be different in terms of volume occupied even allowing for the various densities of the finds categories and the soil matrix. It is important to recognise that all of the statistical analyses are for the durable portion of the original refuse assemblage.

Vertical distribution

UNIT G

This is the smallest quantity of bulk finds of all the LBA units. Such finds as are present are thinly spread with no artefact groups. The analysis concentrates on 16.896*

as the main group context, with an underlying layer 16.901*. The majority of the bulk finds comes from the former deposit, while material from the latter is confined to the central part of the trench. In 16.896* there is again a concentration of material in the central squares 56/12 and 57/12–13. This is a low overall figure compared with the overlying units. Average sherd and animal bone weight are in the middle of the range shown by all LBA units (including the flood-reworked deposits), although this may prove to be greater than the average for sub-soil contexts in other areas of the site.

UNIT H

Considerable quantities of bulk finds are located in this thin spit. With only $0.28m^3$ of soil removed across the whole trench there is a density of approximately $220kg/m^3$, the highest within the Area 16 East units. A

Table 7: Bulk finds densities and average weights by amalgamated context and stratigraphic units

Unit	Context	Soil Volume (m³)	Pot Density (kg/m³)	Burnt Flint (kg/m³)	Animal Bone (kg/m³)	Total Density (kg/m³)	Pot Mean wt (g)	Bone Mean wt (g)	Burnt Flint %
16.M	16.807*	0.1630	3.99	54.75	0.86	61.53	5.0	1.5	
16.M	16.813*	0.1225	5.19	63.06	1.01	71.32	3.9	1.4	
16.M	16.814*	0.5025	4.75	48.01	1.24	55.44	3.7	1.3	
16.L	16.819*	0.6275	7.41	76.02	1.95	87.52	4.2	1.8	
16.L	16.820*	0.5025	9.70	109.26	2.72	126.00	5.2	1.9	
16.K	16.822*	0.4450	16.91	111.67	5.36	138.18	6.1	2.6	
16.K	16.824*	0.4500	15.18	60.11	4.82	84.27	6.8	3.2	
16.K	16.829*	0.1787	34.66	96.36	8.99	149.87	6.9	3.1	
16.J	16.830*	0.1150	5.87	7.83	1.02	26.86	6.0	1.6	
16.J	16.834*	0.3575	13.07	36.25	3.31	55.47	8.2	3.4	
16.J	16.836e*	0.1085	36.16	84.79	7.10	161.67	9.3	4.5	
16.J	16.836w*	0.2025	22.24	54.81	4.10	89.84	12.6	5.1	
16.J	16.849*	0.0350	33.20	129.46	10.91	203.86	7.5	2.4	
16.J	16.865*	0.0787	74.28	157.53	16.28	274.00	9.4	5.0	
16.I	16.868*	0.1845	33.40	63.90	10.43	138.96	9.5	5.1	
16.H	16.872*	0.1775	20.66	145.59	16.75	226.05	10.4	6.0	
16.H	16.876*	0.0650	53.42	118.62	30.40	246.17	8.3	4.8	
16.HJ	16.878*	0.0050	125.20	342.00	32.20	581.40	9.8	2.8	
16.H	16.890*	0.0333	45.17	64.56	32.19	149.19	17.9	9.7	
16.G	16.896*	0.3375	0.76	9.35	0.88	12.21	5.9	3.3	
16.G	16.901*	0.2300	0.23	0.45	0.10	0.83	8.7	1.6	
16.M	Total	0.7880	4.66	51.74	1.24	59.17	3.9	1.3	90
16.L	Total	1.1300	8.43	90.80	2.30	104.64	4.7	1.8	89
16.K	Total	1.0737	19.14	87.52	5.74	117.53	6.6	2.9	78
16.J	Total	0.8972	23.16	55.88	4.92	97.36	9.3	3.8	67
16.I	Total	0.1845	33.40	63.90	10.43	138.96	9.5	5.1	59
16.H	Total	0.2758	31.34	129.45	21.83	221.51	10.1	5.9	71
16.G	Total	0.5675	0.55	5.74	0.57	7.60	6.2	3.1	84

Flint % calculated as percentage of pottery, burnt flint and bone weights total.

number of artefact groups (see Table 1) have been amalgamated into the three main layer components 16.872*, 16.876* and 16.890*. There is a concentration of finds towards the eastern end of the trench for all three main categories in terms of both number and weight. 58% of the total unit weight is burnt flint, with 18% in the clay, stone and struck flint category, an unusually high proportion. Potsherd and bone fragments show the highest average weight of all the units, suggesting that there was little traffic across the deposits, or that they were rapidly covered.

UNIT I

This unit only covers the squares eastward from 56/12 and again had a high concentration of finds from a small soil volume. Overall not the heaviest assemblage – some 25 kg of finds recovered from approximately 0.18m^3 of soil. Several artefact clusters were detectable within the broader matrix and have been re-absorbed into the main spit 16.868*. The main category of find by weight is again burnt flint, but this has fallen to about 46%, whilst the 'others' category rises to its highest at 22%. Interestingly this unit has the highest pottery density and high average bone and sherd weights, being only slightly lower than unit H. Looking at individual squares, it is noticeable that the bone weights vary more than the pottery.

UNIT J

The largest amalgamation of contexts, with major spits/layers 16.830*, 834*, 836e*, 836w*, 849* and 865* in addition to nineteen identified artefact groups (see Table 1). The spits involved removed about 0.9m^3 of soil and showed an overall drop in finds density in comparison to H and I. The finds by weight percentages still have a broad mix, with 57% of the total being burnt flint and a reduction to 14% for the 'other' component. The animal bone and pot average weights are similar to I, although more variable on a square by square basis. There is no obvious pattern to this.

Within unit J, soil body 16.836 west contained a disproportionate number of pot groups. Although these make up over half of the weight of the pottery in this layer, curiously they do not give rise to a greater pot density than the unit J average.

UNIT K

This unit has the highest bulk finds weight, though not the greatest density since the three main spits of soil had a total volume of 1.07m^3. There was only one artefact group; this lack of concentrations marks an important difference between units J and K. There is also some change between the three main spits; there is an increas-

ing dominance in the burnt flint percentage towards the upper one 16.822*, particularly at the expense of pottery. There is a drop from 7–3% in the combined clay, stone and struck flint category. There appears to be no significant variation in the average bone and sherd weights when viewed as metre square or context group totals, but as a unit grouping these are noticeably lower than for the unit J total.

UNIT L

A large weight of finds from the largest volume of soil, 1.13m^3, gives this unit a similar appearance in bulk find statistics to unit K. It contains no artefact clusters and is divided between two spits. The overall density breaks down to a fluctuating pattern when viewed square by square, with the suggestion that the south-western squares had less recoverable material. Burnt flint constitutes 87% of the total finds weight, with the 'other' category reducing to 3%, while animal bone has little more than a token presence at 2%. Average bone weight has decreased further, here about a third of that seen in unit H, while sherd size is about half.

UNIT M

For a consideration of the bulk finds, 16.801 is ignored as a modern reworking of little relevance to the LBA sequence. Thus this unit consists of three main spits. It is also important to note that the uppermost layer 16.807 was an initial cleaning layer and bulk finds retrieval may have been lower as a result.

The total soil volume is the third largest at 0.79m^3. The total finds weight is comparable with H, but the density is second lowest, ahead of only unit G. Again there are no artefact groups, and the assemblage is dominated by burnt flint at 88%. Animal bone is again at a very low level, as are 'other' finds, and there is a remarkable uniformity to the three spit assemblages, suggesting a process of homogenisation of any original patterning. The average sherd and animal bone weights are the lowest of all the units containing LBA material.

Horizontal distribution

In addition to the vertical dimension outlined above, the horizontal finds patterning for both layers and units was considered. This section will concentrate on the latter, although the layer information remains in archive. The seven squares along 12 m north were taken as a transect through the deposits, and the variation in the density of the three main materials and the combined stone, clay and struck flint category noted. The results are shown in Table 8 below.

Data supplied by Morven Leese (Table 9) shows a

Table 8: Variation in bulk finds densities by metre square along grid 12.00 North

Unit	Grid E	Pot (kg/m³)	Burnt Flint (kg/m³)	Bone (kg/m³)	Other (kg/m³)	Total (kg/m³)
16.G	53.00	0.55	20.00	1.30	0.00	21.85
	54.00	0.52	5.79	0.17	0.03	6.51
	55.00	0.88	6.50	0.08	3.40	10.85
	56.00	0.94	10.86	0.17	0.00	11.97
	57.00	0.08	26.40	1.24	0.75	28.47
	58.00	0.00	0.33	0.10	0.23	0.67
	59.00	0.32	0.00	0.10	0.15	0.57
16.H	53.00	9.30	92.50	2.70	0.40	104.90
	54.00	6.05	30.50	5.10	106.70	148.35
	55.00	8.43	50.00	3.37	15.63	77.43
	56.00	6.31	625.91	6.89	22.04	661.16
	57.00	56.50	150.50	74.90	2.50	284.40
	58.00	38.17	108.57	48.06	9.60	204.40
	59.00	42.03	87.24	26.53	16.96	172.76
16.I	56.00	16.30	65.00	12.90	10.50	104.70
	57.00	21.65	39.33	5.63	2.21	68.83
	58.00	45.63	105.38	16.34	14.55	181.91
	59.00	22.40	50.00	10.25	62.29	144.95
16.J	53.00	24.67	105.00	3.55	9.42	142.63
	54.00	13.89	52.87	7.09	8.13	81.97
	55.00	11.45	64.85	13.01	3.79	93.10
	56.00	26.39	52.00	2.95	9.01	90.34
	57.00	31.31	39.39	4.34	11.65	86.69
	58.00	43.79	80.86	5.51	10.54	140.70
	59.00	33.31	97.33	7.31	12.21	150.16
16.K	53.00	9.94	101.85	3.43	8.26	123.47
	54.00	14.16	68.82	5.41	1.89	90.29
	55.00	12.09	98.80	5.29	3.51	119.69
	56.00	25.55	96.73	6.67	4.99	133.93
	57.00	22.19	86.52	9.08	3.19	120.98
	58.00	18.18	119.85	6.78	5.28	150.09
	59.00	28.72	113.85	9.98	10.12	162.68
16.L	53.00	7.20	96.93	2.66	2.19	108.98
	54.00	7.30	87.50	2.07	6.82	103.69
	55.00	7.27	71.84	2.73	2.28	84.13
	56.00	10.22	77.95	1.79	1.41	91.36
	57.00	9.83	63.95	2.16	2.96	78.89
	58.00	8.86	44.17	2.11	1.90	57.03
	59.00	7.76	107.81	1.41	1.58	118.56
16.M	53.00	3.58	54.29	0.63	2.27	60.76
	54.00	3.98	52.27	0.98	0.78	58.02
	55.00	3.77	42.86	0.66	2.16	49.44
	56.00	4.97	58.33	1.52	1.00	65.83
	57.00	4.98	50.74	1.19	0.98	57.88
	58.00	2.10	35.56	0.53	0.53	38.73
	59.00	2.38	45.83	0.42	1.03	49.67

Table 9: The coefficients of variation and supporting data for metre squares along grid 12.00 North

Unit/ Stats	Pottery	Burnt Flint	Animal Bone	Other Materials
G				
Range	0.94	26.40	1.22	3.40
Mean	0.47	9.98	0.45	0.65
Std Dev	0.36	9.94	0.56	1.24
CV	77.37	99.60	124.17	190.38
H				
Range	50.45	595.41	72.20	106.30
Mean	23.83	163.60	23.94	24.83
Std Dev	21.12	207.54	28.00	36.93
CV	88.63	126.86	117.00	148.73
I				
Range	29.33	66.05	10.71	60.08
Mean	26.50	64.93	11.28	22.39
Std Dev	13.04	28.95	4.52	27.09
CV	49.23	44.59	40.04	121.02
J				
Range	32.34	65.61	10.06	8.42
Mean	24.53	69.64	7.10	8.57
Std Dev	11.67	22.98	3.96	3.24
CV	47.56	33.00	55.83	37.80
K				
Range	18.78	51.03	6.55	8.23
Mean	18.69	98.06	6.66	5.31
Std Dev	7.08	16.98	2.26	2.94
CV	37.88	17.32	33.99	55.34
L				
Range	3.02	63.64	1.30	5.41
Mean	8.35	78.58	2.13	2.73
Std Dev	1.28	21.27	0.46	1.87
CV	15.38	27.06	21.48	68.47
M				
Range	2.88	22.77	1.10	1.74
Mean	3.68	48.55	0.85	1.25
Std Dev	1.13	7.70	0.40	0.68
CV	30.68	15.86	47.05	54.57

Key: Std Dev = Standard deviation; CV = Coefficient of variation (the relative standard deviation as a percentage of the mean)

further statistical analysis of these results. The main measurement in this respect is the coefficient of variation (CV in the table) calculated by taking the standard deviation as a percentage of the mean. The higher the CV the less homogeneous the artefact assemblage. For CVs in excess of 100% the likelihood is that it consists of a number of sub-populations, in archaeological terms representing more than one spatially discrete dumping episode.

Given that the trench is an arbitrary slice through the deposits, it is unclear if the centre of the deposit has been uncovered, or just a thin slice of the periphery. Significant variation can be detected within the earliest units, G and H, and to a lesser extent in I. Unit G consists of a relatively small amount of archaeological material within a large soil body and the statistics may thus be unreliable as a result; they do, however, broadly reflect those for unit H. The high CVs suggest that there is not a uniform dumping regime across this area at this early stage. Discrete groups, particularly of the animal bone, are identifiable rather than a general thin spread. The high CV for the 'other' materials reflects biases caused by a few finds of relatively heavy stone in certain squares.

Unit H also has localised concentrations. It may be that some of these dumps of material represent 'industrial', or at least non-domestic, activity; witness the re-use of the burnt flint for pottery production (14 kg in 16.882.1–2, square 56/12), and the concentrations of fired clay in 16.872, 875 and 899/900. The 'other' component in these lower assemblages is again notably variable (see Table 9), probably due to the distribution of stone fragments. CV figures from unit I are artificially reduced because it is limited to four grid squares rather than seven.

The seven metre squares are in fact remarkably uniform when analyzed horizontally for stratigraphic units J-M. Local variations do of course exist, as in the dropping away of recovered finds from unit L upwards, as outlined above. However, across the transect each of units J-M has a consistent artefact 'signature', as defined by quantity, variation, spread and condition, thereby supporting their definition as separate archaeological groupings. The internal homogeneity of each suggests a pattern formed by a uniform dumping regime and/or a particular set of post-depositional transformations. Although artefact groups are a major component of unit J (see Table 1), causing localised concentrations, they are all attributable to domestic refuse and are mostly pottery. The exceptions are a discarded hearth (16.845) and a burnt flint concentration (16.861). The remaining bulk finds in J seem to be broadly similar square by square, although the variation in the average bone and sherd sizes reinforces the frequent localised dumping that typifies this level. Interestingly the increase in the size of sherds is not necessarily reflected in a similar increase in bone, suggesting at least a different pre-incorporation regime for the two materials. Also this unit has the lowest CV for the 'other' category, supporting the notion that this unit predominantly consists of rapidly accumulating 'everyday' domestic material.

In the higher units, K-M, a variety of factors influences the summary statistics. The CVs here show less spatial variation in the assemblage than in the lower units, although there is little consistency about the material categories unit by unit. Slower accumulation leading to prolonged exposure will tend to even out the disparities, while the flood reworking argued for unit M has had some interesting consequences. The burnt flint CV is the lowest for all layers suggesting a uniform spread with a surprisingly narrow range. Much of the animal bone has been lost or become degraded through ground water attack and provides an unreliable statistic. Although one might perhaps expect water-reworked clusters amongst such material, none were identified.

Statistical analysis of the densities of bulk finds

MORVEN LEESE

The aim of this investigation was to study relationships between the various types of material discarded in the occupation deposits of Area 16 East. The data consist of the densities of pottery, bone and burnt flint, and of the remaining recurrent material combined (fired clay, stone and struck flint). Data were available for each of twenty-one amalgamated contexts within the area, as well as unit totals based on weights and soil volumes aggregated over all the relevant contexts for each stratigraphic unit.

Details of the statistical methods used may be found in the user guide to the package SPSS-PC, which was used for all the calculations, or in standard texts such as Snedecor and Cochran (1991).

The densities for some of the contexts were based on very low soil volumes. The worst case was a very localised context, 16.878 (unit HJ), for which the volume calculated is thought to be misleading; it was omitted from further analysis. Density data for the remaining twenty contexts were used to assess correlations between different types of material and the degree of variation within and between phases. The soil volumes, and hence the densities, are subject to errors due to the approximation of contoured surfaces by planes. Such errors affect all materials to the same extent and therefore correlation between types of materials can justifiably be based on the specific context data. Temporal trends, on the other hand, are more reliably reflected by the unit totals since these are based on aggregated soil volumes where absolute errors in soil volume will not have increased, and will thus be proportionately rather smaller. The data are shown in Table 7, which also shows the percentage of burnt flint in relation to the total of burnt flint, pottery and bone (this is shown below to be a significant feature of the data).

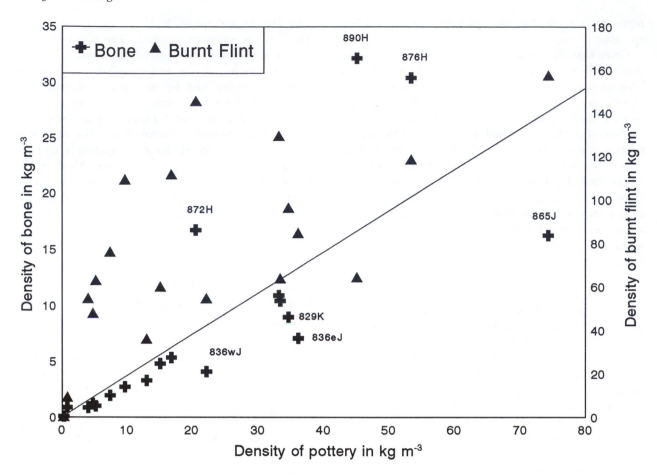

Fig. 52 *Bone and burnt flint densities (vertical axis) versus pottery density (horizontal axis) in kg m⁻³. The line represents the overall bone/pottery ratio. The seven contexts having the highest deviations from the line are indicated separately.*

Summary statistics

Table 10 gives the correlation coefficients between the densities of the three main types of material, i.e. burnt flint, pottery and bone, and their means and standard deviations computed over all contexts (except 16.878). The table shows that the amounts of all three materials are positively correlated, especially pottery and bone, and to a lesser extent pottery and burnt flint. The individual densities are also shown in Fig. 52, where the strong bone/pottery and weaker burnt flint/pottery correlations can be seen. At lower values of bone and pottery there is a fairly constant ratio of pottery to bone of 2.7:1 (as indicated by the line), although higher values are more spread out. The fact that all three relatively high bone/pottery cases are in unit H and three out of four low bone/pottery ratios are in unit J is worth noting and may have some archaeological significance.

Principal components analysis

The aim of a principal components analysis is to reduce correlated sets of variables to smaller numbers of linear combinations of the variables (components) which express the variation in the data. This type of analysis can be useful in suggesting combinations of the original variables which might be worth investigating. For these data, the first component accounts for 90% of the variation and is positively correlated with all three types. It is thus correlated with total density. The second component (accounting for a further 10% of the variation) is positively correlated with bone and pottery and negatively with flint. As already shown, bone and pottery are highly correlated with one another, and the principal components analysis places bone and pottery in

Table 10: Summary statistics for pottery, burnt flint and animal bone for the Area 16 East assemblage *en masse*

n=20	Correlation coefficient			Mean (kg/m³)	Std. Dev.
	BF	P	B		
Burnt Flint BF	1	0.66	0.52	74.6	44.6
Pottery P		1	0.78	21.8	19.8
Bone B			1	8.0	9.4

opposition to flint. Thus the percentage of pottery and bone taken together (or its complement the percentage of flint) is a feature of the data which may have significance.

Variability among contexts

Fig. 53 shows the individual densities, their totals, and the percentage that burnt flint represents of each total. There appears to be a trend towards increasing relative amounts of burnt flint in the later contexts but the situation is more confused in the earlier contexts where the variability between contexts is greater, especially for burnt flint. This observation is confirmed by a test for equality of variances (Bartlett-Box F). The following four groups of contexts were taken: H with I, J, K and L with M, the data being grouped in order to give a reasonable number of values to compare, and the data were log-transformed to bring them closer to normality. The test was applied to both the raw densities and also to the percentage of burnt flint. The test indicated a statistically significant increase in variability, at the 5% significance level, in the density of burnt flint and also

in the percentage of burnt flint of the total, the values of both these quantities becoming more stable in the later deposits, consistent with a greater degree of mixing.

As noted earlier, general trends in the percentage of burnt flint, and in the raw densities, are better considered in relation to the aggregated unit totals because variation, such as that discussed above, is averaged out. The unit totals are now discussed.

Temporal trends based on unit totals

The variation between unit totals was compared to that within units, as reflected in the variation between contexts placed in the same unit. Because the normality of the data is difficult to assess, a non-parametric form of analysis of variance (Kruskal-Wallis) was used. Two types of data were considered, the raw densities of pottery, bone and burnt flint and the percentage of burnt flint (of the total of pottery, bone and burnt flint). The former might be regarded as reflecting the overall level of activity and the latter, the balance of various types of activity.

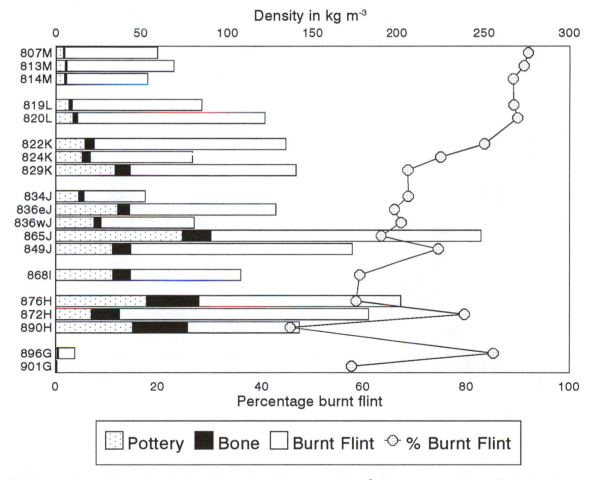

Fig. 53 *Pottery, bone and burnt flint densities for amalgamated contexts in kg m⁻³. The percentage of burnt flint is also shown. Contexts are in stratigraphic order.*

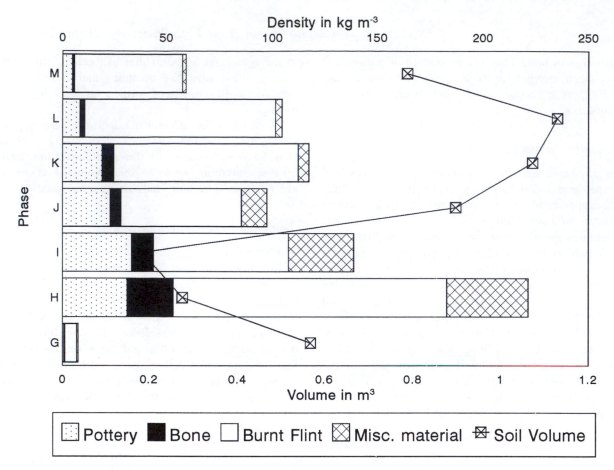

Fig. 54 *Unit density totals for pottery, bone and burnt flint and for 'other' materials. The soil volume in m³ is also shown.*

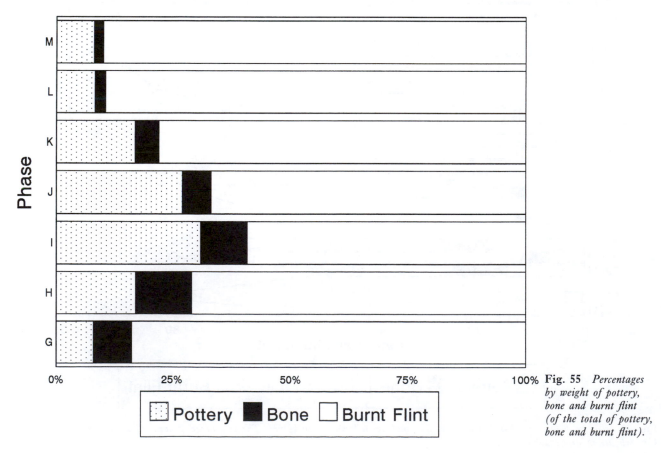

Fig. 55 *Percentages by weight of pottery, bone and burnt flint (of the total of pottery, bone and burnt flint).*

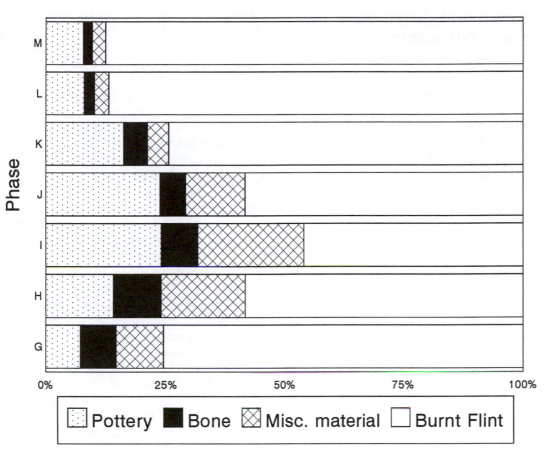

Fig. 56 *Percentages by weight of pottery, bone, burnt flint and 'other' material (of the total of pottery, bone, burnt flint and 'other' material).*

The raw densities of pottery, bone and burnt flint are shown in Fig. 54 along with the densities of the other material. From unit to unit the pottery and bone densities differ significantly (at approximately the 5% level) on the basis of an analysis of variance between and within units. The burnt flint density was too variable from context to context to show any significant trends, but the relative proportion of flint did follow a pattern, as noted in the discussion of the context data. The burnt flint percentages are shown for the unit totals, in Fig. 55. Fig. 56 shows the percentages including the 'other' material, where it can be seen that the latter follows the pattern of the bone and pottery rather than the burnt flint. The percentage of burnt flint, in relation to the total of bone, pottery and burnt flint, shows significant differences from unit to unit at the 5% level, and reaches a minimum relative to bone and pottery in unit I. It can be shown that this pattern is unlikely to have arisen entirely by chance.

Conclusions

The densities of bone and pottery are correlated with one another, and both decrease towards the later phases.

While there is a constant ratio of bone to pottery in most contexts, those in unit H have a relatively higher proportion of bone and three contexts in unit J have a relatively higher proportion of pottery. The density of burnt flint is also correlated with bone and with pottery, but to a lesser extent, and it does not show such a clear time trend. However, a pattern has emerged in the *relative proportion* of burnt flint compared to bone and pottery: this is at a minimum in unit I. The pattern of the 'other' material matches that of the pottery and bone, rather than that of the burnt flint. The density of burnt flint, and the proportion of burnt flint compared to pottery and bone, is less variable among later contexts, perhaps due to mixing.

To summarise, assuming that observational bias has not influenced the data, there appears to be a gradual decrease in discard activity relative to sediment accretion through time, as reflected in the total densities of pottery, bone and burnt flint; this is accompanied by a change in the balance of discard types, the proportion of pottery and bone compared to burnt flint reaching a relative peak in unit I.

Composition and distribution of the special finds assemblage

TONY SPENCE

There are nearly 170 special finds from the two seasons of excavation in Area 16 East. Details of location, category and dimensions are given in Table 12 along with the British Museum registration number, and concordances with catalogue numbers for those published in greater detail in the relevant sections elsewhere in this volume.

The 2 m wide trench through the Late Bronze Age deposits, reducing to 1 m for the Neolithic, gives little prospect for sensible statistical analyses particularly given the low number of finds by unit or category. This, taken with the many other factors that artificially distort distributions (such as excavator experience, material survival or changes in awarding special find status), makes interpretation of these assemblages particularly difficult.

The majority of the data in Table 12 is self-evident. However, the last two columns provide a little information on the formation of the deposits. An examination of the condition of the artefacts supports the interpretations of different rates of dumping. The clay material for example shows a general improvement in condition the lower its position in the sequence, although differences in fabrics will influence this (see Chapter 10). The bone finds also follow this pattern; flood reworking in the upper levels may well have damaged worked bone beyond recognition, accounting for their absence from unit M. (The only bone special find from this unit is a small human skull fragment, 1985 sf 225). Stone special finds are generally found in good condition throughout the sequence, but this subset is dependent on the survival of evidence for working. The apparently unworked stone material shows differential decay/abrasion through the sequence according to raw material durability (Chapter 9).

A study of the completeness data does little more than indicate the fragility of a material and the possible utility of a damaged object. Clay objects appear as fragments, except where they are small, easily lost items such as the clay disc (C38) or fall rapidly into disuse, as is the case for the pottery test piece (C19). Stone is seemingly reduced to a small size before being discarded, presumably because of its continuing utility for various purposes. Set against this is the appearance of complete items in several of the materials. They may be the results of casual loss rather than deliberate discard. Most obviously of the latter category is the pottery production evidence (Chapter 6): some of the pebble pounders, the large quern fragment and three bone tools are complete and usable. These would appear to be a prime example of Schiffer's *de facto* refuse

(1976), i.e. material that still has use potential but has been abandoned. Conversely there are other items, such as the tweezers (M24) or awl (M21), that seem more likely to have become incorporated after loss. Their presence says something about either the ubiquity of the metal or the house-keeping practices of the early first millennium. However, the idea that all the material recovered from these deposits is deliberately discarded refuse, and that all represents the same dumping regime, needs to be treated with caution.

A basic distribution of material type by stratigraphic unit can be used to highlight broad trends in the deposition, supporting observations made elsewhere about the general conditions of formation of the Late Bronze Age deposits (see Table 11). Unit M has lost the less durable and lighter materials during flood reworking. There appears to be a general similarity in the composition of Units L-I, with low numbers of organic materials and higher numbers of metal, stone and clay. Unit H has a strong emphasis on stone and coprolites, although they need not necessarily be linked to the same depositional factors. In the pre-dumping unit G there are no special finds, reflecting the general paucity of cultural debris at this level.

In studying the spatial patterning a few observations may be drawn. There are notable concentrations of special finds in 59 east (i.e. in 2 metre squares) in units K, I and H with 14, 9 and 10 respectively. The bulk find record also shows increasing material towards the eastern end of the trench in the two lower units, so this is perhaps unsurprising. The only other metre square pair that breaks double figures for a single phase are those at 56 east in unit K.

The quantities of special finds generally increase with the volume of soil excavated. When ranked in order of their density per unit volume they show, moreover, a

Table 11: Distribution of special finds materials by stratigraphic unit (LBA only)

Unit	G	H	I	J	K	L	M
Amber				1	1	1	
Antler			1	1	1		
Animal Bone		2	2	3	4	1	
Fired Clay		6	6	5	16	9	4
Flint		1			2	1	3
Human Bone							1
Metal		1	3	2	3	7	4
Organics		6		1	1		
Stone		7	6	10	15	10	4
Vitreous					1		
Total	0	23	18	23	44	29	16

Unmodified flint pebble objects (hammerstones and possible striker) are entered as stone. Joining objects and those duplicated in general or sub-type columns of Table 12 (i.e. not material) are counted as one.

good correlation with the ranked densities of the corresponding bulk finds.

Certain materials tend to be found in clusters rather than as individual finds. This is a product of raw material abundance and durability, and the use to which the original object was put. An examination of the distribution of material type by stratigraphic unit and grid reveals groups of clay, stone and organic (coprolite) material types, whereas bone and copper alloy are more sparsely distributed.

One change in the assemblage can be detected. There is a presence of materials related to what could loosely be termed 'industrial' activities throughout the unit sequence H-M. These include mould fragments, and a variety of stone fragments interpreted as hammers and abraders. In addition there is the group of pottery production equipment. However, from unit J upwards there is an increase in what might be termed 'craft' related items; bone awls, spindlewhorls and light copper alloy tools for example. With an increase in the quantity of likely quern fragments it is possible that there is an increasing 'domestic' component in the refuse.

Below the LBA horizon the material remains are much thinner. There are two groups of special finds that deserve a brief mention here. The flint artefacts are unspectacular in both their diversity and their quantity, but are generally in good or fair condition. They are found in complete or near complete state (see Chapter 9 for a selection). Also from the top of the Neolithic levels come two rather battered human skull fragments (HB5–6). These are in the flood reworked deposits and thus have no obvious contextual significance. As with that from unit M (HB47), these will be reported in a later volume, where all human skeletal material from the site will be drawn together.

Special Finds Catalogue

The following table consists of all special finds recovered from Area 16 East during excavation and post-excavation. Both the 1985 and 1986 seasons are included. For convenience finds are ordered by material followed by object type.

Cat. No. — This cross-refers to those finds fully described and illustrated in the relevant catalogue sections of this report. Only the most significant or representative items have been treated in this way. The codes assigned in this volume follow on from those published in the 1978 excavation report.

AM = amber
B = animal bone and antler
C = clay
FL = struck flint
HB = human bone
M = metalwork
S = stone including chalk.

Material — The description of the material from which the object is made. (In the case of composite artefacts it will be listed under both materials. However these items will only have one British Museum registration number.)

General type — A general indication of what the object is. A single object may have more than one entry if it has possible multiple uses or identifications.

Sub-type — A more detailed classification of form or source material.

Unit — The stratigraphic unit from which the artefact originated.

Context — The Area code and context number of the originating layer/feature.

Grid E, Grid N — The easting and northing on the site grid. Where both coordinates end in 00 the object was not recorded in situ, and thus can only be placed in its metre grid square. There will be no level for these latter examples.

Level (mOD) — The height O.D. of the three-dimensionally recorded items.

ERB Code — The season in which the find was excavated, preceded by the site code ERB.

sf No. — The special find number allocated in finds processing. (N.B. each season this was reset at 1 for each Area.)

Reg. No. — The final number in the British Museum registration sequence P1989 10–1 1ff.

L, W, T	Dimensions to the nearest mm. When axes are arbitrary orthogonal ones, the measurements are entered in descending order. With annular forms L serves as height or thickness of the band, W as external diameter and T as width of band.

wt — Weight to nearest gramme.

Cond. — Condition, referring to the physical state of the object. The following codes are used:

- a = abraded (specialised form of 'poor')
- f = fair
- g = good
- p = poor (includes burnt, fragile, powdery, laminated etc.)

Comp. — Completeness, in so far as can be determined given the artefact's condition. The following codes are used:

- c = complete
- f = fragment
- lf = large fragment, lacking only minority
- nc = near complete, lacking tiny ends or corners.

Other abbreviations used in the Table:

- adj. = adjacent
- asym. = asymmetric
- chis. = chisel
- frag. = fragment
- glob. = globular
- hu. = human
- opp. = opposing
- ornmt = ornament
- terml = terminal
- whet. = whetstone

Table 12: Special finds from Area 16 East ordered by material then type

Cat. No.	Material	General type	Sub-type	Unit	Con-text	Grid E	Grid N	Level (mOD)	ERB Code	sf No.	Reg No.	L mm	W mm	T mm	wt g	Cond	Comp
	amber	bead		16.L	16.820	53.56	12.71	14.54	ERB85	093	1	5	11	4	0.2	p	f
AM2	amber	bead	asym. glob.	16.J	16.836	59.29	12.47	14.30	ERB85	154	2	10	16	6	1.6	f	c
AM1	amber	bead	wedge	16.K	16.824	54.57	13.57	14.42	ERB85	123	3	5	12	4	0.4	p	c
B23	antler	cheekpiece?		16.K	16.822	54.00	13.00	0.00	ERB85	137	4	35	5	2	1.4	f	f
B22	antler	handle		16.J	16.865	57.59	12.55	14.30	ERB85	126	5	118	23	20	37.5	g	c
	antler	off-cut	tine	16.I	16.868	58.24	12.06	14.26	ERB85	162	407	44	13	12	5.0	g	c
B17	bone	awl	metapodial	16.J	16.834	54.00	12.00	0.00	ERB85	219	6	40	9	5	1.7	g	f
B16	bone	awl	metapodial	16.J	16.836	56.00	12.00	0.00	ERB85	155	7	61	21	13	4.4	g	c
B15	bone	awl	metapodial	16.J	16.865	58.00	12.00	0.00	ERB85	173(i)	8	62	21	14	8.5	g	f
B15	bone	awl	metapodial	16.I	16.868	58.50	12.64	14.26	ERB85	160(i)	8	35	7	4	8.5	g	f
B18	bone	needle	slender	16.K	16.829	59.00	13.00	0.00	ERB85	218	9	37	4	3	0.5	f	f
	bone	perforated		16.L	16.819	53.00	12.00	0.00	ERB85	222	10	22	15	14	0	f	f
	bone	perforated		16.L	16.819	57.00	12.00	0.00	ERB85	237	11	28	11	1	0.3	g	f
B24	bone	plaque		16.K	16.824	57.00	13.00	0.00	ERB85	226	12	56	25	5	5.6	g	lf
	bone	point	slender	16.K	16.824	55.00	13.00	0.00	ERB85	141	13	14	3	3	0.1	f	f
B21	bone	polisher	carpal	16.I	16.873	58.00	12.00	0.00	ERB85	217	14	107	17	7	1.7	g	c
	bone	polisher?	tusk	16.K	16.824	56.00	13.00	0.00	ERB85	220	15	90	20	15	19.6	g	nc
B20	bone	spatula	rounded	16.J	16.834	56.15	14.00	14.37	ERB86	010	16	159	30	23	43.2	g	c
B19	bone	spatula	rounded	16.H	16.872	57.40	13.92	14.27	ERB85	169(ii)	17	94	26	5	36.8	g	c
B19	bone	spatula/tally		16.H	16.872	57.00	13.00	0.00	ERB85	181(ii)	17	160	29	19	13.8	g	c
	bone	worked?		16.H	16.896	57.00	12.00	0.00	ERB86	021	18	31	9	13	1.7	f	f
S228	chalk	ring/pendant		16.I	16.868	59.00	13.00	0.00	ERB85	207(iii)	19	12	22	18	6.8	f	f
S228	chalk	ring/pendant		16.I	16.875	59.00	13.00	0.00	ERB85	205(iii)	19	12	18	15	4.3	f	f
C37	clay	bead		16.M	16.814	57.16	12.49	14.57	ERB85	039	20	14	17	8	3.6	p	lf
C38	clay	disc		16.J	16.865	57.00	12.00	0.00	ERB85	230	21	23	20	5	2.5	g	c
C36	clay	disc/whorl?		16.K	16.829	55.00	13.00	0.00	ERB85	139	22	26	19	10	4.2	f	f
	clay	faced	1 face	16.L	16.819	54.65	12.95	14.57	ERB85	056	23	37	16	32	16.9	a	f
	clay	faced	1 face	16.L	16.820	53.91	12.77	14.51	ERB85	094	24	27	22	10	6.2	a	f
	clay	faced	1 face	16.L	16.820	58.89	12.98	14.44	ERB85	086	25	50	34	16	22.6	p	f
	clay	faced	1 face	16.K	16.822	55.08	12.26	14.50	ERB85	111	26	30	23	14	9.4	a	f
	clay	faced	1 face	16.K	16.822	59.71	13.34	14.42	ERB85	110	27	30	28	12	6.8	a	f
	clay	faced	1 face	16.J	16.836	58.55	12.65	14.31	ERB85	114	28	72	61	61	361.9	a	f

Table 12: Special finds from Area 16 East ordered by material then type (continued)

Cat. No.	Material	General type	Sub-type	Unit	Con-text	Grid E	Grid N	Level (mOD)	ERB Code	sf No.	Reg No.	L mm	W mm	T mm	wt g	Cond	Comp
	clay	faced	1 face/skin	16.K	16.822	59.82	12.74	14.39	ERB85	097	29	54	38	17	40.4	a	f
C19	clay	faced	test piece	16.I	16.875.3	59.00	13.00	0.00	ERB85	237	30	87	68	34	138.7	g	c
	clay	impressed	1 wattle?	16.K	16.822	56.00	12.00	0.00	ERB85	213	31	21	19	21	7.0	a	f
C30	clay	impressed	2 wattles	16.J	16.834	54.00	13.00	0.00	ERB85	238	32	39	18	18	10.0	g	f
C27	clay	impressed	3 wattles	16.L	16.820	59.85	13.54	14.43	ERB85	087	33	28	26	18	14.0	a	f
C28	clay	impressed	3 wattles	16.K	16.822	54.00	13.00	0.00	ERB85	228	34	18	20	19	5.5	f	f
C31	clay	impressed	3 wattles	16.K	16.824	56.73	13.43	14.39	ERB85	125	35	102	85	40	195.2	g	f
C21	clay	impressed	keying	16.I	16.868	59.00	12.00	0.00	ERB85	231	36	29	20	10	4.5	g	f
C22	clay	impressed	keying	16.H	16.872	58.00	13.00	0.00	ERB85	232	37	40	24	21	13.7	g	f
C23	clay	impressed	keying	16.I	16.875.3	59.00	13.00	0.00	ERB85	233	38	51	31	17	19.2	g	f
C24	clay	impressed	keying	16.I	16.875.3	59.00	13.00	0.00	ERB85	234	39	30	26	22	11.0	f	f
C25	clay	impressed	keying	16.I	16.875.3	59.00	13.00	0.00	ERB85	235	40	31	28	18	9.4	g	f
C26	clay	impressed	keying	16.H	16.894	59.00	13.00	0.00	ERB85	236	41	31	24	16	8.4	g	f
	clay	impressed	perforated	16.M	16.814	59.05	14.00	14.38	ERB85	084	42	88	49	28	59.8	f	f
C30	clay	impressed	string	16.J	16.834	54.00	13.00	0.00	ERB85	238	32	39	18	18	10.0	g	f
C20	clay	impressed	?thatch	16.K	16.829	58.00	12.00	0.00	ERB85	229	43	29	43	25	20.4	f	f
	clay	impressed +faced		16.K	16.829	53.29	12.98	14.39	ERB85	129	44	63	44	17	51.7	a	f
C29	clay	impressed +faced	1 wattle/pit	16.K	16.829	54.33	12.15	14.44	ERB85	128	45	40	37	22	35.9	g	f
	clay	impressed?		16.H	16.896	55.00	13.00	0.00	ERB86	026	46	31	24	10	6.1	a	f
	clay	impressed?	1 wattle?	16.K	16.824	56.00	12.00	0.00	ERB85	203	47	27	18	13	4.6	f	f
	clay	loomweight?		16.K	16.823	54.91	13.08	14.47	ERB85	113	48	37	27	26	27.8	a	f
	clay	loomweight?		16.H	16.872	58.00	13.00	0.00	ERB85	201	49	59	33	32	35.3	a	f
	clay	mould		16.L	16.820	57.36	12.71	14.48	ERB85	085	50	28	23	13	6.6	a	f
	clay	mould		16.K	16.822	56.00	13.00	0.00	ERB85	223	51	22	19	8	3.2	a	f
C33	clay	mould		16.K	16.822	56.00	13.00	0.00	ERB85	227	52	19	11	6	3.2	a	f
C32	clay	mould	socket	16.L	16.820	56.10	13.00	14.47	ERB85	078	53	49	35	10	18.7	f	f
	clay	mould?		16.M	16.807	59.00	13.00	0.00	ERB85	020	54	21	16	3	1.5	a	f
	clay	mould?		16.M	16.814	52.00	12.00	0.00	ERB85	092	55	27	17	9	2.7	p	f
	clay	mould?		16.L	16.820	55.14	13.64	14.50	ERB85	088	56	21	15	9	2.0	a	f
	clay	mould?		16.K	16.822	53.00	12.00	0.00	ERB85	214	57	24	17	9	2.1	a	f
	clay	mould?		16.K	16.822	56.00	12.00	0.00	ERB85	215	58	22	17	8	2.4	a	f
	clay	mould?		16.I	16.868	59.00	12.00	0.00	ERB85	187	59	59	32	14	16.6	a	f
	clay	mould?		16.H	16.872	55.00	13.00	0.00	ERB85	194	60	25	16	7	2.3	a	f
	clay	mould?		16.H	16.887	59.06	13.80	14.25	ERB85	179	61	24	18	8	27.3	a	f
	clay	shaped		16.L	16.819	55.79	12.82	14.50	ERB85	067	62	45	30	28	47.9	f	f
C34	clay	spindlewhorl		16.L	16.819	56.40	13.50	14.52	ERB85	059	63	28	38	27	16.5	g	f
C35	clay	spindlewhorl		16.J	16.836	58.00	12.98	14.31	ERB85	153	64	18	33	15	13.2	g	f
M21	cu alloy	awl		16.L	16.819	59.44	12.14	14.44	ERB85	047	65	28	2	2	0.4	f	c
M22	cu alloy	blade? tang?	chis./tracer	16.L	16.819	59.47	12.26	14.43	ERB85	050	66	7	6	2	0.4	f	f
	cu alloy	blob		16.M	16.807	52.25	12.62	14.68	ERB85	009	67	17	14	13	5.3	p	?
	cu alloy	blob		16.L	16.819	56.57	13.25	14.49	ERB85	062	68	17	11	7	1.1	p	?
	cu alloy	blob		16.K	16.824	59.38	13.92	14.37	ERB85	127	69	8	4	3	0.1	p	f
	cu alloy	blob	tabular	16.K	16.822	54.17	13.19	14.50	ERB85	107	70	19	14	7	3.2	p	c?
	cu alloy	blobs		16.L	16.819	59.33	12.22	14.43	ERB85	037	71	15	14	11	1.8	p	?
M28	cu alloy	ingot	thin edge	16.L	16.820	54.00	13.00	0.00	ERB85	122	72	33	27	13	25.3	f	f
M20	cu alloy	knife	blade tip	16.HJ	16.878	59.68	13.94	14.24	ERB85	178(iv)	73	99	29	5	37.4	p	f
M23	cu alloy	needle?	slender	16.J	16.834	54.42	13.28	14.37	ERB85	142	74	47	1	1	0.3	f	f
M26	cu alloy	pin	wart-headed	16.H	16.872	57.58	13.88	14.27	ERB85	170	75	53	7	6	1.2	p	nc
	cu alloy	point	rounded	16.L	16.819	53.26	12.85	14.55	ERB85	042	76	39	4	4	1.4	p	f

Table 12: Special finds from Area 16 East ordered by material then type (continued)

Cat. No.	Material	General type	Sub-type	Unit	Con-text	Grid E	Grid N	Level (mOD)	ERB Code	sf No.	Reg No.	L mm	W mm	T mm	wt g	Cond	Comp
	cu alloy	ribbon		16.M	16.814	59.66	12.30	14.49	ERB85	036	77	12	9	1	0.1	p	f
	cu alloy	sheetlike		16.M	16.814	58.33	13.72	14.47	ERB85	033	78	5	5	1	0.1	p	f
	cu alloy	sheetlike		16.K	16.824	56.16	12.72	14.43	ERB85	120	79	5	5	1	0.1	p	f
	cu alloy	small frag.		16.L	16.819	52.34	12.78	14.56	ERB85	063	80	7	5	4	0.1	p	f
	cu alloy	socketwall	mouth	16.M	16.814	59.02	12.11	14.54	ERB85	035	81	13	7	3	1.0	f	f
M24	cu alloy	tweezers		16.J	16.836	58.29	13.30	14.32	ERB85	152(v)	82	43	7	2	3.1	p	c
M25	cu alloy	tweezers?	hinge	16.I	16.868	59.16	12.41	14.25	ERB85	161	83	18	3	2	0.7	p	f
M27	cu alloy	wire ornmt?	coil terml?	16.I	16.868	56.49	12.50	14.33	ERB85	163	84	17	3	2	0.3	f	f
FL19	flint	arrowhead	leaf	16.H	16.887	59.39	12.20	14.21	ERB85	180	85	41	21	6	4.4	g	nc
FL29	flint	arrowhead?	blank?	16.F	16.921	57.00	12.00	0.00	ERB86	022	86	37	18	5	2.4	f	lf
FL17	flint	flake	hollow retouch	16.M	16.807	56.00	13.00	0.00	ERB85	013	87	50	22	12	12.9	p	c
	flint	flake	retouched	16.E	16.922	53.00	12.00	0.00	ERB86	025	88	36	22	7	5.2	f	c
	flint	flake	retouched?	16.L	16.819	52.00	12.00	0.00	ERB85	149	89	30	19	3	2.3	g	c
S213	flint	hammer	pebble	16.I	16.868	57.50	12.80	0.00	ERB85	209	90	117	92	72	993.6	g	c
S211	flint	hammer	pebble	16.H	16.872	54.00	13.00	0.00	ERB85	192	91	51	46	35	134.3	f	c
S212	flint	hammer	pebble	16.H	16.872	57.45	13.85	0.00	ERB85	200	92	120	117	53	764.2	g	lf
S210	flint	hammer	pebble	16.H	16.872	58.00	13.00	0.00	ERB85	190	93	94	63	80	487.9	g	f
S209	flint	hammer	pebble	16.H	16.876	59.00	13.00	0.00	ERB85	216	94	68	61	57	325.7	f	c
FL22	flint	knife	plano-convex	16.F	16.921	58.37	13.33	13.91	ERB86	006	95	27	42	6	5.6	g	c
	flint	knife?		16.M	16.814	57.35	13.24	14.54	ERB85	034	96	42	25	8	6.9	f	c
	flint	notched	3 notches	16.K	16.822	57.57	13.87	14.41	ERB85	083	97	37	30	10	9.5	g	c
FL23	flint	point	thick	16.B	16.955	58.00	12.00	0.00	ERB86	014	98	52	40	10	17.4	g	c
FL20	flint	scraper	end	16.E	16.924	55.00	12.00	0.00	ERB86	023	99	43	26	9	8.5	g	c
FL21	flint	scraper	end	16.B	16.952	56.00	12.00	0.00	ERB86	027	100	54	23	7	6.5	g	c
FL18	flint	scraper	end+side	16.M	16.814	56.00	12.00	0.00	ERB85	055	101	41	38	18	24.2	g	c
	flint	scraper?		16.K	16.824	59.96	13.69	14.36	ERB85	117	102	25	15	4	1.9	p	f
FL24	flint	serrated		16.F	16.920	54.75	13.48	14.13	ERB86	005	103	44	23	5	4.8	g	c
FL25	flint	serrated		16.E	16.923	54.14	12.40	14.03	ERB86	009	104	55	16	4	3.3	g	c
FL26	flint	serrated		16.B	16.934	57.00	12.00	0.00	ERB86	029	105	41	32	11	9.6	g	c
FL27	flint	serrated		16.C	16.945	54.00	12.00	0.00	ERB86	028	106	31	14	4	1.5	g	lf
FL28	flint	serrated		16.B	16.952	55.00	12.00	0.00	ERB86	030	107	34	21	7	3.8	g	c
S208	flint	striker	pebble	16.H	16.872	58.00	13.00	0.00	ERB85	193	108	109	21	19	65.6	g	c
HB47	hu. bone	skull frag.		16.M	16.814	57.00	13.00	0.00	ERB85	225	405	19	19	5	1.0	f	f
HB5	hu. bone	skull frag.		16.F	16.921	59.19	12.65	13.88	ERB86	007	109	69	39	7	13.2	a	f
HB6	hu. bone	skull frag.		16.F	16.921	59.20	13.08	13.88	ERB86	008	110	37	34	6	5.6	a	f
M29	lead	casting jet	1 feeder	16.I	16.868	57.43	12.93	14.26	ERB85	164	111	37	43	5	154.7	p	c
	organics	coprolite		16.K	16.822	54.00	13.00	0.00	ERB85	136	112	21	20	—	—	f	f
	organics	coprolite		16.H	16.872	56.00	12.00	0.00	ERB85	199	113	19	15	—	—	p	f
	organics	coprolite		16.H	16.872	56.00	13.00	0.00	ERB85	196	114	—	—	—	—	f	f
	organics	coprolite		16.H	16.887	59.00	12.00	0.00	ERB85	183	115	46	27	25	14.3	g	c
	organics	coprolite		16.B	16.953	57.00	12.00	0.00	ERB86	015	116	27	18	—	—	p	f
	organics	coprolite	impressed	16.H	16.872	55.00	12.00	0.00	ERB85	197	117	50	33	—	—	f	f
	organics	coprolite	impressed	16.H	16.887	59.00	12.00	0.00	ERB85	184	118	42	37	21	—	f	f
	organics	coprolite	impressed	16.H	16.887	59.00	12.00	0.00	ERB85	198	119	58	44	—	—	f	c?
M24	organics	fibres		16.J	16.836	58.29	13.30	14.32	ERB85	152(v)	82	—	—	—	—	-	f
M20	organics	fibres		16.HJ	16.878	59.70	13.90	14.24	ERB85	178(iv)	73	—	—	—	—	-	f
S217	stone	abrader	3 faces	16.L	16.820	54.12	12.29	14.52	ERB85	073	120	96	86	49	370.9	p	f
S218	stone	abrader	grooved	16.L	16.820	55.00	13.00	0.00	ERB85	090	121	25	21	10	12.2	p	f
S216	stone	abrader	pebble	16.J	16.834	55.56	13.85	14.38	ERB85	145	122	57	45	30	104.0	f	f
S214	stone	hammer	pebble?	16.I	16.868	57.75	13.75	0.00	ERB85	210	123	84	81	73	693.2	g	f

Table 12: Special finds from Area 16 East ordered by material then type (continued)

Cat. No.	Material	General type	Sub-type	Unit	Con-text	Grid E	Grid N	Level (mOD)	ERB Code	sf No.	Reg No.	L mm	W mm	T mm	wt g	Cond	Comp
S215	stone	hammer/ grinder	pebble	16.J	16.834	53.81	12.63	14.41	ERB85	143	124	53	48	38	217.4	f	c
	stone	pebble	1 face	16.K	16.822	58.55	12.22	14.38	ERB85	101	125	58	52	16	82.6	g	f
	stone	pebble	3 faces?	16.L	16.819	57.80	13.43	14.52	ERB85	046	126	36	30	28	43.3	g	f
	stone	pebble	enhanced?	16.M	16.814	56.00	12.00	0.00	ERB85	054	127	41	32	20	35.8	g	f
	stone	pebble	enhanced?	16.L	16.819	56.00	13.00	0.00	ERB85	102	128	33	32	21	33.1	g	f
S222	stone	quern	tabular	16.I	16.868	57.90	14.00	13.34	ERB86	011	129	212	168	52	2732.2	g	lf?
S226	stone	quern?		16.K	16.824	55.36	12.92	14.44	ERB85	130	130	83	71	34	436.5	g	f
S221	stone	quern?		16.HJ	16.895	59.00	13.00	0.00	ERB85	202	131	56	40	43	110.4	g	f
S224	stone	quern?	cuboid	16.K	16.829	59.60	13.32	14.33	ERB85	140	132	90	86	31	396.0	g	f
S227	stone	quern?	faces adj.	16.L	16.819	54.00	12.00	0.00	ERB85	098	133	129	59	31	222.2	f	f
S225	stone	quern?	faces adj.	16.K	16.824	59.61	13.03	14.37	ERB85	121	134	82	65	43	347.3	g	f
S223	stone	quern?	trapezoid	16.J	16.849	57.10	13.61	14.33	ERB85	156	135	144	133	39	813.3	g	f
S219	stone	whetstone	tabular	16.I	16.868	57.00	13.00	0.00	ERB85	171	136	108	54	14	159.7	g	c
	stone	whetstone?	cuboid	16.K	16.822	59.53	13.39	14.40	ERB85	095	137	82	79	30	406.7	g	c
S220	stone	whet.?/ mould?	faces adj.	16.K	16.824	59.81	13.39	14.37	ERB85	119	138	49	45	25	64.4	g	f
	stone	worked		16.M	16.813	57.19	13.89	14.61	ERB85	021	139	64	60	30	162.0	g	c
	stone	worked	2 faces?	16.M	16.814	58.13	13.96	14.51	ERB85	041	140	54	46	16	64.3	a	f
	stone	worked		16.M	16.814	59.00	13.00	0.00	ERB85	148	141	60	48	38	95.4	g	f
	stone	worked	3 faces	16.L	16.819	54.00	12.00	0.00	ERB85	064	142	70	55	38	141.6	p	f
	stone	worked	1 face	16.L	16.819	55.30	13.88	14.53	ERB85	065	143	22	17	17	8.7	p	f
	stone	worked	1 face	16.L	16.819	59.27	12.84	14.45	ERB85	053	144	37	33	22	31.6	f	f
	stone	worked	cuboid?	16.L	16.820	54.70	12.12	14.52	ERB85	074	145	55	36	33	148.9	f	f
	stone	worked	2 faces? opp.	16.K	16.822	53.35	12.34	14.51	ERB85	096	146	49	39	27	51.4	g	f
	stone	worked		16.K	16.822	54.92	13.25	14.47	ERB85	108	147	30	22	17	16.0	f	f
	stone	worked		16.K	16.822	55.08	13.19	14.45	ERB85	116	148	48	46	36	65.4	g	f
	stone	worked	1 face	16.K	16.822	57.13	13.06	14.41	ERB85	103	149	41	26	18	34.6	f	f
	stone	worked		16.K	16.822	59.00	13.00	0.00	ERB85	157	150	56	46	38	81.0	g	f
	stone	worked		16.K	16.824	58.95	13.29	14.39	ERB85	124	151	44	39	31	107.1	p	f
	stone	worked		16.K	16.829	59.93	12.34	14.32	ERB85	132	152	60	39	38	64.5	f	f
	stone	worked	2 faces opp.	16.K	16.829	56.66	13.40	14.36	ERB85	075	153	75	44	27	134.7	f	f
	stone	worked	plano-convex	16.K	16.829	59.55	13.92	14.37	ERB85	133	154	70	61	33	122.0	g	f
	stone	worked		16.J	16.834	53.00	12.00	0.00	ERB85	167	155	52	40	27	79.9	a	f
	stone	worked		16.J	16.836	57.00	13.00	0.00	ERB85	168	156	45	36	31	54.2	g	f
	stone	worked		16.J	16.865	58.00	12.00	0.00	ERB85	174	157	47	18	18	17.5	g	f
	stone	worked		16.J	16.865	58.00	12.00	0.00	ERB85	175	158	49	29	12	13.4	g	f
	stone	worked		16.I	16.868	57.99	14.00	13.33	ERB86	012	159	93	55	58	468.8	f	f
	stone	worked	faces adj.	16.I	16.868	59.90	12.44	14.27	ERB85	159	160	68	67	64	383.5	g	f
	stone	worked		16.H	16.872	56.00	13.00	0.00	ERB85	204	161	38	24	17	15.4	f	f
	stone	worked?	cuboid?	16.L	16.819	54.00	12.00	0.00	ERB85	104	162	22	20	12	7.2	p	f
	stone	worked?		16.J	16.834	55.83	13.33	14.36	ERB85	144	163	53	48	38	30.9	f	c
	stone	worked?	flake?	16.J	16.836	55.00	12.00	0.00	ERB85	176	164	41	33	8	10.4	g	f
	stone	worked?		16.J	16.865	56.00	12.00	0.00	ERB85	165	165	35	32	20	30.3	g	f
	stone	worked?		16.H	16.885	54.00	12.00	0.00	ERB85	182	166	62	60	66	235.0	f	f
	stone	worked		16.E	16.927	59.00	12.00	0.00	ERB86	024	167	20	17	16	8.1	a	f
	vitreous	lump	?modern	16.K	16.829	59.00	13.00	0.00	ERB85	166	406	23	21	11	3.1	g	f

Joining finds are shown by a lower case roman numeral in brackets after the sf No.

CHAPTER 7

The Neolithic pottery

IAN LONGWORTH AND GILLIAN VARNDELL

Of a total sherd count of 331, 80% is represented by plain wall sherds. The remainder consists of rims, decorated wall sherds and other featured sherds such as recognisable shoulders, necks etc. A minimum number of thirty-two vessels was estimated from the featured sherds, given the number of actual and probable joins. No further statistical treatment of this small assemblage is attempted.

Form and decoration

The range of rim forms, simple and heavy, is not extensive and there are no extreme forms. Overall a general tendency towards the everted was noted. Among the rims classified as heavy, two have incipient collars (NP59, 60); otherwise treatment is not elaborate.

Open vessel forms include simple hemispherical bowls (e.g. NP54), shouldered bowls (e.g. NP53), and shallow bowls with or without shoulder (NP57, 75). Shoulders are not sharp. Closed forms are represented by bowls with an upright or hollow neck.

The decorative range is narrow and tends to be made with either a pointed implement or flake, or fingernail and tip. Rim decoration is commonly incised, either deeply (slashes) or more shallowly (strokes). There may be diagonal slashes externally, vertical strokes internally, diagonal (and sometimes curvilinear) incisions on top and internally, incisions across the rim, or diagonal incisions below the rim. Fingernail impressions may occur on the rim top, and on the lip internally or externally. Elsewhere on the vessel the following techniques were noted: haphazard fingernail impressions on the body, incised herringbone on the body, incised lines externally on body (possibly), deep pits beneath the rim, fingertip impressions in the neck. There is one example of a plain, horizontal lug.

Affinities

The heavy rims, shouldered bowl shapes and incised/impressed decoration place the assemblage within the Earlier Neolithic regionalised decorated bowl tradition. However, at least eight vessels have marked Ebbsfleet traits – the closed forms with upright or hollow necks (NP55, 64, 70, 73, 74 and 77) sometimes with inturned rims (NP64, 70 and 74), pits or impressions in the neck (NP66, 67 and 73). Sherds from these vessels are in fabric and condition indistinguishable from the decorated bowl assemblage. They may be contrasted with the Ebbsfleet pottery from the nearby causewayed enclosure at Staines where open forms, heavier and more elaborate rims, and impressed cord and bird bone decoration are present (Robertson-Mackay 1987). The assemblage from Area 16 East is too small to say more; study of the remaining areas promises to shed more light. However, the definition of, and the chronological and regional variation within, the style we now call Ebbsfleet need further study.

The single sherd with random fingernail impressions (NP68) is reminiscent of the Peterborough tradition, while the sherd with herringbone decoration (NP84) may be chronologically closer to Beaker, though the fabric is indistinguishable from the bulk of the assemblage (group T:I). The execution is unlike other examples of herringbone decoration noted on Neolithic pottery from the rescue excavation of 1978 (Kinnes 1991), which occur on rim, neck and just below (NP15, 24 and 39). It is more precise and placed, probably, well down the body. In addition the context, unit F, allows deposition as late as the second millennium BC. The eroded rim sherd (unit B, uncatalogued) already mentioned has no distinguishing features aside from its fabric, which does occur in the Earlier Neolithic assemblage reported on previously (Kinnes 1991, 158).

Cross-context joins

NP77 is represented by sherds from different contexts: 16.922 53/12 (unit E) and 16.929 53/12 (unit D). NP64 (unit B) and NP74 (unit C) are also very similar to the preceding – given the variations in shape and execution of decoration to be found on one vessel, all these sherds might be from the same pot.

Catalogue of illustrated sherds

The examples illustrated are representative of the assemblage. Numbers carry on the sequence begun in the rescue volume (Kinnes 1991) and refer directly to illustrations (Figs 57–9). The catalogue is arranged according to stratigraphic unit beginning with the earliest; the context number and site grid references follow the catalogue number.

R = rim; Dec = decoration; T = fabric temper.

Four fabric groups were distinguished by eye.

T:I   The largest group. Burnt flint, fine to coarse in graded sequence with no hard divisions. Both plain and decorated sherds may have very large inclusions.

T:II   A substantial minority of sherds had a fairly fine, sandy temper, occasionally micaceous.

T:III   A small group with mainly fine, crushed burnt flint grits.

T:IV   One sherd only had virtually no visible temper (Unit C, 16.944 5913, plain rim sherd).

Unit B

NP53 (reconstructed bowl): 16.952 56E/12N, 16.953.2 56E/12N, 953.6 56E/13N, 953.7 56E/13N
12 plain sherds including 6 rim. R: simple, pointed, inturned. T:I.
Reg. P1989 10–1 168

NP54: 16.955 59E/12N
3 plain rim sherds. R: flattened, everted. T:I.
Reg. P1989 10–1 169

NP55: 16.955 59E/12N
1 plain rim and 1 wall sherd. R: simple, rounded, everted. T:I.
Reg. P1989 10–1 170

NP56: 16.952 56E/12N
1 plain rim sherd. R: simple, rounded, upright. T:I.
Reg. P1989 10–1 171

NP57: 16.955 58E/12N
2 plain rim and 2 wall sherds. R: expanded, everted. T:I.
Reg. P1989 10–1 172

NP58: 16.955 59E/12N
2 plain rim sherds. R: T-shaped. T:I.
Reg. P1989 10–1 173

NP59: 16.955.5 59E/12N
1 plain sherd. R: incipient collar. T:I. Probably same vessel as NP60.
Reg. P1989 10–1 174

NP60: 16.934 57E/12N
1 plain sherd. R: incipient collar. T:I.
Reg. P1989 10–1 175

NP61: 16.952 56E/12N
1 rim sherd. R: expanded, everted. Dec: diagonal fingernail impressions on outer rim and vertical on bevel; vertical to diagonal inside. Possible row of horizontal fingernail impressions externally, beneath rim. T:I.
Reg. P1989 10–1 176

NP62: 16.953 56E/12N
1 plain rim sherd. R: heavy type but damaged and unclassifiable. Depressions below neck are voids left by filler. T:I.
Reg. P1989 10–1 177

NP63: 16.953 57E/12N
1 rim sherd. R: expanded, everted. Dec: vertical incised lines on inner lip. T:I.
Reg. P1989 10–1 178

NP64: 16.956 54E/12N
1 rim sherd. R: simple, flattened, inturned. Dec: diagonal incised lines on outer lip. T:I.
Reg. P1989 10–1 179

NP65: 16.952 56E/12N
1 rim sherd. R: everted, T-shaped. Dec: row of diagonal slashes beneath rim (and possibly on rim top). T:I.
Reg. P1989 10–1 180

NP66: 16.952.3 56E/12N
1 rim sherd. R: expanded, everted. Dec: deep fingertip impressions in neck. T:I (micaceous).
Reg. P1989 10–1 181

NP67: 16.953.3 57E/12N
1 rim sherd. R: internally thickened, everted. Dec: deep, circular pits beneath rim. T:I.
Reg. P1989 10–1 182

NP68: 16.955.4 59E/12N
1 wall sherd, probably lower body. Dec: random fingernail impressions externally. T:I.
Reg. P1989 10–1 183

NP69: 16.955 59E/12N
1 wall sherd with part of plain, imperforate lug: T:I. The lug has been formed unusually, being both applied and pinched out (there is a marked corresponding internal dent).
Reg. P1989 10–1 184

Unit C

NP70: 16.944 58E/12N
2 plain rim sherds. R: simple, inturned; thumb groove internally beneath rim. T:I.
Reg. P1989 10–1 185

NP71: 16.944 58E/12N
1 plain rim sherd. R: simple, pointed. T:I.
Reg. P1989 10–1 186

NP72: 16.944 59E/12N
1 plain rim sherd. R: T-shaped. T:IV.
Reg. P1989 10–1 187

NP73: 16.944 58E/12N
1 rim sherd. R: Thickened, rounded, upright. Dec: remains of one, perhaps two, deep pits in neck made with tapered implement. T:I.
Reg. P1989 10–1 188

NP74: 16.945 54E/12N
1 rim sherd. R: simple, rounded, inturned. Dec: diagonal incised lines beneath rim externally. T:I.
Reg. P1989 10–1 189

Unit D

NP75: 16.929 53E/12N
1 plain rim sherd. R: simple, flattened, upright. T:II.
Reg. P1989 10–1 190

NP76: 16.940 54E/12N
4 rim sherds. R: expanded, everted. Dec: incised lines across rim top. T:I.
Reg. P1989 10–1 191

Units D, E

NP77: 16.929 53E/12N; 16.922 53E/12N
2 rim sherds. R: simple, rounded, upright. Dec: diagonal slashes on outer lip. T:I.
Reg. P1989 10–1 192

Unit E

NP78: 16.923 54E/12N
2 plain rim sherds. R: internally thickened and rolled. T:I.
Reg. P1989 10–1 193

NP79: 16.922 53E/12N
1 rim sherd. R: flattened, externally thickened. Dec: light diagonal incised strokes in neck. T:I.
Reg. P1989 10–1 194

NP80: 16.923 54E/12N
1 wall sherd. Dec: ?lightly incised lines externally. T:I.
Reg. P1989 10–1 195

Unit F

NP81 16.921 (general)
1 plain rim sherd. R: simple, rounded, upright. Shallow thumb groove internally beneath rim. T:I.
Reg. P1989 10–1 196

NP82 16.921 54E/12N
1 rim sherd. R: internally thickened, everted. Dec: incised diagonal lines on rim top. Internal surface lost. T:II.
Reg. P1989 10–1 197

NP83 16.921 (general)
1 rim sherd. R: flattened, externally thickened. Dec: diagonal incised lines on rim top. T:I.
Reg. P1989 10–1 198

NP84 16.921 56E/12N
1 wall sherd. Dec: incised herringbone, carefully executed. T:I.
Reg. P1989 10–1 199

NP85 16.921 53E/12N
1 wall sherd. Dec: no formal decoration, but internally grass-wiped. T:I.
Reg. P1989 10–1 200

Two further sherds are worthy of mention. One (unit B, 16.934 57E/12N) is a simple rim sherd in a distinctive fabric, well fired with sparse ferruginous sand filler. The sherd is very weathered. The other (unit E, 16.923 54E/12N) is possibly a flat base sherd; the fabric conforms to T:I.

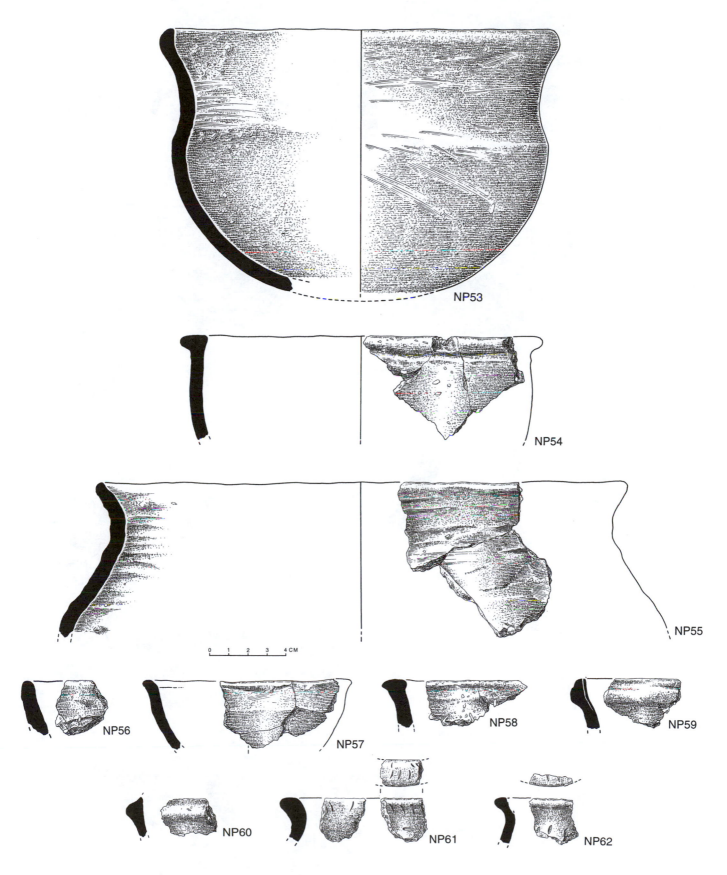

NP53

NP54

NP55

0 1 2 3 4 CM

NP56

NP57

NP58

NP59

NP60

NP61

NP62

Fig. 57 *Neolithic pottery, unit B. Scale 1/2.*

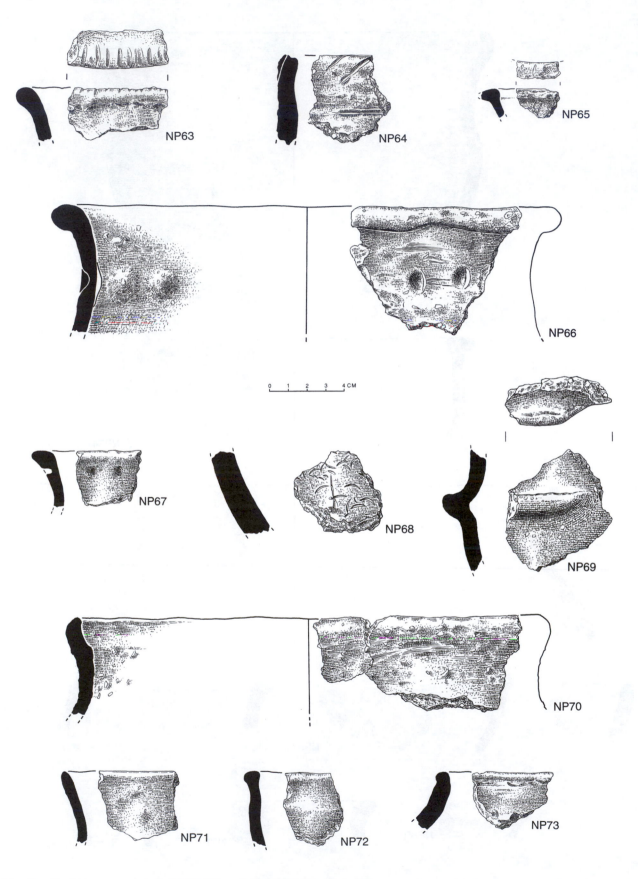

Fig. 58 *Neolithic pottery, unit B (NP63-69), unit C (NP70-73). Scale 1/2.*

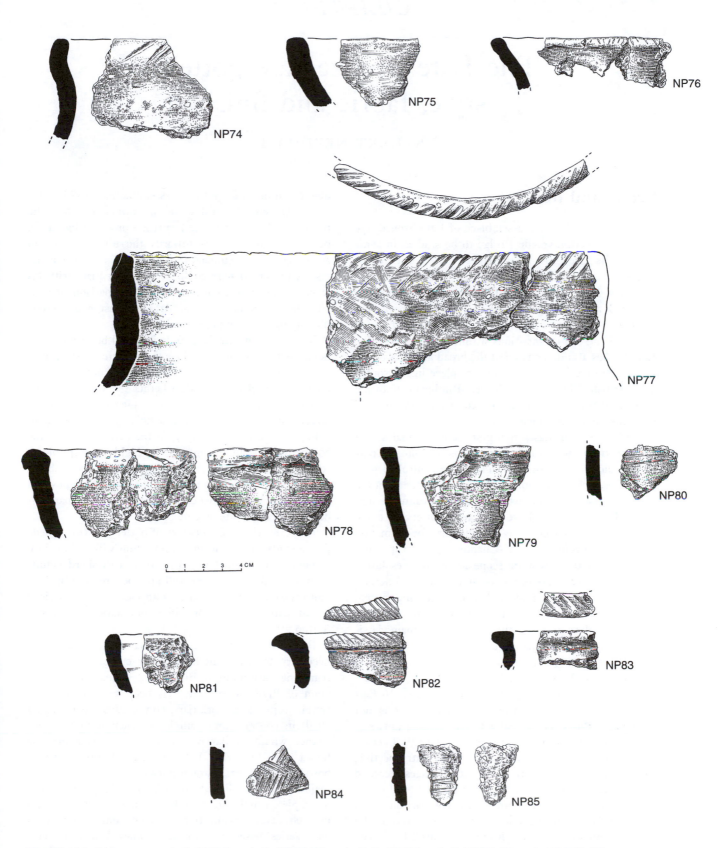

Fig. 59 *Neolithic pottery, unit C (NP74), unit D (NP75-76), units D–E (NP77), unit E (NP78–80), unit F(NP81–85). Scale 1/2.*

CHAPTER 8

The Late Bronze Age pottery: style, fabric and finish

STUART NEEDHAM

Scope and methods

This is the third trench assemblage of Late Bronze Age pottery from Runnymede Bridge to be studied in some depth; the previous assemblages were from rescue phases of the investigations in Area 2 and Area 6 (Longley 1980; Longley 1991). Their publication has provided a considerable body of information on the ceramic repertoire of the site, with some indications of temporal and spatial variations within the site's deposits. Longley has also demonstrated the broad affinities of the site assemblage in terms of both its place in the south-east British PDR (Post Deverel-Rimbury) tradition (Barrett 1980) and its links with contemporary Urnfield elements on the continent.

With Area 16 East, the first detailed analysis of material from the research excavations, the aims of pottery studies have broadened. The more controlled pace of the research excavations has allowed better retrieval, documentation and contexting of finds; meanwhile new lines of investigation have emerged. Pottery is being used more extensively now as evidence for formation processes and refuse history (Chapter 4), whilst it is also believed that there is more scope for greater resolution of chronological developments and ceramic function. With these aims in mind, a detailed recording system has been devised to serve as an archive database from which to analyse pottery issues. Most of the main classificatory codes used to date are defined in Table 16. It is hoped that the system can continue to be employed as successive zonal assemblages from the site are studied.

Although the following analysis of the Area 16 East assemblage looks at a variety of attributes, it is not intended at this stage to deal with all potential causes of variation in ceramic assemblages (e.g. Plog 1980). In effect the aspects considered here are rather introspective, being concerned with establishing the changes recorded locally; broader matters such as the function and status of particular classes of pottery and comparisons with other contemporary site assemblages are reserved until a broader suite of contexts at Runnymede itself have been studied.

Orton has recently reviewed means and ends in the quantification of pottery assemblages (1993). He acknowledged the value of quantification for the purposes of understanding formation process (ibid. 176), but his main thrust is towards the ultimate goal of assessing life assemblages of pots. The Runnymede results presented here could be seen to equate with his level (iii) objective, concerning the comparison of sub-assemblage compositions in Area 16 East and thereby identifying any composition change.

To implement this level fully it would be necessary to define pottery types and then to estimate vessel-equivalents (Orton 1975). In the absence of such definition there is a problem assessing whether the various sample populations in the Area 16 East sequence represent the target populations (i.e. life assemblage) in a consistent manner. There is anyway a further complication: the comparison of sub-assemblages is highly susceptible to the incorporation of parts of individual vessels at different horizons. This problem of secondary deposition is unlikely to arise when making gross comparisons between distinct site assemblages.

However, the basic measure of pottery at Runnymede in the study of assemblage composition will be based on recognised individual vessels, rather than sherd counts or weight (although these will also be presented). This 'pottery-as-vessels' approach is an essential prerequisite to estimating proportions in a population of vessels (Orton 1993, 177).

Before the Area 16 East material is described, it is necessary to say something about current limitations regarding terminology. Broad morphological classification of PDR assemblages has been kept deliberately simple in previous work (jars, bowls, cups – e.g. Barrett 1980) in contrast for example to schemes in northern France where similar but wider form ranges may be found (e.g. Talon 1987). Even so, attribution to jar or bowl status is not a straightforward matter. The great majority of published British vessels have rather incomplete profiles, or even lack diameter estimates, and in such cases classification rests on comparisons with 'type series' based on complete profiles. Whilst it seems to the writer that there is some degree of form standardisation in PDR ceramics, both at site and regional levels, there seem nevertheless to be other forms present which are eclectic in their use of attributes. Attribution to a defined form or class thus becomes problematic and is undoubtedly influenced by such factors as the quality of ware or finish and the researcher's preconceptions. Ultimately it is hoped that the large Runnymede assemblage will allow consideration of both general classes and more specific forms, but this cannot be tackled prematurely. Such issues as the correlation of fabrics to profiles and surface finish, or the estimation of vessel volumes, will be worth investigating. Many of these higher questions depend on a good sample of substantial or complete profiles which will take time to build up. In the meantime it has seemed most fruitful to concentrate on a series of traits to explore the extent of variation present within a localised vertical sequence. The traits studied are diverse, involving morphology, angles, fabric and surface finish.

Even the large Area 16 East assemblage (9,505 sherds weighing almost 70 kg), featuring much early-stage refuse with a reasonable number of recognised joins/belongs, contains only a modest number of complete or near-complete profiles. Consequently it is intended in this report to use the terms 'bowl' and 'jar' very loosely, and often to use merely 'vessel'. No attempt is made to quantify bowls and jars as proportions of the unit or total assemblages beyond a very rough, partly intuitive, estimation. On the other hand, quality of ware can be assessed in a systematic fashion for all sherds, or any defined sub-set, and its quantification can be a valid description of one aspect of the local sequence.

For the purposes of this study of style, fabric and finish, all featured sherds have been considered (but not all catalogued) in the rims, bases and decorated categories, whilst only a selection of undecorated shoulder/carination sherds were extracted for study (although where these have been linked to fuller profiles they are automatically included). A total of 470 vessels (many represented by individual sherds) were thus under study. Selection of 204 vessels for the catalogue presented here aimed to:

1. show complete or near-complete profiles;
2. show a representative form range, including any idiosyncratic features;
3. show all types of decoration present.

This was done initially for the whole trench assemblage without regard to the stratigraphic sequence, but some minor adjustments were subsequently made to the context groups to reflect better the perceived character of sub-assemblages. Nevertheless, there is an increased risk of biases having been introduced for the upper context groups. As they yielded few substantial profiles, the more unusual rim forms and sherds featuring decoration are likely to be over-represented in the catalogue

at the expense of some plain and simple forms, which are otherwise well illustrated in lower context groups.

The pottery has been divided according to the stratigraphic units (G–M), most of which give conveniently-sized groups. Although there is scope for breaking some into finer stratified groups, it is not considered to help in interpretation; indeed for trend evaluation some units have been lumped together. The seven groups thus defined are de facto a chronological sequence, though it must be understood at the outset that this is a sequence of *final incorporation* and not invariably one of initial discard, still less one of production. The questions of re-use, reworking and redeposition should be prominent in interpreting the sequence, as highlighted by Lambrick (1984), and moreover need to be addressed initially to resolve the matter of phase attribution for multi-unit vessels.

Phasing of multi-unit vessels

Before a sequence, albeit a sequence of final incorporation, can be faithfully reconstructed it is necessary to resolve the problem of multi-unit vessels. These are the cases of single pots whose constituent sherds have been dispersed vertically through the stratigraphy being thus represented at more than one level. To avoid double-counting such examples (i.e. those occurring in more than one sub-assemblage) one must decide which level is likely to be the closest in time to their initial discard. This will be the earliest deposit known to have incorporated relevant sherds, but even this will be later than use and initial discard by a variable interval. Of course in the majority of cases, where a particular vessel is only recognised at a single level or stratigraphic unit, one has little option but to take this as the most appropriate one. In fact intensive searching for joining and belonging sherds within the Area 16 East deposit (Chapter 4) yielded a fair number of joins and belongs, a proportion coming from more than one stratigraphic unit (Table 17).

In a high-activity area the dispersal of interrelated material through a vertical sequence is to be expected. One obvious mechanism responsible is that of redeposition of material following the disturbance of pre-existing deposits so that some material ends up in stratigraphically later contexts (Chapter 4). In Area 16 East there is little evidence to suggest that specific contexts, once fully sealed by succeeding dumps, saw disturbance *within* the excavated trench. This would imply that the immediate 'source' of late-deposited sherds lay beyond the excavated area, perhaps from the periodic clearance of surfaces or the digging of features. Apparent secondary deposition could on occasion have an alternative explanation if parts of broken vessels had a continuing utility around the settlement so that not all of the vessel was discarded simultaneously (as discussed in Chapter 4). Noteworthy in this context is the pottery crock (context 16.862) beneath a cluster of burnt flint which was probably used as a carrying tray (Plate 16).

Further hypothetical causes of stratigraphical separation have been set out in Chapter 4, focusing in particular on downwards abraded relationships. From the point of view of phasing, most of the pathway combinations envisaged, although variable in outcome, are nevertheless concomitant with taking the lowest stratified sherd(s) as the best indication of phase of discard (though still only a *terminus ante quem*). This assumption will only fail when the stratigraphy has been misunderstood either because of an unrecognised feature (Fig. 48D) or because of poor recognition of stratigraphic boundaries between deposits of different ages such that some sherds become misattributed.

Several possible factors might be considered in deciding whether misunderstood stratigraphies account for 'anomalous' relationships. Sherd abrasion and quantity (expressed in weight) have already been introduced in the above discussion. These do not always work in concert and can therefore give contradictory indications as to the best unit attribution. When those two factors do reinforce one another, they can help confirm the degree of protection or attrition suffered, but do not distinguish potential protection in a previous depositional context, nor potential intrusion into a lower stratigraphic position. One should note also the occurrence of differential condition for sibling sherds within a single context, although in Area 16 differences tend to be small. Uneven firing may play a part in causing such variation.

Where a number of sherds are involved which do not show entirely consistent abrasion and size patterns from one context to another, then it is a problem to decide what rules should be applied. At an elemental level, when is a larger sherd (or set of sherds) to be regarded as significantly larger? Certainly one would not want to attach much significance to the comparison between one sherd of, for example, 10g weight and another single sherd in a higher stratification of 25g.

Further complications can arise from the degree of separation of contexts. Two vessel portions from contiguous contexts either side of a unit boundary (often an arbitrary divide) might best be regarded as coming from essentially the same horizon close to the 'transition' or 'interface'. Where there is wide separation of different parts of a vessel (e.g. P661 in units H, and K-M) it might seem more likely that the 'earliest' piece was in fact intrusive, a conclusion that tends to be resisted in cases where the various units were contiguous. However, this assumption would deny some of the more unusual pathway combinations that are feasible. Throughout, one has to keep in mind that even the earliest context

recorded for a vessel may itself be significantly later than initial discard.

The difficulties are not inconsiderable and it has seemed preferable to take a simple approach in phasing. While the process of downward intrusion cannot be ruled out, it is hard to evaluate and the assumption has been made hereafter that this was of minor occurrence when compared to stratigraphically upward movement. The pottery has been grouped according to a straightforward premise of upward redeposition from the lowest stratigraphic horizon in which the vessel is represented, but at the same time 'flags' have been inserted to denote where evidence exists that *might* argue for counter processes.

The system employed is as follows:

1. 'Vessel phase' cites the full unit representation of the vessel (regardless of relative conditions/quantities), in unit sequence: e.g. HIJ;
2. The vessel is always placed with the earliest unit group represented;
3. Where there are grounds for suspecting that this *might* have resulted in incorrect phasing, one or more higher units are flagged with an asterisk: e.g. HI*J, suggesting that the sherd(s) in H may have been intrusive from I.

The criteria for such a flag are that a higher stratified sherd (group) is:

(a) overall less abraded than the lowest sherd/group, *unless* it is much smaller (i.e. < 25% the size, very approximately);
(b) much larger (>x4) than the lowest sherd/group, but is *not* more abraded.

Character of the sub-assemblages

The character will be described first in terms of the individual sub-assemblages for the stratigraphic units. Thereafter particular attributes are looked at with regard to sequence trends.

Unit G (Fig. 60)

Only a single sherd was catalogued from this context group which is poor in artefacts. It is a simple tub-like vessel (P650).

Unit H (Figs 60–7)

Thirty-seven vessels are represented in the catalogue, of which twenty-one include sherds from higher-stratified units. In seven cases the sherds in H are perhaps at risk of being intrusive from a later deposit (P656, P659,

P674, P679, P686, P687 and P854). One of these (P679) is an unusual form of jar or bucket which can be best matched in middle- to late-dated contexts in the Area 6 sequence (units 6.E onwards: P222, P304 and P549). Such a date range may not post-date unit H. The other potentially intrusive vessels are entirely in keeping with the H assemblage.

Cups/bowls and jars seem to be roughly equally represented. Three reconstructed profiles indicate cups, whilst a fourth, very thin-walled sherd should also be a cup (P651-4; Plate 19). The wares are fine and semi-fine. P654 has a light internal bevel with a slight internal hollowing for the upper part of the neck.

As with the cups, bowls are plain and relatively unelaborate but often burnished. Hollow-necked bowls with rather weak carinations are present (P656-659), while a second series has rounded profiles and out-turned rims, either slack (P662-664) or more globular (P666-667). Not all of these are fine wares and size is variable, P667 in particular being large. P665 may have something in common with the latter series but it could be a deeper tub-shaped vessel. Two thin-walled vessels with marked carinations (P668-669), the former being burnished, could belong either to bowls or jars.

Most of the thicker-walled coarse wares can be regarded as jars, amongst which moderately shouldered profiles with a gently concave neck predominate (P670-676, 854). Shoulders are generally angular though still obtuse. Three different varieties of rim decoration are present. Another hollow-necked vessel, P678, is unusual in its pronounced concavity with a shoulder diameter narrower than the body below. The bucket-like vessel with slightly flared neck (P679) has already been discussed above, whilst P680 seems to be a standard convex-walled bowl/jar. Other sherds show the presence at this stage of decoration inside the rim (P682), decorated neck cordons (P683) and strap handles (P684).

Unit I (Figs 68-9)

One of the twelve catalogued vessels from unit I might belong to a higher-stratified context (P693).

Cups/bowls predominate over jars in the catalogued group for unit I. Notable are two thin-walled cups with different rim profiles (P688, 689) and the burnished bowl with a flattened band at the carination. The larger coarse-ware vessels reflect the range seen in unit H (P693-94), whilst strap handles also continue, albeit with different cross-sections represented (P696-97). The fingered treatment on body sherd P695, although not 'formal', appears to be of decorative intent and distinct from the more usual body surface treatment of finger smearing.

Unit J (Figs 69-77)

Fifty-one vessels are represented in the catalogue. Two multi-unit vessels are considered at risk of being intrusive into unit J contexts (P712, 714).

This relatively large unit assemblage also shows a degree of diversity in forms. Capacities, however, concentrate on moderate sizes with little evidence for cups or small bowls and only a modest number of large vessels (P724-31). Where profiles are sufficiently intact, most vessels are relatively deep and many might be described either as deep bowls or jars. There is a continuation of plain hollow-necked carinated 'bowls', again with weak to moderate carinations, in a variety of wares including some rather crudely made (P701-04). P707-09 represent a large variant characterised by thin walls, burnished surfaces, a deep neck slightly out-turned at the top, and flattened rims. Two also have light internal bevels.

More globular vessels are also present (P710-11) in one case with a short upright neck surviving. P713 shows a distinctive much thickened upright neck, but could have had either a globular or shouldered body. P714 and P715 should come from barrel or biconical profiled forms, the former vessel also having a pie-crust rim. The series P716-19 come from modest diameter cylindrical necks with slight lip expansion. P716 is in fine ware with burnishing and an internal bevel. Some of this group might represent cylinder-neck jars.

Ten coarse-ware vessels are standard jars (or jar/bowls) with shortish hollow necks above relatively weak shoulders (P720-29). Rim tops are decorated in two cases (P725, 729), but otherwise roughly flattened causing irregular internal and/or external lipping. P722 carries finger-tipping on the shoulder. P731 can be regarded as a distinct form with lower shoulder and more biconical profile up to its gently expanded lip. Two further rims carry decoration (P734-35), whilst two body sherds show contrasting decorative techniques: neat incised geometric (P740) and plastic finger-pushed cusps (P741). A variety of base forms is attested including two finer wares with omphalos (P742-43), the former in fact having been created by a small foot-ring. Rim P739 seems out of keeping in a Late Bronze Age context and is better regarded as residual from the Middle Neolithic assemblage.

Unit K (Figs 78-82)

Sixty vessels have been catalogued of which seven have sherds from higher-stratified units (in each case unit L).

Numbers of bowls and jars seem to be reasonably balanced, although probably weighted towards the latter, and therefore also towards coarser wares.

One fine-ware sherd appears to be from a shallow dish

(P751), whilst a weakly carinated cup is also represented (P752). The coarse-ware sherd P753 is likely to be from a bowl, but identifiable bowls are fine and exhibit an interesting range of profiles (P754–59), to which may be added non-reconstructible sherds (P760–63). There is variation in wall thickness as well as in many nuances of profile, mostly being variations on carinated forms. P758 is noteworthy for its bevelled band above the carination, P760 has a corrugated upper neck, whilst P759 is a neat, apparently globular bowl furnished with a ridge and groove just below its upright lip. The beaded rim and gritless fabric of P761 suggest that it belongs to an established class of beaded biconical bowls. Another novel fine ware (P764) has a well-defined lip and fairly thick walls; its extant profile suggests a deepish globular vessel.

The range of jars and/or coarse wares also suggests some development from lower stratified forms. Moderate-to weakly-shouldered forms are still predominant (P767–73), although with variation in detail. Some rims are lipped, especially when decorated along the top, but the heavy out-turned moulding of P767 is more unusual. P778 is a curious vessel, thick-walled, yet lightly burnished. It has a silty fabric with light flint gritting. There are similar fine-burnished sherds with medium-thick near-straight walls below flat or internally bevelled rims (P779–80), apparently from fairly large vessels. P781 would seem to have had a very short neck with two rows of diagonal impressions at shoulder and neck, whilst P782 has a club rim apparently at a constricted mouth.

Decoration is noticeably more common in this assemblage, particularly a variety of finger treatments to rims, shoulders, necks and cordons. Cordons are sited in two cases in the neck (P772, P799), and one on a belly (P800). Apart from grooves, used in a few instances to define rim mouldings, other decoration is confined to curved combing on a fine-ware body sherd (P798), light scratches on a set of sherds of unusually soft fabric (P797) and diagonal tooled lines below the rim of P795.

Fine-ware bases include one with an omphalos (P806). P788 has a possible lid seat in its neck.

Unit L (Figs 82–3)

This context suite is thought to have included heavily reworked components which probably explains why very few of the 'vessels' presented constitute more than one sherd. There is also a risk of later conflation of material deposited during the LBA at different stratigraphic horizons, although generally those horizons are likely to have been the uppermost layers of the sequences locally around Area 16 East.

The group of thirty-four catalogued vessels should not be regarded as representative of the unit L assembl-age. Because few substantial profiles are reconstructible from the assemblage, sherds have been chosen to illustrate decorative treatment or some other noteworthy feature. Consequently both decoration and unusual morphology will appear over-represented. Nevertheless, there is no doubt from consideration of all featured sherds that these are important aspects of the L assemblage.

The most complete bowl profile has a modest carination beneath a near cylindrical neck (P811). P812 on the other hand appears to be from a more tripartite profile. P813, in extremely fine ware with geometric incised decoration, can be attributed to a class of jars with flared necks (e.g. Longley 1980, 70; Type 18). Other fine-ware sherds exhibit additional rim forms: flat-topped (P814), out-turned lips (P815–16), or pinched-out lip with broad flat top (P817). As with the finer wares, coarse wares show a good range of rim profiles and wall thickness (P819–31).

A few sherds have lid seats, either as internal hollowing (P819–21) or by provision of an internal flange (P818); this last vessel has a closed mouth and is a burnished ware. Decorative techniques are diverse and executed by incision (P813), combing (P833), rilling (P832), stamping (P822, 835, 837) and rocking (P834), as well as various finger treatments on rims, neck cordons or shoulders. The external rim position seen on P823 seems to come into use at a late stage of the LBA sequence. One fine-ware base has a pronounced foot-ring (P842).

Unit M (Fig. 83)

Nine sherds have been catalogued and are subject to similar biases as those represented in unit L. Most elements seen on unit M pottery can be found in unit L or a little lower. The strap handle (P853) has a different cross-section from any of those found lower in the sequence.

Trends through the stratigraphic sequence

Fabric and finish

All catalogued sherds have been classified with regard to the following aspects of fabric and surface finish: grit density, grit size, inclusion type, surface treatment and the colours of inner face, outer face and core (which relate to firing conditions). Grit density and size were judged by inspection of ancient (clean) breaks. In addition certain special features were noted relating to the occurrence of laminar structure, additional grits or vegetal material on bases, or refiring. All these categories are coded to aid tabulation and computerisation; the definition of codes is presented in Table 16.

The paste of both fine and coarse wares is generally hard-fired; only occasional sherds are noticeably flaky, crumbly or friable throughout the body, in some cases evidently due to poor firing rather than the nature of the paste.

The terms *grit density* and *grit size* are used in this report to allow the possibility that the easily visible grits are not always the sole tempering agent. Sand is a common additional inclusion in this assemblage and in some cases at least is suspected of being a deliberately added temper. Grit density and size categories thus refer only to the flint grit inclusions, which dominate the fabrics (184 of 205 vessels). Other inclusions are less frequent and perhaps mostly derive from the clays used; they are dealt with below. The boundaries for grit size are slightly modified from those adopted by Longley (1991, 163); in particular it was found that an upper threshold of 1 mm maximum size was more practicable for defining the smallest grit range (code 11–'fine'), as opposed to Longley's 0.5 mm.

There are some noteworthy shifts in the nature of flint gritting from top to bottom of the Area 16 East sequence (Figs 84–5). The distribution of grit density in the lower assemblages (units H and I) shows a marked peak for 'moderate' density (03). This is progressively eroded and by unit K 'light' gritting (02) predominates instead. This is just part of an overall shift towards the addition of less grit since 'dense' gritting (04) diminished whilst 'sparse' and 'absent' (01,00) gritting became relatively more common. Units L and M show a similar overall emphasis to the unit K assemblage but without signs of a peak for light gritting.

Grit size also seems to change. The larger size ranges (13, 14, 15) are well represented in units H and I, though still outnumbered by sherds with finer grits (11, 12). The latter categories, however, become more and more predominant through units J, K, L and M. It should be recognised of course that the distributions presented here represent just a sample of the entire Area 16 East assemblage, but that the sampling is unlikely to have been biased in these respects.

The shift towards sparser tempering with grit which was also of a finer grade, can probably be linked to the parallel increase in the percentage of sandy wares. Earlier studies have pointed to this inverse relationship which seems to be widespread in lowland Britain and is taken to be a chronological development (in the local context: Longley 1980, 40; Needham and Longley 1980, 413).

The presence of sand in the Area 16 East pottery was noted in 39% of unit H and I catalogued pottery, rising steadily to 67% in units L and M (Table 13). Humphrey could find no evidence from the thin-sectioned sherds

Table 13: The percentage incidence of sand and iron-rich pellet inclusions in the Late Bronze Age pottery (catalogued)

Stratigraphic unit	Sand (26–27)	Fe-rich (23)
L & M	67%	12%
K	55%	20%
J	43%	24%
H & I	39%	31%

that the sand was a deliberate addition (below). It would seem that sandier clays were being deliberately sought later in the occupation and that lesser quantities of flint filler were added.

Less frequent inclusions in the Area 16 East pottery are shell (small amounts in 2 sherds), occasional sandstone lumps (2 sherds), other non-angular grits (8 sherds) and iron-rich pellets (45 sherds). While their presence is noted in the catalogue, no attempt has been made to quantify the densities of these inclusions. The iron-rich pellets, when examined under thin-section (below), prove to be glauconite inclusions, almost certainly deriving from the clays selected for potting. There is a consistent decline in the proportion of pottery showing these inclusions, from about 30% in units H and I to 12% in units L and M (Table 13). Thin-sectioning also picked up the presence of argillaceous pellets in a number of sherds, but as these can be difficult to identify in hand specimen no attempt has been made to document their occurrence in the full catalogued group. Four sherds from units K to M also have tiny voids which are taken to be burnt-out organic matter.

Few base fragments have been classified in detail owing to their limited variation, but there is an indication of change in the way their undersides were treated (Fig. 86). In units H and I there is a fairly even distribution of bases with added flint grit (08), vegetal matter (09), or neither. Above these deposits vegetal inclusions disappear rapidly, whilst in unit K additions of either kind are exceptional. Further area assemblage studies must be awaited to see whether this pattern is general for the site.

Surface treatment again seems to attest changing techniques in pottery production, although care must be exercised in interpreting the histograms (Fig. 87) because taphonomic factors may have had a disproportionate effect on sherd surface survival. Taking initially the overall percentages for burnished ware (codes 30–2), smooth/even-walled ware (defined here as category 33 without any second treatment present), and the various rough-finished wares (34–7), a striking feature is the apparently consistent rise in smooth/even ware from 8% at base to 30% at top of the stratigraphic sequence. It is possible that some sherds thus classified in units L and M have lost the burnished 'skin' due to natural weathering processes and again in unit K owing to longer average refuse-cycles. To set against this argument it may be seen that recognisable burnished ware itself remains at a similar level (*c*.30%) through units J-M, but is somewhat more common (*c*.43%) in units H and I). In other words, most of the variation in smooth/even wares appears instead to be inversely related to rough-surfaced wares. This suggests that the main cause is the replacement of some rough wares by vessels with a smoother standard of finish, but does not entirely exclude the possibility that some smooth even-walled vessels were originally burnished and have therefore been mis-classified.

There may be some more refined variation within the broad classes of surface treatment considered so far. The character of the burnish changes; in units H and I a good proportion of burnished vessels have an uneven or 'rough' burnish (30). The proportion diminishes to low levels higher in the stratigraphy where smooth burnishes (31) predominate. Ripple burnish (32) is a minor component throughout. Amongst the rougher surface treatments finger-smearing (36) and grass-wiping (37) are noteworthy in early sub-assemblages whilst higher up they decline leaving 'undistinguished' surfaces (34). The decline is extreme in units L and M, perhaps partly due to the preferential erosion of subtle grass-wiping marks.

Decoration

Decoration is being considered from the point of view of position on the vessel (codes a-j), technique (codes A-H) and specific forms (codes 01–97). Starting with general issues, it would be useful to quantify the proportion of decorated vessels, rather than decorated sherds. In fact the frequency of decoration within a particular context group cannot be straightforwardly calculated. The proportion of decorated/undecorated total sherds will severely under-represent decorated vessels where decoration tends to be confined to limited zones on the pots. A better evaluation comes from considering just featured sherds and 'vessels' (including those not published in the catalogue). Some 'plain' sherds/vessels might omit decoration that was placed elsewhere on the pot; this will again tend to under-represent decorated wares. Conversely however, some decorated body sherds (shoulders, walls etc. – which are designated as featured sherds) may come from the same vessels as others (e.g. decorated rims) already contributing to the decoration frequency count, because the two portions are not recognised as belonging together. This would enhance the apparent frequency and run counter to the former bias. Calculation of

Table 14: Frequency of decoration on LBA pottery rims

Stratigraphic unit	No. of vessels with rim present	No. of rims decorated	Proportion of rims decorated
L & M	83	19	23%
K	96	16	17%
J	77	10	13%
H & I	62	7	11%

decoration frequency among featured sherds is then only a crude estimation of proportions of vessels decorated. It should, however, reflect real differences in trend between sub-assemblages. It is anyway doubtful whether greater precision could be achieved at a site like Runnymede given the extent of redeposition and rather variable patterns of refuse cycle.

One facet of decoration that may be quantified relatively closely is the frequency of rim decoration. Using all vessel rims represented in Area 16 East (including uncatalogued vessel rims) the proportions shown in Table 14 were obtained. The proportion of rims decorated seems effectively to double between units HI and LM. In fact it is possible that this under-represents the degree of change since any reworked earlier material in units L and M are likely to have led to dilution of the contemporary frequency.

The incidence of decoration positions is shown in Fig. 88, which illustrates a change from conservative, mainly rim decoration in H-J, to much more diversification in the positioning of decoration thereafter. A rise in neck and shoulder decoration relative to rim decoration is well shown.

In the histograms for decorative technique (Fig. 89) the most obvious distinctions between sub-assemblages are the additions of finger-nail technique (C) and stabbed/stamped/impressed motifs (F) to the repertoire from unit K upwards. Larger samples in future will be needed to see whether these distinctions show up consistently. There is some evidence also that the balance between simple finger-impressed techniques (B) and more carefully finger- or tool-moulded forms (D) changes significantly, with the former only slightly in the majority in lower units but becoming much more dominant high up. Combing (G) is, as always, at a very low frequency, but it does occur from unit J upwards.

Individual types of decoration are generally too few in number in Area 16 East to give any firm indications of changes; however, a few observations may be made at this stage (Fig. 90). Amongst rim types, decoration on the outside lip of the rim, either by finger impression or slash (01, 15), occurs only in units K and upwards (six examples). Basic finger-tipping of the rim top occurs throughout the sequence. Although, as noted above, rim decoration is much less frequent towards the base of the sequence, it is noteworthy that the detailed forms present in units H and I are diverse.

Once body decoration becomes more common, above unit J, the overall balance of motifs would appear to be constant with greatest incidence in two general categories, simple finger-tip designs on shoulders/carinations, and 'geometric' designs. Many of the latter are simple parallel-groove designs. These categories extend back to unit J, and they appear to increase in step with the emergence of body decoration. Body designs based on finger-nail and incised slashes, however, may have gained currency a little later. Amongst the 'other' group are two small fragments of distinctive combed curvilinear motifs, both occurring in unit K.

Pot profiles

Rim forms (Fig. 91) are most commonly round-topped (code 02) or flat-topped (09, 10), but there is a clear drift from a predominance of the rounded form lower in the stratigraphy to flattened rims higher up. This may in part be explained by the increase in rim decoration where finger-tipping frequently creates, or is given, a flat platform. This could also account for the occurrence of more unrestrained lipping on flattened rims (10 rather than 09) in higher units when compared with H and I. The demise of simple rounded rims could be seen to be offset by the development of various externally rolled or beaded forms which generally also have rounded tops (03, 05, 12). The tapered rim form 01 is overwhelmingly a feature of units J and K, whilst other thickened forms, often 'club-like' (06, 07, 08, 11), occur throughout and peak in J. These features give the rim assemblage in J an unusually even spread, the common forms (02, 09, 10) being not much more numerous, than the rarer ones (01, 03–08, 11–12), in ratio 24:15.

Neck and shoulder/carination forms have also been classified (codes 21–38 and 51–61 respectively), but there is little to note from their distribution in the Area 16 East sequence. Angled and concave necks and, less common, straight and convex forms are all present throughout the stratigraphic sequence. Both strongly angled and strongly concave forms (21, 24, 32) are rather exceptional in an assemblage dominated by shallow or moderately hollowed necks. Special internal features deserve some comment. Internal bevels (44, 45) are present throughout the sequence in small numbers, which fluctuate between about 8% and 18% of rim sherds catalogued (Table 15). Slight internal hollowing (43) is a less frequent feature, but does seem to increase from *c.*2.5% to 11% occurrence from units HI up to LM. Well-developed hollowing and internal flanging, both providing lid seats (41, 42), occur once each in the upper stratigraphy (K and L).

Where they may be assessed with some confidence,

Table 15: The occurrence of special internal features on LBA pottery (sample: catalogued sherds)

Stratigraphic unit	Codes			No. of rims considered
	41 & 42	43	44 & 45	
L & M	1	3	4	28
K	1	2	5	43
J	0	1	7	39
H & I	0	1	3	38

the angles of mouths, upper bodies and base walls have been classified using simple categories: strongly out-sloped, moderately out-sloped, slightly out-sloped, vertical, slightly in-sloped, moderately in-sloped, strongly in-sloped. These define codes MA1–MA7 respectively for mouths, UB2–UB7 for upper bodies, and BW1–BW5 for base walls. In looking at the sequence (Fig. 92), there is a problem in that vessels reconstructed to give angles become infrequent above unit J due to changing formation process and are virtually non-existent in units L and M. The lower units, H, I and J, show similar distributions peaking strongly at MA3, slightly out-turned mouths, and UB5, slightly in-turned upper bodies. Unit K, however, seems to show a shift to more contracted profiles on average with MA3 and MA4 roughly equally represented, and similarly UB5 and UB6.

Base forms are typical of PDR assemblages with the coarser wares generally having feet pinched out to varying degrees (codes 84–7). The finer wares usually have a distinct though obtuse angle at the wall/base junction. Six vessels in Area 16 East exhibit an omphalos or pushed up base, these being distributed through units H (1 example), I (1), J (3) and K (1), whilst two further vessels, from units J and L, each have a foot-ring (P742, P842).

Conclusions

One of the main lines of enquiry in analysing the Area 16 East pottery has been a search for temporal (vertical) trends since there is little scope for seeing horizontal patterning. To state (as above) the truism that the stratigraphic sequence through the LBA dark earth deposits is a chronology of deposition, or rather, of final incorporation, does not automatically mean that assemblage change through that sequence would have been a function of gross change in the site's ceramic repertoire. There is always a possibility that some changes will instead relate to the changing activity status of the particular zone. This could either work directly, through the abandonment of ceramics from specific activities in close proximity or indirectly, in accordance with the proportion and history of the reworked contribution.

We are also to some extent hamstrung by the poor resolution possible in independently dating the duration of deposition. For example, if overall duration was very short, this would lessen (though not rule out) the likelihood of gross ceramic assemblage change. A starting point for the dark earth sequence is provided by the radiocarbon evidence, which for the lower layers calibrates to fairly restricted calendar ranges. These give a preferred date either side of 800 cal BC for unit H. The dating for units J and K is later, but has a wide permissible band.

In the absence of any independent estimate of duration, one is left to look at the range and diversity of change, rather than its rate, in both the ceramics and the associated debris. Investigation of a good number of independent aspects of the pottery has allowed a variety of changes to be documented through the four defined sub-assemblages (for units HI, J, K and LM). The fact that differences, sometimes substantial ones, have been identified in various aspects of fabric, form and decoration might favour a predominantly chronological, rather than functional, explanation, although both probably interplay.

Trend indicators considered to be potentially meaningful are summarised in Fig. 93. A few of these may be interdependent, but most are not. Form does not appear to offer many such indicators, but this is partly because it has only been possible to use individual aspects of pots statistically, whereas there may also be significant changes in trait combinations which would, it is hoped, in due course allow definition of vessel forms. Most of the attributes show a progression through all four stratigraphic stages. Only rarely are there any trend reversals, these relating to specific minority rim forms. The progressive nature of most change need not be interpreted in purely chronological terms; taphonomic factors could theoretically give rise to some such changes given the sequence in formation process envisaged, with early-stage refuse (H-J) giving way to refuse of longer average life-cycle (K) and then to flood-reworked material with potential for extensive mixing of deposits. In this way the sequence could be seen to have trapped material from a progressively wider catchment within the settlement. For such a process to be the major cause of the variations encountered, it would imply that the very local ceramic assemblage assumed to be responsible for the early-stage refuse in H-J was a distinct sub-set of the contemporary overall site assemblage and that this sub-set distinguished itself in a number of ways, relating to fabric, finish, frequency of decoration and form, i.e. it was functionally specific. One way of assessing the relative contribution of taphonomic as opposed to chronological factors is to make inter-comparisons with other sequences, both those on site and those from other sites. As already mentioned, at least some of the changes identified in Area 16 East are broadly matched by the suggested sequence for south-east England, notably the increasing frequency of decoration (Barrett 1980) and the increase in sandy wares with reduction of the flint grit added. Many of the other features may not yet have been sought in analyses; some might prove to be site-specific developments.

There are grounds for concluding that there is a significant chronological depth to the Area 16 East deposits, sufficient to witness developments in ceramic style and manufacture on and around the site. During this period the character of pottery refuse also seems to have changed in response to activities around Area 16 East. Preparation of pottery temper and perhaps other aspects of pottery production seem to have taken place actually in amongst the early rubbish dumps (units H and I; see below). However, it seems unlikely that any significant quantity of associated potsherds was directly related to these activities which are instead superimposed on early-stage refuse from eating areas (Chapter 14). The modifications to the form range seen in unit J, plus the density of pot groups there, suggest new inputs, with more emphasis on the dumping of small storage and cooking vessels and less on tableware. This could point to a reorganisation of domestic space. The range of rim forms would stem from either one eclectic household assemblage or perhaps hint at contributions from different households in the neighbourhood. Temporal conflation is thought not to be a major factor in this context since much of unit J material is fresh and the unit formed rapidly. By unit K, however, it would seem that the dumping pattern had altered and might be interpreted as reflecting the shifting away of local residential accommodations. Such a shift might only be in the order of tens of metres to have a tangible effect on the character of debris accumulating. The unit K sub-assemblage can perhaps be regarded as a 'background' assemblage accumulated over a moderate time-span, its mixture of wares and detailed forms having origins in a broad functional catchment within the site. Further diversity in the sub-assemblage could have come from an increase in residual pot sherds of much earlier discard dates.

Catalogue of the illustrated Late Bronze Age pottery

Table 16: Definitions of codes classifying LBA pottery traits, and abbreviations used in Tables 18 and 19.

Portion represented

B – Base
C – Carination
R – Rim
S – Shoulder

Fabric and finish (see Table 18)

Grit density

00 None
01 Sparse
02 Light
03 Moderate
04 Dense

> Density of easily visible grit inclusions; does not take account of any sand or finer particles present. Divisions are subjective

Special features

07 Laminar structure visible in body thickness
08 Additional gritting on base
09 Concentrated vegetal impressions in base
10 Refired sherd

Grit size (measurements refer to maximum dimensions of grits exposed in breaks and surfaces)

11 Fine: almost exclusively 0–1 mm size range
12 Fine and medium: 0–1 mm numerically predominant, but also some in 1–3 mm range
13 Fine plus: much fine grit 0–1 mm, but also medium (1–3 mm) and large (3–6 mm) present
14 Medium and large: 1–3 mm range predominant; variable amounts fall into 0–1 mm and 3–6 mm ranges
15 Large: major components falls within 1–6 mm range; fine (0–1 mm) and very large (>6 mm) grits may also be present

Inclusions type

20 Voids (burnt out organic)
21 Angular burnt flint
22 Grog
23 Fe-rich pellets (some, possibly all, are argillaceous pellets)
24 Shell
25 Silt (difficult to determine macroscopically when grit density moderate or dense)
26 Fine sand (either fine or fine-medium)
27 Coarser sand (medium or coarser grade)
28 Sandstone lumps
29 Non-angular grits (likely flint)

Surface treatment

30* Rough burnish: partial polish; surface left rather uneven; generally poor finish
31* Smooth burnish and regular
32* Ripple burnish: distinct and regular ripple-effect left by tool marks, possibly deliberately; good, but not necessarily 'high' burnish
33 Smooth/even: wall thickness well controlled; surface grits flush; category may include sherds where originally burnished surface has flaked/dissolved away, perhaps especially where fabric is sandy
34 Undistinguished surface
35 Rough with scoremarks: rather rough, uneven; scoremarks not necessarily co-aligned and likely due to dragged grits
36 Rough with finger-smearing or dimpling: rather rough, uneven; widespread finger treatment, may be deliberate effect
37 Rough with striations: rather rough, uneven; light striations suggestive of grass-wiping or similar

* These codes may be further qualified by: **E** – exterior surface, **I** – interior surface

Colour (of exterior, core, interior)

bk black   **d** dark
br brown   **l** light
bf buff
gr grey
or orange
pk pink
rd red

Decoration (see Table 18)

Zone of decoration

a Rim (includes external lip; such examples are distinguished by distinct decorative forms – e.g. 1, 15)

Exterior:

b Underlining rim
c Neck
d Between neck and shoulder/carination
e At shoulder
f Lower body
g Foot

Interior:

h Inside mouth
i Below neck
j Body chamber
- uncertain zone
def Crosses multiple zones

Technique of decoration

A Finger-pinched
B Finger-impressed
C Finger nail
D Moulded cable, rilling etc. (can be carried out with finger, but individual finger marks tending to coalesce into broader morphology)
E Stylus drawn/incisions/slashes
F Stabbed/impressed/stamped
G Combed (in effect a specialised form of E)
H Rocked

Forms of rim decoration

01 Finger-tip or 'scallop' impressions on outer lip of rim
02 Pie-crust: contiguous broad finger-tipping
03 Pie-crust specifically along inner edge
04 Slightly spaced pie-crust
05 Spaced notching by finger tip (thinnish rims)
06 Scalloped pie-crust
07 Cable moulded, outer edge of rim
08 Feeble cable moulding rim on top
09 Contiguous diagonal scallops (ovate)
10 Spaced diagonal scallops (ovate)
11 Spaced deep diagonal grooves
12 Spaced shallower diagonal strokes
13 Spaced lunettes (often slightly diagonal), usually finger nail
14 Internal vertical strokes from rim
15 Strokes on external lip of rim
16 Triangular finger treatment
17 Stabbed rim top, spaced row

N.B. Codes for other forms of decoration will be set out in a future volume. They include:

20–27 for cordon decoration
30–58 for various neck/shoulder/body forms of finger tip/nail decoration

60–86 for various 'geometric' designs involving lines and furrows
90–94 for curvilinear motifs
95–97 other forms

Form (see Table 19)

Rim form
01 Distinct taper to thin edge
02* Rounded/undiagnostic (can be sporadic lipping)
03* With external beading, not heavy but neat
04 Unexpanded, neat beading created by groove, furrow or crease – internal (I) or external (E)
05* Usually rounded and externally rolled – not sporadic; intentional, but may undulate
06 Club profiles giving heavier mouldings – asymmetric towards interior (I) or exterior (E)
07 Distinct out-facing bevel on thickened rim
08 Strongly thickened giving fairly symmetrical triangular section
09* Flattened top, not necessarily evenly but fairly systematically (may also be flattened lipping)
10* Flattened top with lipping, internally (I) and or externally (E); (lipping may be variable/erratic and a by-product of decorative treatment – but is not suppressed)
11 Thickened, giving diamond profile
12 Rolled out, but very irregular and/or squashed (but not erased)
13 Distinct in-facing bevel (bevel must be at rim, not below)

* These forms may be further qualified by: **T** – significant thickening of wall close to rim

Neck form
Simple angled forms:
21 High-placed angle; short, strongly out-turned lip (*c*.90°)
22 High-placed angle; short, moderately out-turned lip
23 High-placed angle; short, slightly out-turned lip
24 Lower-placed angle; very strongly out-turned mouth (*c*.90°)
25 Lower-placed angle; moderately out-turned mouth
26 Lower-placed mouth; weakly out-turned mouth

Non-angled forms:
27 Pronounced convex upper body
28 Slightly convex upper body
29 Straight upper body profile
30 Slightly concave neck
31 Moderately concave neck; fairly even curvature
32 Strongly concave neck; fairly even curvature
33 Asymmetrically curved neck; curve tighter towards top
34 Asymmetrically curved neck; curve tighter towards shoulder/carination
35 Definite 'S' curve (generally slack)
36 Sinuous upper profile with central bulb
37 Sinuous upper profile with central hollowing
38 Squat hollow neck

Special rim/neck internal features
41 Protruding internal ledge, providing 'lid seat'.
42 Moderate hollow seating, potential 'lid seat'
43 Slight internal hollowing
44 Distinct fashioned bevel inside rim creating 'lip bevel' (not concave bevels).
45 Distinct fashioned bevel at neck

Shoulders/carination/belly form
Simple angled forms:
51 Weak, but angled rather than curved
52 Moderate angle
53 Strong angle
54 Very strong angle (*c*.90°)

Curved forms:
55 Weak curve
56 Moderate curve
57 Strong curve

Other forms:
58 Basically straight (buckets/tubs)
59 Beaded angle
60 Faceted belly; two flanking angles of varied strength
61 Double-moulded shoulder/carination

Base form
Raised bases:
71 Medium height foot-ring
72 Small foot-ring; definite bump and fairly flat inside ring
73 Vestigial foot-ring; slight but neat protrusion enclosing flattish base
75* Moderately strong omphalos (centre raised)
76* Shallow omphalos
77 Very slight hollow base, uncertainly deliberate

* These forms may be further qualified by: **R** = rounded instead of angular base angle; **F** = flattened surface around perimeter of base

Flat bases:
81 Rounded exterior angle
82 Simple angle
83 'Foot-plinth': effectively vertical-sided before out-turn into lower body
84 Vestigial foot
85 Small foot
86 Strong, sharp foot; fairly regular
87 Strong, irregular foot

Supplementary base profile features:
91 Dished interior surface
92 Fairly prominent central internal swelling

Dimensions
Th Average wall thickness, excluding rim, in millimetres

(Other dimensions are in archive or may be taken from the drawings)

Handle form (Hd)
Strap handles:
H1 Roughly oval section
H2 Very elongate section, oval or 'D'-shaped
H3 Bulbous 'D' section
H4 Sub-rectangular section

(Non-strap forms of handles are not represented in Area 16 East)

Component angles

	Mouth	Upper body	Base wall
Strongly out-sloped (*c*.45° or more)	MA1	(UB1)	BW1
Moderately out-sloped (*c*.60°)	MA2	UB2	BW2
Slightly out-sloped (*c*.80°)	MA3	UB3	BW3
Vertical (*c*.90°)	MA4	UB4	BW4
Slightly in-sloped (*c*.80°)	MA5	UB5	BW5
Moderately in-sloped (*c*.60°)	MA6	UB6	-
Strongly in-sloped (*c*.45° or more)	MA7	UB7	-

Notes: Mouth angle includes the upper neck; curved profiles averaged. Upper body angle refers to average angle between middle of neck and shoulder/carination; not always definable.

Base wall angle refers to angle at which very base of wall springs from base itself, ignoring effects of any foot present.

Table 17: Late Bronze Age pottery: vessel numbers, contexts and constituent sherd data. N.B. Vessel numbers continue the sequence published in Longley 1991

Vessel No.	Sub	Vessel phase	Context	Sub-context	Unit	Grid East	Grid North	Weight (g)	No. of sherds
P650	a	G	16.896		16.G	55.00	13.00	13	1
	b	G	16.896		16.G	55.00	12.00	11	1
P651		H	16.891.	3,5,17	16.H	59.00	12.00	201	7
P652	a	HI	16.892		16.H	59.00	13.00	67	1
	a	HI	16.878		16.HI	59.00	13.00	12	1
	b	HI	16.875		16.I	57.00	13.00	2	1
P653	a	HI	16.868		16.I	57.00	13.00	2	1
	b	HI	16.872		16.H	57.00	13.00	1	1
P654		HI	16.887		16.H	59.00	12.00	21	2
		HI	16.878		16.HI	59.00	13.00	7	2
		HI	16.876		16.H	58.00	12.00	3	1
P655		H	16.872		16.H	54.00	12.00	9	1
P656	b	HI*	16.876		16.H	58.00	12.00	20	1
	a	HI*	16.890		16.H	59.00	12.00	12	1
	c	HI*	16.868		16.I	58.00	12.00	7	1
	d	HI*	16.868		16.I	57.00	13.00	11	1
P657		H	16.897.	75,84–86	16.H	58.00	13.00	60	4
P658	a	H	16.897.	70–71	16.H	58.00	13.00	35	3
	a	H	16.897.	76–78,80	16.H	58.00	13.00	30	5
	a	H	16.897.	118,119	16.H	58.00	13.00	8	3
	a	H	16.897		16.H	58.00	13.00	7	2
	b	H	16.897.	79,116	16.H	59.00	13.00	—	2
	c	H	16.897.	120	16.H	59.00	13.00	—	2
P659		HI*J	16.866		16.I(J)	59.00	12.00	600	20
		HI*J	16.865		16.J	58.00	12.00	10	1
		HI*J	16.868		16.I	59.00	12.00	15	2
		HI*J	16.872		16.H	57.00	13.00	23	2
		HI*J	16.876		16.H	58.00	12.00	28	1
		HI*J	16.875.	1	16.I	59.00	12.00	5	1
P660		HI	16.868		16.I	57.00	13.00	3	1
		HI	16.872		16.H	57.00	13.00	9	2
P661	a	HKLM	16.894		16.H	59.00	13.00	17	1
	a	HKLM	16.807		16.M	58.00	13.00	12	1
	b	HKLM	16.824		16.K	59.00	12.00	7	1
	b	HKLM	16.820		16.L	57.00	13.00	6	1
P662	a	HI	16.891.	15	16.H	59.00	12.00	22	1
	b	HI	16.878		16.HI	59.00	13.00	11	2
P663		H	16.891.	11,13	16.H	59.00	12.00	49	3
P664	a	HI	16.875.	1	16.I	59.00	12.00	11	1
	b	HI	16.876		16.H	58.00	12.00	4	1
P665		H	16.897.	111,114	16.H	58.00	13.00	33	2
P666		H	16.872		16.H	57.00	13.00	19	1
P667	a	HJ	16.872		16.H	57.00	13.00	46	3
	b	HJ	16.834		16.J	55.00	13.00	12	1
	c	HJ	16.872		16.H	57.00	13.00	28	2
	d	HJ	16.872		16.H	57.00	13.00	6	1
P668	a	H	16.887		16.H	59.00	12.00	13	3
	b	H	16.887		16.H	59.00	12.00	9	1
P669	a	HIJ	16.872		16.H	57.00	12.00	91	5
	b	HIJ	16.878		16.HI	59.00	13.00	44	3
	c	HIJ	16.887		16.H	59.00	12.00	8	1
	d	HIJ	16.834		16.J	54.00	13.00	20	1
P670	a	H	16.897.	49,51	16.H	58.00	13.00	88	2
	a	H	16.897.	53,55,57	16.H	58.00	13.00	115	4

Table 17: Late Bronze Age pottery: vessel numbers, contexts and constituent sherd data.

Vessel No.	Sub	Vessel phase	Context	Sub-context	Unit	Grid East	Grid North	Weight (g)	No. of sherds
	a	H	16.897		16.H	58.00	13.00	4	1
	b	H	16.891.	6–9	16.H	59.00	12.00	116	4
P671	a	HIJ	16.879.	4,9–10	16.I	58.00	13.00	90	3
	a	HIJ	16.879.	12	16.I	58.00	13.00	—	1
	a	HIJ	16.872		16.H	58.00	13.00	125	5
	b	HIJ	16.879.	6–7,11	16.I	58.00	13.00	48	3
	b	HIJ	16.870		16.J	58.00	13.00	13	1
	c	HIJ	16.872		16.H	58.00	13.00	56	4
	c	HIJ	16.897		16.H	58.00	13.00	2	1
	c	HIJ	16.897.	41,44	16.H	58.00	13.00	92	3
	c	HIJ	16.897.	45,65–67	16.H	59.00	13.00	54	4
	c	HIJ	16.897.	71,82–83	16.H	58.00	13.00	37	3
	d	HIJ	16.897.	139	16.H	59.00	13.00	10	1
P672	a	H	16.889.	1–7,9–14	16.H	59.00	12.00	375	13
	a	H	16.890		16.H	59.00	12.00	—	2
	b	H	16.887		16.H	59.00	12.00	4	1
	c	H	16.890		16.H	59.00	12.00	—	1
P673	a	HI	16.888.	5,6	16.H	59.00	12.00	162	2
	b	HI	16.878		16.HI	59.00	13.00	45	2
P674	a	HIJ*K	16.851		16.J	55.00	13.00	200	3
	a	HIJ*K	16.853.	1–3	16.J	56.00	13.00	180	3
	a	HIJ*K	16.860.	9	16.J	55.00	13.00	60	1
	a	HIJ*K	16.868		16.I	57.00	13.00	65	2
	b	HIJ*K	16.852.	13–18	16.J	56.00	13.00	131	6
	b	HIJ*K	16.852.	20–21	16.J	56.00	13.00	25	3
	b	HIJ*K	16.854.	14–18	16.J	56.00	13.00	100	6
	b	HIJ*K	16.836		16.J	56.00	13.00	5	1
	c	HIJ*K	16.836		16.J	56.00	12.00	196	2
	c	HIJ*K	16.849		16.J	56.00	13.00	28	1
	c	HIJ*K	16.835.	85	16.J	56.00	12.00	92	1
	d	HIJ*K	16.872		16.H	57.00	13.00	40	1
	d	HIJ*K	16.865		16.J	58.00	13.00	48	2
	d	HIJ*K	16.856.	6–7	16.J	56.00	13.00	52	2
	d	HIJ*K	16.856.	10,12	16.J	56.00	13.00	54	2
	d	HIJ*K	16.849		16.J	54.00	13.00	46	1
	d	HIJ*K	16.829		16.K	57.00	13.00	57	1
	e	HIJ*K	16.857.	1	16.J	56.00	13.00	20	1
	f	HIJ*K	16.862.	29	16.J	57.00	13.00	24	2
	g	HIJ*K	16.853.	4	16.J	56.00	13.00	54	2
	h	HIJ*K	16.834		16.J	55.00	13.00	34	1
	i	HIJ*K	16.834		16.J	57.00	12.00	15	1
	i	HIJ*K	16.836		16.J	56.00	12.00	13	2
P854		HJ*	16.872		16.H	54.00	12.00	798	1
		HJ*	16.867.	1–5,7,14	16.J	53.00	12.00	—	9
		HJ*	16.867.	16–20,22	16.J	53.00	12.00	—	6
		HJ*	16.848.	21	16.J	54.00	12.00	—	1
P675	a	H	16.897.	72–74	16.H	58.00	13.00	86	3
	a	H	16.897.	104,121	16.H	58.00	13.00	84	3
	a	H	16.897.	141,175	16.H	58.00	13.00	41	2
	b	H	16.897.	108,133	16.H	58.00	13.00	24	2
	c	H	16.890		16.H	59.00	12.00	27	1
P676		HI	16.868		16.I	57.00	12.00	39	1
		HI	16.878		16.HI	59.00	13.00	20	1
P677		H	16.872		16.H	57.00	13.00	105	2
P678	a	HI	16.873		16.I	58.00	12.00	50	4
	b	HI	16.872		16.H	57.00	12.00	30	4

Table 17: Late Bronze Age pottery: vessel numbers, contexts and constituent sherd data.

Vessel No.	Sub	Vessel phase	Context	Sub-context	Unit	Grid East	Grid North	Weight (g)	No. of sherds
P679	a	HI*J	16.872		16.H	57.00	13.00	11	1
	a	HI*J	16.869		16.J	58.00	13.00	10	1
	a	HI*J	16.868		16.I	57.00	13.00	15	1
	b	HI*J	16.868		16.I	58.00	12.00	42	1
	b	HI*J	16.868		16.I	57.00	13.00	7	1
	c	HI*J	16.865		16.J	58.00	13.00	16	1
	c	HI*J	16.868		16.I	58.00	12.00	12	1
	d	HI*J	16.868		16.I	58.00	12.00	15	1
	e	HI*J	16.868		16.I	59.00	12.00	44	1
	f	HI*J	16.865		16.J	58.00	12.00	7	1
P680	a	H	16.897.	61–62	16.H	59.00	13.00	24	2
	a	H	16.897.	90–94	16.H	59.00	13.00	99	8
	a	H	16.897.	105,134	16.H	59.00	13.00	20	3
	b	H	16.897.	60,87,89	16.H	59.00	13.00	59	4
	b	H	16.897.	93,100	16.H	59.00	13.00	10	2
P681		H	16.898		16.H	59.00	13.00	14	2
P682		H	16.887		16.H	59.00	12.00	2	1
P683		H	16.876		16.H	59.00	12.00	23	1
P684		HI	16.878		16.HI	59.00	13.00	41	2
P685		HI	16.871		16.I	59.00	12.00	47	1
		HI	16.878		16.HI	59.00	13.00	18	1
P686		HJ*	16.872		16.H	56.00	13.00	45	1
		HJ*	16.860.	10–12	16.J	55.00	13.00	61	4
		HJ*	16.857.	3–4	16.J	56.00	13.00	90	2
P687	a	HJ*	16.865		16.J	55.00	12.00	15	1
	a	HJ*	16.849		16.J	54.00	12.00	28	1
	a	HJ*	16.836w		16.J	55.00	12.00	20	1
	a	HJ*	16.834		16.J	54.00	12.00	9	1
	b	HJ*	16.834		16.J	55.00	12.00	25	2
	c	HJ*	16.836w		16.J	54.00	12.00	16	1
	c	HJ*	16.872		16.H	54.00	13.00	15	1
P688		I	16.868		16.I	57.00	13.00	1	1
P689		I	16.868		16.I	57.00	13.00	1	1
P690	a	IJ	16.868		16.I	57.00	13.00	39	3
	b	IJ	16.868		16.I	56.00	12.00	5	1
	c	IJ	16.849		16.J	56.00	13.00	15	1
P691	a	IJ	16.848.	25	16.J	53.00	12.00	24	1
	a	IJ	16.868		16.I	56.00	12.00	12	1
	b	IJ	16.834		16.J	55.00	12.00	26	1
P692		I	16.868		16.I	59.00	12.00	48	1
P693	a	IJ*	16.836e		16.J	57.00	12.00	88	3
	b	IJ*	16.836e		16.J	58.00	13.00	12	1
	c	IJ*	16.835.	65,67	16.J	57.00	12.00	111	2
	d	IJ*	16.865		16.J	57.00	12.00	16	1
	d	IJ*	16.868		16.I	57.00	12.00	16	1
P694	a	I	16.881.	1–3	16.I	57.00	13.00	222	3
	b	I	16.881.	4	16.I	57.00	13.00	119	1
P695		I	16.868		16.I	57.00	12.00	62	1
P696		I	16.868		16.I	58.00	12.00	18	1
P697		I	16.871		16.I	59.00	12.00	21	1
P698		I	16.868		16.I	58.00	13.00	25	2
P699	a	I	16.868		16.I	57.00	13.00	23	3
	b	I	16.868		16.I	57.00	13.00	5	1
P700	a	J	16.836		16.J	58.00	13.00	3	1
	a	J	16.836		16.J	59.00	12.00	15	1
	a	J	16.836		16.J	58.00	12.00	63	4

Table 17: Late Bronze Age pottery: vessel numbers, contexts and constituent sherd data.

Vessel No.	Sub	Vessel phase	Context	Sub-context	Unit	Grid East	Grid North	Weight (g)	No. of sherds
	a	J	16.863.	12,20–22	16.J	58.00	12.00	80	4
	b	J	16.836		16.J	58.00	12.00	3	1
P701	a	JK	16.836w		16.J	56.00	13.00	71	2
	a	JK	16.829		16.K	56.00	13.00	48	1
	b	JK	16.849		16.J	53.00	12.00	24	1
P702		J	16.846.	3,7–10	16.J	58.00	12.00	118	5
		J	16.846.	13–15	16.J	58.00	12.00	114	3
P703		JK	16.829		16.K	56.00	13.00	14	1
		JK	16.836		16.J	59.00	12.00	74	2
P704		J	16.860.	5	16.J	55.00	13.00	63	2
P705	a	JK	16.822		16.K	58.00	12.00	5	1
	b	JK	16.836		16.J	58.00	12.00	4	1
	c	JK	16.865		16.J	56.00	12.00	5	1
P706		J	16.849		16.J	53.00	12.00	3	1
P707	a	JK	16.854.	32–34,38	16.J	56.00	13.00	12	5
	a	JK	16.824		16.K	58.00	13.00	6	1
	b	JK	16.854.	30	16.J	56.00	13.00	22	3
P708		J	16.849		16.J	57.00	13.00	58	2
		J	16.865		16.J	57.00	13.00	31	1
P709	a	J	16.862.	6–7	16.J	57.00	13.00	15	2
	a	J	16.865		16.J	58.00	13.00	7	1
	b	J	16.834		16.J	55.00	13.00	8	1
P710	a	J	16.836		16.J	59.00	12.00	120	7
	b	J	16.836		16.J	59.00	12.00	148	9
P711		J	16.836		16.J	57.00	12.00	39	3
P712	a	JK*	16.824		16.K	57.00	12.00	9	1
	b	JK*	16.824		16.K	56.00	13.00	5	1
	c	JK*	16.836		16.J	57.00	12.00	3	1
	d	JK*	16.822		16.K	55.00	12.00	3	1
P713		J	16.865		16.J	59.00	12.00	17	1
P714	a	JK*	16.824		16.K	57.00	12.00	13	1
	b	JK*	16.824		16.K	55.00	13.00	4	1
	c	JK*	16.836w		16.J	56.00	12.00	2	1
P715		J	16.865		16.J	57.00	12.00	18	1
P716	a	J	16.869		16.J	59.00	13.00	10	1
	a	J	16.836		16.J	59.00	12.00	10	1
	b	J	16.834		16.J	58.00	13.00	6	1
P717		J	16.834		16.J	53.00	12.00	6	1
P718		JK	16.836		16.J	55.00	12.00	17	1
		JK	16.829		16.K	57.00	13.00	38	2
P719		JK	16.865		16.J	58.00	13.00	6	1
		JK	16.829		16.K	56.00	12.00	24	1
P720	a	J	16.852.	5–6	16.J	56.00	13.00	22	2
	a	J	16.845		16.J	57.00	13.00	37	1
	b	J	16.865		16.J	57.00	12.00	—	1
P721		J	16.864.	1–3	16.J	58.00	12.00	178	10
P722	a	J	16.836		16.J	58.00	12.00	53	1
	b	J	16.865		16.J	59.00	12.00	10	1
P723		JL	16.820		16.L	55.00	12.00	8	1
		JL	16.862.	1	16.J	57.00	13.00	20	1
P724	a	J	16.854.	8,27	16.J	56.00	13.00	49	3
	a	J	16.854.	31,35	16.J	56.00	13.00	24	2
	a	J	16.854.	37,41	16.J	56.00	13.00	51	2
	b	J	16.855.	2,4	16.J	56.00	13.00	69	2
P725	a	JK	16.860.	4	16.J	55.00	13.00	32	1
	a	JK	16.856.	5,16	16.J	56.00	13.00	39	2

Table 17: Late Bronze Age pottery: vessel numbers, contexts and constituent sherd data.

Vessel No.	Sub	Vessel phase	Context	Sub-context	Unit	Grid East	Grid North	Weight (g)	No. of sherds
	a	JK	16.852.	2–4	16.J	56.00	13.00	95	4
	a	JK	16.834		16.J	55.00	13.00	4	1
	a	JK	16.829		16.K	57.00	13.00	78	5
	b	JK	16.857.	6,8,9	16.J	56.00	13.00	41	4
	b	JK	16.856.	2,15	16.J	56.00	13.00	83	3
	b	JK	16.852.	10–11	16.J	56.00	13.00	65	3
	b	JK	16.829		16.K	57.00	13.00	112	6
P726	a	JK	16.862.	9,13–14	16.J	57.00	13.00	136	3
	a	JK	16.862.	17–19	16.J	57.00	13.00	52	3
	a	JK	16.862.	32,38	16.J	57.00	13.00	36	3
	a	JK	16.862		16.J	57.00	13.00	5	1
	a	JK	16.860.	3,6	16.J	55.00	13.00	85	2
	a	JK	16.836w		16.J	55.00	13.00	26	1
	a	JK	16.829		16.K	56.00	13.00	61	1
	a	JK	16.829		16.K	55.00	13.00	7	2
	b	JK	16.862.	2–3,34	16.J	57.00	13.00	47	3
	b	JK	16.829		16.K	57.00	13.00	72	1
P727	a	J	16.835.	8,11–22	16.J	56.00	12.00	1019	35
	a	J	16.835.	24–29	16.J	57.00	12.00	—	—
	a	J	16.835.	33–35	16.J	56.00	12.00	—	—
	a	J	16.835.	37–40	16.J	56.00	12.00	—	—
	a	J	16.835.	42,44	16.J	56.00	12.00	—	—
	a	J	16.835.	46,49	16.J	57.00	12.00	—	—
	a	J	16.835.	52,59,60	16.J	57.00	12.00	—	—
	a	J	16.836		16.J	56.00	12.00	22	2
	b	J	16.835.	5,9–10	16.J	57.00	12.00	182	3
	c	J	16.835.	54,55	16.J	57.00	12.00	99	2
	c	J	16.865		16.J	57.00	12.00	17	1
	d	J	16.865		16.J	57.00	12.00	44	1
	e	J	16.835.	25,31	16.J	56.00	12.00	—	2
P728	a	JK	16.836e		16.J	59.00	12.00	20	1
	a	JK	16.824		16.K	59.00	12.00	27	1
	b	JK	16.829		16.K	54.00	12.00	7	1
P729		J	16.867.	6,24–26	16.J	53.00	12.00	122	4
P730		J	16.849		16.J	57.00	13.00	45	2
P731		JK	16.863.	1,4,7–10	16.J	58.00	12.00	670	17
		JK	16.863.	13–15	16.J	58.00	12.00	—	—
		JK	16.863.	23–30	16.J	58.00	12.00	—	—
		JK	16.862.	20–23, 30,31	16.J	57.00	13.00	170	6
		JK	16.829		16.K	57.00	13.00	28	1
P732		J	16.849		16.J	56.00	13.00	82	1
P733		J	16.836		16.J	56.00	13.00	7	1
P734		JKL	16.822		16.K	59.00	12.00	5	1
		JKL	16.820		16.L	58.00	12.00	3	1
		JKL	16.836e		16.J	58.00	12.00	4	1
P735		J	16.834		16.J	55.00	13.00	8	1
P736		J	16.865		16.J	59.00	13.00	10	1
P737		J	16.865		16.J	57.00	12.00	3	1
P738		J	16.834		16.J	55.00	12.00	8	1
P739		J	16.868		16.I	58.00	12.00	48	1
P740		J	16.865		16.J	58.00	12.00	3	1
P741		J	16.834w		16.J	56.00	12.00	39	1
P742	a	JK	16.834		16.J	55.00	12.00	9	1
	b	JK	16.829		16.K	57.00	13.00	8	1
P743		J	16.865		16.J	58.00	13.00	8	1
P744		J	16.834		16.J	54.00	13.00	12	1

Table 17: Late Bronze Age pottery: vessel numbers, contexts and constituent sherd data.

Vessel No.	Sub	Vessel phase	Context	Sub-context	Unit	Grid East	Grid North	Weight (g)	No. of sherds
P745		J	16.865		16.J	58.00	13.00	32	1
P746		J	16.865		16.J	55.00	12.00	61	2
P747		J	16.845		16.J	57.00	13.00	173	1
P748	a	J	16.865		16.J	57.00	12.00	55	1
	b	J	16.865		16.J	58.00	12.00	45	1
	c	J	16.836e		16.J	57.00	13.00	13	1
P749	a	JK	16.834		16.J	54.00	12.00	31	1
	b	JK	16.824		16.K	55.00	13.00	70	2
	c	JK	16.829		16.K	55.00	13.00	24	1
P750	a	JK	16.836e		16.J	58.00	12.00	55	2
	b	JK	16.834		16.J	55.00	13.00	26	1
	c	JK	16.829		16.K	53.00	12.00	26	1
P751		K	16.822		16.K	56.00	12.00	3	1
P752		K	16.822		16.K	56.00	13.00	2	1
P753		K	16.829		16.K	55.00	13.00	19	1
P754		K	16.829		16.K	56.00	13.00	50	9
P755	a	K	16.824		16.K	59.00	12.00	55	4
	b	K	16.824		16.K	58.00	13.00	11	1
P756		K	16.822		16.K	55.00	13.00	14	1
P757	a	KL	16.822		16.K	54.00	13.00	6	1
	a	KL	16.819		16.L	53.00	13.00	2	1
	b	KL	16.819		16.L	57.00	12.00	2	1
P758		K	16.829		16.K	58.00	12.00	120	3
P759		K	16.824		16.K	54.00	12.00	5	1
P760		K	16.829		16.K	58.00	12.00	5	1
P761		K	16.822		16.K	55.00	13.00	2	1
P762		K	16.824		16.K	57.00	12.00	2	1
P763		K	16.824		16.K	57.00	13.00	5	1
P764		K	16.822		16.K	57.00	13.00	17	1
P765		K	16.829		16.K	55.00	13.00	12	1
P766		K	16.822		16.K	59.00	12.00	22	1
P767		K	16.829		16.K	57.00	13.00	35	1
		K	16.824		16.K	57.00	13.00	27	1
P768	a	KL	16.820		16.L	55.00	13.00	36	1
	b	KL	16.822		16.K	55.00	13.00	26	1
	c	KL	16.822		16.K	56.00	12.00	9	1
P769		K	16.824		16.K	59.00	12.00	39	1
P770		K	16.824		16.K	55.00	12.00	15	1
P771	a	KL	16.824		16.K	—	—	57	1
	a	KL	16.824		16.K	58.00	13.00	8	1
	b	KL	16.824		16.K	57.00	13.00	40	1
	c	KL	16.822		16.K	59.00	13.00	78	1
	d	KL	16.820		16.L	56.00	12.00	7	1
P772	a	K	16.824		16.K	57.00	13.00	19	1
	b	K	16.822		16.K	55.00	12.00	21	1
P773		K	16.822		16.K	57.00	13.00	34	1
P774		K	16.824		16.K	59.00	12.00	31	1
P775	a	KL	16.820		16.L	54.00	12.00	20	1
	b	KL	16.819		16.L	58.00	12.00	12	1
	c	KL	16.824		16.K	56.00	12.00	14	1
P776		K	16.829		16.K	59.00	12.00	20	1
P777		K	16.824		16.K	57.00	13.00	65	1
P778		K	16.824		16.K	56.00	13.00	76	1
P779		K	16.822		16.K	53.00	12.00	9	1
P780		K	16.824		16.K	58.00	13.00	4	1
P781		K	16.822		16.K	58.00	13.00	33	1

Table 17: Late Bronze Age pottery: vessel numbers, contexts and constituent sherd data.

Vessel No.	Sub	Vessel phase	Context	Sub-context	Unit	Grid East	Grid North	Weight (g)	No. of sherds
P782		K	16.824		16.K	59.00	13.00	5	1
P783		K	16.824		16.K	57.00	12.00	2	1
P784		K	16.824		16.K	59.00	12.00	3	1
P785		K	16.824		16.K	56.00	13.00	5	1
P786		K	16.824		16.K	55.00	12.00	5	1
P787		K	16.829		16.K	55.00	13.00	7	1
P788		K	16.822		16.K	57.00	13.00	9	1
P789		K	16.824		16.K	57.00	13.00	11	1
P790		K	16.829		16.K	56.00	13.00	19	2
P791		K	16.822		16.K	59.00	12.00	7	1
P792		K	16.824		16.K	59.00	12.00	12	1
P793		K	16.822		16.K	55.00	13.00	5	1
P794		K	16.822		16.K	55.00	13.00	2	1
P795		K	16.824		16.K	55.00	13.00	17	1
P796	a	KL	16.820		16.L	58.00	12.00	7	1
	b	KL	16.822		16.K	58.00	13.00	14	1
P797	a	KL	16.824		16.K	58.00	13.00	3	1
	b	KL	16.819		16.L	55.00	12.00	5	1
	c	KL	16.820		16.L	56.00	12.00	3	1
P798		K	16.822		16.K	56.00	12.00	5	1
P799		K	16.822		16.K	59.00	12.00	28	1
P800		K	16.829		16.K	59.00	12.00	50	1
P801		K	16.822		16.K	58.00	13.00	38	1
P802		K	16.824		16.K	54.00	12.00	43	1
P803	a	K	16.822		16.K	59.00	12.00	6	1
	b	K	16.822		16.K	58.00	13.00	6	1
P804	a	KL	16.822		16.K	56.00	13.00	10	1
	b	KL	16.820		16.L	58.00	13.00	6	1
P805		K	16.822		16.K	56.00	12.00	8	1
P806		K	16.824		16.K	57.00	12.00	8	1
		K	16.824		16.K	58.00	12.00	9	1
P807	a	K	16.824		16.K	58.00	13.00	11	1
	b	K	16.829		16.K	58.00	13.00	17	1
P808		K	16.822		16.K	55.00	12.00	24	1
P809		K	16.824		16.K	59.00	13.00	50	2
P810		K	16.824		16.K	59.00	12.00	71	1
P811		LM	16.820		16.L	59.00	13.00	21	2
		LM	16.807		16.M	59.00	13.00	10	1
P812		L	16.820		16.L	59.00	13.00	10	1
P813		L	16.819		16.L	55.00	12.00	3	1
P814		L	16.820		16.L	58.00	13.00	4	1
P815		L	16.820		16.L	53.00	12.00	3	1
P816		L	16.819		16.L	56.00	13.00	2	1
P817		L	16.819		16.L	57.00	13.00	3	1
P818		L	16.819		16.L	56.00	13.00	9	1
P819		L	16.820		16.L	53.00	12.00	6	1
P820		L	16.819		16.L	53.00	13.00	8	1
P821	a	L	16.820		16.L	57.00	13.00	11	1
	b	L	16.820		16.L	58.00	12.00	5	1
P822		L	16.820		16.L	58.00	12.00	3	1
P823		L	16.820		16.L	58.00	12.00	9	1
P824		L	16.820		16.L	59.00	13.00	1	1
P825		L	16.819		16.L	55.00	13.00	4	1
P826		L	16.819		16.L	54.00	13.00	4	1
P827		L	16.819		16.L	55.00	13.00	3	1
P828		L	16.820		16.L	56.00	12.00	21	1

Table 17: **Late Bronze Age pottery: vessel numbers, contexts and constituent sherd data.**

Vessel No.	Sub	Vessel phase	Context	Sub-context	Unit	Grid East	Grid North	Weight (g)	No. of sherds
P829		L	16.820		16.L	56.00	12.00	9	1
P830		L	16.819		16.L	54.00	13.00	19	1
P831		L	16.819		16.L	55.00	12.00	10	1
P832		L	16.819		16.L	58.00	13.00	4	1
P833		L	16.819		16.L	53.00	12.00	3	1
P834		L	16.820		16.L	58.00	13.00	5	1
P835		L	16.820		16.L	58.00	13.00	4	1
P836		L	16.820		16.L	57.00	12.00	24	1
P837		L	16.820		16.L	55.00	13.00	10	1
P838		L	16.820		16.L	58.00	13.00	8	1
P839		L	16.819		16.L	59.00	12.00	32	1
P840		L	16.819		16.L	54.00	12.00	12	1
P841		L	16.819		16.L	57.00	12.00	17	1
P842		L	16.819		16.L	56.00	12.00	6	1
P843		L	16.820		16.L	58.00	12.00	19	1
P844		L	16.819		16.L	54.00	12.00	38	1
P845		M	16.814		16.M	55.00	12.00	4	1
P846		M	16.814		16.M	54.00	12.00	1	1
P847		M	16.814		16.M	56.00	13.00	1	1
P848		M	16.814		16.M	57.00	12.00	8	1
P849		M	16.814		16.M	57.00	13.00	2	1
P850		M	16.813		16.M	57.00	13.00	16	1
P851		M	16.814		16.M	58.00	13.00	4	1
P852		M	16.814		16.M	58.00	12.00	10	1
P853		M	16.814		16.M	54.00	13.00	15	1

P854 see after P674

Table 18: Late Bronze Age pottery: fabric, representation and decoration details
(for abbreviations and code definitions see Table 16)

Vessel No.	Portion(s) represented	Fabric & finish	Exterior colour	Interior colour	Core colour	Decoration	Sim*
P650	R16%	03/12/21/23/34	l.br/gr.br	d.gr/l.br	d.gr	-	Y
P651	R95% B100%	02/09/12/21/30/37	l.br/d.gr/rd	l.br/gr	l.gr	-	Y
P652	R75% S&B100%	03/12/21/30E	bk/br	l.br/gr	l.gr/pk	-	Y
P653	R C	02/11/21/31IE	d.gr	d.gr	gr.br	-	Y
P654	R35% C	03/07/11/21/26/31IE	d.gr	d,gr	d.gr	-	Y
P655	R	02/11/21/25/32IE	gr.br	d.gr.br	gr	-	Y
P656	R S	03/12/21/25/30IE	l.br/gr	gr.br/or	d.gr/or.br	-	N
P657	R15% C	01/07/13/21/(23)/26/30E	br/or	d.gr/or	gr.br/d.gr	-	Y
P658	R15% C	01/07/13/21/23/26/32E	l.br/d.gr.br	gr	gr.br	-	Y
P659	R&S60% B75%	02/09/14/21/32E	br/gr	d.gr/bk	gr	-	Y
P660	R12%	03/12/21/?26/31	d.gr.br	d.gr.br	l.gr/or.br	-	Y
P661	R16%	01/12/(?23)/26/33	bf/gr	bf	gr	-	N
P662	R S	03/12/21/?25/30I/31E	d.gr	d.gr.br	gr.br	-	Y
P663	R S	02/11/21/(23)/26/30IE	br/bf	gr.br	gr/l.or	-	Y
P664	R (S)	03/12/21/(23)/25/34	d.gr	bf	gr/l.br	-	Y
P665	R14%	03/10/12/21/(23)/25/37	l.gr/or/d.gr	d.gr/l.gr	d.gr/l.gr	-	Y
P666	R C	02/11/21/26/31IE	l.br	l.br	gr	-	Y
P667	R19% S	03/14/21/23/34	l.gr/d.gr/rd.br	d.gr/gr	gr/l.gr	-	N
P668	R11% C	02/13/21/25/31E	br	d.gr	gr.br	-	Y
P669	R12% S	03/14/21/(23)/26/30/37	d.gr.br/br	br	gr	-	N
P670	R21% C	03/14/21/25/(28)/(29)/37	l.br/d.gr.br	d.gr	d.gr	-	Y
P671	R34% S	04/15/21/(23)/25/(28)/37	d.gr.br	gr.br/l.br	gr/br	-	Y
P672	R2% S17% B12%	03/14/21/29/35/37	gr/l.br	gr/bf	gr	a/B/03	Y
P673	R19% S	03/07/12/21/25/37	gr.br/l.gr	d.gr	gr.br	a/E/11	Y
P674	R S43% B42%	02/09/14/21/23/(24)/26/36/37	d.br/bf/l.or	l.or.br/gr.br	l.gr	-	N
P854	R55% S55%	03/14/21/23/35/36	rd.br/d.gr	gr.br/l.br	gr	-	N
P675	R S B	03/07/13/21/26/37	br/d.gr.br	d.gr.br	d.gr	-	Y
P676	R	04/14/21/25/37	or.br/gr.br	bf/gr.br	l.gr/or.br	a/B/02	Y
P677	R10.5%	04/14/21/34	l.br/l.gr/or	l.gr	l.gr	-	Y
P678	R24% S	04/14/21/26/37	d.gr.br/br	l.br/gr.br	br	-	Y
P679	R35%	03/13/21/25/37	bf/l.or.br	bf	gr/bf	-	Y
P680	R34% C	04/12/21/(23)/26/36	d.br	or.br	gr.br/l.br	-	Y
P681	R10%	02/12/21/33	gr.br	gr/l.br	gr	-	Y
P682	R	03/12/21/34	l.br	l.br	gr	h/E/14	Y
P683	N9%	03/07/14/21/26/33	l.br	or	l.gr	c/D/25	Y
P684	H	04/07/14/21/25/30	d.gr.br/l.br	-	gr.br	-	Y
P685	B58%	04/12/21/25/31E	d.gr.br/br	br/gr.br	gr	-	N
P686	B33%	02/08/09/12/21/23/27/36/37	bf	bf/gr.br	d.gr/l.gr	-	Y
P687	B78%	03/07/08/12/21/(23)/25/36	d.gr/gr.br	gr.br	gr	-	N
P688	R8.5%	03/11/21/30E	d.br	gr.br	l.gr.br	-	Y
P689	R7.5%	03/11/21/26/31IE	gr.br	d.gr.br	l.br	-	Y
P690	R17% C	03/15/21/25/37	l.or.br/gr/bf	d.gr/l.or.br	gr/l.or.br	-	Y
P691	C17% B	03/08/14/21/26/37	gr.br/bf	d.gr	d.gr	-	N
P692	R7% S10%	01/11/23/26/31IE	d.gr/l.br	gr	gr	-	Y
P693	R16% S	03/07/12/21/25/35	d.gr.br/br	d.gr.br/gr/bf	l.gr	-	N
P694	R S	03/07/14/21/(23)/25/36/37	br/gr.br	gr/l.br	gr/br	a/B/16	N
P695	?S	03/07/14/21/26/37	gr.br	gr.br/br	gr	?e/B/57	Y
P696	H	03/12/21/25/33	br/gr.br	-	gr.br	-	Y
P697	H	03/12/21/26/34	d.gr	-	d.gr	-	Y
P698	B25%	04/11/21/31IE	d.gr	d.gr	gr.br	-	Y
P699	B75%	02/07/11/21/30IE	gr.br	gr.br	br	-	Y
P700	R25% C B40%	00/26/32IE	gr.br/l.br	gr	gr/bf	-	Y
P701	R C27% B	03/09/12/21/25/35	gr.br/bf	gr.br	d.gr	-	Y
P702	R55% C	02/07/13/21/25/30IE	d.gr.br/br	d.gr	d.gr	-	Y
P703	R35% S	01/12/21/23/26/34	br/gr	br/l.br	gr	-	N

Table 18: Late Bronze Age pottery: fabric, representation and decoration details

Vessel No.	Portion(s) represented	Fabric & finish	Exterior colour	Interior colour	Core colour	Decoration	Sim*
P704	R C(12%)	03/12/21/(23)/26/32IE	d.gr.br	d.gr	gr/pk	-	Y
P705	R C	03/07/12/21/25/30E	d.gr	br	br	-	Y
P706	R	01/12/21/?25/31IE	d.gr	d.gr	gr	-	Y
P707	R8% C	03/12/21/31IE	d.gr/l.br	d.gr	gr	-	Y
P708	R C13%	04/12/21/30IE	gr.br	d.gr	gr	-	Y
P709	R18% C	03/12/21/25/31IE	d.br	br	gr.br	-	N
P710	S20% B60%	04/12/21/(23)/31IE	d.gr/br	br/gr	gr	-	Y
P711	R17%	02/12/21/23/26/34	gr.br	d.gr.br	d.rd.gr	-	Y
P712	R S	02/11/21/(23)/26/31IE	br	gr.br	gr.br	-	Y
P713	R23%	02/12/21/25/30E	l.gr.br	l.gr.br	l.gr	-	Y
P714	R13%	02/12/21/34	bf	l.gr/bf	l.gr	a/B/09	Y
P715	R7%	02/12/21/(25)/34	bf/l.gr	l.gr/bf	gr	-	Y
P716	R18%	01/11/21/23/26/32IE	gr.br/l.gr/or	d.gr	gr	-	Y
P717	R10%	02/12/21/34	gr.br	gr.br	gr	c/E/70	Y
P718	R17%	04/14/21/25/37	gr.br	l.br	l.br	-	Y
P719	R16%	03/14/21/25/37	d.gr.br	d.gr.br	gr	-	Y
P720	R15% S	03/14/21/25/36/37	gr.br	gr.br	d.gr/gr.br	-	N
P721	R9% S B	03/07/14/21/(23)/36/37	br/d.gr.br	gr.br/br	gr	-	Y
P722	R14% C	02/12/21/26/37	gr.br	gr.br	gr	e/A/37	Y
P723	R18% S	03/12/21/(23)/25/34	bf/gr.br	bf/br	gr	-	N
P724	R23% S	04/14/21/23/26/37	d.gr/br/rd.br	rd.br	l.gr/rd.br	-	Y
P725	R20% S S19%	03/07/13/21/25/35/37	d.br	d.br/rd.br	d.gr	a/D/08	N
P726	R38% C	04/14/21/(23)/26/36/37	br/gr.br	br/gr.br	gr.br	-	N
P727	R17% S B60%	03/08/14/21/25/36	d.gr/gr.br/bf	l.br/gr.br	l.gr.br	-	Y
P728	R9% S	01/07/13/21/23/25/37	or.br	gr.br/l.br	l.gr/or	-	Y
P729	R14% S	03/14/21/25/36	l.gr/gr	gr/br	gr	a/B/16	Y
P730	R10%	03/14/21/25/35	d.gr.br	d.gr.br/br	gr	-	Y
P731	R33% S B	04/15/21/(23)/36	d.gr/br	d.gr/l.br	d.gr	h/F/14	Y
P732	R	01/12/21/26/33	or.br	l.gr	l.gr	-	Y
P733	R (?S)	02/07/11/21/26/30IE	d.gr.br	d.gr	br	-	Y
P734	R	03/12/21/25/34	gr.br	gr.br	gr.br	a/B/09	Y
P735	R	03/07/12/21/34	br/gr.br	br	gr.br	a/D/08	Y
P736	R	03/07/12/21/26?/33	br	br	gr.br	-	Y
P737	R S	01/11/21/26/33	l.or	l.or	l.or	-	Y
P738	R	02/11/21/26/-	or.br	or.br	or.br	-	Y
P739	R	03/12/21/34	or.br	or.br	gr	?a/?B/?03	Y
P740	W	00/25/31IE	d.gr	d.gr	gr	-/G/83;?j/D/86	Y
P741	W	03/07/12/21/26/37	l.br	l.gr/l.br	gr/bf	f/B/58	Y
P742	B38%	01/11/26/29/31I/33E	d.gr	d.gr	d.gr	-	Y
P743	B	02/11/21/(?26)/33	gr.br	d.gr	gr.br	-	Y
P744	B20%	03/07/08/12/21/26/33	gr	gr	br	-	Y
P745	B10%	04/07/12/21/25/33	d.gr.br	gr.br	d.gr.br	-	Y
P746	B70%	02/07/12/21/26/37	gr.br	gr.br	gr	-	Y
P747	B40%	03/08/14/21/26/34	l.br	gr	gr	-	Y
P748	B	03/07/08/14/21/25/36	br	l.br	gr	-	Y
P749	B33%	02/08/?10/14/21/26/34	gr.br/or.br	gr	gr	-	Y
P750	B34%	03/07/08/10/12/21/26/37	l.br/gr.br	d.gr/gr.br	l.gr	-	N
P751	R8%	02/11/21/26/31IE	d.gr.br	br/d.gr	gr.br	-	Y
P752	R11% C	00/26/33	l.gr.br	gr	gr	-	Y
P753	R C	02/07/12/21/26/34	d.gr	d.gr.br/br	gr	-	Y
P754	R C17%	03/12/21/25/31E	br/d.gr	gr.br	gr	-	Y
P755	R10% C21%	02/12/21/26/30E/32I	d.gr/bf	d.gr	l.gr/l.or	-	Y
P756	R9% S	03/07/12/21/?25/31E	l.br/gr	gr.br	gr	-	Y
P757	R17%	02/12/21/33	bf/gr	gr	gr	-	Y
P758	C15% B	02/12/21/25/31IE	gr.br/bf	d.gr.br	gr	-	Y
P759	R7%	02/07/11/21/26/33	d.gr/l.br	or.br	l.gr.br	c/D/62	Y

Table 18: Late Bronze Age pottery: fabric, representation and decoration details

Vessel No.	Portion(s) represented	Fabric & finish	Exterior colour	Interior colour	Core colour	Decoration	Sim*
P760	R	02/11/21/26/31E	gr.br	gr	gr.br	-	Y
P761	R	00/25/31E	l.gr	l.gr	l.gr	-	Y
P762	R	02/11/21/26/31IE	br	br	br	-	Y
P763	R	01/11/27/33	br/bf	bf/gr	l.gr	-	Y
P764	R ?S	02/11/21/25/33	gr.br	gr.br	gr.br	-	Y
P765	R8%	03/07/12/21/37	l.br	l.br	l.gr	c/C/51	Y
P766	R13	02/07/14/21/34	d.gr	d.gr	d.gr	-	Y
P767	R10% S	02/?10/21/25/34	bf.gr	gr	gr	-	Y
P768	R15% S	02/07/12/21/25/37	d.gr/gr.br	gr.br	gr.br	-	Y
P769	R S	03/15/21/25/37	d.gr.br	br/gr.br	gr	-	Y
P770	R7% S	03/12/21/26/37	gr.br	d.gr	gr	-	Y
P771	R12% S B21%	03/12/21/(23)/26/35/36/37	bf/l.gr/or	gr.br/l.gr	gr	a/D/08; e/B/35	Y
P772	R S	02/07/14/21/(23)/27/(29)/33	d.gr.br	d.gr.br	gr	a/BD0108;c/A/21	Y
P773	R S	03/12/21/26/34	gr/bf	gr	gr.br	a/B/02;e/B/41	Y
P774	R	03/12/21/25/36	l.br	l.br	l.gr	a/D/08	Y
P775	R	03/?10/14/21/25/34	gr.bf	gr.bf/or	l.gr/or	a/B/09	N
P776	R (S)	03/14/21/25/36?	gr.br	gr.br	d.gr	-	Y
P777	R	02/12/21/25/30IE	gr/bf	gr/bf	gr	-	Y
P778	R C	01/12/21/(23)/26/32I	or/bf	or/bf	bf	-	Y
P779	R	02/12/21/26/31IE	gr/bf	gr/bf	l.gr.br	-	Y
P780	R	03/12/21/26/31IE	l.br	bf	gr	-	Y
P781	S	03/12/21/(23)/26/37	br	d.gr	gr	e/CE/53	Y
P782	R	02/10/12/20/21/26/34	l.gr	gr	l.gr	-	Y
P783	R	03/12/21/34	gr.br	gr.br	gr.br	-	Y
P784	R	01/11/21/26/31IE	or.br	gr	gr	-	Y
P785	R	02/12/21/23/26/37	gr.br	gr	l.gr.br	-	Y
P786	R	02/14/21/34	or.br	or.br	gr	-	Y
P787	R	02/12/21/26/?33	gr.br	gr.br	gr/bf	-	Y
P788	N	03/14/21/25/37	d.gr.br	d.gr.br	gr/l.br	-	Y
P789	R S	02/12/21/25/34	gr.br	d.gr.br	d.gr.br	-	Y
P790	R	04/14/21/26/37	gr.br	gr	gr	-	Y
P791	R	03/10/12/21/25/33	or	bf	l.gr	a/D/06	Y
P792	R	03/12/21/26/?30E	gr.br	br	gr	a/D/08	Y
P793	R	01/25/34	gr.br	bf/or	bf	a/C/13;a/C/15	Y
P794	R	02/11/21/25?/34	bl	bl	d.gr	a/B/03	Y
P795	R	03/12/21/26/37	gr.br	br/gr.br	gr.br	c/E/66	Y
P796	N	03/14/21/25/37	gr.br	d.gr.br	gr.br	c/C/51	Y
P797	W B	02/07/11/21/23/26/33	bf	bf/gr	l.gr	f/E/85	Y
P798	W	00/26/31IE	gr.br	gr.br	gr.br	-/G/94	Y
P799	N	02/11/21/26/33	bf	bf.gr	d.gr	c/D/24	Y
P800	S	03/14/20/21/26/34	l.br	l.br	l.gr	?ef/20	Y
P801	S15%	00/07/23/24/25/?26/35	or.bf	or.bf	l.gr	e/B/41	Y
P802	S	04/14/21/25/37	d.gr/br	or.br	gr	e/B/32	Y
P803	S	02/12/21/26/33	br	d.gr/gr,br	d.gr	e/B/32	N
P804	S	02/12/21/26/34	d.gr.br	d.gr.br	d.gr.br	e/CE/53	Y
P805	W	02/14/21/26/33?	bf	gr	gr	?def/BC/50	Y
P806	B45%	02/11/21/25?/31IE	d.gr	gr.br	br	-	Y
P807	R B35%	03/11/21/(23)/25/(29)/31IE	d.br	d.gr.br	d.br	-	Y
P808	B	01/07/26/29/31E	gr/br	gr	gr	-	Y
P809	B18%	02/14/21/25/34	rd.br	d.gr	d.gr	-	Y
P810	B10%	03/07/08/14/21/26/34	bf	l.br	l.gr/or.br	-	Y
P811	R15% C	01/11/21/26/31IE	or/gr	l.or	gr	-	Y
P812	R	02/12/21/25/32E	gr.br	gr	gr	-	Y
P813	R	00/25/31IE	bf	bf	d.gr	h/E/70	Y
P814	R	00/26/31IE	l.gr.bf	bf	l.gr.bf	-	Y
P815	R	02/12/25/30IE	d.gr	gr.br	gr.br	-	Y

Table 18: Late Bronze Age pottery: fabric, representation and decoration details

Vessel No.	Portion(s) represented	Fabric & finish	Exterior colour	Interior colour	Core colour	Decoration	Sim*
P816	R	03/12/26/31E	br	br	gr.br	-	Y
P817	R	03/12/26/31E	gr.br	gr.br	gr.br	-	Y
P818	R	02/11/21/(26)/31E	bl	bl	d.gr	-	Y
P819	R	02/12/21/(23)/26/34	gr/l.br	or.br	or.br	a/D/08	Y
P820	R	03/12/26/34	d.gr.br	l.br	gr.br	a/B/09	Y
P821	R	02/12/21/25/33	d.or	gr.br	gr	-	Y
P822	R	03/07/12/21/26/34	l.br	l.br	l.br	a/F/17	Y
P823	R	02/11/21/27/33	br	gr	d.gr	a/B/01	Y
P824	R	02/11/21/26/34	l.br	l.br	gr	a/B/05	Y
P825	R	02/11/21/26/33	l.br	l.br	l.br	h/C/14	Y
P826	R	03/12/20/21/26/34	or	bf	l.gr	-	Y
P827	R	02/?10/11/21/26/34	gr	gr	or	-	Y
P828	R S	04/14/21/26/34	gr.br	d.gr	gr.br	-	Y
P829	R	03/12/21/26/33	l.br	gr.br	gr	-	Y
P830	R	02/12/21/25/30IE	gr.br/bf	bf	bf	-	Y
P831	R	03/14/21/34	gr.br	d.gr	d.gr	-	Y
P832	W	01/11/21/26/31E	bf.gr	bf.gr	d.gr	-/D/86	Y
P833	W	00/26/33	bf	d.gr	d.gr	-/G/82	Y
P834	W	03/14/21/25/34	br	gr.br	gr.br	-/H/95	Y
P835	W	03/12/21/26/37	bf.gr	gr	gr	?cd/F/97	Y
P836	N	01/11/21/25/33	bf	bf.gr	gr	c/A/21	Y
P837	N	03/07/12/21/26/33	bf/l.gr	bf.gr	gr	c/F/96	Y
P838	S	02/07/12/21/25/34	gr.br	d.gr/br	gr.br	d/B/31	Y
P839	S	03/10/12/21/25/33	bf.gr	bf.gr	l.gr/or	e/B/44	Y
P840	S	02/11/21/23/26/34	bf/gr	bf	gr	e/B/32	Y
P841	S	03/12/21/(23)/34	l.gr	gr	l.gr	e/C/53	Y
P842	B	03/08/11/21/31I/33E	l.br	gr	l.gr/or.br	-	Y
P843	B15%	03/07/08/12/21/25/33	d.gr/or.br	br	gr.br/or	-	Y
P844	B8%	01/12/21/26/35	bf	d.gr	d.gr	-	Y
P845	R	00/26/31IE	bf	bf	gr	i/E/70	Y
P846	W	02/11/21/33	br	d.gr	bf	?c/E/61	Y
P847	R	00/26/33	gr	gr	gr	-	Y
P848	R	03/12/21/26/34	gr.br	gr.br/br	gr	a/C/13	Y
P849	R	03/12/21/26/34	d.gr.br	gr.br/bf	l.gr	a/C/15	Y
P850	R	01/11/21/23/26/(29)/31IE	d.gr/br	gr.br	gr.br	-	Y
P851	R	03/11/21/26/34	gr	gr	gr	-	Y
P852	R	02/11/20/21/23/27/33	d.gr	d.gr	gr/or.br	-	Y
P853	H	02/12/21/27/(29)/33	or.br	-	l.gr/l.or	-	Y
P854 see after P674							

* N denotes that some sherds of the vessel in different contexts are *not* in a similar state of abrasion.

Table 19: Late Bronze Age pottery: morphological attributes, angles and dimensions
(for abbreviations and definitions of codes see Table 16)

Vessel No.	B.M. Reg. P1989 10–1	Rim	Neck	Sp	S/C	Base	Th	Hd	MA	UBA	BWA
									Component angles		
P650	201	02	28	-	(55)	-	6.5	-	5	5	-
P651	202	02	28	-	58	77	5.0	-	3	3	2
P652	203	02	30	-	51C	82	4.0	-	3	5	2
P653	204	09	30	-	51C	-	3.0	-	-	-	-
P654	205	01	26	43	51C	-	4.0	-	3	3	-
P655	206	02	22	45	-	-	5.5	-	-	-	-
P656	207	02	31	-	56S	-	7.5	-	-	-	-
P657	208	02	30	-	51C	-	8.0	-	4	5	-
P658	209	02	30	-	51C	-	8.0	-	4	5	-
P659	210	02	29	-	51C	82	6.0	-	5	5	2
P660	211	09	23	-	-	-	4.0	-	3	4	-
P661	212	02	-	-	-	-	6.0	-	2	-	-
P662	213	02	23	-	56	-	5.0	-	-	-	-
P663	214	09	23	-	55	-	6.0	-	-	-	-
P664	215	02	30	-	(55?)	-	5.5	-	-	-	-
P665	216	09	30	-	(55?)	-	6.5	-	4	5	-
P666	217	04E	33	-	56	-	4.5	-	-	-	-
P667	218	10E	33	-	56S	-	5.5	-	3	6	-
P668	219	02	22	44	52C	-	5.0	-	3	5	-
P669	220	09	31	-	52S	-	5.0	-	4	6	-
P670	221	03	30	-	52C	-	7.5	-	4	5	-
P671	222	02	30	-	52S	-	8.0	-	3	5	-
P672	223	10E	30	-	52C	-	8.0	-	3	5	2
P673	224	02	31	-	56S	-	6.0	-	4	6	-
P674	225	02	31	-	52C	85	9.0	-	3	6	3
P854	407	02	31	-	52S	-	7.0	-	3	6	-
P675	226	02	31	-	52S	82	6.0	-	3	5	2
P676	227	06E	22	-	-	-	7.0	-	-	-	-
P677	228	02	33	-	-	-	8.0	-	2	5	-
P678	229	02	32	44	52S	-	8.0	-	2	6	-
P679	230	09	26	-	(55)	-	7.0	-	3	4	-
P680	231	09	28	-	51/55C	-	6.0	-	5	5	-
P681	232	09	-	-	-	-	5.0	-	3	-	-
P682	233	02	-	-	-	-	6.0	-	-	-	-
P683	234	-	-	-	-	-	6.5	-	-	6	-
P684	235	-	-	-	-	-	-	H2	-	-	-
P685	236	-	-	-	-	82	5.0	-	-	-	1
P686	237	-	-	-	-	84	7.0	-	-	-	3
P687	238	-	-	-	-	85	5.5	-	-	-	2
P688	239	02	26	-	-	-	2.5	-	3	5	-
P689	240	09	35	-	-	-	3.0	-	3	-	-
P690	241	02	30	-	55C	-	5.5	-	3	4	-
P691	242	-	-	-	51C	84	7.0	-	-	5	2
P692	243	09	31	-	60C	-	5.0	-	2	5	-
P693	244	02	30	-	51S	-	8.0	-	5	6	-
P694	245	02	31	-	56S	-	8.0	-	-	-	-
P695	246	-	-	-	(51)	-	9.0	-	-	-	-
P696	247	-	-	-	-	-	-	H3	-	-	-
P697	248	-	-	-	-	-	-	H1	-	-	-
P698	249	-	-	-	-	82 91	5.5	-	-	-	1
P699	250	-	-	-	-	76F	4.5	-	-	-	2
P700	251	01	30	-	51C	77?	5.0	-	4	5	1
P701	252	01	31	-	52C	82	7.0	-	3	5	3
P702	253	12	31	-	52C	-	7.0	-	3	5	-
P703	254	02	31	-	56S	-	6.0	-	3	6	-

Table 19: Late Bronze Age pottery: morphological attributes, angles and dimensions

Vessel No.	B.M. Reg. P1989 10–1	Rim	Neck	Sp	S/C	Base	Th	Hd	Component angles MA	UBA	BWA
P704	255	02	30	-	55C	-	6.0	-	-	-	-
P705	256	02	30	-	52C	-	5.0	-	-	-	-
P706	257	02	35	43	-	-	4.5	-	-	-	-
P707	258	09	23	45	51C	-	4.5	-	2	4	-
P708	259	09	33	-	51C	-	5.0	-	3	5	-
P709	260	09	23	45	52C	-	4.5	-	3	5	-
P710	261	-	-	-	51C	91 82	6.0	-	-	5	2
P711	262	02	22	45	(52)	-	6.0	-	4	7	-
P712	263	01	31	-	51	-	4.5	-	-	-	-
P713	264	08	32	-	-	-	3.0	-	4	7	-
P714	265	10IE	29	-	-	-	5.0	-	5	-	-
P715	266	01	30	44	-	-	6.5	-	6	6	-
P716	267	01	22	44	-	-	5.0	-	2	4	-
P717	268	07	-	-	-	-	4.5	-	2	4	-
P718	269	02	30	-	-	-	7.0	-	3	4	-
P719	270	05	30	-	-	-	5.5	-	3	4	-
P720	271	06E	30	-	51S	-	6.0	-	3	4	-
P721	272	09	30	-	51S	85	7.0	-	3	5	3
P722	273	09	34	-	52C	-	6.0	-	3	5	-
P723	274	10I	34	-	52S	-	6.0	-	4	6	-
P724	275	02	31	-	52S	-	7.5	-	3	5	-
P725	276	10IE	31	-	56S	-	8.0	-	3	5	-
P726	277	10I	30	-	52S	-	8.5	-	4	5	-
P727	278	10E	31	-	51S	87	6.5	-	3	5	2
P728	279	06E	33	-	(52)	-	6.0	-	4	6	-
P729	280	10E	31	-	56S	-	7.0	-	4	6	-
P730	281	02	26	-	-	-	6.5	-	3	5	-
P731	282	02	33	-	56S	82	8.0	P2	3	6	3
P732	283	01	30	-	-	-	7.5	-	-	-	-
P733	284	10IE	29	-	-	-	5.0	-	-	--	-
P734	285	10IE	(30)	-	-	-	5.0	-	-	-	-
P735	286	10IE	(30)	-	-	-	5.0	-	-	-	-
P736	287	03	25	45	-	-	6.5	-	-	-	-
P737	288	09	22	-	52	-	4.0	-	-	-	-
P738	289	07	-	-	-	-	7.0	-	-	-	-
P739	290	11	35	44	-	-	9.0	-	-	-	-
P740	291	-	-	-	-	-	4.5	-	-	-	-
P741	292	-	-	-	-	-	8.0	-	-	-	-
P742	293	-	-	-	-	72	5.0	-	-	-	1
P743	294	-	-	-	-	76	5.0	-	-	-	2
P744	295	-	-	-	-	(76)	5.5	-	-	-	1
P745	296	-	-	-	-	84	6.0	-	-	-	1
P746	297	-	-	-	-	83	6.0	-	-	-	1
P747	298	-	-	-	-	84	0.0	-	-	-	1
P748	299	-	-	-	-	85	8.0	-	-	-	3
P749	300	-	-	-	-	85	8.0	-	-	-	3
P750	301	-	-	-	-	86	8.5	-	-	-	3
P751	302	09	28	-	-	-	3.5	-	1	-	-
P752	303	01	30	-	52C	-	3.5	-	4	4	-
P753	304	02	30	-	51C	-	6.0	-	-	-	-
P754	305	02	33	-	56C	-	4.0	-	3	6	-
P755	306	02	23	-	52C	-	6.0	-	3	4	-
P756	307	03(09)	30	-	55C	-	4.5	-	3	5	-
P757	308	09	30	-	-	-	4.0	-	3	-	-
P758	309	-	-	-	60C	83	6.5	-	-	6	1
P759	310	-	?	-	56	-	3.5	-	-	7	-

Table 19: Late Bronze Age pottery: morphological attributes, angles and dimensions

Vessel No.	B.M. Reg. P1989 10–1	Rim	Neck	Sp	S/C	Base	Th	Hd	Component angles MA	UBA	BWA
P760	311	01	36	-	-	-	4.5	-	-	-	-
P761	312	03	29	-	-	-	4.0	-	-	-	-
P762	313	09	22	45	-	-	3.5	-	-	-	-
P763	314	02	33	-	-	-	4.5	-	-	-	-
P764	315	01	21	44	(?55)	-	6.5	-	-	-	-
P765	316	12	33	-	-	-	5.5	-	3	5	-
P766	317	02	27	-	(55)	-	6.5	-	6	5	-
P767	318	05	26	-	51	-	7.5	-	4	5	-
P768	319	10E	33	-	51S	-	6.5	-	4	6	-
P769	320	09	33	-	52S	-	7.0	-	-	-	-
P770	321	12	31	-	52S	-	5.0	-	4	6	-
P771	322	10IE	31	-	52S	85	8.0	-	4	6	2
P772	323	09	30	-	51S	-	7.0	-	-	-	-
P773	324	Un	33	-	-	-	7.0	-	-	-	-
P774	325	10I	31	-	-	-	7.0	-	-	-	-
P775	326	10I	30	-	-	-	7.0	-	-	-	-
P776	327	09	25	-	-	-	6.5	-	-	-	-
P777	328	02	33	-	-	-	8.0	-	-	-	-
P778	329	09	30	-	52C	-	10.0	-	-	-	-
P779	330	09	29	-	-	-	5.5	-	-	-	-
P780	331	13	30	44	-	-	6.0	-	-	-	-
P781	332	-	-	-	53	-	7.0	-	-	-	-
P782	333	06IE	31	-	-	-	4.0	-	-	-	-
P783	334	10IE	-	-	-	-	4.5	-	-	-	-
P784	335	04I	-	-	-	-	6.5	-	-	-	-
P785	336	04I	-	-	-	-	4.5	-	-	-	-
P786	337	09	28	--	-	-	5.0	-	-	-	-
P787	338	09	-	43	-	-	6.0	-	-	-	-
P788	339	-	25	42	-	-	6.5	-	-	-	-
P789	340	02	30	-	51S	-	4.5	-	-	-	-
P790	341	09	30	-	-	-	7.0	-	-	-	-
P791	342	01	-	-	-	-	7.0	-	-	-	-
P792	343	09	-	-	-	-	8.0	-	-	-	-
P793	344	09	-	-	-	-	6.5	-	-	-	-
P794	345	06IE	-	-	-	-	4.5	-	-	-	-
P795	346	10E	(26)	43	-	-	6.0	-	-	-	-
P796	347	-	-	45	-	-	5.5	-	-	-	-
P797	348	-	-	-	-	82	5.5	-	-	-	2
P798	349	-	-	-	-	-	5.5	-	-	-	-
P799	350	-	-	45	-	-	7.5	-	-	-	-
P800	351	-	-	-	(56)	-	8.0	-	-	-	-
P801	352	-	-	-	55	-	9.0	-	-	-	-
P802	353	-	-	-	51	-	7.0	-	-	-	-
P803	354	-	-	-	51	-	6.0	-	-	-	-
P804	355	-	-	-	51	-	7.0	-	-	-	-
P805	356	-	-	-	-	-	6.5	-	-	-	-
P806	357	-	-	-	-	76R	4.5	-	-	-	1
P807	358	-	-	-	-	82 92	6.5	-	-	-	2
P808	359	-	-	-	-	-	6.0	-	-	-	2
P809	360	-	-	-	-	85	7.0	-	-	-	2
P810	361	-	-	-	-	84	13.0	-	-	-	1
P811	362	02	30	-	52C	-	4.5	-	4	4	-
P812	363	03	34	-	-	-	5.0	-	-	-	-
P813	364	04IE	-	-	-	-	5.0	-	-	-	-
P814	365	09	30	-	-	-	5.0	-	-	-	-
P815	366	05	-	-	-	-	5.0	-	-	-	-

Table 19: Late Bronze Age pottery: morphological attributes, angles and dimensions

Vessel No.	B.M. Reg. P1989 10–1	Rim	Neck	Sp	S/C	Base	Th	Hd	Component angles MA	UBA	BWA
P816	367	03	-	-	-	-	3.5	-	-	-	-
P817	368	10E	-	-	-	-	4.5	-	-	-	-
P818	369	06	(29)	41	-	-	5.0	-	-	-	-
P819	370	10E	-	43	-	-	4.0	-	-	-	-
P820	371	09	22	43	-	-	6.5	-	-	-	-
P821	372	02	37	43	-	-	8.0	-	-	-	-
P822	373	06E	(31)	-	-	-	5.0	-	-	-	-
P823	374	09	-	-	-	-	7.5	-	-	-	-
P824	375	10IE	-	-	-	-	4.0	-	-	-	-
P825	376	02	-	-	-	-	4.0	-	-	-	-
P826	377	09	22	45	-	-	5.0	-	-	-	-
P827	378	10E	-	-	-	-	7.5	-	-	-	-
P828	379	?02	31	-	55	-	7.0	-	-	-	-
P829	380	09	-	-	-	-	8.5	-	-	-	-
P830	381	09	30	-	-	-	7.0	-	-	-	-
P831	382	10IE	28	-	-	-	6.5	-	-	-	-
P832	383	-	-	-	-	-	5.5	-	-	-	-
P833	384	-	-	-	-	-	5.0	-	-	-	-
P834	385	-	-	-	-	-	7.0	-	-	-	-
P835	386	-	-	-	-	-	7.5	-	-	-	-
P836	387	-	-	-	-	-	6.5	-	-	-	-
P837	388	-	-	-	-	-	5.0	-	-	-	-
P838	389	-	-	-	55	-	4.5	-	-	-	-
P839	390	-	-	-	52	-	7.5	-	-	-	-
P840	391	-	-	-	(51)	-	6.5	-	-	-	-
P841	392	-	-	-	51	-	8.0	-	-	-	-
P842	393	-	-	-	-	71	5.0	-	-	-	1
P843	394	-	-	-	-	82 91	7.0	-	-	-	2
P844	395	-	-	-	-	82	9.0	-	-	-	2
P845	396	02	22	45	-	-	5.0	-	-	-	-
P846	397	-	-	-	-	-	4.0	-	-	-	-
P847	398	03	29	-	-	-	3.0	-	-	-	-
P848	399	09	-	-	-	-	7.0	-	-	-	-
P849	400	03	-	-	-	-	4.0	-	-	-	-
P850	401	09	28	44	-	-	6.0	-	-	-	-
P851	402	10I	28	-	-	-	4.5	-	-	-	-
P852	403	09	-	44	-	-	8.0	-	-	-	-
P853	404	-	-	-	-	-	8.0	H4	-	-	-
P854 see after P674											

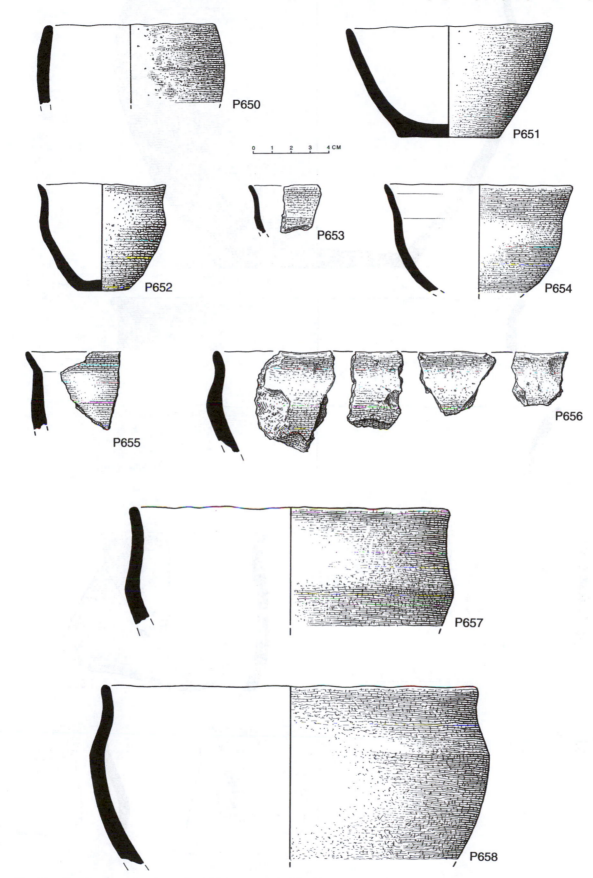

Fig. 60 *Late Bronze Age pottery, unit G (P650), unit H (P651–658). Scale 1/2.*

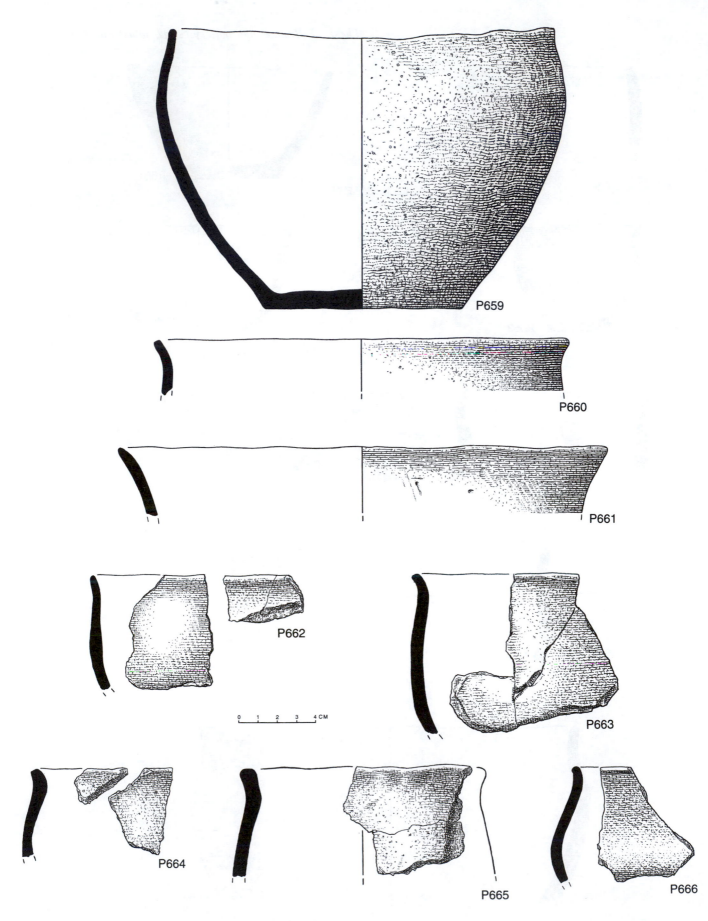

Fig. 61 *Late Bronze Age pottery, unit H. Scale 1/2.*

P659

P660

P661

P662

P663

P664

P665

P666

0 1 2 3 4 CM

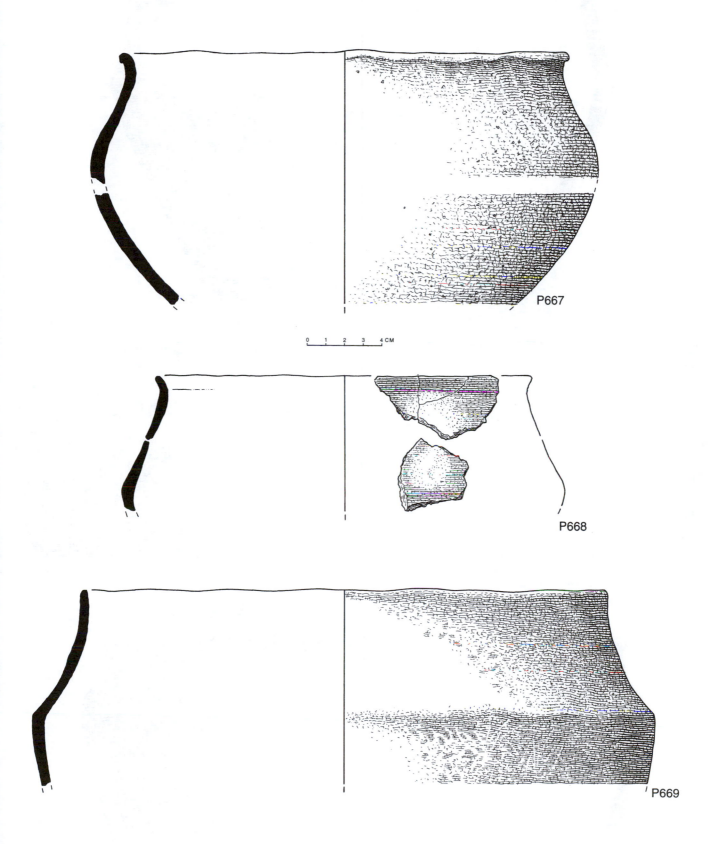

Fig. 62 *Late Bronze Age pottery, unit H. Scale 1/2.*

135

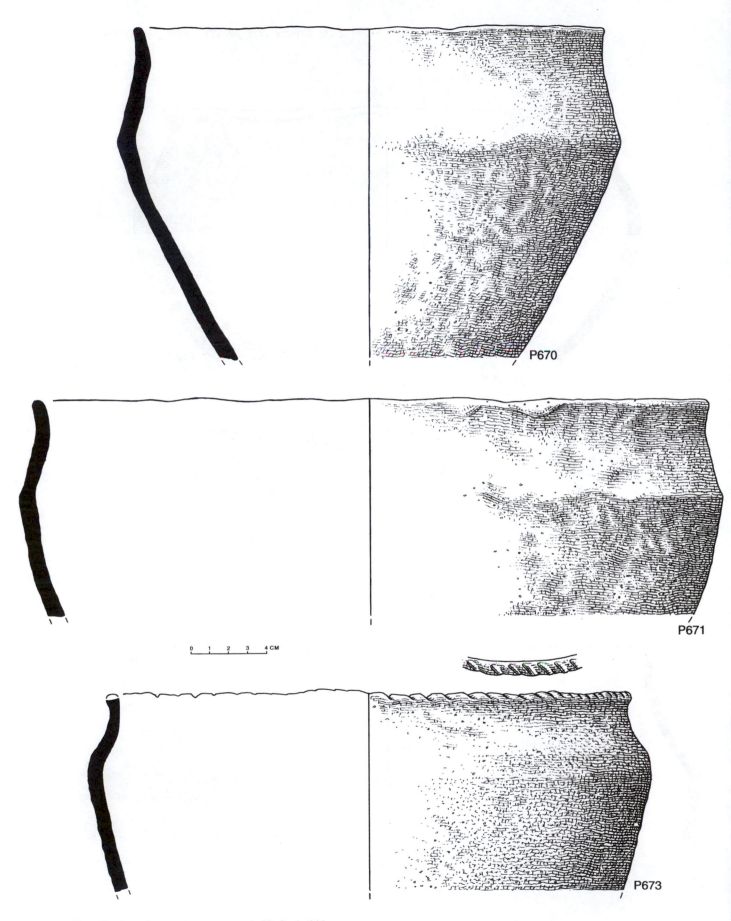

Fig. 63 *Late Bronze Age pottery, unit H. Scale 1/2.*

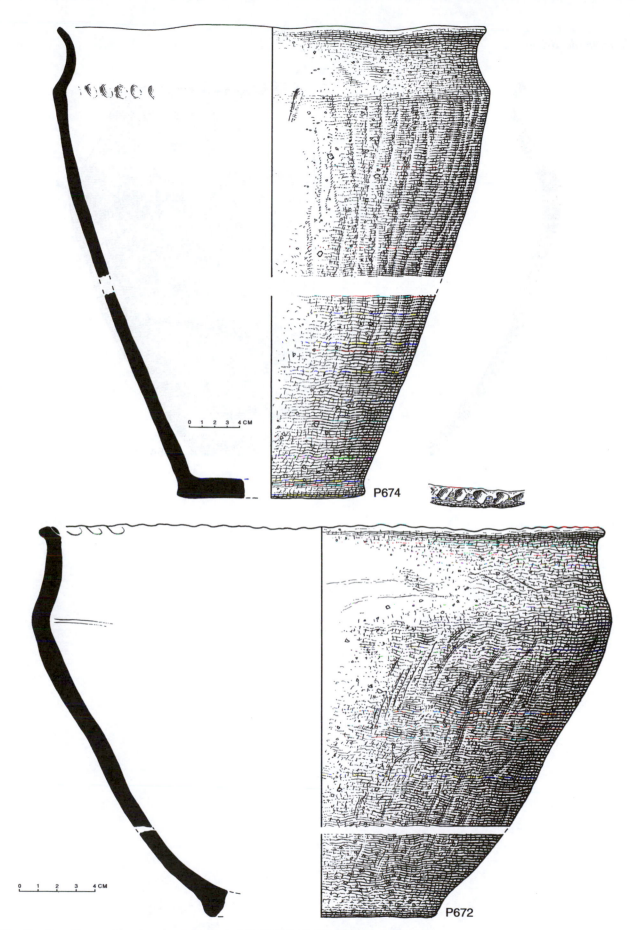

Fig. 64 *Late Bronze Age pottery, unit H. Scale 1/3 (P674) & 1/2 (P672).*

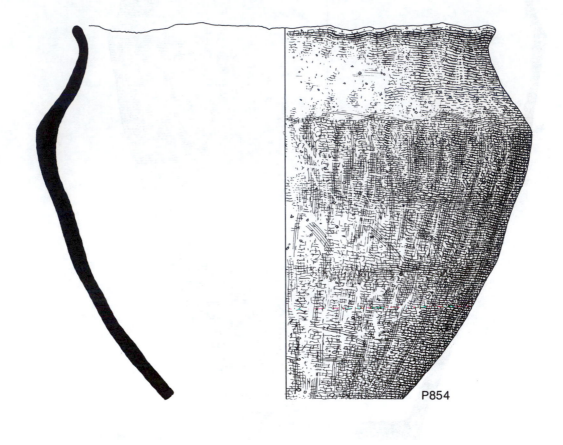

P854

Fig. 65 *Late Bronze Age pottery, unit H. Scale 1/2.*

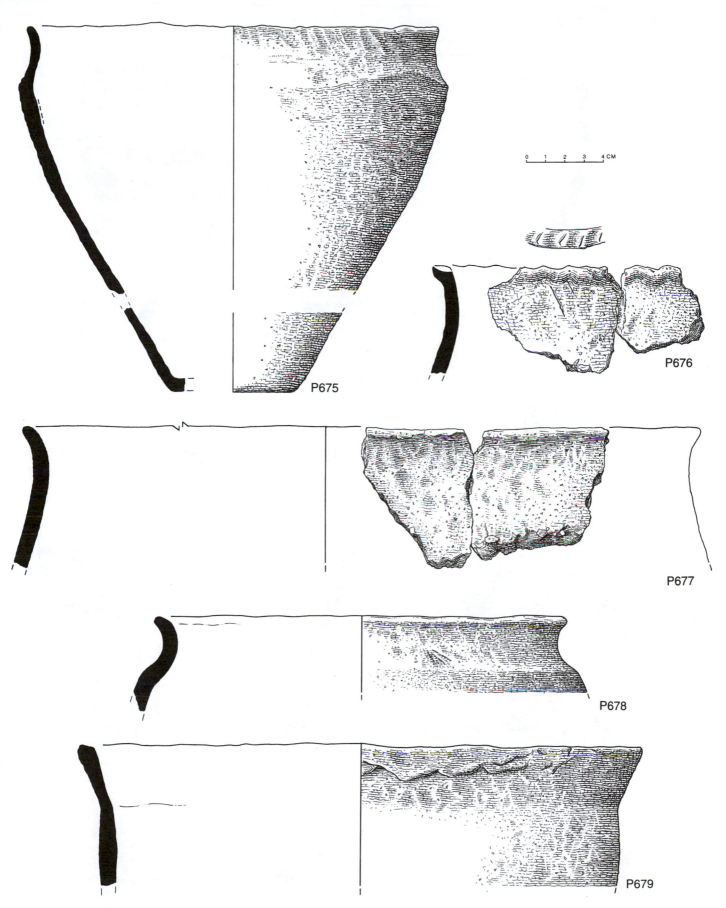

Fig. 66 *Late Bronze Age pottery, unit H. Scale 1/2.*

P675
P676
P677
P678
P679

0 1 2 3 4 CM

139

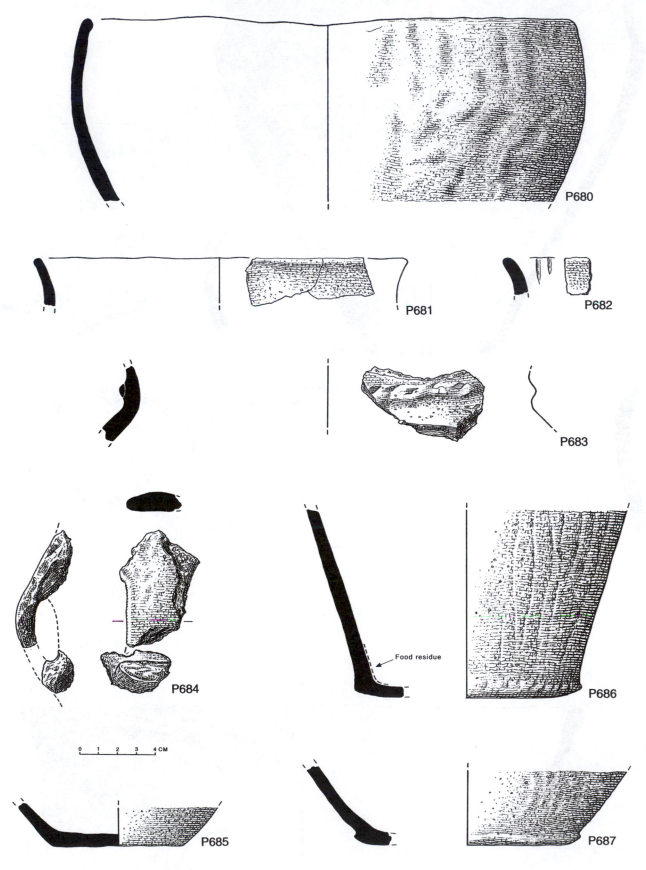

Fig. 67 *Late Bronze Age pottery, unit H. Scale 1/2.*

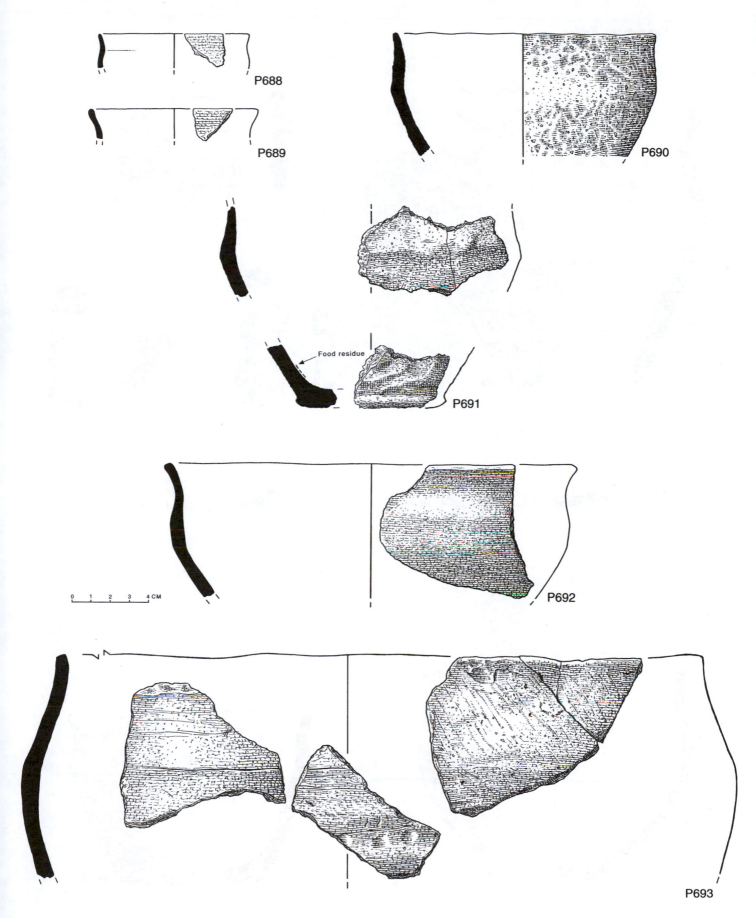

P688

P689

P690

Food residue

P691

P692

0 1 2 3 4 CM

P693

Fig. 68 *Late Bronze Age pottery, unit I. Scale 1/2.*

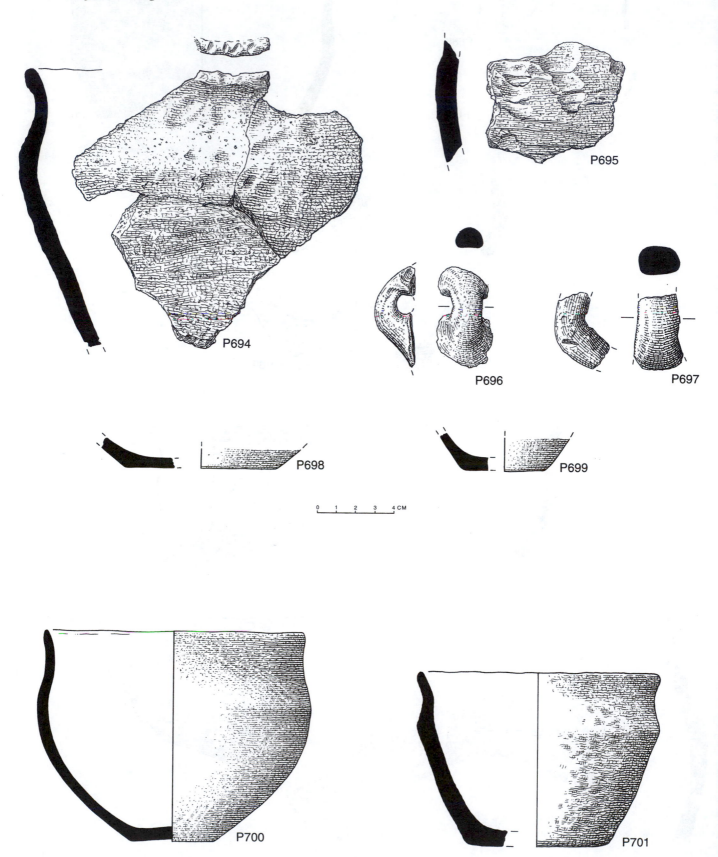

Fig. 69 *Late Bronze Age pottery, unit I (P694–699), unit J (P700–701). Scale 1/2.*

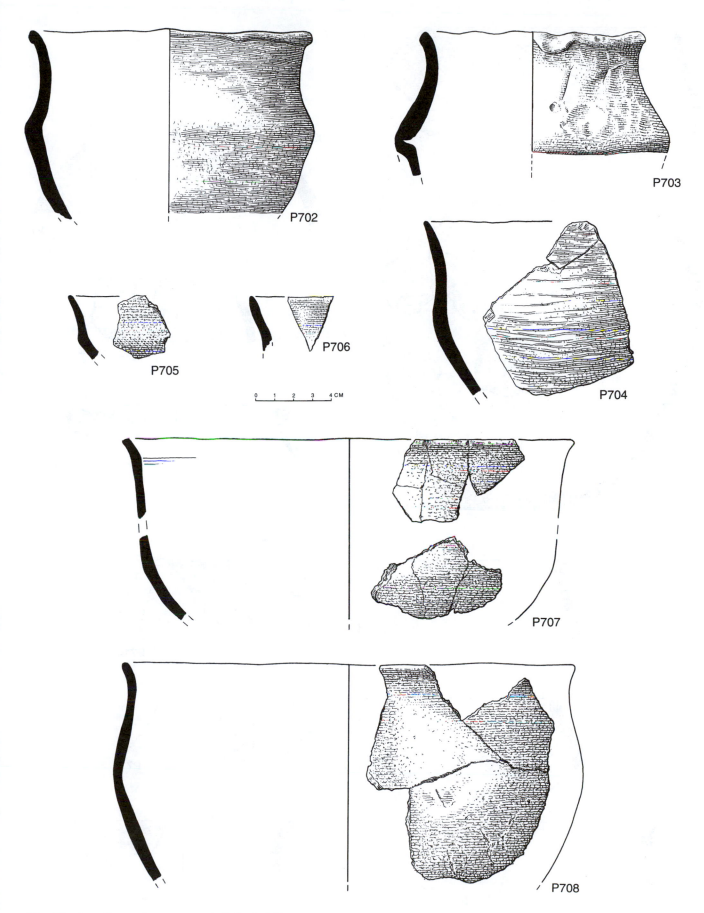

P702

P703

P705

P706

P704

P707

P708

0 1 2 3 4 CM

Fig. 70 *Late Bronze Age pottery, unit J. Scale 1/2.*

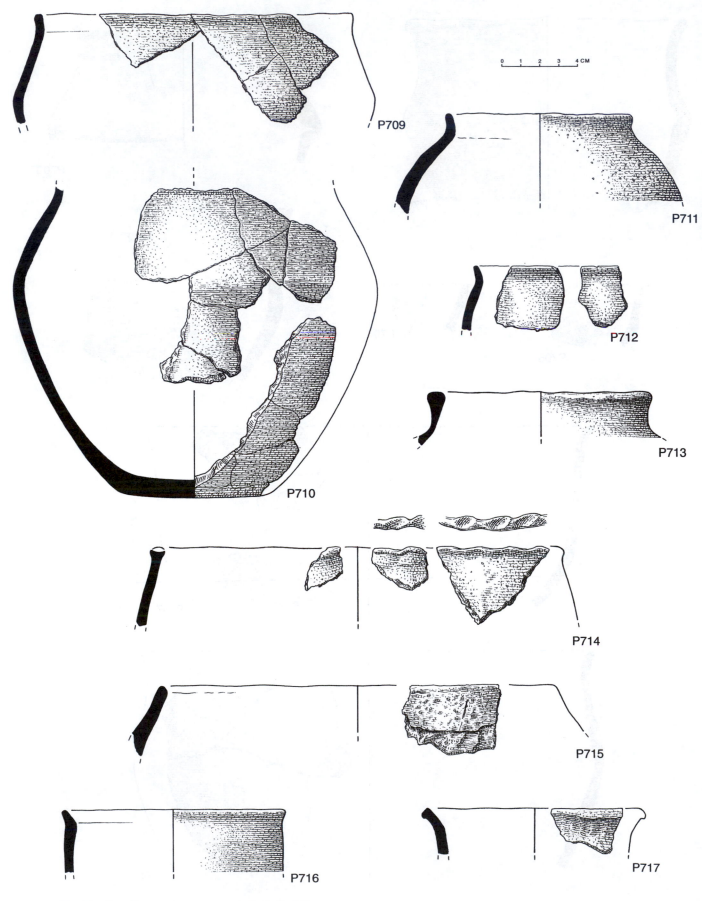

Fig. 71 *Late Bronze Age pottery, unit J. Scale 1/2.*

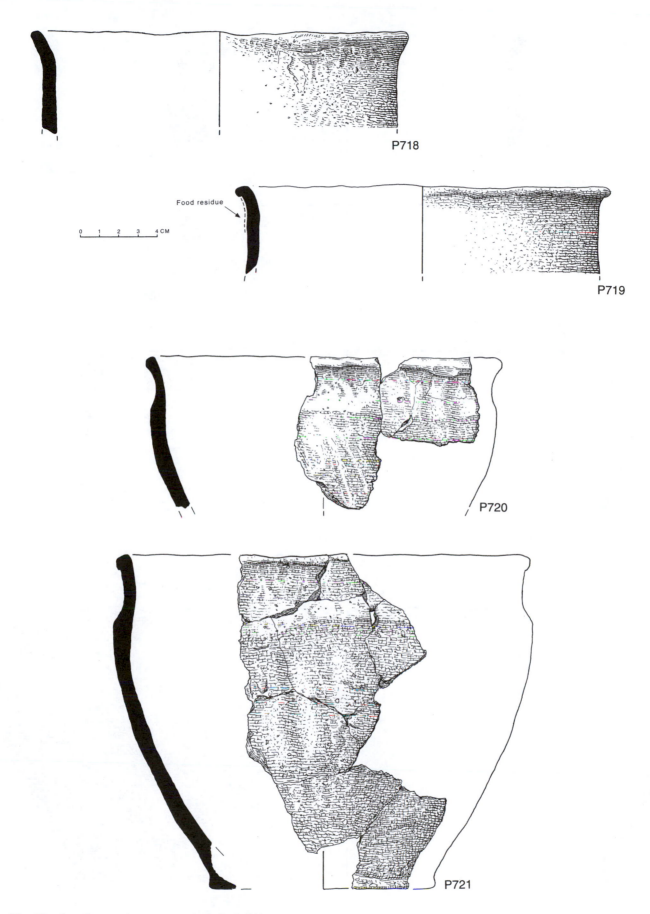

Food residue

0 1 2 3 4 CM

P718

P719

P720

P721

Fig. 72 *Late Bronze Age pottery, unit J. Scale 1/2.*

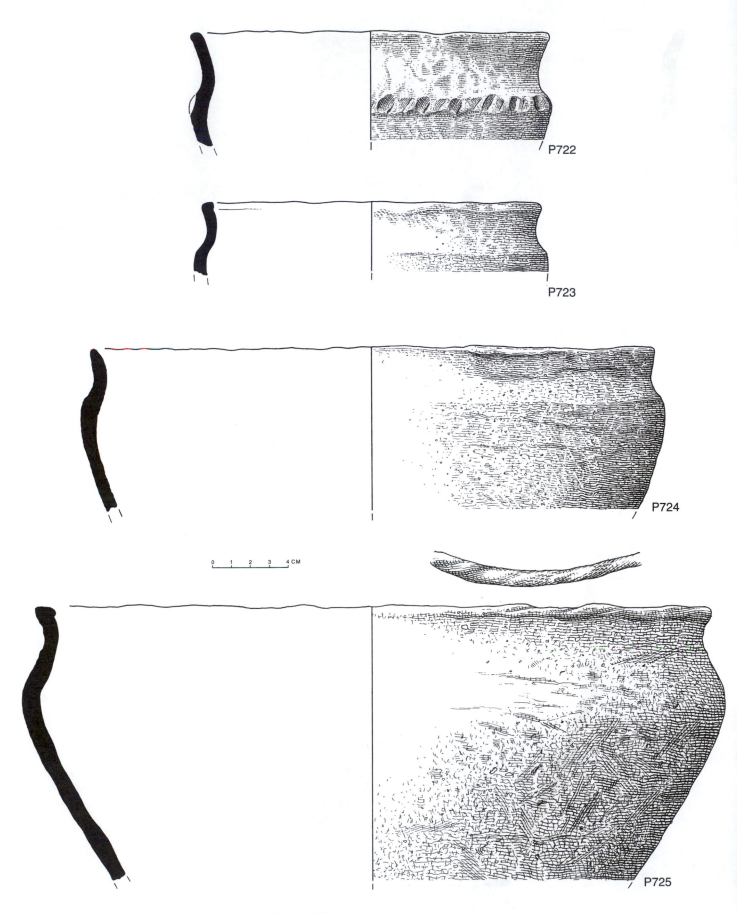

Fig. 73 *Late Bronze Age pottery, unit J. Scale 1/2.*

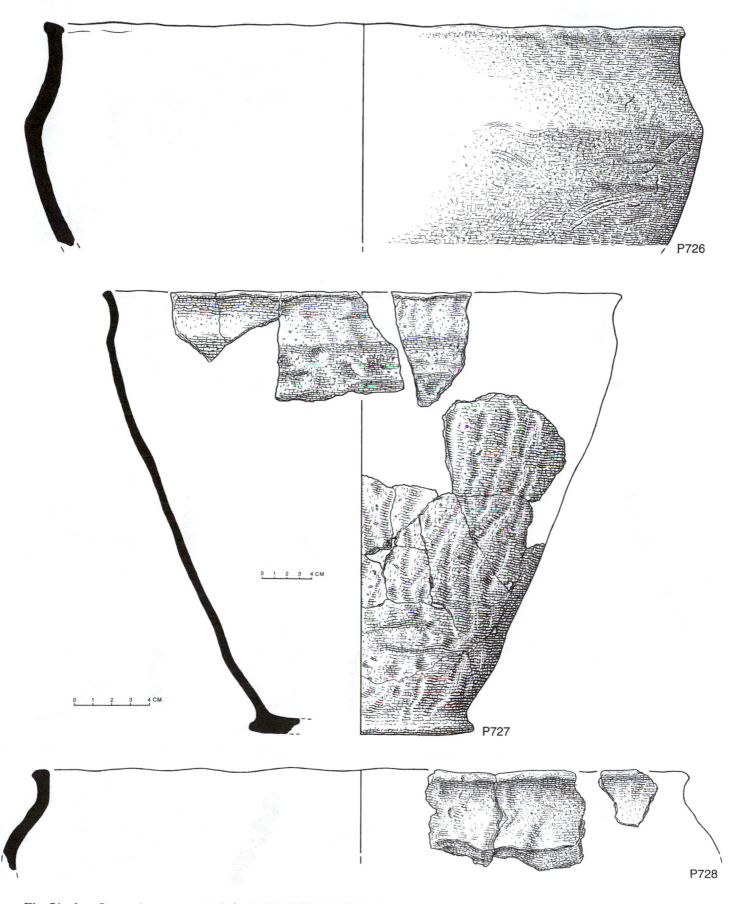

P726

P727

P728

Fig. 74 *Late Bronze Age pottery, unit J. Scale 1/3 (P727) & 1/2 (rest).*

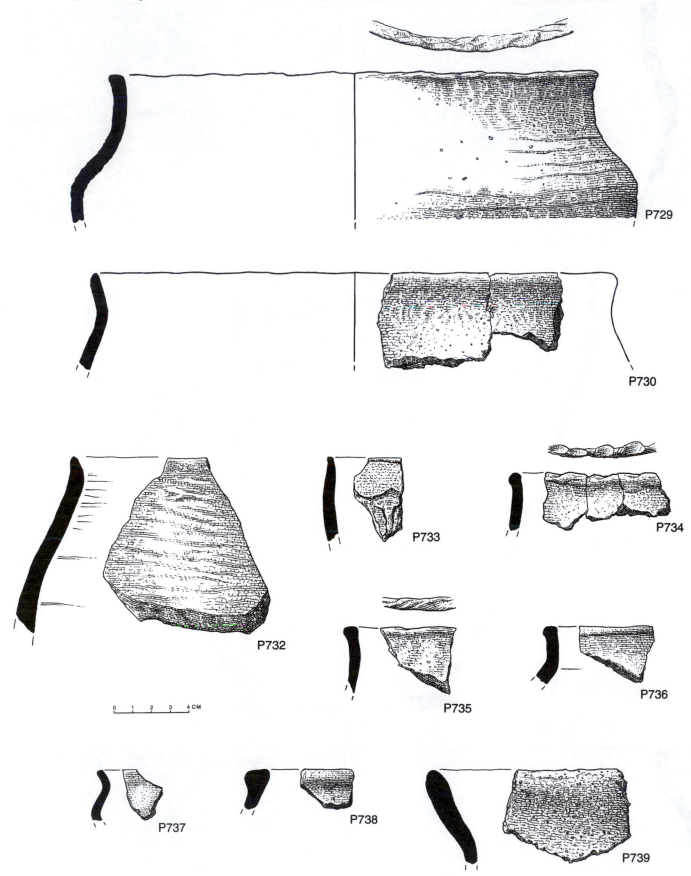

Fig. 75 *Late Bronze Age pottery, unit J. Scale 1/2.*

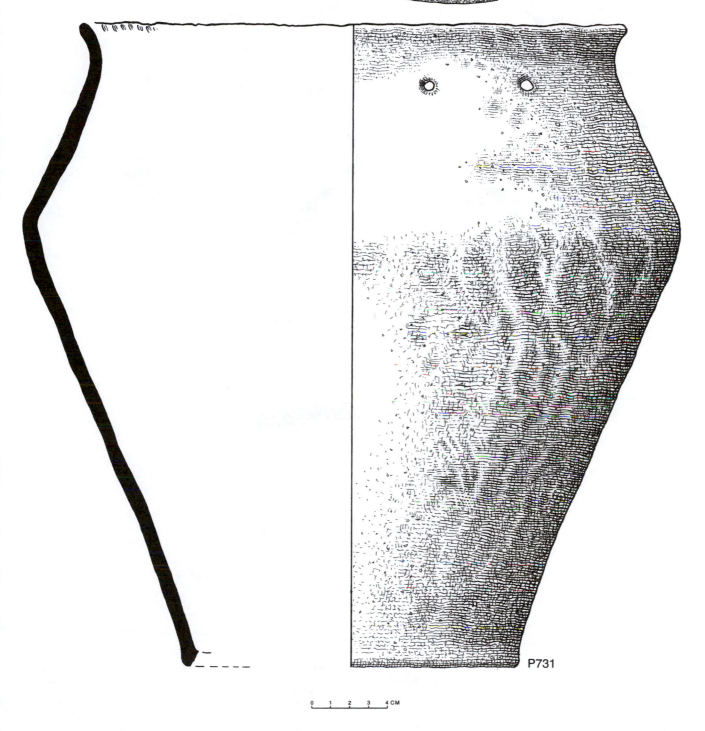

P731

Fig. 76 *Late Bronze Age pottery, unit J. Scale 1/2.*

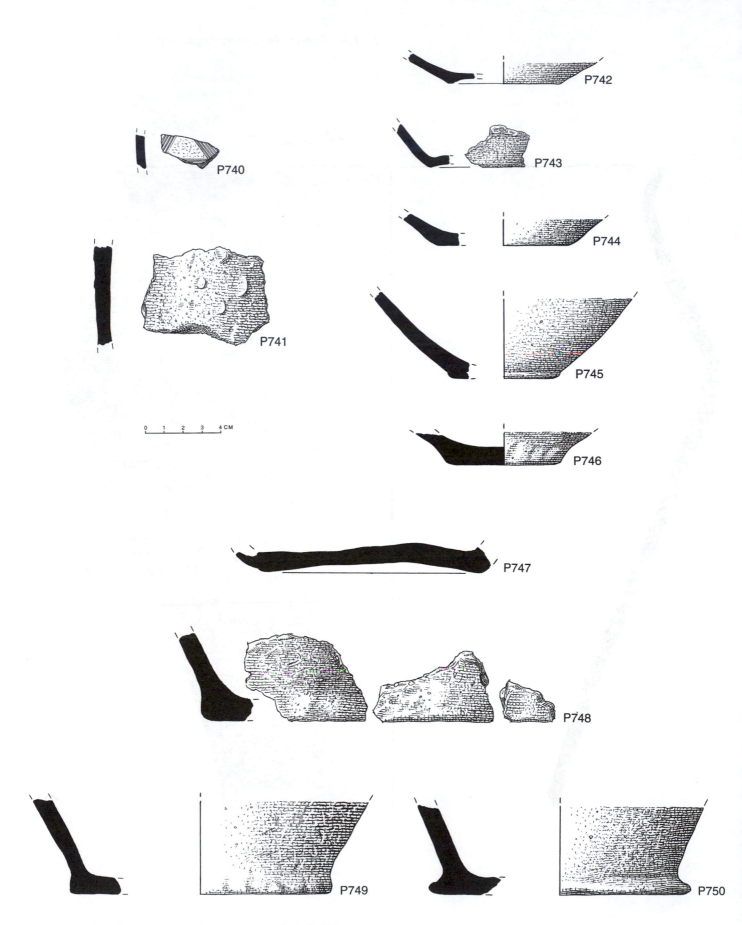

Fig. 77 *Late Bronze Age pottery, unit J. Scale 1/2.*

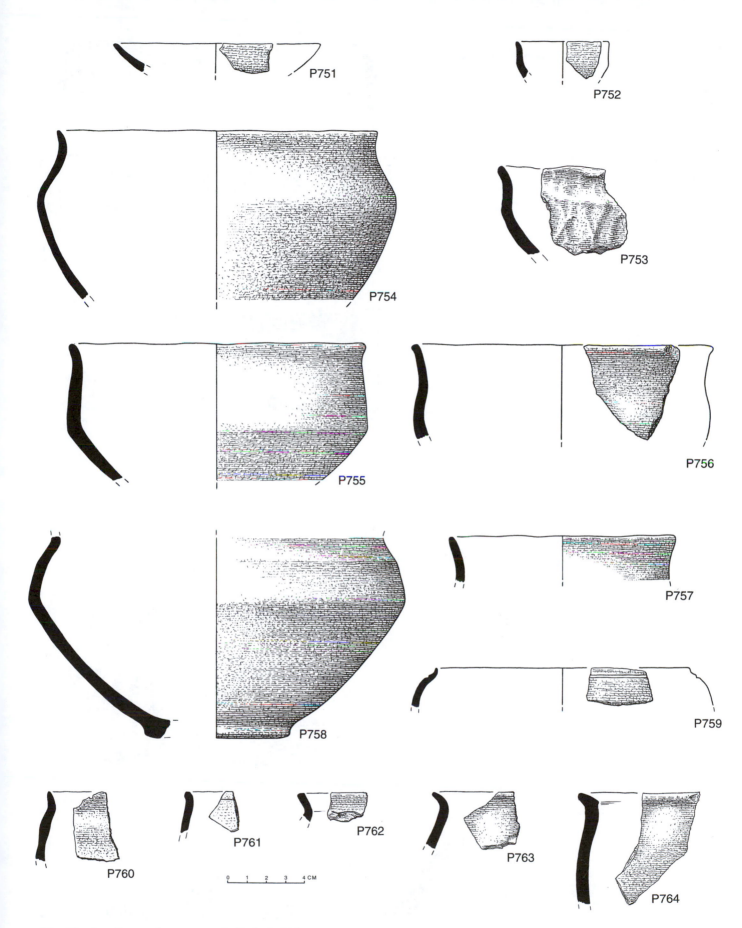

P751

P752

P754

P753

P755

P756

P758

P757

P759

P760

P761

P762

P763

P764

0 1 2 3 4 CM

Fig. 78 *Late Bronze Age pottery, unit K. Scale 1/2.*

151

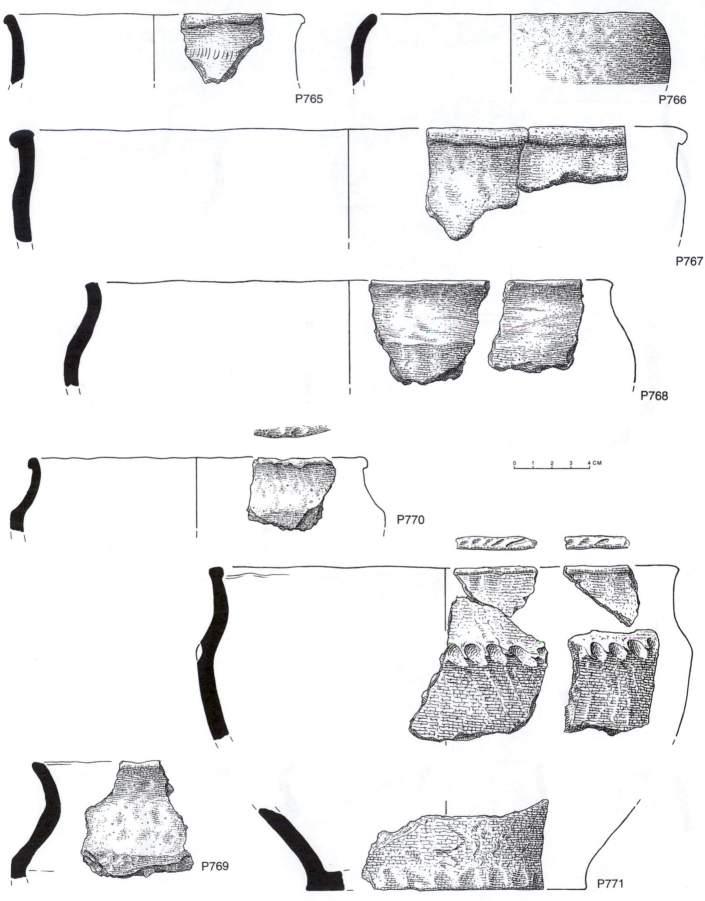

Fig. 79 *Late Bronze Age pottery, unit K. Scale 1/2.*

P765

P766

P767

P768

P770

P769

P771

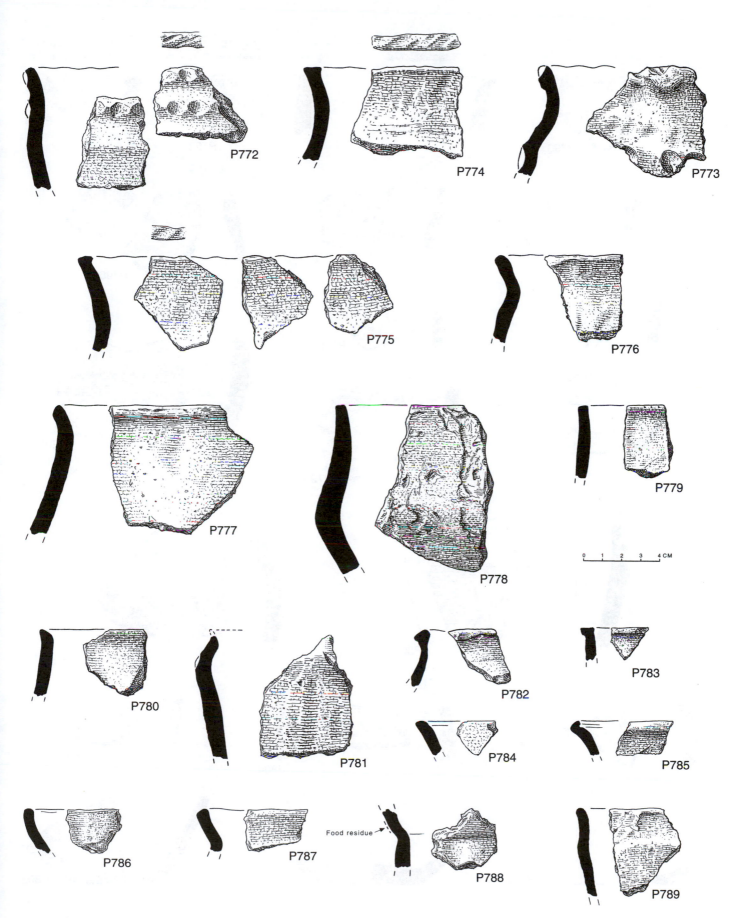

Fig. 80 *Late Bronze Age pottery, unit K. Scale 1/2.*

P772

P774

P773

P775

P776

P777

P778

P779

P780

P781

P782

P783

P784

P785

P786

P787

Food residue

P788

P789

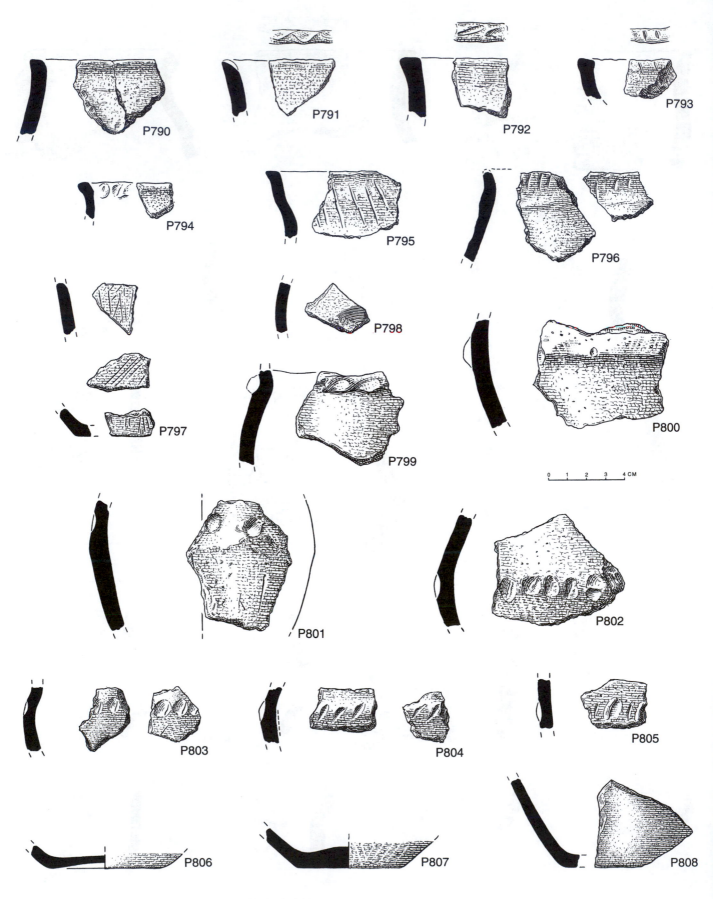

Fig. 81 *Late Bronze Age pottery, unit K. Scale 1/2.*

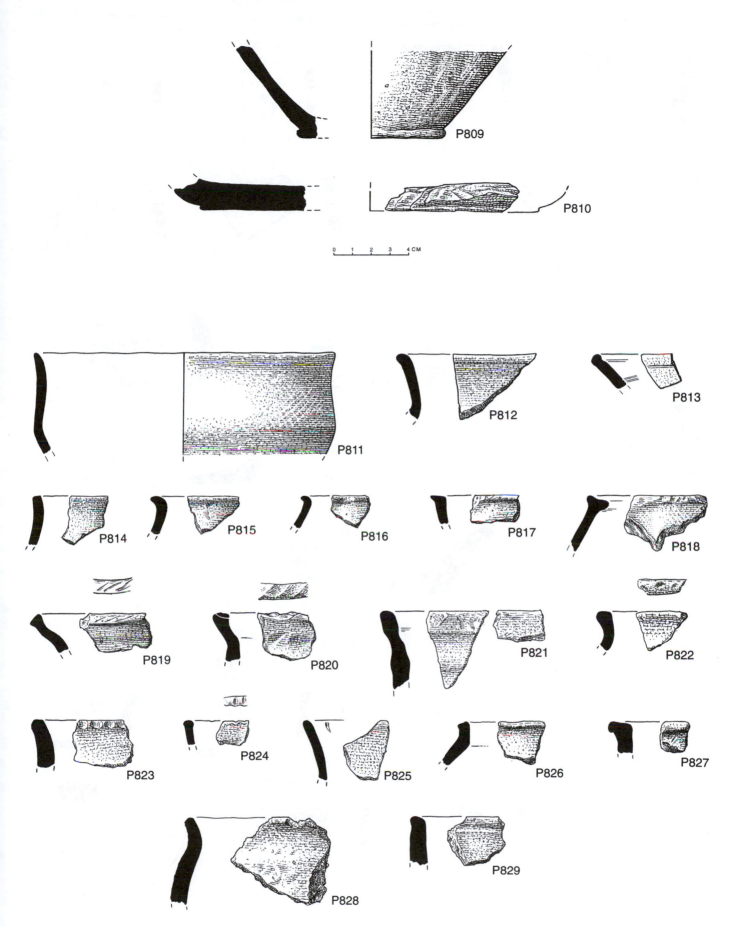

Fig. 82 *Late Bronze Age pottery, unit K (P809–810), unit L (P811–829). Scale 1/2.*

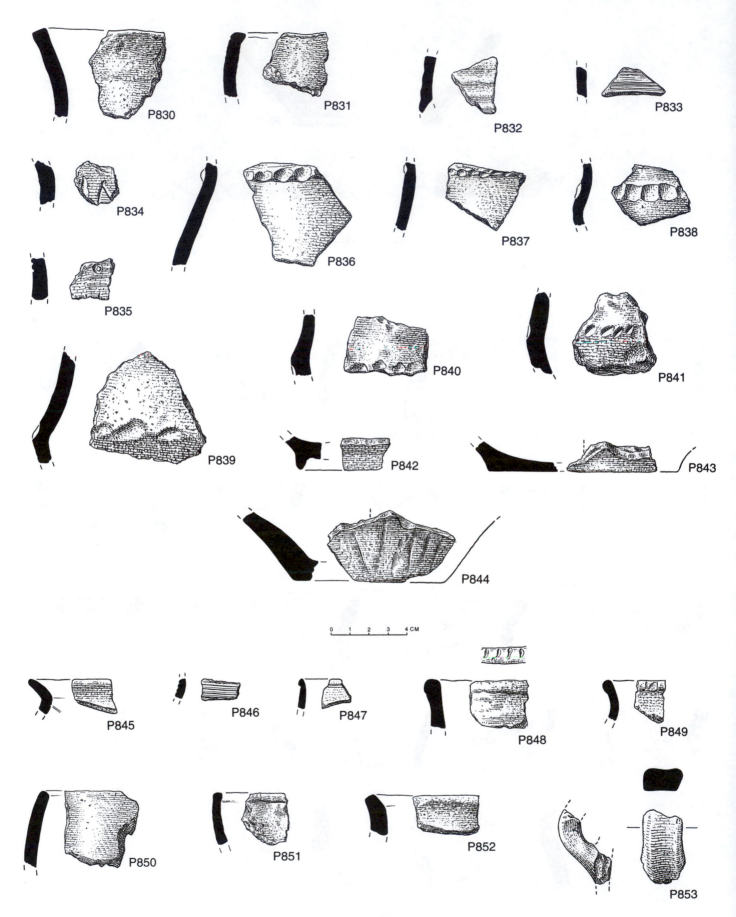

P830

P831

P832

P833

P834

P835

P836

P837

P838

P839

P840

P841

P842

P843

P844

0 1 2 3 4 CM

P845

P846

P847

P848

P849

P850

P851

P852

P853

Fig. 83 *Late Bronze Age pottery, unit L (P830–844), unit M (P845–853). Scale 1/2.*

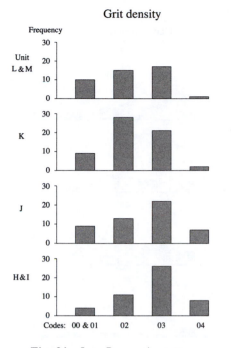

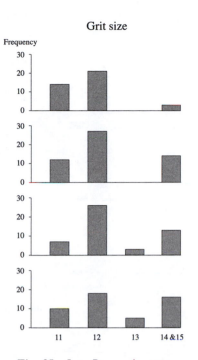

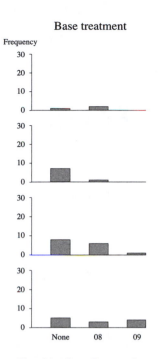

Fig. 84 *Late Bronze Age pottery, sequential distribution of grit density (sample: catalogued vessels).*

Fig. 85 *Late Bronze Age pottery, sequential distribution of grit size (sample: catalogued vessels).*

Fig. 86 *Late Bronze Age pottery, sequential distribution of base treatment (sample: catalogued vessels).*

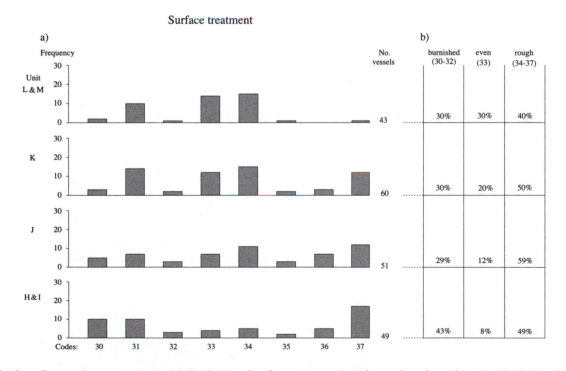

Fig. 87 *Late Bronze Age pottery, sequential distribution of surface treatments (sample: catalogued vessels); a) individual surface categories; b) percentage trends in burnished, even and rough surfaced wares. NB. A few vessels were classified with more than one surface treatment type and are therefore double-counted in the histograms.*

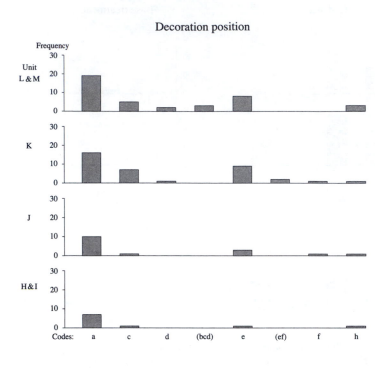

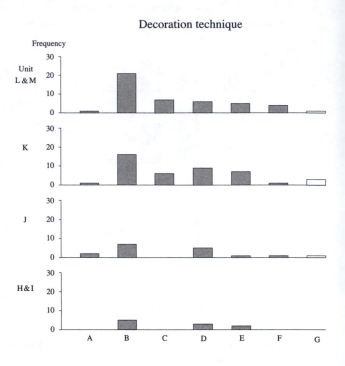

Fig. 88 *Late Bronze Age pottery, sequential distribution of decoration position (sample: all decorated sherds/vessels).*

Fig. 89 *Late Bronze Age pottery, sequential distribution of decoration technique (sample: all decorated sherds/vessels).*

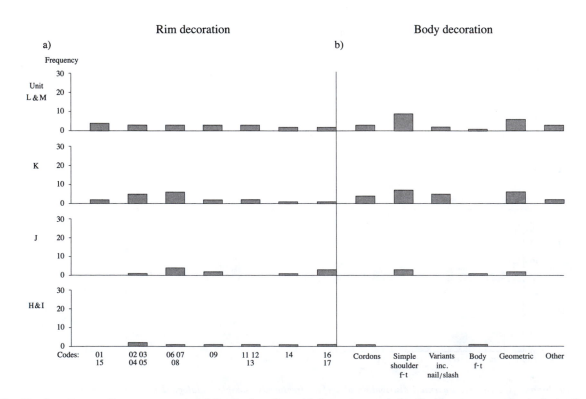

Fig. 90 *Late Bronze Age pottery, sequential distribution of general decoration types (similar types are grouped together): a) rim decoration; b) body decoration (sample: all decorated sherds/vessels).*

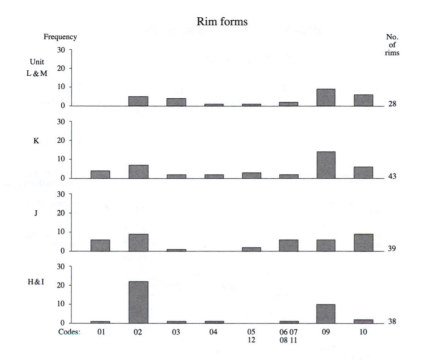

Fig. 91 *Late Bronze Age pottery, sequential distribution of rim forms; some infrequent forms are grouped with similar types; (sample: catalogued vessels).*

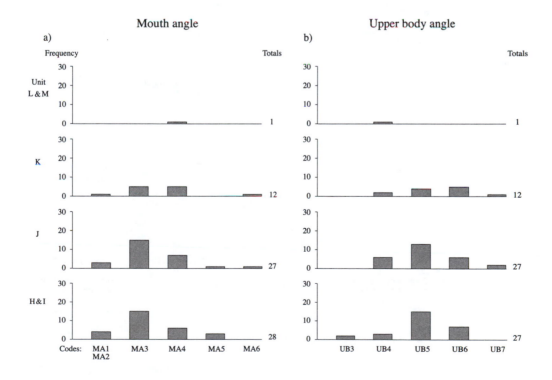

Fig. 92 *Late Bronze Age pottery: sequential distribution of measurable angles of: a) mouth, b) upper body; angles were only ascertainable for minority of catalogued vessels; (sample: catalogued vessels).*

159

Ceramic change indicators

Stratigraphic Units

Attribute	HI	J	K	LM
FABRIC				
Grit density	Peaks at moderate	⟶ Peaks at light		Light/moderate
Grit size	Balanced grit size distribution	⟶		Predominantly small-medium grits
Paste	Minority of sandy wares	⟶		Majority of sandy wares
	Large minority of glauconitic	⟶		Small minority of glauconitic
SURFACES				
Base treatment	Mixed treatment	Decline in vegetal addition	Decline in flint addition	
General surface	Good % burnished	Decline in burnish		
	Mixed burnishing technique	⟶		Smooth burnish dominant
	Small minority smooth/even	⟶		Substantial minority smooth/even
	Coarser wares grass-wiped	⟶		Coarser wares non-descript
DECORATION				
Position	Small minority of rims decorated	(increasing) ⟶		
	Virtually no shoulder decoration	(increasing) ⟶		
Type			Finger-nail added	
			Stabbed etc. motifs added	
			Rim outer lip dec. added	
FORM				
Rim	Rounded rims predominant	⟶		Flattened rims predominant
		Tapered rims significant		
		Club rims significant		
			Internal rim hollowing/lid seats significant	
Body	Slightly out-turned mouths predominant	⟶		Small degree of mouth contraction overall

Key : ⟶ Gradual change through sequence

Fig. 93 *Summary of major indicators for ceramic change in LBA Area 16 East.*

Petrology of selected Late Bronze Age pottery

SYLVIA HUMPHREY

Twenty-two sherds of pottery were selected for thin-section analysis (see Table 20). The materials have been grouped according to the nature of the clay and the aplastic inclusions.

1. GLAUCONITIC CLAY WITH FLINT

Sherd P674.

Consists of glauconitic clay, containing sparse to common pellets of glauconite with a diameter of up to 0.50 mm, typically 0.25 mm. Common sub-angular flint ranging in size from silt grade (rare), up to 1.50 mm, typically 0.50 mm, in diameter is the main aplastic component. Sparse sub-angular fine sand to silt and rare sub-angular to sub-rounded medium sand are also present. Argillaceous inclusions, which are probably iron-rich, up to 1 mm in diameter are sparse. Fine mica and feldspar are rare to very rare.

2. WELL-SORTED VERY FINE SAND TO SILT AND FLINT

Sherds P702, P758 and P767.

Inclusions consisting of abundant sub-angular to sub-rounded well sorted very fine sand to silt. Angular to sub-angular flint is common in sherd P767 and varies in size from silt grade up to 2.50 mm in diameter. Flint in P702 is sparse, sub-angular to sub-rounded, typically 0.20 to 0.30 mm in diameter. P758 and P767 contain very rare glauconitic pellets, typically 0.05 mm in diameter. Fine mica, up to 0.20 mm, and feldspar (P758 only) up to 0.05 mm, are rare.

Groups 3a and 3b are broadly similar. Flint is more abundant in 3b.

3A. SPARSE TO COMMON SILT AND POORLY SORTED SAND

Sherds P657, P692, P700b and P808.

Contains abundant poorly sorted sub-angular to sub-rounded fine to medium sand. Sub-angular silt is sparse to common. Flint is rare, ranging in size from silt-grade up to 1.0 mm in diameter. Argillaceous inclusions occur in P657 and P692. They are rounded in shape, and probably iron-rich, with size varying from 0.50 mm up to 5.0 mm. Fine mica, typically up to 0.05 mm, and feldspar, typically 0.05 to 0.10 mm, are rare.

3B. POORLY SORTED SAND WITH FLINT

Sherds P663, P666, P704, P716a, P722b and P778.

Poorly sorted sand, mainly fine to medium grade is abundant. Rare coarse sand also occurs in P666, P716a, P722b and P778. Sub-angular to sub-rounded silt is sparse to common. In P663, P666, P704 and P716a flint is common. It varies in size from silt grade up to a maximum diameter of 1.5 mm (P716a), and is generally sub-angular to sub-rounded. Flint is sparse to common in P722b, and sparse in P778. P716a also contains sparse argillaceous inclusions, with diameters of less than 1.0 mm, which are probably iron-rich. Flakes of mica are rare to very rare, typically up to 0.10 mm in length. Rare feldspar, typically 0.05 mm in diameter, was detected in P663, P704 and P778.

Groups 4a and 4b contain similar suites of aplastic inclusions in two different clays.

4A. FLINT IN A FINE CLAY MATRIX

Sherds P672, P757b and P766.

Contains sparse to common flint, ranging in size from silt grade up to 2.0 mm in diameter. The finer material is typically angular to sub-angular, whereas the coarser grains are usually sub-rounded. P757b contains rare sub-angular to sub-rounded silt as the only other significant aplastic material. P672 contains sparse to rare sub-angular silt, with the addition of rare coarse (sub-rounded) to fine (sub-angular) sand. Silt is sparse in P766. P757b also contains sparse argillaceous inclusions, up to 3.0 mm in diameter. P766 contains rare argillaceous inclusions. Flakes of mica, typically 0.02 to 0.05 mm long, are rare to very rare.

4B. CALCAREOUS CLAY WITH FLINT

Sherd P715.

Consists of a clay with sparse to common fine calcareous material, including rounded grains up to 1.0 mm in diameter and numerous microfossils. Common sub-angular to sub-rounded flint, ranging in size from silt grade up to 2.50 mm, is the main aplastic constituent. Sparse silt is typically sub-angular. Rare medium to fine sand is sub-angular to sub-rounded. Very rare fine glauconitic pellets with a diameter of up to 0.03 mm are also present. The thin section is rather dark in appearance, and glauconite may be more abundant than is apparent. Rare argillaceous inclusions are less than 1 mm in diameter and probably iron-rich. Rare flakes of mica, up to 0.10 mm in length, are also present.

5. FLINT AND SPARSE TO COMMON SILT

Sherds P670a, P679e, P701a and P705c.

Inclusions of flint, typically sub-angular to angular, and ranging in size from silt-grade up to 2.50 mm in P670a, are common. P670a, P679e and P701a contain sparse to common sub-angular very fine sand to silt, and rare to very rare sub-rounded medium sand. P705c contains sparse to common sub-angular to sub-rounded very fine sand to silt. A single argillaceous inclusion was present in P701a and P705c. Very rare flakes of mica, up to 0.10 mm long, are also present. Rare feldspar up to 0.10 mm was detected in P705c.

Table 20: Thin-sectioned LBA pottery

Cat. No.	B.M. Res. Lab. No.	Unit	Fabric group
P657	43580U	16.H	3a
P663	43572U	16.H	3b
P666	43571W	16.H	3b
P670a	43589Y	16.H	5
P672	43568X	16.H	4a
P674b	43569V	16.H	1
P679e	43587R	16.H	5
P692	43575Z	16.I	3a
P700b	43576X	16.J	3a
P701a	43588P	16.J	5
P702	43579R	16.J	2
P704	43570Y	16.J	3b
P705c	43583Z	16.J	5
P715	43585V	16.J	4b
P716a	43573S	16.J	3b
P722b	43586T	16.J	3b
P757b	43574Q	16.K	4a
P758	43578T	16.K	2
P766	43584X	16.K	4a
P767	43591Z	16.K	2
P778	43577V	16.K	3b
P808	43582Q	16.K	3a

Discussion

Of the twenty-two samples that have been examined in thin section all are flint-tempered. Grog was not detected in any of the sections, although argillaceous inclusions which can resemble grog are sometimes present. The absence of grog implies that naturally occurring tempering materials were readily available in the vicinity of the site.

Glauconitic pellets occur in fabric group 1 (P674b), and also as occasional grains in some other sherds. Glauconite (an iron-rich mineral) is a minor constituent of the London Clay which outcrops close to Runny-mede. It is probable that the London Clay was exploited as a source of raw materials for the production of pottery on the site. Glauconite also occurs in Cretaceous strata, where it is far more abundant. Group 1 may be derived from Cretaceous material, whereas the other sparsely glauconitic sherds may originate from Tertiary deposits (e.g. London Clay and Bagshot Beds).

Flint varies in abundance from sherd to sherd. Particularly sandy/silty sherds tend to contain less flint, for example P758 and P808. Thus the potters may have judged the appropriate amount of flint by the working properties of the clay. The nature of the sand and silt is variable. The very fine fabrics, such as group 4a (flint in a fine clay matrix) contain rare silt, whereas group 2, which is also a fine fabric, contains abundant very fine sand and silt (the sand grades imperceptibly into silt). The degree of siltiness or sandiness of the pottery, and how well sorted these components are, is dependent on the composition of the clay from which they were constructed. There is a clear distinction between sherds containing poorly-sorted and well-sorted sand which suggests that at least two different clay sources were exploited. However, this difference could be explained by material having been collected from different horizons within the same deposit. There is no evidence to suggest that medium to coarse sand (when it is present) has been deliberately added. This material is typically rounded to sub-rounded, supporting the theory that it is integral to the clay matrix. The calcareous clay of P715 consists of fine calcareous material in a clay matrix. This material may have been obtained from the highly calcareous floodplain alluvium in the vicinity of Runnymede.

Pottery production evidence

STUART NEEDHAM

Certain finds, particularly some stone artefacts and burnt flint groups, can be interpreted as relating to the early stages of pottery production. In isolation the individual categories involved can have alternative functional interpretations, but the close proximity of some of the material allows a functionally interrelated activity set to be interpreted (taking note of Schiffer's cautionary words about the significance of associations in refuse – Schiffer 1987, 19–21). The key finds are pounders (hammerstones), lower 'quernstones' and clusters of crushed burnt flint or uncrushed burnt cobbles (Plate 20). Possibly also of relevance are: a relatively artefact-free lens of sandy clay (contexts 16.830/869/870), likely burnishing tools of bone (Plate 21), and a fired clay test-piece in a pottery fabric.

The worked and utilised stone is discussed in detail elsewhere (Chapter 9). Crucial to the argument is a group of four pebble pounders/crushers of moderately large size (Cat. Nos. S210, S212, S213, S214), three of which are incomplete. All show signs of battering at one or more points indicating their use in percussion or pressure against hard/sharp objects. The four (plus a possible fifth in photographs at 57.8E/13.4N) come from a limited part of Area 16 East centred on grid square 57/13 around a cluster of burnt flint cobbles on a pottery crock (16.861/862), all at a similar horizon (Fig. 23). The close relationship between burnt flint and pottery in context 16.861/862 gives the impression that the part-vessel was actually being used as a tray to hold or carry the burnt flint nodules. Broken ceramics are known to be used in various ways in different cultural settings (Schiffer 1987, 30, 49). Again in close proximity were one complete and two fragmentary lower 'quernstones' (Cat. Nos. S222, S223; uncat. 1986 sf12) and it is suggested that the pounder/crushers were being used against these to crush burnt flint into small grits. Although the flint nodules of 16.861 were essentially unbroken (albeit heat-stressed), a small cache of crushed burnt flint, context 16.883, was recovered in very close proximity at 57.3/13.5, while layer 16.868 yielded a cluster of medium-sized fragments in grid square 57/12.

Burnt flint clusters were also recorded elsewhere in the trench (Table 21), mainly again in the lower stratigraphy (units H-J: 16.882.1, 882.2, 874, 858), but one cluster of nodules occurred as high as the unit K/L interface (16.823). Context 16.882 comprises two contiguous large spreads, at least 1.8 m across. There was a noticeable difference in the size grading; 16.882.2 had a sizeable component of more or less complete nodules in addition to others broken down to medium-sized fragments; 16.882.1 comprised overall much finer material dominated by medium to small fragments and with rather few nodules. However, even the 'small' end of this spectrum was rarely of the grit size encountered in the coarse pottery or indeed in cache 16.883. Contexts 16.823 and 16.874 were, like 16.861, essentially of nodules, not always heat-stressed, whereas 16.858 was of medium-sized fragments.

As with the burnt flint, some hammerstones occur apart from this focus (Cat. Nos. S209, S211, S215), the last being from a significantly higher context. A range of further quernstone fragments, dealt with in Lorrain Higbee's report (Chapter 9), are distributed through the deposits.

Not all the burnt flint groups described need have had the same origin or purpose. Some of the fracturing could, for example, be a byproduct of heating in cooking, which is believed to be the prevalent source of burnt flint across the site at large. On the other hand, in some of the contexts there are clear indications of a systematic attempt to break down burnt nodules. Given also their spatial cohesion, it is possible to view a number of the clusters as raw material 'fossilised' at different points of the grit production process. In the focal zone, for example, in addition to the stone crushing equipment described there is burnt flint at three stages: intact nodules (16.861), partly fragmented (16.868) and thoroughly crushed (16.883). The early-stratified clusters just to the west (16.882.1 and 882.2; unit 16.H) also seem to illustrate preliminary stages in the reduction and a pounder was again found nearby (S211) in the same stratigraphic unit. The large spread of burnt clay contiguous with them (16.899) seems likely to have been functionally related, perhaps, for example, the base of a pottery firing site. This invites comparison with other possible pairings: burnt flint 16.874 close to burnt clay spread 16.875, and the burnt clay hump 16.845 alongside the focal zone defined above (although this is regarded as redeposited – Chapter 10).

It is suggested then that in and around Area 16 East the preparation of flint temper for pottery was a regular if not necessarily persistent pursuit over a period spanning units H to early J. Phasing of some of the relevant evidence may not be precise. The thickness of the larger stone objects relative to that of soil spits excavated around them allows alternative context attribution and it is thus possible that the apparent stratigraphic span of the relevant finds in the focal zone is exaggerated. From plans and photographic records

Table 21: Summary of burnt flint clusters

Unit	Context	Grid	Character	Sampling
K/L	16.823	53/12–54/12	burnt and unburnt cobbles, minimal fracturing	sub-sampled
J	16.858	53/12	heavily burnt and fragmented	none
J	16.861	57/13	thoroughly burnt nodules, with only limited fragmentation	sample/all
I	16.868	57/12	mainly well burnt and fragmented to medium sized chips	sample (?all)
I	16.874	59/12	burnt cobbles	none
H	16.882.1	56/12	well burnt; some cobbles, mainly medium to small fragments	all
H	16.882.2	55/12	well burnt; many cobbles and medium-sized fragments	all
I(H)	16.883	57/13	small cache of relatively well crushed grits <10 mm size (see Table 22).	all

N.B. 'Cobble' is used to indicate a complete gravel pebble, or a large piece thereof retaining substantial areas of the cortex; sizes centre on the range 4–7 cm.

most of the elements can be viewed as coming from a limited 'horizon' (e.g. Fig. 23; Cat. Nos. S210, S212, S213, S214, S222, S223; uncat. sf12; contexts 16.861–862, 883, 868 57/12), roughly equating with stratigraphic unit 16.I. Even if this set had a limited time span, however, the evidence from elsewhere in the trench points to a longer chronology for the activity.

The near-sterile deposit 16.830/869/870 could be relevant to the interpretation offered. The conclusion has been drawn above (Chapter 3) that this was probably a deliberate dump and it was noted in the field as clay with sandy elements. It seems entirely possible that this was clay intended for potting; unfortunately sampling to allow this hypothesis to be investigated was overlooked. It may be significant that this dump was 'abandoned' during the accumulation of unit J deposits (around context 16.836 east) above which level there is no particularly strong evidence for continued grit production. Following this interpretation, the abandoned potting clay dump would mark the effective cessation of pottery production at Area 16 East.

The question arises as to what quality of ware the raw materials in Area 16 East were intended for. The best evidence comes from the most finely crushed flint deposit, 16.883. This was carefully retrieved *en masse* and sieved through meshes of 1, 2 and 4 mm which gave the size fractions presented in Table 22.

The 1–2 mm fraction contained a substantial minority of soil and other non-flint matter, whilst the 0–1 mm was even more heavily contaminated making quantification difficult (22 g of mainly silt). The largest grits mainly ranged up to 9 mm in maximum dimension, with just nine fragments of larger size still.

Working on the assumption that this cache was already fully prepared ready for adding to the clay, and allowing for some of the larger pieces to be picked out by hand, the size distribution would certainly seem to match that in some of the coarsest pottery on the site. It may thus have been destined for direct use. Alternatively, further crushing or simple sieving by the LBA potters could have easily resulted in a finer overall grade of temper. Some indication that fine wares were also

Table 22: Size distribution of flint grits in cache 16.883. N.B. The percentages exclude estimated extraneous matter.

Size range	Weights	Estimated weight less extraneous	Approximate percentages
0–1 mm	22.0g	-	-
1–2 mm	19.8g	12g	13%
2–4 mm	42.9g	42g	45%
>4 mm	39.0g	39g	42%
Totals		93g	100%

being produced nearby is provided by certain bone tools which are perhaps best interpreted as for burnishing (Chapter 11, Cat. Nos. B19, B20, B21). All come from around the focal zone, two at low stratigraphic levels (units H and I), whilst the third (B20) was somewhat higher, in unit J. If the surface of the already leather-hard pots needed to be slurried to facilitate burnishing, then it seems possible that the cups nearby (P651, 652) were receptacles to hold a small amount of water for that purpose. Equally finger dips like this could be useful for smoothing joins during pot construction.

Evidence for prehistoric pottery production is notorious for its invisibility (Gibson and Woods 1990, 43–4, 56). This is thought to be due in large measure to the fact that the pottery can be successfully 'open' fired (in bonfires) at modest temperatures (i.e. usually under 800 C) without the necessity for any definite kiln structure. In this practice even the degree of burning of the underlying surface would be slight, except perhaps after prolonged heating. Given these circumstances, the evidence most likely to be forthcoming would take the form of raw materials and tools required in the manufacturing process – exactly the range of evidence which has been isolated amongst the Area 16 East assemblage. However, we have also suggested tentatively that the in situ burnt clay bed 16.899 and perhaps also the disturbed one 16.875, could mark the sites of pottery firing. Such an identity would imply more controlled firing by use of a superstructure (a kiln), or at least repeated firing on a specially-prepared bed. The pottery clay lump C19, if correctly interpreted as a firing test-piece (Chapter 10), would lend support to the view that firing sites were in or close to Area 16 East.

In addition to achieving only moderate temperature, open firing tends to be rapid and economical of fuel; rapid firing gives added necessity for temper, or 'opening materials', since these aid the escape of water, as well as reducing shrinkage and cracking during drying (Gibson and Woods 1990, 27). Angular inclusions are better so as not to weaken the pottery unnecessarily (ibid. 28), thus presumably explaining the long-term popularity of crushed burnt flint as a tempering agent. Gibson and Woods suggest that flint needed to be heated to 400 C to release water of chemical composition and also facilitate crushing in order to produce chunky, non-sharp, but still angular fragments (1990, 31–2).

When firing is rapid and effectively uncontrolled there is always a risk of water failing to escape the clay body, thus leading to spalls and waster pots (ibid. 267–8). Wasters would therefore be another likely indication of nearby firing. In this context pot P703 in Area 16 East may have spalled during firing, although it needs to be borne in mind that wasters would not necessarily be so seriously damaged as to prevent use.

CHAPTER 9

The lithic finds

Imported stone: morphology and utilisation

LORRAIN HIGBEE

A total assemblage of 406 stones have been catalogued in archive (illustrated pieces appear in Figs 94–5), the majority of which are considered to be imported by human agency since they are not present within local alluvial deposits. Analysis of the material shows that a minimum of forty-five stones exhibit characteristics indicative of utilisation. Of these approximately twenty-two show clear signs of having been dressed and worked, whilst a further twenty-three pieces may possibly have been worked since they have similar morphological features. Most of the material is fragmentary and few of the stone pieces within the assemblage can be positively identified as artefact types. Hence, only tentative interpretations have been included here, where appropriate.

The large LBA assemblage has been organised into broad petrological groups following the proposition that morphological and technological studies need to take account of the relationship between the physical properties of the stone and its possible usage (Needham 1991, and Table 23 below).

Neolithic stone

Very few stones were recovered from Neolithic contexts and only one shows signs of utilisation: A16 1986 sf24 is a piece of friable light pink sandstone with a smooth surface, possibly due to grinding, and exhibiting hints of fine pecking. It is probably of Tertiary sarsen.

Late Bronze Age stone (Figs. 94–5)

The assemblage is mainly composed of various types of sandstone, which range in durability from hard to very friable, with other lithologies, such as limestone and chalk, occurring much less frequently.

HARD SANDSTONE

Within this category two main groups of Greensand have been identified on the basis of petrology (see Humphrey below). One has been identified as probably originating from Lodsworth, West Sussex (Freestone 1991), whilst the other as yet remains unprovenanced. The majority of Greensand fragments are from the latter group.

Four main sub-groups may be suggested based on different combinations of worked features:

1. pecking and grinding marks on one face with coarsely dressed edges (Cat. Nos. S219, S220, S226 and A16 1985 sf168), some of which appear to be of a much more regular shape, whilst others show evidence, in the form of blackened surfaces, of having been heated. It was thought that S220 might be a mould for casting metal; however, non-destructive XRF analysis of its surface found no trace of metal. Of special note is sf133 upon which the features categorising this sub-group are most evident. The high points of the pitted surface caused by deep pecking have been ground smooth and flat. This example shares some technical affinities with Area 6 S39 and a smaller fragment Area 6 S33 which have been identified by Needham (1991) as saddle querns or other heavy duty equipment. However, the petrography of these two pieces is different from sf133, for they have been attributed to the Lodsworth source (Freestone 1991; Humphrey below);
2. one ground surface: represented by A16 1985 sf103, which also has faint striations, and A16 1985 sf175, which is polished over at least 30% of its surface;
3. one or more dressed faces, represented by A16 1985 sf204;
4. one pecked face (Cat. No. S221).

Of the total of eight fragments designated as Lodsworth, only two exhibit signs of having been worked in the form of grinding and dressing either on the same face or different faces. For example, sf116 has a smooth ground slightly convex face and coarsely dressed edges.

MEDIUM–HARD SANDSTONE

There are seventy-eight Tertiary sarsen pieces with nine examples exhibiting signs of working. Three have pecked, ground and coarsely dressed surfaces (Cat. Nos. S217, S227 and A16 1985 sf124). The latter in this group (sf124) in particular shows grinding striations. The other six pieces have one ground surface (Cat. No. S216 and A16 1985 sf53, 65, 165, and 182 and 1986 sf24). In addition twenty-nine pieces may be described as hematitic sandstones, three of which show signs of working. Two have smooth flat surfaces from grinding and coarsely dressed edges (Cat. No. S225 and A16 1985 sf75), whilst the third (A16 1985 sf64) has three coarsely dressed faces on two adjoining sides and a bevelled edge where the two join. One example from this group has been examined petrographically (see 1985 sf21 below).

FRIABLE SANDSTONE

Due to the textural nature of this category identifiable worked surfaces rarely survive. Hence of a total of eighty-four pieces only one (Cat. No. S218) shows good evidence for having been worked. This working takes the form of three regular grooves running the length of the worked surface. Some of this friable sandstone is also hematitic and one piece (1985 sf132) has been sectioned by Humphrey (see below).

COARSE-GRAINED SANDSTONE

There are a total of fourteen pieces in this category of which at least six show signs of having been worked and utilised. The majority have had at least two treatments applied to them (grinding/pecking with dressing) either on the same surface (Cat. No. S222), or different faces (Cat. Nos. S223, S224; A16 1985 sf159 and 1986 sf12). On the other hand, A16 1986 sf176 only has pecking on one surface. Three examples of this group have been sectioned and identified as sandy limestones (see below).

PEBBLES (FLINT AND STONE)

There are thirty-five pieces in this group which is composed mostly of flint, whose sources are presumably the gravels of the Thames. At least twelve show various degrees of utilisation in the form of extensive abrasion at one end, indicative of percussion against materials of similar durability. These items can thus be regarded as hammerstones, pounders or pestles. Six pebble pounders, or fragments thereof, come from Area 16 East (Cat. Nos. S209–S214). Of special note is S212 which has battering of similar form on three corners. A smaller pebble (Cat. No. S215) is more cuboid and perhaps shaped all round. It seems to have been used for both hammering and grinding. There is also a possible striker (S208), which utilised an elongate flint pebble.

Of the other lithologies in this group many have not been identified. However, they exhibit general modific-

ations to their natural form, an example being A16 1985 sf101 which is a fragment of a large pebble with one flat abrasion face. The pebble is of a fine-grained sandstone, perhaps a Tertiary.

CHALK AND TUFA

There are five pieces of chalk which have survived, of these only two show signs of working. These two pieces (Cat. No. S228) in fact fit together (at an ancient break) to form a semicircle with an off-centre hole. The object might represent some form of personal adornment (i.e. a pendant) or alternatively a small weight. Neolithic and Bronze Age deposits at Grimes Graves have yielded a variety of perforated chalk objects, generally rather crudely shaped; they could have served a variety of functions (Varndell 1991, 101–3).

Nine pieces of tufa survive. All are natural amorphous lumps presumably originating in a tufa bed such as that seen elsewhere underlying the river channel and lower floodplain silts (Area 6 layer 42: Needham 1991, 53).

Discussion

Considerable understanding of the basic economy of a site can be gained from the nature of the stone artefacts and the sources of the raw materials. As with the stone assemblage described by Needham (1991) Area 16 East assemblage contains few clearly identifiable types. Overall the assemblage may reflect a series of both specialist and domestic activities.

The character of the Area 16 East assemblage, in terms of both lithology and morphological attributes, is broadly similar to that for Area 6 on the eastern edge of the site. A wide variety of possible functions has been advanced by Needham (1991) and it seems likely that many of these account for the assemblage under study. One particular additional component in Area 16 East, however, is the pebble pounder. These are discussed elsewhere (Chapter 8) in conjunction with other evidence to argue for pottery temper production. Such pounders, used against hard surfaces such as quern stones, also offer a potential means of crushing weakly cemented sandstones, a practice that has been inferred from circumstantial evidence (Plate 20).

Besides these specialist activities some of the stone pieces, particularly the pebbles, may have been used daily as pot boilers, while decent sized blocks once redundant from other activities could have surrounded hearths. No in situ evidence for this exists at Runnymede, but some pieces show evidence of contact with heat in the form of blackened surfaces. The tools required for the dressing and working of stone, i.e. heavy mauls, have not obviously been recovered during the excavation, but these themselves might ultimately have been broken down. The survival of a few stone flakes, mostly of Tertiary sandstone (not illustrated) with marked bulbs of percussion, again suggests that there was some degree of control over fracturing (cf. Needham 1991, 132). It is evident from this assemblage that a number of different lithologies were utilised for a number of different functions. The full range of lithologies represented here have a variety of sources, some local (sarsens from the Bagshot Table), and some from distances of up to 25 km or more (mostly the hard sandstone group), thus giving some indication of their importance to the economy at Runnymede.

Table 23: Stone groups by context and weight.
N.B. Neolithic and Late Bronze Age contexts.

Context	Unit	Stone group	Weight (g)	Percentage	Total weight (g)
16.807	16.M	Gr1	19.9	41	48.0
		Sar	28.1	59	
16.813	16.M	Gr1	6.9	49	14.0
		Sar	7.1	51	
16.814	16.M	Gr1	71.4	39	182.6
		Misc	5.0	3	
		Misc P	60.2	33	
		Sar	18.8	10	
		Sd.1	9.4	5	
		Sand	17.8	10	
16.819	16.L	Gr1	119.4	33	360.8
		Gr2	5.8	2	
		Hemsd	21.2	6	
		Misc P	130.2	36	
		Sar	20.8	6	
		Sar F	24.1	7	
		Sd.1	36.4	10	
		Sand	2.9	1	
16.820	16.L	Fis.st	15.0	1	1134.8
		Gr1	381.0	34	
		Misc P	25.2	2	
		Q	31.8	3	
		Sar	490.8	43	
		Sar F	13.9	1	
		Sd.1	166.7	15	
		Sand	10.4	1	
16.822	16.L	Gr1	63.8	29	219.3
		Misc P	19.0	9	
		Sar	122.0	56	
		Sar F	14.5	7	
16.823.1>	16.K	Sar	91.5	58	157.0
		Sar F	65.5	42	
16.824	16.K	Gr1	3.1	1	603.4
		Gr2	10.7	2	
		Hemsd F	11.0	2	

Context	Unit	Stone group	Weight (g)	Percentage	Total weight (g)
		Misc	279.1	46	
		Sar	284.6	47	
		Sar F	12.3	2	
		Sd.1	2.6	0	
16.829	16.K	C	8.2	2	420.1
		Gr1	11.1	26	
		Hemsd	18.7	4	
		Misc P	75.0	18	
		Sar	193.2	46	
		Sar F	9.6	2	
		Sd.1	4.3	1	
16.830	16.J	Sd.1	15.2	100	15.2
16.834	16.J	Gr1	60.3	15	397.8
		Misc P	249.0	63	
		Sar	6.8	2	
		Sar F	81.7	21	
16.836	16.J	F1 P	429.7	42	1025.9
		Gr1	115.9	11	
		Misc P	103.6	10	
		Sar	191.4	19	
		Sar F	183.9	18	
		T	1.4	0	
16.849	16.J	Gr1	229.1	71	321.6
		Sar	18.0	6	
		Sar F	37.9	12	
		Sd.1	31.9	10	
		T	4.7	1	
16.865	16.J	C	4.3	1	844.9
		Gr1	164.2	19	
		Hemsd	17.0	2	
		Misc	180.8	21	
		Misc P	57.5	7	
		Sar	176.6	21	
		Sar F	242.3	29	
		Sd.1	2.2	0	
16.868	16.I	C	67.3	9	777.0
		Gr1	142.8	18	
		Hemsd	6.1	1	
		Misc	51.4	7	
		Misc P	232.1	30	
		Sar	129.8	17	
		Sar F	147.5	19	
16.869	16.J	Gr1	6.7	1	1076.1
		Hemsd	914.6	85	
		Hemsd F	13.3	1	
		Misc	7.1	1	
		Misc P	6.3	1	
		Sar	88.6	8	

Table 23: (continued)

Context	Unit	Stone group	Weight (g)	Percentage	Total weight (g)
		Sar F	35.3	3	
		T	4.2	0	
16.872	16.H	Gr1	7.9	1	726.9
		Misc P	45.5	6	
		Sar	207.2	29	
		Sar F	466.3	64	
16.873	16.I	Hemsd	10.2	6	161.5
		Sar F	151.3	94	
16.875	16.I	Sar	8.7	100	8.7
16.875.4	16.I	Sar	10.8	100	10.8
16.876	16.H	C	14.4	3	482.9
		Gr1	15.3	3	
		Hemsd	2.5	1	
		Hemsd P	228.8	47	
		Misc P	37.9	8	
		Sar	138.3	29	
		Sar F	45.7	9	
16.878	16.HJ	Hemsd	6.9	3	250.0
		Sar	132.4	53	
		Sar F	91.7	37	
		Sd.1	19.0	8	
16.882.2	16.H	Sar	157.4	100	157.4
16.887	16.H	Hemsd	4.1	1	321.6
		Misc P	95.4	30	
		Sar	105.0	33	
		Sar F	117.1	36	
16.890	16.H	Sar F	25.7	100	25.7
16.894	16.H	Hemsd	6.4	100	6.4
16.896	16.G	Misc	6.0	100	6.0
16.897	16.H	Hemsd	2.7	100	2.7
16.898	16.H	Gr1	3.7	1	418.7
		Misc P	111.7	27	
		Sar	298.9	71	
		Sar F	4.4	1	
16.900.1	16.H	Sar	12.4	100	12.4
16.900.2	16.H	Sar F	2.0	100	2.0
16.903.1	16.HJ	Sar	4.0	100	4.0
16.905.1	16.I	Misc	4.8	100	4.8
16.907.1	16.-	Misc P	7.5	100	7.5
16.908	16.G	Gr2	130.8	100	130.8
16.921	16.F	Hemsd	7.6	1	704.5
		Sar	682.8	97	
		Sar F	14.1	2	

Context	Unit	Stone group	Weight (g)	Percentage	Total weight (g)
16.931	16.D	T	2.1	100	2.1
16.935	16.D	Hemsd	37.0	100	37.0
16.945	16.C	Sar	31.0	100	31.0
16.954	16.B	Sar	68.0	81	83.5
		Sar F	15.5	19	
16.955	16.B	Sar	36.2	65	55.4
		Sar F	19.2	35	

Abbreviations

C = crystal; Ch = chalk; Fis.st = Fissile Siltstone; Fl = Flint; Gr1 = Unprovenanced Greensand; Gr2 = Lodsworth Greensand; Hemsd = Hematitic Sandstone; Misc = Miscellaneous/unclassified; Q = Quartz; Sand = Sandstone; Sar = Tertiary Sarsen; Sd.1 = Sandy Limestone; T = tufa
F = friable; P = pebble

Petrology of selected stone samples

SYLVIA HUMPHREY

Nine fragments of worked stone from Area 16 East were sampled for thin-section analysis and examined with a petrological microscope. The samples were selected with a view to consolidating formerly established petrographic groupings (Freestone 1991) and additionally identifying any novel elements within this particular assemblage. Two are catalogued objects (below).

Greensands

Sandstones in this group contain glauconite and are typically greenish in hand specimen. Two types were recognised which correspond to those suggested by Freestone (1991).

LODSWORTH STONE

Samples: 16.814 59E/13N sf148 (BM Lab No. 46303X); 16.822 55E/13N sf116 (46305T)
A fine grained, well-sorted glauconitic sandstone. The common sub-angular quartz grains and glauconitic pellets are typically 0.2 mm in diameter and are set in a fine siliceous matrix. This material is a Lower Cretaceous Greensand. When compared with the previously examined thin sections from Area 6, one sample (sf148) matched very closely S33, S39, S156, S170 and S186. These samples had been tentatively identified as originating from the Greensand outcrop at Lodsworth, West Sussex. Comparison with a hand specimen and

thin section again indicated that Lodsworth is probably the source of this stone.

The second sample in this group (sf116) is very similar in hand specimen and thin section to samples of the Lodsworth material, but distinctive cherty stringers that are characteristic of the Lodsworth rock were not observed.

OTHER GREENSANDS

Samples: 16.822 53E/12N sf96 (46304V);
16.829 55E/13N sf133 (46306R)

A highly glauconitic sandstone consisting of common, poorly sorted sub-angular to sub-rounded quartz 0.2 to 1 mm in diameter and common to abundant glauconitic pellets of similar dimensions, set in a fine brown matrix. Feldspar and zircon occur rarely. The main difference between this group and the Lodsworth material is the degree of sorting. S164 from Area 6 is a particularly close match in thin section with sf133. Sf96 is very similar in thin section to sf133, but in hand specimen is reddish-brown in colour, which may indicate that the stone has been burned. This stone probably has a provenance in south-east England other than Lodsworth.

Sandy limestones

LITHIC CALCARENITE

Sample: 16.849 57E/13N sf156, Cat. No. S223, (46309W)

This sample bears a very strong resemblance to S187 of the previous report. It consists of common sub-rounded quartz, typically 0.2 to 0.5 mm in diameter, common rounded micritic pellets, typically 0.5 mm and numerous fossil fragments in a generally micro-sparite matrix. Glauconite is a minor component. It is not possible to indicate a firm provenance for this stone, but Robin Sanderson (pers. comm.) has suggested that a source in the Jurassic Portlandian strata which outcrop adjacent to the Chiltern Hills to the south-east of Oxford, should be considered.

LITHIC BIO-SPARITE

Samples: 16.829 59E/13N sf140, Cat. No. S224 (46308Y);
16.868 59E/12N sf159 (46310Z)

Consists of sub-rounded quartz sand, typically 0.2 to 0.3 mm in diameter, with sparse coarse sand, consisting in part of lithic fragments of varied rock type up to 3 mm in diameter, common fossil fragments and sparse glauconite, typically 0.2 to 0.3 mm, set in a sparry/micritic matrix. Rare grains of zircon are also present. In some parts of the sections (especially sf159) the rock is more sandy and could perhaps be termed a calcareous sandstone. These stones cannot be precisely provenanced but Robin Sanderson (pers. comm.) has suggested that they may be sandier variants of Kentish Rag.

Fine sandstones

QUARTZ ARENITE

Sample: 16.813 57E/13N sf21 (46302Z)

Consists of slightly interlocking quartz grains, typically 0.1 to 0.2 mm in diameter. This rock is similar but not identical to the sarsen reported by Freestone (1991).

FINE HEMATITIC SANDSTONE

Sample: 16.829 59E/12N sf132 (46307P)

This sandstone is generally similar to the fine sandstone described above, but it contains sparse muscovite (mica) flakes, and there is a hematitic coating on the individual quartz grains.

Conclusion

Although it is only possible to suggest a reasonably secure provenance for the samples sf116 and sf148 which are similar to Lodsworth Greensand, it seems probable that the sandy limestones and calcareous sandstones were also obtained from relatively distant sources – near Oxford and in Kent respectively. Some of the stone may have been collected from superficial deposits.

Catalogue of selected lithic finds

LORRAIN HIGBEE AND TONY SPENCE

As few flint finds came from Area 16 East, they are not discussed as a discrete group in this report. Selected pieces are catalogued and illustrated here and it is worth remarking that one Neolithic leaf arrowhead (FL19) was recovered from a clear LBA context.

Where flint pebbles have been used in percussive mode, rather than as a resource for manufacturing flint flakes and blades, these have been catalogued and discussed with the stone finds. The catalogues group finds by type or function, although not all these divisions are clear cut.

Stone

Key

Morphology:
a – round/oval pebble;
b – sub-cuboid, sub-rectangular etc.
c – angular
d – amorphous
e – struck flake
f – tabular
g – trapezoid

Nature of working:
a1 – enhanced surfaces on pebbles, e.g. polish or faceting
a2 – pecking
a3 – coarse dressing, roughish shaped surface, no individual peck marks
a4 – fine dressing; evenly shaped, not necessarily smooth surface
a5 – smooth surface (or parts) from grinding
a6 – polished high gloss surface (or parts)
a7 – battered apex or surface

Examples: a3–4, intermediate or spanning both treatments
a3/5, two treatments superimposed on one face
a3, a5, different treatments on different parts of the stone

S208   Pebble striker (flint); Layer 16.872, 58E/13N (sf193) Fig. 94
Opaque grey pebble with off-white cortex; flakes removed from one end possibly by ?natural agent, subsequently battered.
L 109 mm; MW 21 mm; MT 19 mm; wt 65.6 g.
Morphology: a; Working: a7.
Reg. P1989 10–1 108

S209   Pebble pounder (flint); Layer 16.876, 59E/13N (sf216) Fig. 94
Opaque grey pebble with rough brown cortex, small areas of batter with some spalling.
L 68 mm; W 61 mm; T 57 mm; wt 325.7 g.
Morphology: a; Working: a7.
Reg. P1989 10–1 94

S210   Pebble pounder (flint); Layer 16.872, 58E/13N (sf190) Fig. 94
Fragment of large pebble pounder with pale yellow-ochre core and ruddy brown cortex with ochre patches; pronounced battering at end; slight burning?
L 94 mm; W 63 mm; ET 80 mm; wt 487.9 g.
Morphology: a; Working: a7.
Reg. P1989 10–1 93

S211   Pebble pounder (flint); Layer 16.872, 54E/13N (sf192) Fig. 94
Opaque grey pebble with yellowy brown cortex; a few flakes detached from various points, battered on most apices.
L 51 mm; W 46 mm; T 53 mm; wt 134.3 g.
Morphology: b; Working: a7.
Reg. P1989 10–1 91

S212   Pebble pounder (flint); Layer 16.872, 57.45E/13.85N (sf200) Fig. 94
Opaque grey pebble with off-white cortex; obvious signs of batter due to percussion on three corners.
L 120 mm; W 117 mm; T 53 mm; wt 764.2 g.
Morphology: a/d; Working: a7.
Reg. P1989 10–1 92

S213   Pebble pounder (flint); Layer 16.868, 57.5E/12.8N (sf209) Fig. 94, Plate 20
Off-white and pale orangey/brown pebble, small area of batter at one end.
L 117 mm; W 92 mm; T mm; wt 993.6 g.
Morphology: a; Working: a7.
Reg. P1989 10–1 90

S214   Pebble pounder (fine, medium-hard sandstone); Layer 16.868, 57.75E/13.75N (sf210) Fig. 94, Plate 20
Very pale grey; naturally fissured with one end battered due to percussion.
L 84 mm; W 81 mm; T 73 mm; wt 693.2 g.
Morphology: a; Working: a7.
Reg. P1989 10–1 123

S215   Hammer/grinder (?coarse-grained sandstone); Layer 16.834, 53.81E/12.63N (sf143) Fig. 94
Off-white/grey; battered on several corners; localised abrasion facets.
L 53 mm; W 48 mm; T 38 mm; wt 217.4 g.
Morphology: b; Working: a4, a5, a7.
Reg. P1989 10–1 124

S216   Abrader (medium-hard sandstone); Layer 16.834, 55.56E/13.85N (sf145) Fig. 94
Pinky grey pebble; one end abraded to facets; opposing break also abraded?
L 57 mm; W 45 mm; T 30 mm; wt 104.0 g.
Morphology: a; Working: a5.
Reg. P1989 10–1 122

S217   Abrader (medium-hard sandstone); Layer 16.820, 54.12E/12.29N (sf73) Fig. 94
Pale pink sarsen; ?worked face triple-faceted; apex bears two ground facets.

L 96 mm; W 86 mm; T 49 mm; wt 370.9 g.
Morphology: c; Working: a3, a5.
Reg. P1989 10–1 120

S218   Grooved abrading stone (friable sandstone); Layer 16.820, 55E/13N (sf90) Fig. 94
Pale grey: three deep striations (a3) across smooth, flat face
L 25 mm; W 21 mm; T 10 mm; wt 12.2 g.
Morphology: c; Working: a3/6.
Reg. P1989 10–1 121

S219   Whetstone (siltstone); Layer 16.868, 57E/13N (sf171) Fig. 94
Light grey brown; two very flat, relatively smooth surfaces, ?natural cleavage planes; probably dressed sides, one straight, flat and smooth from grinding.
L 108 mm; W 54 mm; T 14 mm; wt 159.7 g.
Morphology: f; Working: ?a4/5.
Reg. P1989 10–1 136

S220   ?Whetstone/mould (hard sandstone); Layer 16.824, 59.81E/13.39N (sf119) Fig. 95
Orangey grey, brown; two smooth, flat faces meeting at bevel in obtuse angle; rest fractured.
L 49 mm; W 45 mm; T 25 mm; wt 64.4 g.
Morphology: c; Working: a5–6.
Reg. P1989 10–1 138

S221   ?Quern (hard sandstone); Layer 16.895, 59E/13N (sf202) Fig. 95
Light pinky grey with black patches possibly due to burning; deeply pecked flat surface, high points of which have been smoothed due to grinding.
H 56 mm; EW 40 mm; ET 43 mm; wt 110.4 g.
Morphology: c; Working: a2/5.
Reg. P1989 10–1 131

S222   Quern (coarse-grained sandstone); Layer 16.868, 57.90E/14.00N (1986 sf11) Fig. 95, Plate 20
Off-white to light grey brown; main face flat and even with traces of pecking, smoothed by grinding/rubbing; large part of original object present, although removals from either end and one side are evident. Traces of white siliceous rock along one edge.
L 212 mm; W 168 mm; T 52 mm; wt 2732.2 g.
Morphology: f; Working: a2/5, a3.
Reg. P1989 10–1 129

S223   ?Quern (sandy limestone – see Humphrey above); Layer 16.849, 57.10E/13.61N (sf156) Fig. 95
Yellowish-white; (1) pecking over most of one flat surface; large quarter circle hollow in one corner – possibly accidental flaking; (2) opposite side smoother but also has similar shaped hollow in one corner; (3) two sides coarsely dressed.
L 144 mm; W 133 mm; T 39 mm; wt 813.3 g.
Morphology: f; Working: a2/3, a4, a3.
Reg. P1989 10–1 135

S224   ?Quern (sandy limestone – see Humphrey); Layer 16.829, 59.60E/13.32N (sf140) Fig. 95
Yellowy grey; (1) smooth flat surface due to grinding, edges of this face appear to have been rounded; (2) coarse dressing on at least two sides.
L 90 mm; EW 86 mm; T 31 mm; wt 396.0 g.
Morphology: f; Working: a4–5, a3.
Reg. P1989 10–1 132

S225   ?Quern (hard sandstone); Layer 16.824, 59.61E/13.03N (sf121) Fig. 95.
Dark maroon; flat dressed surface with possible traces of pecking; two sides may be shaped.
L 82 mm; W 65 mm; T 43 mm; wt 347.3 g.
Morphology: g; Working: a5/?a2, a3–4.
Reg. P1989 10–1 134

S226   ?Quern (Greensand); Layer 16.824, 55.36E/12.92N (sf130) Fig. 95
Greeny grey; (1) smooth slightly convex face with many calcareous filaments across its surface; (2) opposite face and two adjacent sides coarsely dressed with rounded edges.
L 83 mm; W 71 mm; T 34 mm; wt 436.5 g.
Morphology: f; Working: a5, a2–3.
Reg. P1989 10–1 130

S227   ?Quern (fine-grained sandstone/sarsen); Layer 16.819, 54E/12N (sf98) Fig. 95
Pale pink off-white; (1) smooth gently concave face, a few small chips in surface possibly due to pecking before utilisation as grinding surface; (2) extant convex side coarsely dressed.
L 129 mm; W 59 mm; T 31 mm; wt 222.2 g.
Morphology: c; Working: a5/?a2.
Reg. P1989 10–1 133

S228   Ring/pendant (chalk); Layer 16.875, 59E/13N (sf 205), 16.868, 59E/13N (sf 207) Fig. 95
Dirty white; two fragments fitting together to form semi-circle with off-centre hole, presumably half of an annular object; the faces are essentially flat, but converge towards one side; most of exterior side is flattened.
D 41 mm; MT 12 mm; MW of band 18 mm; d of perforation 10 mm; wt 11.1 g.
Morphology: annular disc; Working: a, a4–5 .
Reg. P1989 10–1 19

Flint

LATE BRONZE AGE CONTEXTS

FL17   Hollow-retouched flint flake; Layer 16.807, 56E/13N (sf13) Fig. 96
Milky brown flint with inverse semi-abrupt retouch on right side. Slight battering on left dorsal face, broken proximal end; abraded sporadically on lateral margins.
L 49.9 mm; MW 22.3 mm; T 11.8 mm; wt 12.9 g.
Reg. P1989 10–1 87

FL18   Flint side/end scraper; Layer 16.814, 56E/12N (sf55) Fig. 96
Complete scraper on thick dark grey flake with chalky cortex. Direct abrupt to semi-abrupt retouch

to distal end and right lateral.
L 40.7 mm; MW 37.6 mm; MT 17.6 mm; wt 24.2 g.
Reg. P1989 10–1 101

FL19   Flint leaf arrowhead; Layer 16.887, 59.39E/12.20N (sf180) Fig. 96
Leaf shaped arrowhead in mid-brown flint. Bifacially flaked with extensive retouch around edges. Tip angled – possibly reworked after damage.
A black deposit adhering to dorsal surface has been analysed by Yvonne Shashoua (Department of Conservation, BM) using the Fourier Transform Infrared spectrum technique. From the results obtained it was concluded that the arrowhead was likely to have residues of a tar-like adhesive on its surface, probably a distillate of wood. Further characterisation would require gas chromatography/mass chromatography.
L 41.1 mm; MW 21.3 mm; MT 5.6 mm; wt 4.4 g.
Reg. P1989 10–1 85

NEOLITHIC AND SECOND MILLENNIUM CONTEXTS

FL20   Flint end scraper; Layer 16.924, 55E/12N (1986 sf23) Fig. 96
Mid grey-brown flake with orange band under cortex on left side and distal end. Very abrupt direct retouch on distal end and abrupt direct retouch on right side.
L 43.0 mm; W 25.8 mm; T 8.5 mm; wt 8.5 g.
Reg. P1989 10–1 99

FL21   Flint end scraper; Layer 16.952, 56E/12N (1986 sf27) Fig. 96
Milky grey flint blade with abrupt direct retouch at proximal end, removing butt. Slight natural damage on distal end and right side.
L 54.4 mm; MW 23.3 mm; T 6.6 mm; wt 6.5 g.
Reg. P1989 10–1 100

FL22   Flint knife; Layer 16.921, 58.37E/13.33N (1986 sf6) Fig. 96
Plano-convex knife in yellow-brown flint with white cortex at distal end; direct retouch on all edges except round butt.
L 27.0 mm W 42.0 mm MT 6.1 mm; wt 5.6 g.
Reg. P1989 10–1 95

FL23   Flint point; Layer 16.955, 58E/12N (1986 sf14) Fig. 96
Mid-brown flint flake with white/cream cortex on left and distal end of dorsal surface. Direct abrupt retouch to distal edges to produce offset point.
ML 51.9 mm; MW 39.5 mm; T 9.6 mm; wt 17.4 g.
Reg. P1989 10–1 98

FL24   Serrated flint blade; Layer 16.920, 54.75E/13.48N (1986 sf5) Fig. 96
Utilised brown flint flake with white cortex at distal end. Direct serrated retouch on left; right side reduced by hinge fracture from original flaking.
L 44.2 mm; EMW 22.5 mm; T 4.5 mm; wt 4.8 g.
Reg. P1989 10–1 103

FL25   Serrated flint blade; Layer 16.923, 54.14E/12.40N (1986 sf9) Fig. 96
Utilised blade in mid-brown flint with orange band beneath black cortex at distal end – Bullhead flint. Serrated direct retouch on right side.
L 54.9 mm; W 16.4 mm; MT 4.0 mm; wt 3.3 g.
Reg. P1989 10–1 104

FL26   Serrated flint flake; Layer 16.934, 57E/12N (1986 sf29) Fig. 97
Dark grey flake with wide orange band under light grey cortex on right. Natural termination with relict core edge on distal end; small regular abrupt retouch to left side to create serrated edge.
L 40.5 mm; MW 31.7 mm; MT 10.3 mm; wt 9.6 g.
Reg. P1989 10–1 105

FL27   Serrated flint blade; Layer 16.945, 54E/12N (1986 sf28) Fig. 97
Milky light brown to mid-grey flint flake broken at distal end. Possible direct abrupt retouch to left side giving serrated edge; ?residue above this.
EL 31.4 mm; W 13.8 mm T 3.6 mm; wt 1.5 g.
Reg. P1989 10–1 106

FL28   Serrated flint flake; Layer 16.952, 57E/12N (1986 sf30) Fig. 97
Mid-brown flint flake with yellow-white cortex on right side. Possible direct abrupt retouch on right and particularly left side. Some damage to butt and right distal end.
L 33.8 mm; MW 20.8 mm; MT 7.4 mm; wt 3.8 g.
Reg. P1989 10–1 107

FL29   Retouched flint flake/?incomplete arrowhead; Layer 16.921, 57E/12N (1986 sf22) Fig. 97
Dark brown flint flake, bifacially worked at proximal end; broken at left distal and left side, probably during manufacture of leaf arrowhead.
EL 36.6 mm; EW 17.8 mm; T 4.6 mm; wt 2.4 g.
Reg. P1989 10–1 86

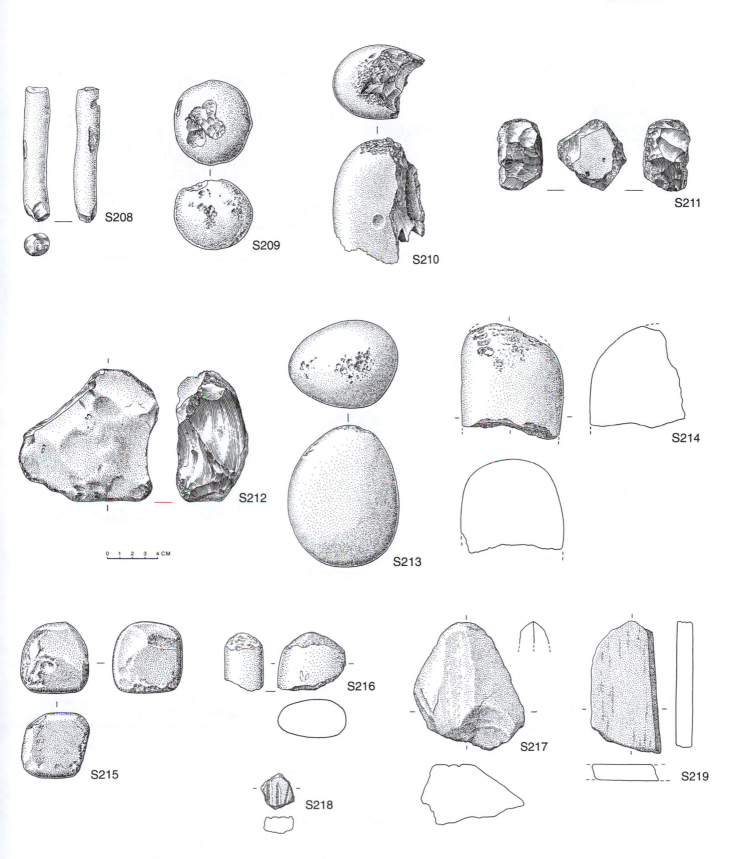

Fig. 94 *Late Bronze Age worked stone: S208–S219. Scale 1/3.*

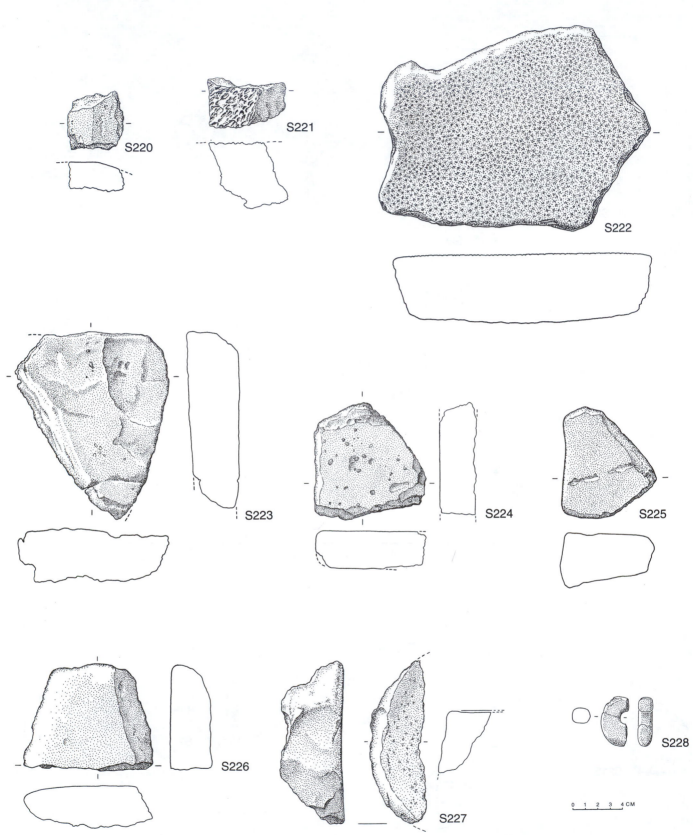

Fig. 95 *Late Bronze Age worked stone: S220–S228. Scale 1/3.*

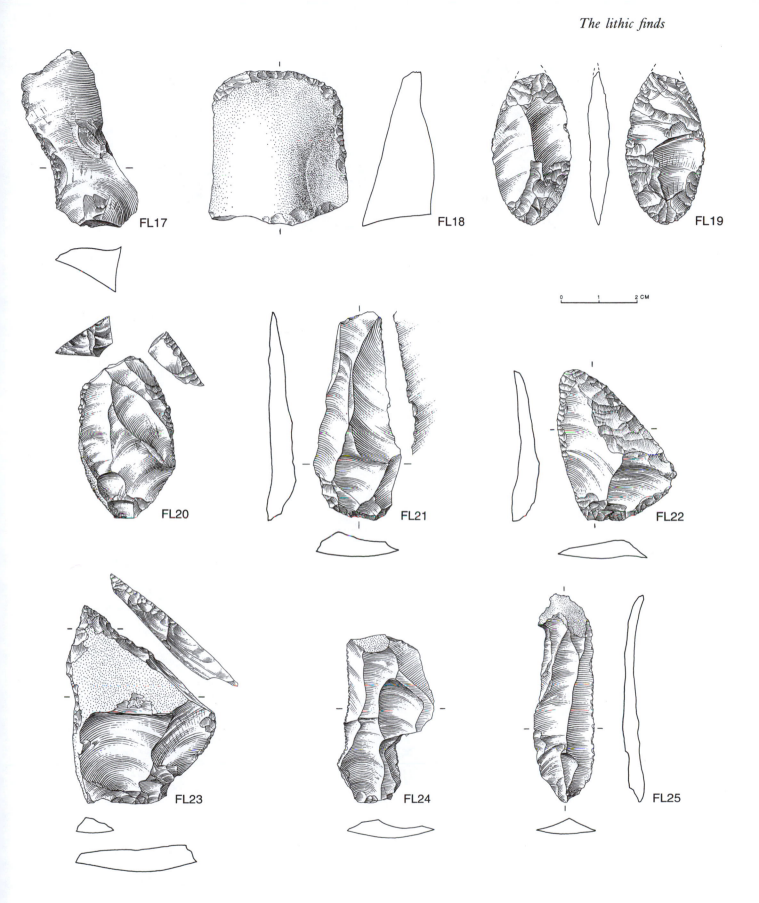

Fig. 96 *Late Bronze Age and Neolithic flint artefacts: FL17–FL25. Scale 1/1.*

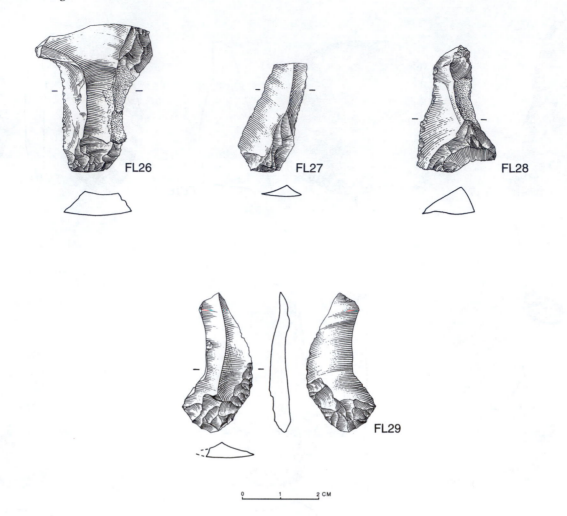

Fig. 97 *Neolithic flint artefacts: FL26–29. Scale 1/1.*

CHAPTER 10

The clay finds

TONY SPENCE

Structural fired or burnt clay is one of the most ignored areas of artefact research. Portable clay artefacts have long been a standard component of finds reports, but daub and other structural clays have received scant attention. The quantity of material that can be recovered from late prehistoric sites may be one reason for the omission; this type of material can be found in large quantities and much may be seemingly undiagnostic. Where resources are limited it is therefore understandable that fired clay will be overlooked in favour of pottery, animal bone and the like. However, the information borne by the structural clay offers great potential for a wider understanding of architectural and environmental aspects of the site. The timber impressions contained on some of the fragments indicate the type of construction linking the familiar post holes and stake holes. The size of these impressions and their frequency reveals much about woodland management and resource availability in the construction of the settlement structures. It is also worth noting that the quantities of clay used for construction and in the non-pottery artefacts will generally greatly exceed that used in pottery production. However, much will not be recovered in the course of excavation as daub survival depends on the firing of the supporting structure.

Previous reports on Runnymede Bridge included some details of the structural fired clays. The 1976 excavation report (Longley 1980) records the presence of large quantities of daub associated with burnt organic material around Area 2 feature 31, the possible round house. This had not been removed after the structure had either accidentally caught fire or been partially demolished to recover reusable timbers, the unwanted remnants having been set alight. The 1978 report (Needham 1991) contains details of only one wattle impressed daub fragment (C18). Both reports illustrate the range of clay objects recovered from the site.

The fired clay from the easternmost thirteen metre squares of Area 16 comprises forty-six finds and some 22 kg of bulk finds, virtually all from the Late Bronze Age deposits. As the Neolithic levels only produced 18 g of material (from six grid squares) they have been ignored in the following report. There have been two avenues of enquiry: an analysis of the fabrics based on macroscopic identification, and a search for impressions and structural information. All grid square contexts producing 5 g or more of the material have been examined.

Fired clay does not represent a single category of material – rather it is a general term for clay-based artefacts and fragments that do not appear to be from pottery vessels. The latter are normally tempered with flint, which is rare in the fired clay. Inevitably some flint does occur in the clay matrix, but in insufficient quantities to suggest it is a deliberate addition.

Pottery aside, the uses of clay on a late prehistoric site can be expected to fall into three main categories. By far the largest is what might be termed 'structural', i.e. daub or clay used in building construction and repair. This material is only unintentionally fired. A smaller group comprises hearth or oven debris, although in practice it may be difficult to separate from daub. A third group comprises artefacts such as mould fragments, loomweights and spindlewhorls. These may have fabrics indistinguishable from pottery vessels.

Fabric analysis and distribution

The majority of the bulk finds would seem to be amorphous fragments of daub, the decayed and abraded result of fired walls and the like. Almost all of the fired clay has been redeposited, thus there is no information on how the daub relates to structures. However, a series of distinctions could be made based on colour and consolidation broadly relating to poor, medium and well-fired material. These represent something of a gradation through a range of factors such as firing temperature, extent of oxidisation or reduction and the initial composition of the clay. It was possible to distinguish two specialised fabrics beyond the basic threefold division. A central problem remains in that redeposited hearth bases, a product of intense burning of the 'natural' cannot be macroscopically divided from the material interpreted as 'daub'. This suggests that the latter, not surprisingly, also utilised a local clay source.

Study of the fired or burnt clay fabrics has not been to the same depth as the pottery fabric analyses. The Runnymede evidence for pottery production in the Late Bronze Age suggests the careful selection of clays, addition of fillers and partial drying prior to firing. For the fired clays it appears that most of the matrices have been poorly mixed and have a fine sandy/silty feel. Occasional voids can be seen in many of the fragments, presumably where organic binding material has been burnt out or rotted away. Although some grass or straw impressions can be seen in a few fragments (see C25) it is by no means certain that this was the only binding agent. Animal hair would seem a likely alternative, although without microscopic analysis this will prove impossible to determine. It is hoped that a scientific analysis of the various fabrics can be included in future volumes on the site. To summarise, the identified groupings are:

Fabric 1 Buff to red clay, well fired, often in irregular nodules or chunks. Generally soft with a tendency to powder if rubbed. Occasional fragments have buff matrix with red 'inclusions' to max. of 5 mm, probably iron-rich pellets naturally occurring in the clay.

Fabric 2 White to grey-white surface, highly fired and friable. Often grades into fabric 1 away from the surface, suggesting it has been subjected to a higher temperature. Smooth matrix with no visible inclusions.

Fabric 3 Yellow to light brown poorly-fired clay with no visible inclusions, often grading from a smooth well-formed surface to an unfired dark earth beneath.

Fabric 4 Dark brown to red hard fabric. Characteristically has swirled texture, uniformly and highly fired, apparently when quite wet. Breaks are sharp and angular.

Fabric 5 Mid-brown, well-fired friable clay with the addition of sand, probably deliberate. Generally a noticeably sandier and therefore coarser version of fabric 2. Some finds in fabric 5 are mould fragments, but a few bear presumed wattle impressions.

Table 24 shows the distribution of fired clay fabrics by stratigraphic unit. Statistics for the individual metre squares within each layer remain in archive. The clay is not evenly distributed through the layer sequence – five contexts account for 50.8% of the total studied weight, having approximately 2 kg or more each. These are dominated by fabrics 1 and 3. Half of the forty tabulated contexts have less than 1% of the assemblage each,

although many of these are in stratigraphic units H and G low in the LBA sequence.

The most common fabric is fabric 1, about 55.6% of the total assemblage. The clay and earth of fabric 3 comprises 34.7% and fabric 2, 6.6%. The more specialised clays, fabrics 4 and 5, constitute a mere 1.3% and 1.8% respectively.

When the fabrics are analysed by stratigraphic unit totals it can be seen that there is a general trend to greater variation lower in the sequence. Part of this is due to survival – particularly true of fabric 3. In the flood reworked deposits (units M and L) its soft fabric has been eroded by water and gravel action. Interestingly it is also present in negligible quantities in unit K, interpreted as being a more gradual accumulation than unit J. A logical explanation is that this soft material will only survive when rapidly buried. The highest survival of the most highly-fired daub fabric, fabric 2, occurs in unit K suggesting that durability is an important factor in this unit at least. Fabric 5 is always present, most plentiful in units L and K where it is 5% of the unit total weights. Fabric 4 is only represented by one or two fragments in each of the units except G, where none was recovered. Unit J context 16.836 contains one sizeable chunk at 120 g.

Table 24: LBA fired clay fabrics by stratigraphic unit (all weights in grams)

Unit	Fabric 1	Fabric 2	Fabric 3	Fabric 4	Fabric 5	Unit Total
16.M	421.1	13.4	0.0	9.1	13.7	457.3
16.L	1079.0	122.4	0.0	23.1	58.0	1283.3
16.K	1587.2	507.6	17.3	1.4	102.0	2215.5
16.J	2506.2	223.0	1800.0	138.1	27.1	4694.4
16.I	1980.5	435.8	1102.3	56.1	101.7	3676.4
16.H	4725.7	147.4	4578.6	57.2	99.7	9608.6
16.G	141.6	4.9	279.2	0.0	7.4	433.1
TOTAL	12441.3	1454.5	7777.4	285.0	409.6	22368.6

To a certain extent the condition and quantities of the fired clay reflect the same story as other material in the dark earth deposits. The distribution patterns match those of pottery and animal bones – a thin even scatter of material in units M, L and K leading to concentrations in J, I and H. The flood reworking in the upper two units has reduced the amount of material when compared to the uppermost in situ deposit, unit K. Generally the size of the surviving fragments is greater in units H to J where the speed of deposit accumulation is taken to be at its greatest. Within these particular units there are also a number of specialised deposits.

The stratigraphically highest concentrated deposit is 16.845.1, isolated at the time of excavation as an in situ artefact group. It consists of 157 g of fabric 1 clay and approximately 1800 g of fabric 3. The gradation to soil on the underside of some of the fabric 3 pieces is entirely consistent with the clay deriving from a hearth, discarded in some periodic cleaning. However, no traces of charcoal can be detected in the flattened surface of the well-fired pieces.

In unit I there is one significant deposit, 16.875. Approximately half the total of 3.1 kg falls into fabric 1, with a further 1.1 kg in fabric 3 and 0.36 kg in fabric 2. This could again indicate a redeposited hearth, although there is a suggestion that the clay may have been from a more specialised structure. A number of fragments have straw or grass impressions (see below) along with 27 g of the fabric 4 clay. However, the most significant feature of this assemblage came from 16.875.3, a lump of clay of pottery fabric weighing 140 g. A wodge of clay had been held in the left hand, divided and the residue fired (see Cat. No. C19; Fig. 98). It is possible that it represents a firing test piece, although it may have acted as a 'gauge-brick', a slab of clay put in the oven on lighting to indicate when the correct baking/firing temperature had been reached. It is worth noting that there are three distinct grass/straw impressions on the underside.

Unit H contains large quantities of fired clay associated with burnt flint. Context 16.872 (particularly the lower part) contains large quantities of fabrics 1 and 3. Once again the bulk of the clay appears to be a dump of hearth material concentrated around squares 55/13 and 56/12. Although there are small quantities of fabrics 4 and 5 (51 g and 80 g respectively), there is no evidence for any particular use. Some of the fabric 5 material (all from the upper spit of 16.872) has rather enigmatic slashing/impressions which have been tentatively interpreted as 'keying' (see Cat. Nos. C21–6).

The only definite in situ spread of burnt clay encountered in the trench occurred lower still (16.899.1–4 and 16.900.1–2, Fig. 19), lying in grid squares 54/12 and particularly 55/12. It is essentially one spread but context 16.900 lies over a post hole and has slumped by 0.08 m as the fill consolidated. The clay falls into fabrics 1 and 3, 16.900 tending to be the more highly fired. No other fabrics were recovered from either context. Even allowing for damage, the limited extent of the burnt clay spread (the dimensions are 1.3 m by 0.5 m) with a depth of 45 mm might suggest that the fire was contained within some boundary. Four of the thickest fragments from 16.900.2 combine to form a flat bed with a maximum length of 152 mm with the possibility that one edge is starting to rise. Generally the clay appears unstructured in its matrix, although one small fragment has a laminar texture. Its beige colour would imply similar firing to the other pieces. No definite structure can be made from the surviving evidence, but this can be regarded as a remnant of an oven or hearth.

The concentrations of burnt clay in units I and H may be significant in relation to other categories of finds. The association with the burnt flint has already been noted, including one cache of 14 kg in square 56/12 (contexts 16.882.1–2). Pounded flint was recovered from 16.883 57/13, and stone pounders from 16.868 and 16.872. The pottery test piece in 16.875.3 comes from nearby 59/13. Clearly pottery was being manufactured in this area at this horizon (as argued in Chapter 8) and it is tempting to see the in situ hearth, overlying an abandoned post hole, as a possible firing site. The maximum thickness of 45 mm indicates contact with considerable heat.

Clay bearing impressions

Only a small proportion of the recovered finds bear impressions, approximately 3.5% by weight or 56 fragments. These fall into six categories: straw/grass (S); 'keying' (K); wattle (W); possible wattle (W?); larger timber (T) and split/flat wood (F). A few fragments fall into two categories and are thus listed in each of the sections in Table 25, except for S-classified material for which only weight is usually recorded.

Fragments bearing recognisable straw or grass impressions were surprisingly few. Thirteen instances were found, mostly on fabric 1 pieces. The scarcity of such marks would seem to indicate that grass was not a regular addition to the structural clay matrix. Notably such marks are absent from the flood-reworked deposits in units M and L where abrasion has generally reduced the fragment size and removed much of the original surfaces. With further study it may prove possible to identify some of the grass species.

While the majority of the impressions are longitudinal, in the case of C20, from 16.829 58/12 it appears as pricking. Although not certainly an organic impression, it is possible that the piece originally came from the top of the wall where it has been pushed against thatch. This surface is irregular, unlike the normally smooth exterior found on many of the fragments. The approximate diameter of each of the marks is 1 mm.

The eleven fragments bearing the 'keying' are difficult to evaluate (Cat. No. C21–6; Fig. 98). They come from the eastern end of the trench and are all confined to units I and H, most notably 16.875. It is therefore conceivable that they were originally part of the same structure/object even though there is variation in the fabrics and no joins could be found. The metrical data in Table 25 record the best preserved impression on each fragment. The origin of these grooves is unclear. The best preserved example, C22 from 16.872 58/13, has a near circular cross-section suggesting that either some organic material has burnt out or rotted away, or that something has been drawn through the surface whilst still damp. In others it seems as though the wet clay has pushed on to a loose network of grass or fibres. The grooves have smooth sides without the characteristic structure of the grass/straw impressions, although this could be put down to the quality of the clay fabric. The majority of the lines are straight, although the longest extant stretch is only 30 mm. In six cases the 'keying' is on the inside, suggesting that the clay has been pushed on to the material, but on two (C22 and 16.875.4 59/13) it is into a flattened face. Context 16.875 59/13 is uncertain in this respect. It may be that these represent a different building technique from the expected wattle and daub structure, of the wood having been replaced by

Table 25: Contexts and characteristics of fired clay fragments bearing impressions

Context	Grid	Type	Frag. wt. (g)	Depth (mm)	Width (mm)	Diam. (mm)	Cover thick (mm)	Fab.
16.829 (C20)	58/12	S	20.5			1		1
16.836	57/12	S	16.8					1
16.865	56/12	S	10.3	1.1	2.2			1
16.865	57/12	S	28.2					1
16.865	59/12	S	2.9					1
16.871.1	59/12	S	5.3					1
16.875	59/12	S	31.4					2
16.875.2	59/12	S	5.1					1
16.875.3	59/12	S	10.3					1
16.887	59/12	S	1.0					1
16.891.1	59/12	S	16.3					1
16.868 (C21)	59/12	K	4.5	1.2	1.8	2		1
16.872 (C22)	58/13	K	13.8	1.7	2.2	2		5
16.875	59/13	K	1.0	0.8	1.4	1		1
16.875.1	59/13	K	15.6	0.7	1.6	2		1
16.875.3 (C23)	59/13	K	19.2	1.7	1.7	1		1
16.875.3 (C24)	59/13	K	11.1	1.5	1.8	1		1
16.875.3 (C25)	59/13	K/S	9.4	1.8	1.4	1		1
16.875.4	59/13	K	10.0	1.4	1.6	1		2
16.875.5	59/13	K	13.6	1.6	2.3	2		2
16.891.1	59/12	K	47.6	2.6	1.9	2		1
16.894 (C26)	59/13	K/S	8.4	1.3	1.7	1		1
16.807	53/12	W	13.8	3.4	9.0	8	18	1
16.807	59/12	W	9.6	2.4	6.9	18	12	1
16.814	56/13	W	1.5	2.2	6.0	6	7	1
16.819	53/12	W	11.1	2.1	5.5	5	16	1
16.819	54/12	W	7.2	3.8	9.3	7	20	1
16.819	55/12	W	5.1	2.6	11.7	16	6	2
				2.7	13.0	18	13	
16.819	56/13	W	2.9	1.3	9.9	17	7	2
16.819	57/12	W	1.4	0.7	9.9	8	6	1
16.819	58/12	W	3.9	2.5	9.7	10	11	1
16.820	53/12	W	21.5	4.1	16.9	23	19	1
16.820	59/12	W	6.3	2.5	12.2	18	10	1
16.820	59/12	W	5.2	2.5	11.1	15	11	1
16.820	59/13	W	6.3	6.3	11.3	8	10	1
16.820 (C27)	59/13	W	13.9	2.4	7.8	10	8	1
				3.1	8.8	10	14	
16.822 (C28)	54/13	W	5.6	1.8	6.2	9	10	2
				1.3	7.8	6	5	
				1.4	4.5	7	5	
16.822	57/13	W	5.1	1.3	8.9	13	4	1
16.829 (C29)	54/12	W	35.9	3.4	14.0	20	14	1
16.829	56/12	W	7.3	1.8	12.1	21	12	5
16.834 (C30)	54/13	W	10.1	1.4	6.8	8	5	5
				2.8	9.3	10	11	
16.836	53/12	W	9.7	3.8	12.3	17	9	1
16.875.2	59/12	W	10.6	2.2	14.1	24	20	1
16.891.1	59/12	W	16.3	3.0	8.9	11	11	1
16.814	58/13	W?	4.6	2.0	8.5	10	11	5
16.820	55/12	W?	6.2	2.9	13.3	25	7	1
16.820	58/12	W?	11.5	1.4	7.3	15	9	1
16.822	59/12	W?	18.1	4.0	12.9	20	5	1
16.822	59/13	W?	240.9	4.0	10.7	15	10	1
16.829	53/12	W?	8.3	4.7	19.0	25	15	5
16.829	54/12	W?	35.9	6.2	10.8	10	8	1
16.829	57/12	W?	8.7	2.4	7.1	9	10	1
16.836	56/12	W?	8.4	2.1	9.0	11		1
16.869	58/13	W?	0.7	1.8	6.9		7	2
16.875.2	59/13	W?	1.9	1.9	13.4	7	6	1
16.885	54/12	W?	5.4	1.2	8.7	20	10	1
16.822	59/12	F	13.5	5.3	15.1		10	1
16.872	56/12	F	24.2	2.6	13.6		9	1
16.875.5	59/13	F	34.3	1.4	13.3		15	1
				3.9	14.1		19	
16.885	54/12	F	33.9	6.0	10.4		12	1
16.824 (C31)	56/13	T	194.9	10.2	37.4	44	23	1
				2.6	21.3	c30		
				4.8	18.1	27		

Key: S = straw or grass impression; K = keying; K/S = keying and straw impressions in different orientations; W = wattle impression; W? = possible wattle impression; F = split or flat wood; T = structural or load-bearing timber

Fully catalogued objects are cross-referenced by their catalogue numbers in the left hand column.

Linear dimensions are of impressions, not fragments.

?bundles of grass or straw. Given that 16.875 is thought to be a displaced hearth or oven/kiln some variation from wall construction techniques might be expected.

The wattle impressions are divided into two groups dependent on certainty of identification. The questionable category, W?, is usually a result of the small size of the fragment bearing the mark or because of a loss of surface detail. Generally only a single wattle is found on each fragment, running parallel to the surviving flat face of the clay, but in four cases multiple impressions have been recorded. The impressions did not allow differentiation between the vertical 'sails' and horizontal 'rods' or 'ethers', although in the case of C28 both are undoubtedly present. In addition to the depth and width of the impression, a suggested diameter to the nearest millimetre and the thickness of the clay covering has been given (Table 25). The average size for all wattles is 13.4 mm, (or 12.7 mm if only the certain category is considered) having a range from 5 to 24 mm, indicative of three to four years growth of, say, hazel (possibly less for willow). This accords well with the Danebury data (Poole 1984) where 'a large proportion of the horizontal rods measure between 14 mm and 16 mm' as well as those used in the Walton Heath and Rowlands trackways in Somerset (Coles and Orme 1977). Morgan's tree-ring study on the Eclipse trackway found a concentration in rods of 12 to 20 mm equating to an age range of five to ten years in the case of hazel, *Corylus avellana* (Morgan in Coles *et al* 1982).

The average clay covering of the Runnymede pieces is 10.3 mm. Multiple impressions normally run in the same direction. One exception (16.822 54/13) has one running at right angles to the other two, pushing them towards the surface (C28). One fragment can be deduced to have adjoined load-bearing timbers (C31; Fig. 98). Here a roundwood post of *c*.44 mm diameter is joined by two smaller round timbers running perpendicularly. Although the clay does not reveal any direct evidence for jointing there is the suggestion that timber 2 is set into a rebate, to judge from the angle of approach. The five cases of flat wood impressions fall into the same size range as the wattles, and there is little reason to suppose that they are anything other than split roundwood. All are fabric 1.

The distribution of the timber impressions deserves some comment. It differs from the straw and 'keying' data in that the majority come from the uppermost units of the trench. Indeed the 'W' category is concentrated around contexts 16.819 and 820, although it shows a good spread within these. Given the nature of these deposits already outlined, there is no surprise that the impressions show a bias towards fabrics 1 and 2 while fabric 3 is entirely absent. It seems that during the gradual accumulation of unit K a succession of fired clay from a building or buildings, presumably destroyed, was

gradually dumped in this area. No specific dump of material following one calamity was identified, so it would seem that the space occupied by the fired structure was not immediately rebuilt.

Portable clay artefacts

TONY SPENCE AND STUART NEEDHAM

Besides the impressed fired clays there are a number of other fired clay items. They fall into three groups: mould fragments, weights and miscellaneous.

Two fragments can be confidently identified as clay mould on the basis of form and fabric (Fig. 99). There are further possible examples amongst the clay assemblage.

The most informative piece, C32, bears part of a neat tubular matrix with bordering grooves. This suggests the casting of a socketed object. About half of the valve cross-section is present and indicates a slightly oval socket. The socket may have been short, confined to a length of 30 mm between encircling ribs, in which case the short extant impressions lying beyond, which are also tubular but of a reduced diameter, would be extraneous to the finished object. This is not an entirely satisfactory solution; one such extension would be expected in order to provide a seat for a gate and suspended core but a lower, second seat would be unnecessary. The alternative is that the matrix (and therefore the finished object) continued beyond the main socket in at least one direction. In this context it may be noteworthy that the impression at the top end as drawn is slightly hollowed in long-section.

Definite identification of the object type cast is thus not possible. The main socket or collar, rimmed by beadings top and bottom, can be matched on a few socketed sickles of either open ring-socket form, such as those from Isleham (O'Connor 1980, Fig. 44.26) or 'Ireland' (Fox 1939, No. 53), or notionally more developed forms such as those from Norwich and 'Ireland' (Fox 1939, Nos. 14 and 41). Socketed sickles have oval-sectioned sockets more often than circular, whilst on the latter cited examples the socket continues beyond the upper rib. These two features seem to correlate with those found on the Runnymede matrix. It may be worthy of note that the nearby hoard from Petters Sports Field contained a mis-cast, and thus presumably locally made, socketed sickle (Needham 1990, 47 No. 78). Occasional socketed knives have spaced ribs encircling an oval socket, as in the Plainseau hoard, Amiens, northern France (Gaucher 1978, 113 L30). Alternatively the object cast may have been an ornamental fitting in the nature of a ferrule or cap-end, either with or without a terminal knob of reduced diameter. Spear ferrules are only rarely ribbed (e.g.

Bramber hoard, Aldsworth *et al* 1981, Nos. 33 and 34); they are also of smaller diameter than the Runnymede matrix.

The second piece (C33) bears a fragment of a matrix with two flat surfaces meeting at an angular junction. It is unclear which part of the cross-section is present, since no original valve edge survives.

The weights include possible loomweight fragments and spindlewhorls. There is little good evidence for loomweights in Area 16 East; better examples come from other parts of the site. Four possible fragments from the 1985 season were recovered, special find Nos. 67, 86, 113 and 201. The first three are shaped clay fragments that could belong to either the characteristic Late Bronze Age pyramidal or the pre-existing cylindrical type. None is large enough to be certain. The fourth find, sf 201 has traces of a perforation 31 mm long and *c*.15 mm in diameter, but no surviving external surfaces. While the other fragments are from unit K, this piece is from the early dumping in unit H at 16.872 58/13. All fall into fabrics 1 or 2.

Evidence for spindlewhorls and other perforated fired clay discs is slightly better. Fragments of two certain examples were recovered, C34 and C35 (Fig. 99). Both are in the hard firing smooth fabric 4. C36 by contrast is a flint gritted pottery fabric with an uncertain central perforation. However, it seems most likely to be a whorl rather than a disc on account of its conical cross-section.

Three miscellaneous finds are worthy of some further attention. The simplest is a globular pottery bead, C37. It has a reduced black fabric and medium flint gritting. It is damaged on part of the circumference, but enough of the perforation survives to note that it was made by a tapering square-sectioned rod, thus potentially a metal awl.

One of the wattle-impressed fragments included in the above analysis (C30) also has evidence for string binding. Curiously this is in the positive, indicating that the wet fabric was pushed into an existing impression. As the clay is fabric 5 there is a chance that this is part of a mould, but the other impressions appear to be *bona fide* wattles.

A further find from 16.865 57/12 (C38) is a thin poorly-fired disc 22 mm in diameter. There are traces of a sparse flint filler within the fabric, and also traces of straw or grass impressions in both surfaces. It has no obvious function and seems too crudely fashioned to be a specific artefact such as a gaming piece.

Conclusions

The analysis of the Area 16 East fired clay is restricted to some extent by an inability to separate daub (i.e. building wall clay) from other structural clays. However, a division largely based on the intensity of firing has enabled some differentiation in primary use. The presence of the one in situ hearth or oven 16.899 and 16.900.2 reinforces the interpretation of other contexts as redeposited material of similar origin. The majority of the impressed marks are of the types to be expected on any settlement site, although the enigmatic 'keying' largely from a restricted deposit associated with pottery production may require further explanation. The general range of special finds recovered reflects the variety of uses that clay is put to on a Late Bronze Age settlement, although there is probably an under-representation of loomweights given the huge quantities of other domestic refuse recovered from the midden.

Catalogue of clay artefacts (Late Bronze Age)

C19 Pottery clay lump; Context 16.875.3, 59E/13N (sf 237) Fig. 98

Buff orange to light grey and black amorphous clay lump in pottery fabric. Medium dense flint inclusions to maximum of 2 mm diameter. Smooth 'underside', slightly buckled into a shallow reverse S profile. Three grass/straw impressions lie over a thumb print. Edge has three clear fingernail impressions and a thickened smooth edge opposite, consistent with the piece having been held in the left hand between finger tips and base of thumb. The 'top' surface has three parallel finger marks apparently scooping the clay out, which may have produced the buckling of the lower face. All marks were made by an adult hand. Two areas of ancient damage on edges of the piece occur where the clay is at its thickest and thinnest. (For a full discussion of the implications of this piece see Chapter 8).

L 85 mm; W 68 mm; MT 36 mm; wt 138.5 g
Reg. P1989 10–1 30

C20 Impressed fired clay; Layer 16.829 58E/12N (sf 229) Fig. 98

Buff/orange amorphous clay lump in vesicular fabric with eight 1 mm diameter pin pricks in irregular concave surface. If the impressions are from thatching, then this piece must have come from the top of a wall, pushed on to the ends of the straw under the eaves. There may be too few marks for this, however.

L 35 mm; W 35 mm; MT 35 mm; wt 20.5 g
Reg. P1989 10–1 43

C21 Impressed fired clay; Layer 16.868 59E/12N (sf 231) Fig. 98

Pinky white to buff orange small fired clay fragment with sparse white inclusions to a maximum of 1 mm. All surfaces irregular, one bearing four longitudinal impressions of ?grass/straw. No detail of stem visible to confirm this, however. In cross-section the best-preserved mark is semi-circular. Paler colouring on impressed surface.

L 30.1 mm; W 19.7 mm; T 10.1 mm; wt 4.5 g
Reg. P1989 10–1 36

C22 Impressed fired clay; Layer 16.872 58E/13N (sf232)
Fig. 98
Red to buff/white irregular fired clay fragment. Very small white inclusions visible in flat surface, vesicular appearance to buff-coloured body. Three parallel impressions in flat face and one intersecting on the diagonal. Variation in depths: top (as drawn) deepest at 1.8 mm, diagonal shallowest at *c*.0.5 mm. Deepest cross-section a little over 3/4 circumference, neatly circular. If organic in origin the material has rotted/burnt away in situ, or been drawn through whilst the clay was on a flat surface. No trace of detail in impression, although thin traces of a residue of dark earth adheres to the clay matrix.
L 40 mm; W 24 mm; T 21 mm; wt 13.8 g
Best preserved impression (top): EL 15.3 mm; W 1.7 mm D 1.8 mm
Reg. P1989 10–1 37

C23 Impressed fired clay; Layer 16.875.3 59E/13N (sf233)
Fig. 98
Sub-triangular, uniformly orange-buff fired clay fragment with no visible inclusions. Regular thickness with one smooth face and scoring/impressions on uneven opposite surface. At least five marks in an irregular zig-zag. No detail within marks, although deepest has U profile. Varying widths between 1–2 mm.
L 49 mm; W 32 mm; T 17 mm; wt 19.2 g
Best preserved impression: EL 17.1 mm; W 2.2 mm; D 1.4 mm
Reg. P1989 10–1 38

C24 Impressed fired clay; Layer 16.875.3 59E/13N (sf234)
Fig. 98
White to buff orange irregular fired clay fragment. Medium dense white inclusions to maximum 1 mm diameter and very occasional iron-rich red inclusions to 2 mm. A small blob of similar fabric clay adhering to one side forms a smooth face; the opposite has three incised parallel marks/lines round in cross-section but with no evidence of their origin.
L 30 mm; W 25 mm; T 22 mm; wt 11.1 g
Best preserved impression: EL 24.9 mm; W 1.8 mm; D 0.8 mm
Reg. P1989 10–1 39

C25 Impressed fired clay; Layer 16.875.3 59E/13N (sf235)
Fig. 98
Orange to grey fired clay fragment with medium dense small whitish inclusions to maximum 1 mm. Dusty surfaces. One smooth face with angled rear bearing four clear grass/straw impressions (and possible traces of others). Fine clay matrix revealing some of the stem 'veins'. Not regularly arranged, which together with the angled fracture of the piece suggests they were originally incorporated in the clay mix.
L 26 mm; W 31 mm; MT 18 mm; wt 9.4 g
Reg. P1989 10–1 40

C26 Impressed fired clay; Layer 16.894 59E/13N (sf236)
Fig. 98
Orange to dark grey irregular fired clay fragment with sparse white inclusions less than 1 mm diameter. One smooth face covered with shallow flat 'grass' impressions and two deeper slashes running across. Deeper of these has circular profile. Reverse has at least four further impressions at *c*.30 angle to the front flat examples. Only one of these rear ones has a clearly round profile, the others are rather abraded and shallow.
L 24 mm; W 31 mm; MT 15 mm; wt 8.4 g
Front diagonal impression: EL 24.4 mm; W1.7 mm; d 2 mm; D 1.5 mm
Reg. P1989 10–1 41

C27 Impressed daub; Layer 16.820, 59.84E/13.54N (sf87)
Fig. 98
Orange to light brown sandy fabric with sparse, small ?chalk inclusions. One smooth face with single rounded wattle impression to reverse. Edges abraded.
EL 26.8 mm; EW 28.7 mm; T 17.2 mm; wt 14.0 g
Wattle: EL 21.5 mm; Ed 8.6 mm
Reg. P1989 10–1 33

C28 Impressed daub; Layer 16.822 54E/13N (sf228) Fig. 98
Wattle impressed fired clay fragment in buff, friable sandy fabric with sparse white inclusions of less than 0.5 mm and some cavities of similar size. Traces of black soil adhering to surface in patches. One flat face with white staining. Three wattle impressions to rear, one perpendicular to and behind the other two.
L 20 mm; W 18 mm; T 19 mm; wt 5.6 g
Wattle 1: EL 10.9 mm; W 6.2 mm; D 1.8 mm. Wattle 2: EL 12.0 mm; W 7.8 mm; D 1.3 mm. Wattle 3: EL 10.3 mm; W 4.5 mm; D 1.4 mm
Reg. P1989 10–1 34

C29 Impressed daub; Layer 16.829, 54.33E/12.15N (sf128)
Fig. 98
Orange buff and red soft sandy fabric with sparse medium ?chalk inclusions. Outer face undulating, one certain wattle impression in reverse, two possible others.
EL 37.6 mm; EW 37.0 mm; MT 26.6 mm; wt 45.9 g.
Wattle 1: EL 32.7 mm; Ed 14.9 mm. Wattle 2: EL 9.0 mm; EW 10.6 mm; T 6.9 mm. Wattle 3: EL 15.4 mm; EW 14.3 mm
Reg. P1989 10–1 45

C30 Impressed fired clay; Layer 16.834 54E/13N (sf238)
Fig. 98
Fragment in sandy, buff to grey fabric with medium dense white inclusions of 0.5 mm diameter. Sparse dark red iron-rich inclusions of similar size. Generally a rough, sandy feel. One flat face with two parallel round wattle impressions behind. One side of the rear timber also has evidence of a longitudinal twisted string. This appears in the positive, implying that clay was pushed into a previous impression and is nothing to do with the wood shown on this fragment. Four segments of a double strand string are revealed.
L 38 mm; W 19 mm; T 19 mm; wt 10.1 g

String impression: L 19 mm; W 4.5 mm; H 3.5 mm
Reg. P1989 10–1 32

C31 Impressed daub; Layer 16.824, 56.73E/13.43N (sf125)
Fig. 98
Faced clay block with depression on reverse. Soft,
smooth surface mid-brown and pale buff; core soft pale
buff with red/brown inclusions. Curving depression on
reverse flanked by two smaller lateral depressions
caused by timbers joining central post.
Face: EL 80.0 mm; EW 64.7 mm; ET 43.3 mm; wt
195.2 g
Depression: EL 56.9 mm; EW 41.8 mm; ED 11.7 mm
Reg. P1989 10–1 35

C32 Mould fragment; Context 16.820, 56.10E/13.00N
(sf78) Fig. 99
Sandy, dull orange fabric; coarse sand grains and one
large inclusion of whitish sandy clay, i.e. grog? May be
a separate slip of clay on reverse face, perhaps part of
outer wrap, but junction with main body not clear. One
intact side (left hand as drawn) with flat contact face (at
valve junction). The top end is regular and may be
original, although some abrasion; bottom end is less
certain. The object was found as two joining fragments
at the same location, but the join has been subject to
some ancient abrasion.
Main part of matrix is a neat concave face probably
forming a slightly oval cross-section. At the lower end
a pronounced narrow groove, to form a transverse
beading, separates a short surviving stretch of
matrix/seat having a slightly smaller diameter. There is
evidence to suggest a similar groove at the break, and
above it again a matrix/seat of smaller diameter, this
time gently hollowed in long profile.
The matrix surface was analysed non-destructively by
X-ray fluorescence but no metals were detected.
Mould: EL (2 parts together) 49 mm; EW 35 mm; MW
contact face 10 mm; wt 18.7 g
Matrix: L (including 2 grooves) 30 mm; MD lower
groove 1.5 mm; estimated diameter of cast tube *c*.25 x
28 mm
Reg. P1989 10–1 53

C33 Mould fragment; Context 16.822, 56E/13N (sf227)
Fig. 99
Sandy buff to pale orange fabric; all edges broken and
abraded. Gently curved back; front with presumed
fragment of matrix, comprising two flat surfaces
meeting at a fairly angular longitudinal junction.
EL 21 mm; EW 18 mm; MT 7.5 mm; wt 3.2 g
Reg. P1989 10–1 52

C34 Spindlewhorl fragment; Layer 16.819, 56.40E/13.50N
(sf59) Fig. 99
Half whorl with ancient break. Surface orange with
buff/grey encrustation; fine almost gritless orange
fabric. Perforation made from one side, angled through
body: irregular D cross-section.
Md 38.4 mm; MT 28.2 mm; d perforation 5.4 mm; wt
16.5 g
Reg. P1989 10–1 63

C35 Spindlewhorl/weight fragment; layer 16.836,
58.00E/12.98N (sf153) Fig. 99
Half whorl in fine almost gritless fabric; surface buff
and black, core black. Irregular D cross-section with
many small (child's?) fingernail impressions on edge,
and ?grass impressions on reduced, 'lower' face. Smooth
angled central perforation pushed through from 'top'.
Md 32.5 mm; MT 18.3 mm; MinT 15.3 mm;
d perforation 7.3 mm; wt 13.2 g
Reg. P1989 10–1 64

C36 Spindlewhorl fragment; Layer 16.829, 55E/13N (sf139)
Fig. 99
Approximate third of whorl/disc with slight trace of
perforation. Orange buff convex 'upper' surface, buff-
grey irregular concave lower; fine flint inclusions in
hard fabric.
Mradius 19.1 mm; MT 9.4 mm; Ed perforation
2.9 mm; wt 4.2 g
Reg. P1989 10–1 22

C37 Bead; Layer 16.814, 57.16E/12.49N (sf39) Fig. 99
Black surface and fabric with sparse flint grits. Sub-
rounded with modern damage to one side. Tapering
square-sectioned perforation.
Md 17.5 mm; MT 14.6 mm; Perforation 3.4 mm top,
2.2 mm bottom; wt 3.6 g
Reg. P1989 10–1 20

C38 Fired clay disc; Layer 16.865, 57E/12N (sf230) Fig. 99
Sub-rounded clay disc in buff-grey sparsely flint gritted
(to maximum 2 mm) fabric. Wedge-shaped cross-
section. Approximately 1/3 original circumference
surviving, thinner edges damaged, but most of object
extant. Grass impressions on both faces, absent only
where surface has spalled presumably during firing.
EL 23 mm; EW 21 mm; Ed 25 mm; MT 6 mm; wt
2.5 g
Reg. P1989 10–1 21

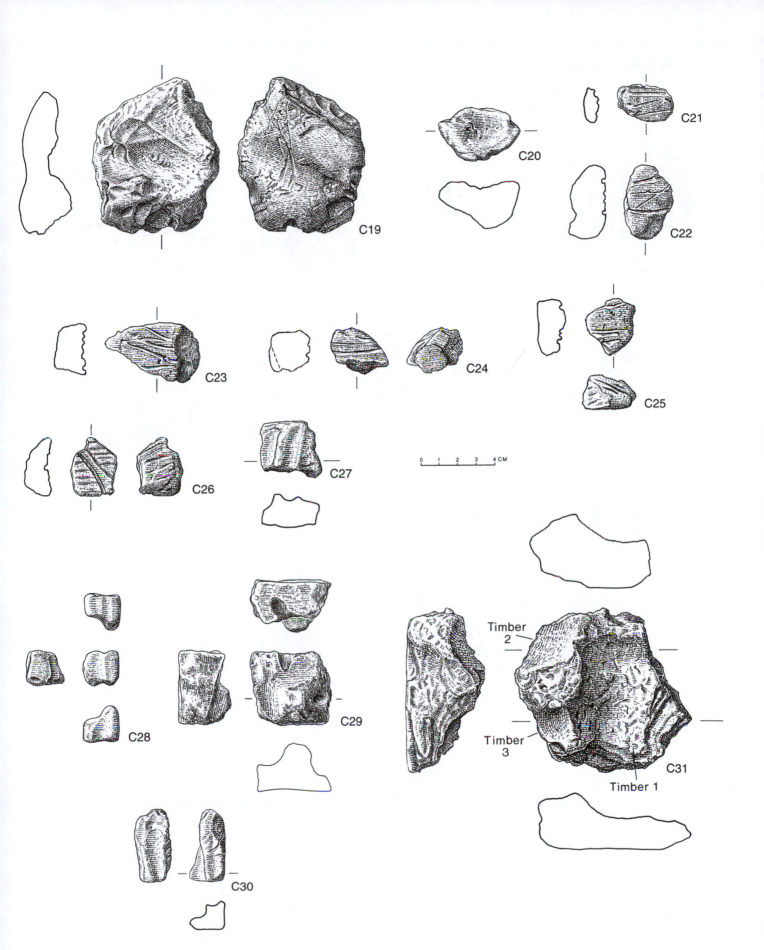

Fig. 98 *Late Bronze Age fired clay: C19–C31. Scale 1/2.*

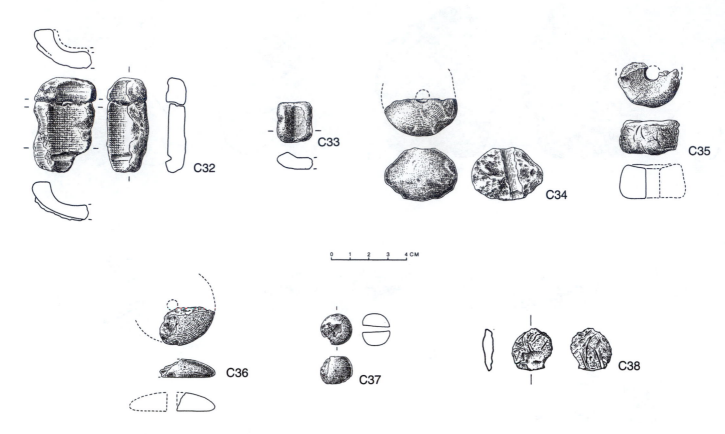

Fig. 99 *Late Bronze Age fired clay: C32–C38. Scale 1/2.*

CHAPTER 11

Metal, amber and worked bone finds

This chapter provides descriptions and illustration of selected objects amongst the remaining special finds categories. Selection is based on the intrinsic interest of the pieces. A full listing of finds of these materials is to be found in Table 12, Chapter 6, where some general points on distribution and representation are made. No overall discussion is offered here; it is better reserved for a future comprehensive look at these material categories across the site. However, a brief discussion may be lodged in catalogue entries for particularly significant finds in terms of function, chronology or links.

Catalogue of copper and lead alloy artefacts

STUART NEEDHAM

M20 Knife blade; context 16.878, 59.68E/13.94N (sf178) Fig. 100, Plate 23
Leaded low-tin bronze (X-Ray Fluorescence); blade fragment from tip end, although tip itself is missing; a bend just above is associated with an invasive fracture. The metal object was found entirely covered on both faces with organic remains, presumably preserved due to metal corrosion inhibiting bacterial action (see Chapter 13). It was lifted as a mini-block for laboratory excavation. Most of the organics have been conserved in situ, but a sample strip has been cleaned down to the underlying metal blade to reveal a near lenticular section with hints of slight hollowing alongside a rounded midrib.
EL 98.5 mm; MW (including attached organics) 28.5 mm; blade W c.24.5 mm; blade T 5.2 mm; wt 37.4 g
Reg. P1989 10–1 73

M21 Awl; context 16.819, 59.44E/12.14N (sf47) Fig. 100
Leaded bronze (XRF); green patina, partially flaked away; broken close to tip, but whole object present. Centre of shank essentially square-sectioned but with two angles faceted; less regular towards tang where end is suddenly brought to a 'chisel-like' edge by bevelling two faces. Section becomes round for short working end.
L 28 mm; MW 2.2 mm; W tang end 2.0 mm; wt 0.4 g
Reg. P1989 10–1 65

M22 Chisel/tracer edge, or tang end; context 16.819, 59.47E/12.26N (sf50) Fig. 100
Leaded bronze (XRF); virtually intact milky green patina; hollows on one side may reflect position of casting flash. A neat wedge-shaped tip brought to a chisel edge by bevels less than 1 mm deep; fine grinding marks associated. Careful working suggests a functioning edge rather than a tang in which case likely function is a light-work chisel or tracer (e.g. for sheet metalwork).
EL 7.5 mm; MW 5.8 mm; MT 2.1 mm; wt 0.4 g
Reg. P1989 10–1 66

M23 Possible needle; context 16.834, 54.42E/13.28N (sf142) Fig. 100
Heavily leaded bronze (XRF); generally textured surface; straight rod of round section, both ends damaged. Top end bifurcates, into two short prongs with slot between; these possibly the stumps of a broken eye of a needle. Slot has corrosion deposit at base, so presumed original; it is also parallel-faced rather than of hourglass profile. Bronze needles are virtually unknown in the British Bronze Age. Recent finds in Wiltshire come from settlement sites, of Late Bronze Age date at Burderop Down and LBA-EIA at Potterne (Gingell 1992, 107; Lawson pers. comm.). Neither example can be regarded as well stratified but the general assemblage associations point to the earlier half of the first millennium BC. The Marlborough Downs sites have also yielded bone needles (Gingell 1992, 114–5 Nos. 2 and 17).
Needles are a component of metalwork assemblages from Swiss Lake sites, e.g. Auvernier (Rychner 1979, 257 Nos. 27–9), whilst one occurs in the final LBA hoard of Vénat, Vendée (Coffyn et al 1981, Fig. XX.15) and several are amongst the diverse assemblage from Fort Harrouard (Mohen and Bailloud 1987, e.g. Pl. 24 No. 58, Pl. 27 No. 48, Pl. 36 Nos. 1 and 30).
EL 46.5 mm; Md 1.4 mm; EL eye 1.2 mm; wt 0.3 g
Reg. P1989 10–1 74

M24 Tweezers; context 16.836, 58.29E/13.30N (sf152) Fig. 100, Plate 23
Leaded bronze (XRF); dull green surface, parts flaked to pale green; pincer ends lacking, likely due to corrosion damage; the two arms expand gently and are not quite co-aligned; usual bow hinge with rectangular-sectioned strip slightly thicker than for arms. Corrosion-impregnated organics are attached, but do not clearly

relate to the object (see Chapter 13). However, organics have been noted on previous tweezer finds (Needham 1980, 20), whilst in the St Andrews hoard, Fife, a pair of tweezer arms are bound together by an organic collar (Cowie pers. comm.; Cowie *et al* 1991) in a similar fashion to those with a metal collar at All Cannings Cross (Cunnington 1923, 119–120 No. 11).
L 43.5 mm; MEW (pincers) 7.4 mm; MinW (hinge) 5.2 mm; T (hinge) 1.7 mm; MinT (pincers) 1.0 mm; wt 3.1 g
Reg. P1989 10–1 82

M25 Strip, possible tweezer fragment; context 16.868, 59.16E/12.41N (sf161) Fig. 100
Bronze (XRF); pale green wholly corroded surface; rectangular sectioned strip changing from squat rectangle at one end to more elongate at other; some bends are probably damage, but narrower end would match curved hinge part of typical LBA tweezers.
EL 17.5 mm; broad end 5.3 x 2.1 mm; narrow end 3.3 x 2.2 mm; wt 0.7 g
Reg. P1989 10–1 83

M26 Pin, wart-headed; context 16.872, 57.58E/13.88N (sf170) Fig. 100
Heavily leaded bronze (XRF); dull green with speckle-pocking; head was encapsulated in corrosion-impregnated organic matter (see Chapter 13); extreme tip of shank lacking – probably excavation damage; slight bends along length. Round sectioned shank expands gently and asymmetrically at the head, perhaps due to ancient damage; below the head four lobes project from four sides of the shank; they are slightly irregular in form, being largely corrosion products.
This pin corresponds well with an established Nordic Late Bronze Age type, the *Warzenkopfnadel*. Four knobs, or warts, distributed around the head is a classic feature, whilst two main variants are recognised, dependent on a straight shank or one bent at the neck (Baudou 1960, 77–8, Karte 38; Laux 1976, 97–9). The Runnymede example belongs to the straight shank variant which is the prevalent form in north-western Germany (Lower Saxony), but is barely known west of the Weser, despite an outlying find from the Thames at Sion Reach (Celoria 1974; Laux 1976; O'Connor 1980, 201–2). Although classified to the same family, the Sion Reach pin is quite different from the Runnymede one as the warts project from a markedly bulbous head. No examples had been recognised in France up until 1981 (Audouze and Gaucher 1981). Datable contexts place *Warzenkopfnadeln* in Montelius IV-V/developed Urnfield period, equatable broadly with the British Late Bronze Age.
EL 52.5 mm; W at lobes 6.7 mm & 5.5 mm; MW head 4.8 mm; d lobes 2.0 – 3.3 mm; wt 1.2 g
Reg. P1989 10–1 75

M27 Wire fragment, ?ornament; context 16.868, 56.46E/12.50N (sf163) Fig. 100
Bronze (XRF); dusty corroded surfaces; apparently broken off a larger object; irregularly curled. Broken end

has roughly round section with signs of twisting. Just before the tight bend this is transformed into flat rectangular section, which continues round the hook to a corrosion damaged end.
If the hook shape is original, this fragment would match the terminals of double-hooked wire bracelets of Middle and Late Bronze Age date. Some British Late Bronze Age examples are of plain wire, but twisted examples can be contemporary as seen for example in the Vénat hoard, Vendée (Coffyn *et al* 1981), or the Lulworth hoard, Dorset (Drew 1935). Further pieces of twisted wire are known from Runnymede (e.g. Needham 1980, No. 26).
EL 16.5 mm; T wire 1.8 mm; MW flattened hook 2.7 mm; wt 0.3 g
Reg. P1989 10–1 84

M28 Ingot fragment; context 16.820, 54E/13N (sf122). Fig. 100
Copper (Atomic Absorption Spectrometry); surfaces somewhat irregular and green; localised corrosion impregnated deposits adhering. Extant faces tend to be slightly convex and converge to an irregular thin edge; other two sides are breaks. Edge fragment apparently from plano-convex ingot.
M dimension 32.5 mm; W 26.5 mm; T 13 mm; wt 25.3 g
Reg. P1989 10–1 72

M29 Lead sprue; context 16.868, 57.43E/12.93N (sf164). Fig. 100
Lead with about 6% tin (AAS; Needham and Hook 1988, 260, 262 No. 4); conical form, symmetrical until close to narrow end which bends; this end is of small, flat, roughly polygonal shape. The upper surface bears a circular dished impression enclosed by a low rim. In profile the rim curves down to the maximum diameter. The dished face is light grey and fairly smooth, whereas the other surfaces are craggy and cracked, grey with brown.
This object is best interpreted as a sprue with a single feeder to the casting from which it was snapped. The dished upper surface may well have resulted from contraction of liquid lead during solidification.
L 36.5 mm; Md 43 mm; dimensions of narrow end (feeder) 5 x 5 mm; wt 154.7 g
Reg. P1989 10–1 111

Catalogue of the amber beads

TONY SPENCE

AM1 Bead; context 16.824, 54.57E/13.57N (sf123) Fig. 101
Near complete; restored from seven fragments. Surface orange-brown to grey; core dull orange. Large perforation circular with slight internal bevel, angled through bead; rounded exterior.
Md 11.9 mm; MT 5.1 mm; d perforation 4.7 mm; wt 0.4 g
Reg. P1989 10–1 3

AM2 Bead; context 16.836, 59.29E/12.47N (sf154) Fig. 101
Near complete with slight ancient damage and recent loss of highly-crazed surface. Surface colour buff and mid-brown; orange to dark red core. Mostly rounded surface with slight facet around smooth perforation.
Md 16.4 mm; MT 10.3 mm; d perforation 4.0 mm; wt 1.6 g
Reg. P1989 10–1 2

Catalogue of the worked bone and antler

STUART NEEDHAM AND DALE SERJEANTSON.

B15 Bone awl (metapodial); context 16.868 58.50E/12.64N (sf160) and 16.865 58E/12N (sf173) Fig. 101
Made on a fused sheep metacarpal, the proximal end removed to leave part of shaft, thinned asymmetrically in profile; some pronounced longitudinal striations probably derive from working; the shaft and point bear fine striations and polish from use and the very tip is lacking.
EL 96 mm; MW 21.3 mm; wt 8.5 g
Reg. P1989 10–1 8

B16 Bone awl (metapodial); context 16.836 56E/12N (sf155) Fig. 101
Made on right metatarsal of sheep or goat by removing proximal end and cutting away posterior face of shaft to create point on remaining anterior face; a transverse cut mark survives at the head of the removed sliver; some more or less longitudinal striations along point, which survives very sharp and bears polish.
L 61.2 mm; MW 21.0 mm; wt 4.4 g
Reg. P1989 10–1 7

B17 Bone awl fragment; context 16.834 54E/12N (sf219) Fig. 101
Shaft fragment of awl close to tip, but broken both ends; hollow-sectioned shaft left after cutting away one face of sheep/goat metatarsal; bears high polish from use, including some round tip fracture indicating continued use after breakage.
EL 39.8 mm; MEW 8.5 mm; wt 1.7 g
Reg. P1989 10–1 6

B18 Bone needle fragment; context 16.829 59E/13N (sf218) Fig. 101
Splinter of bone ground and polished to a cylinder of round section becoming oval towards notched end; species and anatomical part unidentifiable; broken at both ends, the top break retaining half a perforation of hour-glass profile – obtuse cones have been bored from both faces, thereby thinning shaft here. Probable rodent gnawing in middle of fragment.
Bone needles have not often been found British Bronze Age sites, but can for example be documented on Marlborough Downs sites (Gingell 1992, 114–5 Nos. 2 and 17).
EL 36.5 mm; MW 4.0 mm; d at lower break 3.0 mm;

W perforation 0.7 mm; wt 0.5 g
Reg. P1989 10–1 9

B19 Bone spatula (long bone); context 16.872 57.40E/13.92N (sf169) and 16.872 57E/13N (sf181) Fig. 101, Plate 21
Made on a fused distal metatarsal of red deer; the bone was split longitudinally between the condyles, where a chop facet is visible; shaft further whittled and ground to produce long spatulate blade of slight concavo-convex section. One edge of blade has 60 mm length nicked with some forty-three short and near-evenly spaced transverse grooves; they are neat and likely cut with a metal knife; they serve to roughen the edge, but perhaps indicate use as tally-stick; the opposite edge carries twenty-eight similar but fainter nicks over a distance of 30 mm; these may be an earlier-made set more heavily worn by use. A high polish extends over both faces of the blade, including over the tally nicks, but is relatively light on the condyle, the supposed handle; there are cuts on the medial condyle and the lateral edge of the bone made when disarticulating the metacarpal from the proximal phalanx.
The use of red deer, rather than cattle metatarsal permitted a longer implement to be made; deer bones are also denser and thus more robust (Legge pers. comm.).
Spatulae of this type (see for example the Heathery Burn Cave group – Britton 1968) are often regarded as weaving swords for tamping the weft threads. However, an alternative use would be for the burnishing of leather-hard pottery and other materials. The associations in Area 16 East give preference to pottery burnishing, for which the convex face of the spatula would be suited to burnishing hollow necks, whilst the flatter face served for the lower body.
L 251 mm; W butt 28.5 mm; MW blade 25.5 mm; MT 18.8 mm; wt 50.6 g
Reg. P1989 10–1 17

B20 Bone spatula (long bone); context 16.834 56.15E/14.00N (1986 sf10) Fig. 101, Plate 21
Made on the fused distal metatarsal of a mature ox; bone split longitudinally by chopping between the condyles, the one remaining serving as handle; shaft shaped to thin blade of roughly plano-convex section and blunt tongue end, slightly asymmetric and slightly tapered from central swelling; end shaped into obtuse profile by two narrow facets; extensive polish, presumably from use, over blade faces and onto condyle; many striations along blade, or slightly diagonal, could be from use damage and/or original shaping; possible butchery cut marks on diaphysis, close to condyle.
L 160 mm; W butt 29 mm; MT 23 mm; wt 43.2 g
Reg. P1989 10–1 16

B21 Bone burnisher (metatarsal); context 16.873 58E/12N (sf217) Fig. 102, Plate 21
An unmodified or minimally modified metatarsal of an immature sheep; the condyles were unfused and not found with the object, but may still have been attached by cartilage when first in use; the anterior surface of the

bone has been severely reduced to expose the marrow cavity; this wear is associated with irregular longitudinal striations suggesting that the object was rubbed in the direction of its long axis. It is possible that a sliver was originally removed from this face, perhaps indicated by the vestige of a transverse step at the top end; a number of short transverse cut marks appear on the edges of the reduced face; they are rough, irregularly spaced and of uncertain origin or function.

L 109 mm; MW 16.3 mm; MT 16.6 mm; wt 11.1 g
Reg. P1989 10–1 14

B22 Antler handle, ?for knife; context 16.865 57.59E/12.55N (sf126) Fig. 102, Plate 22
Made on the tine of a red deer antler; both ends cut flat, the proximal one retaining sets of parallel striations, probably from grinding; whole of shaft surface covered with longitudinal striations and light polish; deliberate longitudinal groove on concave face is about 1 mm deep; it may have been a start at further shaping, or the beginning of groove-and-splinter, abandoned prior to handle manufacture. Neat cylindrical hole drilled into top end 8.5 mm deep perhaps to allow attachment of inset, pommel or suspension device; two more holes, opposite one another but not co-aligned would allow in two separate pegs, or one curved peg; these enter one side of the socket and would work best in securing a narrow tang by wedging it against the opposite side; a broader tang occupying most of the socket's width would have to be notched on one side very close to its terminal – an unlikely arrangement. The socket-opening is roughly eye-shaped, but could in fact be a two-phase cut: 1. a broad thin socket suitable for a flat tang; this is skew to a perpendicular through the peg holes and seems not to have extended that far; 2. an effectively square socket suitable for a stout narrow tang up to *c*.8 mm thick at the mouth; this is co-aligned with the peg holes.

L 117.7 mm; MW 22.7 mm; W top 12.3 mm; MB 20.0 mm; B top 11.5 mm; D socket 28.0 mm (phase 1 about 16 mm ?); socket opening 16.7 x 11.5 mm; d peg holes 5.0 mm; wt 37.4 g
Reg. P1989 10–1 5

B23 Antler cheek piece fragment; context 16.822 54E/13N (sf137) Fig. 102
Small side fragment showing triple perforation and curved edge to flat end (estimated diameter *c*.12 mm); much of one long side, flanking peg holes, is cut and worn, being one side of strap slot (usually rectangular in shape); two cut facets amongst perforations, but otherwise evenly polished convex exterior; holes are neatly drilled cylindrical.
Although a small fragment its morphology matches closely one end of a class 1 cheek piece.
EL 34.7 mm, EW 12.5 mm; d perforations 3.7–3.9 mm; wt 1.5 g
Reg. P1989 10–1 4

B24 Bone plaque, unfinished; context 16.824 57E/13N (sf226) Fig. 102
Triangular plaque with curved, slightly sinuous profile, made from mandible of large, possibly wild pig; the acute angle is broken off, but otherwise object seems complete; both long sides cut steeply, one having been given a smooth finish and a bordering facet; the other still has the crude scoremarks from deep cutting and a rough irregular flange left after snapping off the presumably unwanted off-cut – this edge seems unfinished; the broad end has been made chisel-like (slightly curved) by grinding the adjacent part of the internal face, the rest of which is rough with remains of cancellous tissue except perhaps along the finished side; the outer convex face is densely covered with transverse striations and other randomly aligned deeper scorings.
A light polish over most might suggest that this object was put into use.
EL 57 mm; MW 24.7 mm; MT 6.4 mm; MT finished side 4.5 mm; wt 5.6 g
Reg. P1989 10–1 12

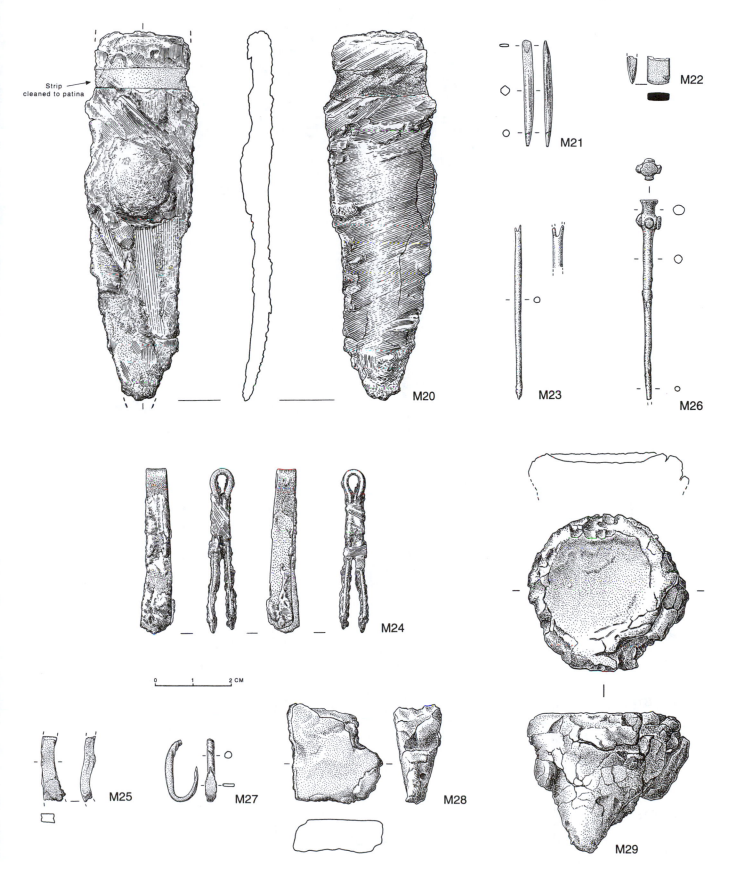

Strip
cleaned to patina

M20

M21

M22

M23

M26

M24

0   1   2 CM

M25

M27

M28

M29

Fig. 100 *Late Bronze Age metal finds: M20–M29. Scale 1/1.*

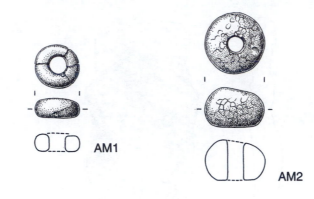

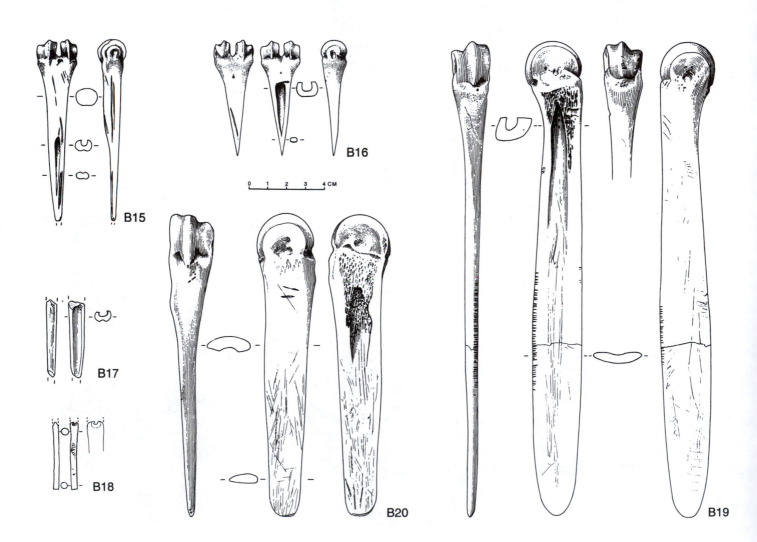

Fig. 101 *Late Bronze Age amber beads: AM1–AM2. Scale 1/1; bone artefacts: B15–B20. Scale 1/2.*

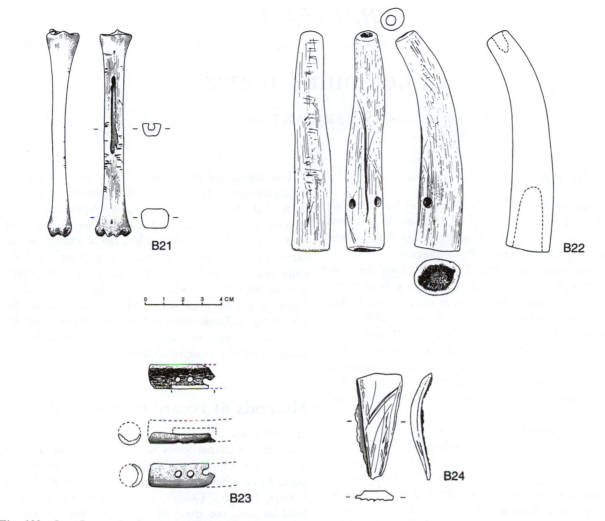

Fig. 102 *Late Bronze Age bone and antler artefacts: B21–B24. Scale 1/2.*

CHAPTER 12

The animal bones

DALE SERJEANTSON

Introduction

The extensive deposits of Neolithic and Late Bronze Age cultural debris revealed at Runnymede includes large quantities of animal bones, most being well preserved by the calcareous silty sediments.

The Neolithic assemblage (Table 29) from Area 16 East, although not very large (765 bones), is of great interest and is discussed in some detail because the broader site is interpreted as a domestic settlement, otherwise rarely recognised for Neolithic Britain. It is from a small area, 7m², with little evidence for structures or site activities, and the bones, along with pottery, dominate the material recovered. Some features of the butchery which have not been noted elsewhere are described.

The sequence of Late Bronze Age deposits in Area 16 East has been the focus of this volume. It is one of the deepest on the site and yielded 6,572 bones from seven interpreted stratigraphic units (Table 42). These provide a welcome addition to the few published assemblages of the early first millennium BC. The LBA assemblage is large in relation to the area excavated, but will still be greatly exceeded by samples from other areas in due course.

Two reports on the animal bones from Runnymede are in print (Done 1980; Done 1991) and a preliminary study of the taphonomy of the bones from Area 16 East and Area 6 has been published (Serjeantson 1991). Some proportions quoted there differ from the final results discussed below, because some contexts have been regrouped in the final phasing. The small number of fish bones from the site as a whole has also been discussed elsewhere (Serjeantson *et al.* 1994).

The methods of recording and analysis are described in full first and are followed by discussion of the Neolithic and Late Bronze Age assemblages. Bone preservation and fragmentation is considered at the beginning of each period section and is followed by description of the bones by stratigraphic unit. For each unit, selection of parts of the carcass and bone alteration as a result of human activity on site is discussed. The species, parts of the carcass and relative numbers are treated thereafter.

This report has placed emphasis on method and on the taphonomy of the animal bone because of the importance of the latter in interpreting the deposits, but also to serve as a preliminary to the discussions to follow in later volumes. Even at this early stage of analysis of the excavated assemblage, it is clear that pigs are relatively more common at Runnymede than on contemporary sites in both the Neolithic and the Late Bronze Age. Consequently the final part of this chapter discusses the role of pigs at Runnymede in both the Neolithic and the Late Bronze Age, whereas consideration of cattle and sheep husbandry is deferred until later volumes.

Methods of recording and analysis

In the first season of the research campaign (1984) it was apparent that animal bones had survived in quantity and in good condition, as had been the case in the rescue work. From 1985 onwards the Centre for Extra-Mural Studies, Birkbeck College, University of London, was involved with the study of the bones, and the author worked on site during the following four seasons (1986–89). In 1986 the bones were listed in a preliminary form. Subsequently it was decided that it was more efficient to make a full record immediately. From the 1987 season onwards as much bone recording as possible was carried out on site each summer, with doubtful identifications being checked later at the Centre for Extra-Mural Studies. Initially, the recording was done on pro forma sheets which were later entered on to database files. From 1991 onwards (during post-excavation) records were entered directly on to computer. Database reports have been created which list the bones by unit and by context. Database archive reports on paper and on disc (in dBase IV) are held at the British Museum and by the author at the Faunal Remains Unit, Southampton. The bones are stored at the British Museum. The small numbers of fish and bird bones have been extracted and are stored separately.

Recovery

Careful emphasis was placed on bone retrieval in the trench, and as the excavations were not taking place in rescue conditions there was no need for compromises to be made in the recovery of finds. The very careful hand retrieval is testified to by the recovery of broken teeth in some deposits and by the high percentage of unidentified fragments in all layers. Where groups of bones appeared to be closely associated, they were excavated as artefact groups and thus contexted in detail (see Chapter 2). The great majority of feature fills were sieved, and in each area of excavation all the sediments from one or two square metres of the area were also sieved (sampling strategy is covered in detail in Research Volume 1, forthcoming).

Identification and recording

Bones of sheep and goat were recorded as sheep/goat, but horn cores, metapodials and deciduous fourth premolars (DPM4) of sheep or goat were distinguished between the two species. No bones of goat were recognised in Area 16 East, although some have been recovered elsewhere on the site. Hence this report refers throughout to 'sheep'. The distinction between wild and domestic pigs is discussed below. None of the cattle bones from Area 16 East was of a size to suggest that they are from the aurochs.

Bones were recorded as certain or probable identifications. The latter was used, for instance, when recording some pieces of long bone shaft of sheep, where roe deer could not be ruled out. The benefit of using the 'probable' category is that parts of some bones were included in the records even where they are less reliably identified. This allowed calculation of MNE to be more realistic.

Teeth were identified to species, as were diagnostic skull fragments. Eruption and wear were recorded following Grant (1975). Ribs and vertebrae were identified to species only where they are substantially complete, or form part of a bone group. The remainder were identified either as cow/deer/horse size ('cow-size') or sheep/pig/dog size ('sheep-size'). Undiagnostic limb-bone splinters were also recorded as either cow-size or sheep-size. Those recorded as cow-size will be mainly from cattle but will also include some of red deer and, in the LBA, of horse. There is evidence elsewhere on the site for a few very large pigs in the LBA, and it is not impossible that ribs from some of these were classed with the cattle-size bones. The sheep-size fragments may include dog and roe deer as well as sheep and pigs, but neither of the first two species is common.

Recording of zones

It was clear that in both periods many bones had suffered heavily from gnawing, which had removed one or both epiphyses of the long bones. Identifiable shaft cylinders and shaft fragments were common. If recording had been restricted to epiphyses only, as has been done elsewhere (Jones *et al* undated; Legge 1981a; Davis 1992), the record of parts of the skeleton present, and consequently interpretation of activities, could have been seriously biased. A system of recording the areas or zones present on each bone was devised, which:

1. shows which areas or 'zones' of a bone are present;
2. allows calculation of Minimum Number of bone Elements (MNE) based on the most frequent part of the bone present; the Minimum Number of Individuals (MNI) can then be calculated from MNE;
3. allows the degree of fragmentation to be quantified.

The system was summarised in the interim report on the taphonomy (Serjeantson 1991) and is described in detail here. The basic premise is similar to that now used by others (e.g. Watson 1979; Rackham 1986; Dobney and Rielly 1988), the main difference being that a uniform number of eight zones per bone is used here as far as practicable. Though this is somewhat arbitrary for an irregular bone such as the pelvis, it makes completion of computer recording sheets or direct entry on to a computer database consistent and speedy to learn and use. Another advantage over other 'zone' recording methods is that it also allows the proportion of the bone present to be calculated consistently.

The current system was developed from that used at the Centre for Extra-Mural Studies from 1979 onwards, devised by A.J. Legge. It was developed in 1986 for recording the bones from Runnymede and has since been used on several other assemblages by the author and others. It is currently routinely used at the Faunal Remains Unit, Southampton. A recording method on the same principle is used for bird bones (Cohen and Serjeantson forthcoming).

The eight-zone system is particularly useful for the main limb bones, which are the bones for which the

Table 26: Description of zones on animal bones: main limb bones, first and second phalanges

Zone	
1	Medial half of proximal epiphysis
2	Lateral half of proximal epiphysis
3	Medial half of proximal shaft
4	Lateral half of proximal shaft
5	Medial half of distal shaft
6	Lateral half of distal shaft
7	Medial half of distal epiphysis
8	Lateral half of distal epiphysis

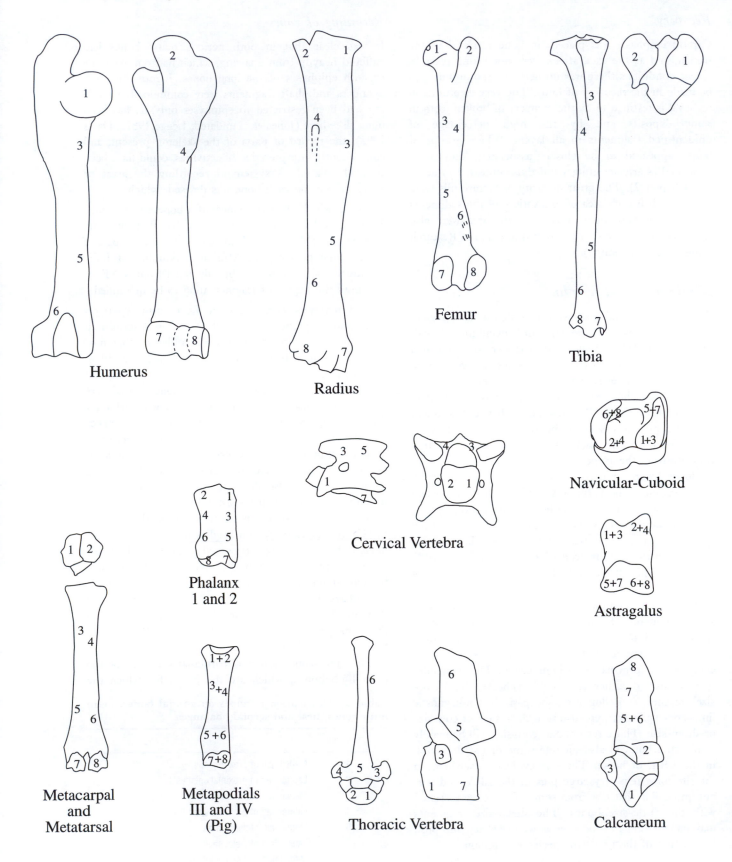

Fig. 103 *Diagrams illustrating the zonation of bones; see Table 27 for full definitions. Bones are not to scale.*

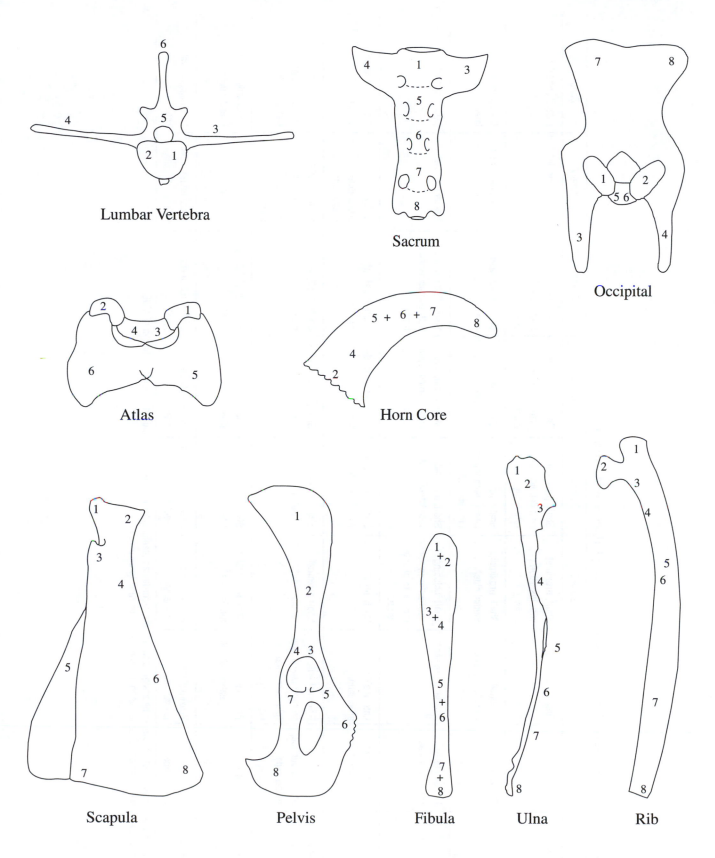

Lumbar Vertebra

Sacrum

Occipital

Atlas

Horn Core

Scapula

Pelvis

Fibula

Ulna

Rib

Fig. 103 (*continued*)

Table 27a: Detailed description of zones: long bones, phalanges and astragalus

Bone	Zone 1	Zone 2	Zone 3	Zone 4	Zone 5	Zone 6	Zone 7	Zone 8
Humerus	Head*	Tuberculum majus*	Shaft, proximal, with insertion of teres	Shaft, proximal, with deltoid tuberosity	Shaft, distal, with medial condyloid crest	Shaft, distal, with lateral condyloid crest	Medial condyle*	Lateral condyle*
Radius	Proximal articular surface, medial part*	Proximal articular surface, lateral part*	Shaft, proximal, medial side*	Shaft, proximal lateral, with top of ulnar groove	Shaft, distal, medial side*	Shaft, distal, lateral side*	Distal articulation, medial side*	Distal articulation, lateral side*
Femur	Femoral head, including fovea	Trochanter major*	Shaft including trochanter minor (horse: trochanter tertius)	Shaft, proximal, with lateral border	Shaft, distal, medial with supracondyloid crest	Shaft, distal, lateral with supracondyloid fossa	Medial condyle*	Lateral condyle*
Tibia	Medial side of articulation*	Lateral side of articulation*	Crista tibia*	Shaft, caudal face, with foramen	Shaft, distal, medial side*	Shaft, distal, lateral side*	Distal articulation, medial side*	Distal articulation, lateral side*
Metapodials (i)	Proximal articular surface, medial side	Proximal articular surface, lateral side (pig, carnivores, etc: = process)	Shaft proximal, medial side*	Shaft, proximal, lateral side*	Shaft, distal, medial side*	Shaft, distal, lateral side*	Medial condyle (horse, pig: medial half of condyle)	Lateral condyle (horse, pig: lateral half of condyle)
Phalanx 1, 2	Proximal articulation, medial side*	Proximal articulation, lateral side*	Shaft proximal, medial side*	Shaft, proximal, lateral side*	Shaft, distal, medial side*	Shaft, distal, lateral side*	Distal articulation, medial side*	Distal articulation, lateral side*
Astragalus	Proximal end, medial side*	Proximal end, lateral side*	Proximal end, medial side*	Proximal end, lateral side*	Distal end, medial side*	Distal end, lateral side*	Distal end, medial side*	Distal end, lateral side*

Note: (i) Unfused condyles which cannot be assigned to side are recorded as medial side, and the number halved for the calculation of MNE
* indicates that over 50% of bone has to be represented for zone to be present.

Table 27b: Detailed description of zones: scapula, pelvis, calcaneum, ulna, fibula, rib and horn core

Bone	Zone 1	Zone 2	Zone 3	Zone 4	Zone 5	Zone 6	Zone 7	Zone 8
Scapula	Dorsal part of articulation, with tuber scapulae	Glenoid*	Origin of spine	Caudal border at neck*	Cranial border*	Caudal border*	Spine at dorsal border	Caudal angle
Pelvis (i)	Ilium, wing with area of articulation with sacrum	Ilium, shaft	Ilium, acetabulum, with ilio-pectineal groove	Ilium, acetabulum	Pubis, acetabulum	Pubis, symphysis	Ischium, acetabulum	Ischium, blade*
Calcaneum	Sustentaculum	Articular facet	Anterior process	Body, proximal part	Body, proximal part	Body, distal part	Body, distal part	Distal epiphysis (tuber calcis)
Ulna	Epiphysis	Body of olecranon	Semilunar notch	Shaft proximal, area of interosseous space	Shaft proximal, area of attachment to radius (sheep, cattle)	Shaft, distal	Shaft, distal with fusion point if immature	Distal epiphysis
Fibula	Proximal epiphysis	Proximal epiphysis	Shaft proximal	Shaft proximal	Shaft, distal	Shaft, distal	Distal epiphysis	Distal epiphysis
Rib (ii)	Head	Tubercle	Dorsal end	Dorsal end	Ventral end	Ventral end	Ventral end	Ventral end
Horn core	Area of attachment to skull, medial side	Area of attachment to skull, lateral side	Bottom half, medial side	Bottom half, lateral side	Top half, medial side	Top half, lateral side	Tip	Tip

Note: (i) it is rare to get zones 3 and 4 separately

(ii) the transition from rectangular cross-section to flat cross-section is taken as the division between the dorsal and the ventral end

* indicates that over 50% of bone has to be represented for zone to be present.

Table 27c: Detailed description of zones: bilaterally symmetrical bones

Bone	Zone 1	Zone 2	Zone 3	Zone 4	Zone 5	Zone 6	Zone 7	Zone 8
Occiput	L condyle	R condyle	L para-mastoid	R para-mastoid	L basilar part	R basilar part	L squamous part	R squamous part
Atlas	L cranial articulation	R cranial articulation	L dorsal side	R dorsal side	L ventral side	R ventral side	L caudal articulation	R caudal articulation
Other vertebrae (i)	L half vertebral body, cranial	R half vertebral body, cranial	L transverse process	R transverse process	L half neural arch	R half neural arch	L half vertebral body, caudal	R half vertebral body, caudal
Sacrum	L half, 1st sacral vert.	R half, 1st sacral vert.	L half, wing	R half, wing	Segment II	Segment III	Segment IV	Segment V

Note: (i) Thoracic vertebrae: neural arch is recorded as zone 5 and distal end of spinous process as zone 6.

fragmentation patterns are usually of most interest. The zones for the main limb bones and first and second phalanges are summarised in Table 26 and Fig. 103.

For mid-line bones such as the vertebrae and the occiput (Fig. 103), zones 1, 3, 5 and 7 are used for the left half of the bone and 2, 4, 6 and 8 are used for the right hand side. There are also adaptations for asymmetrical and irregularly shaped bones such as the scapula, pelvis, ulna, fibula and ribs (Fig. 103).

Zones are recorded as present ('1') or absent ('0'), in eight separate database fields. A zone is recorded as present *either* when a distinct feature on the bone is defined, such as the ulnar groove on the proximal radius shaft of ungulates (cf. Watson 1979) *or* when over 50% of the zone is present. These are defined above (Tables 27a, b and c). Use of the over 50% criterion is indicated with an asterisk.

A standard number of eight zones is not the ideal division of some bones. The top of the trochlea of the distal femur, for instance, is sometimes found on its own yet cannot be zoned using this system. The use of eight zones is excessively detailed for small bones such as the fibula, astragalus and navicular-cuboid, so these, if zoned at all, are divided into four zones (Fig. 103). Of the skull, zones are recorded only for the occipital and the horn cores. Vertebrae and ribs were zoned only when securely identified to species. Mandibles were not zoned for this study. Table 28 summarises which bones were zoned.

Table 28: Zoned and not zoned animal bones

Zoned	Not zoned
scapula	carpals
humerus	small tarsals
radius	sesamoids
ulna	patella
pelvis	small phalanges
femur	lateral metapodials
tibia	disarticulated parts of skull
astragalus	isolated teeth
calcaneum	sternum
metacarpal	hyoid
metatarsal	
phalanx 1	
phalanx 2	
occiput	
horn core	
vertebrae	
sacrum	

Calculation of MNE, MNI and degree of fragmentation

In order to calculate MNE, the number of each zone present for each bone of each relevant species was counted. The most frequent zone is taken to give the MNE. The most frequent element gives the MNI.

The second calculation which can be made is the fraction of the bone present. For this the number of zones on each bone recorded as present are summed. The results are calculated as eighths of a bone, which can also be expressed as a percentage between 12.5% and 100% (Serjeantson 1991). Other systems which allow the calculation of the proportion of the bone present (e.g. Jones *et al*, undated) do not have the advantage of specifying which areas of the bone were present. The results at Runnymede have been used to show how bone fragmentation varied between deposits (Serjeantson 1991).

Tables of anatomical distribution

The tables of anatomical distributions (Tables 33–5 and 47–9) show both the number of identified bones (NISP), the MNE and in the final row, the overall MNI, derived from the most frequent element in the skeleton. For mandibles, MNE has been calculated from the minimum number of jaws. For other bones it has been estimated from a count of the most frequent left, right or midline bone, not taking into account fusion stage or age. Examples of how the MNE count was arrived at is shown in the tables for the anatomical distribution of cattle, pigs and sheep in the Neolithic (Tables 33–5) and in the anatomical distribution of pig in the LBA unit K (Table 50). MNE was calculated using this method for each species from the LBA units (details in archive).

Burnt bones

It was noted when recording started on site that different types of burning were evident on the bones. The incidence and type of burnt bone can provide information on how meat was consumed, how bones were processed and whether some bones were exposed to fire; therefore traces of burning on bones were carefully recorded.

Calcined and charred bones were recorded as 'white', 'black and white', or 'black' as appropriate (Tables 31 and 46). These were straightforward to recognise. Experiments (Gilchrist and Mytum 1986) have shown that this is the colour and texture of bones burned in an open fire at temperatures of 400 C and upwards. As there is no reason to invoke deliberate association with human cremation here, these have been interpreted as bones which have been thrown on to an open fire. Where charred at one end only, bones were recorded as 'black and brown'.

Other types of burning were less easy to recognise with certainty. Many bones in the Bronze Age deposits were brown or pink in colour, but not charred or calcined. Unlike other bones, even those with very good surface preservation, the surface of these pink bones has not been attacked by chemical degradation, soil fauna or rootlet channelling. The colour change was slight, usually only being visible in daylight, and there must be some doubt about whether such bones had indeed been in direct contact with heat. This phenomenon has not been described in other archaeological assemblages. This may be because it is rare, but may also be because the evidence is masked in sediments which stain bones a darker brown. The exceptionally good bone surface preservation was a contributory factor in allowing the burning to be recognised.

A third type of burning was recognised clearly only when a number of butchered long bones from all areas were examined together. Some of the butchered long bones of cattle and fewer of pig and sheep have a patch of burning close to the point of impact where the bone shaft has been smashed. The burnt patch is only slightly darker brown than the rest of the bone and very rarely charred, but there is localised cracking and exfoliation of the bone surface. This was recorded as 'partly burnt'. In the early stages of analysis (including much Area 16 material), recognition of this was still doubtful and such bones were recorded as 'probably burnt'. On some bones no colour change was visible, and there was only the area of exfoliation at the point of impact to suggest that the bone had been exposed to heat. It is likely that this combination of burning with smashing has been under-recorded. This localised patch of burning seems to be similar to that seen on some red deer antlers from other sites where they have been modified to make picks and rakes. It was noted on the antler from Grimes Graves and Durrington Walls (Clutton-Brock 1984), and is also present on some of the worked antler and the bones from the fill of the Stonehenge Ditch (Serjeantson 1995). Experimental work at Durham University has demonstrated that by briefly exposing long bones to open heat on a fire a less strong blow is needed to smash the shaft to extract the marrow (Paul Stokes unpublished). This would seem to offer a satisfactory explanation for this kind of localised burning.

Gnawed bones

Gnawing was recognised when the bone was punctured, or when the end was irregular or 'crenulated' as illustrated by Binford (1981) and as observed on modern gnawed specimens. Many bones have striations or shallow gouges on the surface at the damaged end. On the Runnymede bones the gouge marks are often stained a slightly darker brown than the rest of the bone surface.

Where punctures are present, there is little doubt that the gnawing was the work of carnivores, presumably domestic dogs. Pigs also gnaw bones, destroying the same parts of bones as dogs (Greenfield 1988), but they do not mark them with punctures. The possibility cannot be ruled out that some of the damage observed at Runnymede was due to pigs. A small number of bones have the narrow parallel marks characteristic of rodent gnawing.

The presence and location on the bone of traces of gnawing was recorded (Tables 32 and 45). The proportion on which gnawing was seen will always underestimate the proportion which was in fact attacked by dogs, as they can splinter bones in a way which leaves no tooth mark on the individual splinters. The long bones can fracture spirally just as when smashed by humans to extract the marrow.

Surface preservation and fragmentation

Both the activities which took place at the settlement and post-depositional damage have affected bone preservation. This in turn has an influence on fragmentation, the proportion of identified bones and the relative proportion of teeth and jaws to other bones. These alterations affect interpretation of the bone samples from the individual units and the whole assemblage, and are discussed in detail for each period and unit.

Articulated bones and conjoins

Conjoins in bones, whether unfused bones found with the epiphyses or articulating anatomical elements, are not uncommon on sites of hunter-foragers but are comparatively rare in settlements of farming communities. As well as revealing on-site activities, they indicate that material is close to its original place of deposition and has been little disturbed. Finds of articulated and associated bones were recorded in situ whenever recognised and otherwise during post-excavation; metapodials were kept out to see if further unrecorded associations were present (Serjeantson 1991). These are also discussed for individual units.

The Neolithic assemblage

The assemblage from Area 16 East is of bones which have accumulated in a depression on the settlement with other material such as pottery and flint. Bones were recovered from units B, C, D, E and F (Table 29). Over half of the total of 765 bones (382 bones) are from the lowest unit, B, coming from three bone groups, and this unit is discussed in more detail than the others. The species present are cattle, pig, sheep, red deer and dog.

Table 29: Neolithic animal bones: species present and number of identified bones (n). The percentage of identified bones (%id) is shown in the top half of the table, and the percentage of the total in the lower half.

UNIT	B n	B % id	C n	C % id	D n	D % id	E n	E % id	F n	F % id	total	% id
PIG	81	39.7	13	56.5	7	100.0	16	72.7	3	20.0	120	44.3
CATTLE	106	52.0	9	39.1			4	18.2	8	53.3	127	46.9
SHEEP	14	6.9	1	4.3			2	9.1	2	13.3	19	7.0
RED DEER	3	1.5							1	6.7	4	1.5
DOG									1	6.7	1	0.4
		% total		% total		% total		% total		% total		% total
subtotal identified	204	53.4	23	25.0	7	17.9	22	17.1	15	12.2	271	35.4
SHEEP SIZE	29	7.6	11	12.0	16	41.0	18	14.0	16	13.0	90	11.8
COW SIZE	64	16.8	21	22.8	6	15.4	6	4.7	9	7.3	106	13.9
UNIDENTIFIED	85	22.3	37	40.2	10	25.6	83	64.3	83	67.5	298	39.0
total	382		92		39		129		123		765	

There is a degree of selection of the parts of the carcass discarded in at least two of the bone groups.

Preservation and survival

The surface preservation of much of the Neolithic bone is good, though there is surface erosion on the bones from the upper part of the Neolithic sequence (Table 30). Small patches of dark brown concretion, probably a soil fungus, adhere to most fragments except those which are calcined or charred. Those defined as having 'good' surface preservation are only slightly eroded, while the 'eroded' bone has a cracked surface with the cortex partly flaked off. On some, areas of the exterior surface are a darker brown than the rest of the bone. The possibility was considered that this results from contact with heat, but as it is ubiquitous in the Neolithic layers and is not associated otherwise with evidence for burnt wood, stone or bone, it is interpreted as local contact with more organic material. On a few bones the stain covered the entire bone and preservation was recorded as 'very good'. Bone surface condition was recorded for each bone other than mandibles, teeth and unidentified fragments. Preservation diminishes steadily from the bottom to the top of the sequence, units B to F. In unit B over 90% is well preserved, but the proportion is only 21% in E and less than 2% in F (Table 30).

Although superficially many Neolithic bones looked in good condition, attempts to radiocarbon date some from unit B were unsuccessful, apparently because of poor collagen preservation. This is thought to be due to adverse ground water conditions at some time between the Neolithic and the present.

Two other features of the assemblage reflect the poorer bone survival in the upper Neolithic units. It has already been demonstrated (Serjeantson 1991, 83), that individual bones survive as larger fragments in B than in the units above. The proportion of unidentified bones increases from the lowest unit to the top (Table 29).

Table 30: Neolithic bone surface preservation. Percentages based on bones identified to anatomical element, excluding teeth.

UNIT	B	C	D	E	F
VERY GOOD	1.2	0.0	0.0	3.0	0.9
GOOD	90.4	69.1	43.0	21.2	1.8
ERODED	8.4	30.9	57.0	75.8	97.3
n	239	55	35	66	111

The proportion of bones on which traces of gnawing is clear is quite high, between 9% and 17% of identified bones. When calculated as a percentage of all bones (Table 32), the percentage decreases from the lower to the upper units, from 7% in B to less than 1% in F. The proportion is therefore greater in the units where the bone is less fragmented and better preserved. This is contrary to the finding which might have been expected. It was also noted in the Late Bronze Age assemblage (see below). It must reflect the fact that gnawing cannot be so clearly distinguished where the surface is more damaged and the bones more highly fragmented. It should not be taken to indicate that there was less dog gnawing on bones from units E and F. This is a useful caution against taking crude percentages as a reflection of the amount of dog gnawing, without first understanding the taphonomy.

Table 31: Neolithic burnt bones. Percentage in each unit. (See text for explanation of colours.)

UNIT	B	C	D	E	F
WHITE	0.3	0.0	0.0	0.0	0.8
BLACK and WHITE	0.0	1.1	0.0	0.0	3.3
BLACK	0.3	0.0	0.0	0.0	0.0
BLACK and BROWN	0.5	1.1	0.0	0.8	0.8
BROWN	0.0	0.0	0.0	1.6	0.0
GREY/PINK	0.0	0.0	0.0	0.0	0.8
PARTLY	1.0	0.0	0.0	0.0	0.0
PROBABLY	0.5	0.0	0.0	0.0	0.0
OVERALL % BURNT	2.6	2.2	0.0	2.3	5.7
n	382	92	39	129	123

Table 32: Neolithic gnawed bones. Percentages of identified bones, of identified bones excluding teeth and of total are shown.

UNIT	B	C	D	E	F
% GNAWED					
of total	7.1	4.3	2.6	1.6	0.8
of identified	13.2	17.4	14.3	9.1	6.7
of identified less teeth	13.4	18.2	14.3	10.5	8.3
n	382	92	39	129	123
n identified	204	23	7	22	15
n identified less teeth	201	22	7	19	12

Unit B

Of bones from unit B 53% were identified to species (Table 29). The parts of the anatomy present are set out in Tables 33, 34 and 35. This proportion is high partly because many of the vertebrae and ribs were complete enough for positive identification, but also partly because of the good preservation and relative lack of fragmentation. Burnt bone is rare in unit B: one bone is charred and two partly charred from contact with fire, whilst five were recorded as partly burnt (Table 31).

Though no large sections of carcass were found in articulation, a number of bones in 16.938 and 16.952 were found articulated and several unfused bones were found complete with epiphyses, both comparatively rare features of settlement sites where the great mass of bones of food animals are disarticulated. If these bones were cleared away from where they were first discarded, then they must have been moved to their present location quickly, whilst still articulated by ligaments and even muscle tissue. In 16.938 there were two sets of radius and ulna from two different pigs, two sets of astragalus and calcaneum, again from two different pigs, and an articulating tibia and astragalus. One distal humerus of pig was found complete with its unfused articular end. In bone group 16.952 a further pig

astragalus/calcaneum set was found, whilst two smashed pieces of maxilla are probably from the same skull. Also recovered were a cattle metacarpal with two articulating carpals, articulating cervical vertebrae and a second immature humerus complete with epiphysis.

The proportions of the main species, based on fragment counts, are 52% cattle, 40% pig and 7% sheep. When the fragment counts are taken together with the evidence for fusion (Tables 36–8) and dental age (Table 39), it is clear that in unit B there are bones from at least three cattle, of which one is a calf, four pigs and three sheep. The three deer bones are also from more than one animal. This number of animals could only be consumed over a relatively long period by a

Table 33: Neolithic cattle bones: anatomical distribution. Number of identified bones (NISP), minimum number of elements (MNE) and minimum number of individuals (MNI). Overall MNI in final row.

UNIT	B	C	D	E	F	NISP	MNE L	MNE R
MANDIBLE	5				1	6		1
MAXILLA	5				1	6	2	1
PREMAXILLA	2					2		2
OCCIPITAL	2					2	1	1
TEMPORAL	1					1		
SCAPULA	2					2	2	
HUMERUS	7					7	2	2
RADIUS	2	1				3	1	1
ULNA	3	1				4	1	2
CARPALS	2	1			1	4	2	1
PELVIS	6	1				7	2	1
FEMUR	8	1				9	2	2
TIBIA	6					6	1	2
PATELLA	1					1		
ASTRAGALUS	1					1		1
CALCANEUM	2					2	2	
TARSALS	2			1		3		
METACARPAL	2				2	4	2	2
METATARSAL	1	1				2	1	1
PHALANX 1	4	1				5		
PHALANX 2	1	1				2		
PHALANX 3	1					1		
SESAMOID	1					1		
ATLAS	1					1		
AXIS		1				1		
CERVICAL	5					5		
THORACIC	9			1		10		
SACRUM	2			1		3		
RIB	22					22		
total	106	9	0	4	4	123	2	2

Overall MNI = 2

203

Table 34: Neolithic pig bones: anatomical distribution. NISP, MNE and MNI (as Table 33).

UNIT	B	C	D	E	F	NISP	MNE L	MNE R
MANDIBLE	10	3		1	1	15	1	3
MAXILLA	7		1		1	9	2	2
ID. SKULL	1		1			2		
SCAPULA	5	1				6	1	4
HUMERUS	7			4		11	3	2
RADIUS	8					8	4	3
ULNA	11	2				13	2	6
PELVIS	2			2		4		2
FEMUR	2		2			4	1	1
TIBIA	6	1		1		8	5	2
FIBULA	1					1		
LAT. METAPODIAL	1	1			1	3		
METACARPAL		4		1		5		
METATARSAL	1					1		
METAPODIAL				1		1		
ASTRAGALUS	5			1		6	3	2
CALCANEUM	5		1			6	2	2
TARSALS				1	1	2		
PHALANX 1	2			1		3	1	
ATLAS				1		1		
THORACIC	2	1				3		
LUMBAR	3		1			4		
SACRUM			1	1		2		
RIB	2					2		
total	81	13	7	16	3	120	5	6

Overall MNI = 6

Table 35: Neolithic sheep bones: anatomical distribution. NISP and MNE (as Table 33).

UNIT	B	C	D	E	F	Total NISP	MNE L	MNE R
MANDIBLE					1	1		1
MAXILLA				1	1	2		
HUMERUS	3			1		4	3	1
RADIUS	2	1				3	1	
ULNA	2					2	1	1
PELVIS	2					2		1
FEMUR	3					3	1	2
TIBIA	1					1		1
METATARSAL	1					1		1
total	14	1	0	2	2	19	3	2

overall MNI = 3

small group. Given the degree of preservation and the occurrence of articulated bones, both suggesting rapid formation, we may be dealing with a short-lived accumulation, perhaps even a single episode of deposition if feasting was taking place on a large scale. In comparison with their expected survival rate teeth and jaws are few, whilst bones from the trunk and limb bones are more common than bones from the head or feet.

Unit C

There are ninety-two fragments from unit C, of which 25% were identified to species. The majority are well preserved and only two are burnt. A higher proportion have been gnawed than in Unit B. Thirteen are from pig and nine from cattle; 40% are unidentified fragments. The group includes a complete cattle metatarsal.

Unit D

The bones from unit D are more fragmentary than those from B and C. More than half are eroded and none show burning. Only seven of the thirty-nine bones were identified to species, all from pig. These include two articulating vertebrae.

Unit E

A total of 129 bones was recovered from unit E, only 17% of which were identified to species. The proportion eroded (76%) is greater than D but fewer than F. Three fragments are burnt. The pig bones include limb bones from at least two pigs, as one of the three distal humeri is unfused and another is fused (Table 37).

Unit F

Most fragments (97%) are eroded and the proportion of unidentified fragments (67.5%) is also very high. The bones are more fragmented than in units B to E; only loose teeth, carpals and tarsals survive complete, and only three limb bone fragments have survived in a form which made them recognisable to species. More common is burnt bone; the proportion is 5.7% of all fragments. This may be accounted for by the fact that burnt bone survives decay in the soil better than unburnt bone.

Although the number of identified bones is small cattle, pig, sheep, red deer and also dog bones are present. The dog calcaneum is from an adult animal and is complete and unmodified. The single red deer bone, also a calcaneum is unfused, thus from an immature deer. Both adult and very young cattle are present: a carpal is from a calf, while the upper tooth is from an adult.

Discussion

SITE FORMATION

It is possible to suggest certain elements in the sequence of events which took place before the bones became sealed in the sediments. The number of different animals from which the bones have come is greater than would be generated by a small number of people in a single episode or over a short period. The animals were butchered and consumed and the parts of the carcass dispersed prior to incorporation. The preservation of the bones and their relatively unfragmented nature strongly suggest that a rather short period elapsed between consumption of the meat and the bones being protected from trampling and exposure to the weather, a period perhaps not longer than weeks in summer or a few months in winter. Whether they were protected by being buried or by some other means cannot be established.

It is very rare to find anatomical parts deposited with any pattern in later prehistoric deposits, but in unit C the anatomical elements appear to be selected: in 16.938 these are the limb bones of pig and the thoracic vertebrae and ribs of cattle. One possibility is that these discarded bones are from a household or individuals which had entitlement to the lower front and back leg of a pig, and the trunk of cattle. In 16.952 the selection is similar, with most of the anatomical elements of pigs and sheep coming from the leg and very few from head or feet.

As a whole, the bones from the lower units have suffered little damage other than from dogs after the meat was consumed and the cattle bones smashed for marrow. Nearly all the fragmentation can be accounted for by butchery and carnivore gnawing. The condition of the cattle ribs from unit B in particular shows that bones received little or no exposure to trampling between consumption of the meat and burial. The surface condition also suggests that bones must have been covered within a short time, certainly not more than a season. These were not left strewn around the settlement, but were deliberately cleared up. Others were placed (?together) in an area where they were protected from further trampling. Some were doubtless discarded in the river (Area 6–Done 1991).

The increased damage to the bones from the upper units is subsequent to initial deposition. Some is probably the result of water percolation and rootlet action in situ, but it is likely that most can be attributed to physical transportation with sediments during the post-settlement phases of flooding which are thought to account for stratigraphic units D-F.

Table 36: Neolithic cattle bone fusion. Key: VJU – very immature/porous; UF – unfused; FG – fusing; FUS – fused; %UF – VJU, UF and FG together as a percent of total.

	VJU	UF	FG	FUS	%UF
GLENOID		1			
ACETABULUM				4	
P. RADIUS				1	
D. HUMERUS	1	1	1		
Early fusing subtotal	1	2	1	5	44.4
PHALANX 1	1			3	
D. TIBIA		1			
D. METACARPAL	1			1	
D. METATARSAL		1		1	
Mid fusing subtotal	2	2	0	5	44.4
CALCANEUM	1				
P. FEMUR		2			
P. ULNA		1		1	
P. HUMERUS	1	1	1	1	
P. TIBIA		2			
D. RADIUS					
D. FEMUR					
Late fusing subtotal	2	6	1	2	81.8

Table 37: Neolithic pig bone fusion (as Table 36).

	VJU	UF	FG	FUS	%UF
GLENOID		1		1	
ACETABULUM				2	
P. RADIUS		1	1	4	
D. HUMERUS		2		3	
Early fusing subtotal	0	4	1	10	33.3
PHALANX 1		1		2	
D. TIBIA		1			
M. METAPODIALS			1		
Mid fusing subtotal	0	2	1	2	60.0
CALCANEUM		3	1		
P. FEMUR		1			
P. ULNA		4	1		
P. HUMERUS		1			
P. TIBIA		3			
D. RADIUS		1			
D. FEMUR		1			
Late fusing subtotal	0	14	2	0	100.0

Table 38: Neolithic sheep bone fusion (as Table 36).

	VJU	UF	FG	FUS	%UF
D. HUMERUS			1	2	
P. RADIUS				1	
ACETABULUM				1	
GLENOID					
Early fusing subtotal	0	0	1	4	20.0
1ST PHALANX					
D. TIBIA				1	
D. METACARPAL					
D. METATARSAL					
Mid fusing subtotal	0	0	0	1	0
CALCANEUM					
P. ULNA		2			
P. FEMUR		2		1	
P. HUMERUS		2			
P. TIBIA				1	
D. RADIUS		1			
D. FEMUR		1			
Late fusing subtotal	0	8	0	2	80.0

Table 39: Neolithic cattle and pig: eruption and wear stages of last mandibular premolar (DP4) and molars (M1, M2 and M3), after Grant (1975)

				Grant wear code		
Spec. No.		Side	DP4	M1	M2	M3
CATTLE						
1148	MANDIBLE	R				c
PIG						
1151	MANDIBLE	R	d	g	c	E
1145	MANDIBLE	R	g	h	g	b
1185	MANDIBLE	L	g		h	b
1184	MANDIBLE	R				f

BUTCHERY

The condition of the bones from units B–E allowed butchery evidence to be clearly recognised. Both pig and cattle bones have cut marks; many cattle bones are chopped, but few of pig are (Table 40). Cut marks, especially the heavy cuts at the muscle attachments, were easy to see with the naked eye and a glass. They are characteristic of those made with a flint blade and fall into two types. The first is a series of short repeated cuts with a V-shaped cross-section. The second constitutes longer cuts along the flat part of a bone and is seen on long bones and cattle ribs. The first mode serves to detach ligaments and sinew when disarticulating the bones and further, to detach the muscle. The second serves to fillet meat from the bones. Both types have

been illustrated on other assemblages from Neolithic Europe (e.g. Driesch and Boessneck 1975, Plates 1–6). The proportion of cattle and pig bones with visible cut marks is high and approximately the same for each species: 10% of pig and 11% of cattle. One cut was seen on one of the four red deer bones. There are cuts on the scapula, humerus, radius, ulna, pelvis and ribs of pig, and on the scapula, humerus, radius, pelvis, mandible, thoracic vertebrae and ribs of cattle.

Table 40: Neolithic butchered bones

	Chopped		Cuts		Total
	n	%	n	%	
PIG	2	1.7	12	10.0	120
CATTLE	12	9.4	14	11.0	127
RED DEER	1	25.0	0	0.0	4
CATTLE SIZE	6	5.7	4	3.8	106

Deliberate chopping or smashing was recorded where a percussion mark made the interpretation clear. It was suspected more often than it was recorded, particularly on the cattle-size limb-bone fragments. Nine cattle long bones have been chopped through the shaft, including at least one tibia which has been burned and smashed. None of the pig limb bones has been chopped through the shaft. Similarly vertebrae of cattle but not of pig, were also chopped. One of the four cervical vertebrae of cattle has the articulating process removed, though none is chopped through the body. The most common butchery seen in the thoracic vertebrae of the cattle is removal of the neural spine, again leaving the vertebral body intact: six have the spine removed and three isolated neural spines were recovered. Cattle ribs were chopped into rib 'tablets', some of which survive in longish lengths. To break the rib one or more transverse cuts were made and the rib was then snapped: seven tablets from the middle section of the rib are chopped into lengths between 100 and 200 mm, and four are over 200 mm. The similarity of the number and location of cut marks in cattle and pigs suggests that they were butchered and disarticulated and cooked in a similar fashion, but the midshaft chops suggest that only cattle were exploited for bone marrow.

SPECIES

The great majority of bones are from domestic animals. Only four red deer bones were identified, none being antler. This fits the evidence from other Neolithic sites in Britain that red deer, however important for antler, were only rarely killed for food. The possibility that some of the pig bones are from wild boar is discussed below. None of the cattle bones from Area 16 East was exceptionally large although some, probably from aurochs, have been found in other areas of the site not yet published. The only bone possibly from a bird is a cylinder of long bone with thin walls which was very eroded. A small number of fish bones have been found in Neolithic units elsewhere (Serjeantson *et al.* 1994), but none in this assemblage.

Cattle (47%) and pigs (44%) together make over 90% of the identified bones: only 7% are from sheep. The proportions differ slightly if they are calculated from the MNI, which was calculated for the whole Neolithic sample together (Tables 33–5). The distribution of anatomical parts of both cattle and pig show that post-cranial elements are as common as the head. The minimum number of cattle arrived at in this manner is two and, if ages at death are also considered three, while the figure is six for pigs, based on six right ulnas, and three for sheep, based on three left humeri.

WIDER COMPARISONS

The size of the assemblage is modest, so it will be surprising if the species proportions prove to be exactly the same as for the whole site. Nevertheless, preliminary work on the Neolithic material from elsewhere on the site suggests that Area 16 East is entirely typical. The Neolithic assemblage from Areas 4 and 6 (Table 41) was recovered from river sediments (Needham 1991), so might be expected to reflect different disposal practices to those from the dry land area of occupation; indeed, they are certainly less fragmented than those on the dry land area (Serjeantson 1991). In fact, the proportions from Area 6, with 47% cattle and 41% pig, are closely similar to those from Area 16 East, though there is more variation in the smaller groups from Area 4 (Done 1991).

Table 41: Percentage of cattle, pig and sheep from Runnymede and other Early and Middle Neolithic sites in southern Britain: NISP

	Cattle	Pig	Sheep	n
Runnymede: A16 East	49.1	43.1	7.8	232
Runnymede: A4 stratified contexts	71.8	21.4	6.8	103
Runnymede: A4 U/S	53.1	28.1	18.8	64
Runnymede: A6	47.0	41.1	11.9	219
Staines causewayed enclosure	77.6	10.3	12.1	962
Windmill Hill: primary occupation	60.0	15.8	24.2	570
Windmill Hill: pre-enclosure	70.0	13.4	16.6	187
Hazleton barrow: pre-cairn	36.5	29.1	34.4	244

Comparing Runnymede with the nearest excavated Middle Neolithic site, Staines causewayed enclosure 1 km to the north, however, gives a striking contrast. At Staines, in a topographic environment which must have been closely similar to that at Runnymede, pigs were only 10% of the identified assemblage, sheep 12% and

cattle 78% (Grigson 1987). The possibility that pigs are under-represented at Staines because the bones survived less well than cattle can be effectively ruled out. The sediments at Staines included gravels as well as silts and bone preservation was consequently mixed, but not particularly poor (Grigson – pers. comm.). The difference in proportions does therefore appear to be real. The proportions from Staines are closer to those from the pre-enclosure and primary phases at Windmill Hill causewayed enclosure (Grigson 1965), and to the preliminary results from Hambledon Hill (Legge 1981b). The contrast with Staines suggests strongly that the occupation at Runnymede is indeed of a different nature to that at Staines.

Another substantial sample available for comparison is Hazleton long barrow (Levitan 1990), in an upland setting in the Cotswolds. Here, the proportions of the three main species are more equal, with sheep a little more common than pigs. More domestic Neolithic settlements need to be located and excavated to establish whether the high proportion of pigs seen at Runnymede is characteristic of a domestic assemblage in the Middle Neolithic, or is a phenomenon of the location of the site in the valley bottom.

The Late Bronze Age assemblage

Each of the seven stratigraphic excavation units has over 100 identified bones, except for the lowest unit, G, which pre-dates refuse accumulation, and the uppermost unit, M, where only eighty-one out of 632 fragments were identified. Of the total of 6,572 bones, 1,577 were identified to species (Table 42), and a further 1,885 identified to cattle-size or sheep-size anatomical element (Table 43). Twelve species were identified, of which sheep, pig and cattle together gave over 97% of the finds. A few bones only were found of horse, dog, red deer, badger, otter and cat. A single fish bone is an undiagnostic fragment not identified to species. Of fourteen bones provisionally identified as bird, only three are complete enough for identification.

Rodent remains were recovered from some Late Bronze Age contexts. All identifiable mandibles, skulls and teeth are from the water vole or water rat *Arvicola terrestris*, and the post-cranial bones are compatible with this species, with the exception of a single bone, a femur which is from a smaller rodent. The water vole has been part of the native fauna since the last glaciation. It can swim and at Runnymede was close to a river, a habitat in which it is common today. The most likely origin for rodent bones in archaeological deposits such as these is animals which have dug into the sediments and died in the burrow. The water vole will burrow up to 1 m in soft sediments, so the rodent activity is not necessarily contemporary with formation of the deposits in the Late

Table 42: LBA animal bones: species present and number of identified bones. The percentage of identified bones (% id) is shown in the top half of the table, and the percentage of the total (% tot) in the lower half. NFI – not further identified.

UNIT	G n	G % id	H n	H % id	I n	I % id	J n	J % id	K n	K % id	L n	L %	M n	M % id	total	% id
PIG	2	9.1	87	25.5	31	17.3	84	28.8	139	33.6	100	39.8	18	22.2	461	29.2
CATTLE	5	22.7	101	29.6	49	27.4	73	25.0	110	26.6	69	27.5	28	34.6	435	27.6
SHEEP	15	68.2	150	44.0	97	54.2	128	43.8	155	37.4	65	25.9	28	34.6	638	40.5
HORSE							1	0.3	2	0.5	5	2.0	3	3.7	11	0.7
RED DEER			1	0.3	1	0.6	1	0.3	5	1.2	2	0.8	2	2.5	12	0.8
DOG							1	0.3							1	0.1
OTTER									1	0.2					1	0.1
CAT											1	0.4			1	0.1
BADGER							2	0.7							2	0.1
GOOSE					1	0.2									1	0.1
DUCK											1	0.4			1	0.1
TAWNY OWL													1	1.2	1	0.1
BIRD NFI			1	0.3			2	0.5	2	0.5	6	2.4			11	0.7
FISH			1	0.3							2	0.8	1	1.2	4	0.3
		% tot		% tot		% tot		% tot		% tot		% tot		% tot		% tot
subtotal identified	22	17.1	341	38.1	179	38.0	292	26.3	414	21.5	251	17.8	81	12.8	1580	24.0
SHEEP SIZE	59	45.7	207	23.1	117	24.8	260	23.4	407	21.1	171	12.1	100	15.8	1321	20.1
COW SIZE	17	13.2	111	12.4	34	7.2	138	12.4	153	7.9	65	4.6	46	7.3	564	8.6
CAT SIZE	1	0.8	2	0.2	1	0.2	2	0.2	7	0.4	4	0.3			17	0.3
UNIDENTIFIED	30	23.3	234	26.1	140	29.7	417	37.6	947	49.1	917	65.1	405	64.1	3090	47.0
total	129		895		471		1109		1928		1408		632		6572	
RODENT							5		1		1		2			
total	129		895		471		1114		1929		1409		634			

Table 43: LBA bone fragments identified to pig/sheep size and cattle size. L B = long bone

UNIT	G	H	I	J	K	L	M	TOTAL
Sheep size								
L B SPLINTERS	12	29	19	90	172	91	67	480
VERTEBRA	5	66	22	44	53	19	8	217
SKULL	6	10	3	8	4			31
RIB	36	102	73	118	178	61	25	593
TOTAL	59	207	117	260	407	171	100	1321
Cattle size								
L B SPLINTERS	1	10	2	43	41	25	26	148
VERTEBRA	6	46	16	48	54	25	8	203
SKULL	1	1		15	7			24
RIB	9	54	16	32	51	15	12	189
TOTAL	17	111	34	138	153	65	46	564

Bronze Age. Rodents are shown separately in Table 42. A few amphibian bones were recovered in the sieved material, all compatible with the toad which also burrows into soft sediments.

As with the Neolithic, the assemblage is discussed with three themes in mind. The first is bone survival and other aspects of bone alteration which is compared and contrasted between the units. The origin and nature of the deposits and the activities on site which generated the deposits are discussed separately for each unit. The species are considered last.

Preservation and survival

Where the bone was deeply buried the surface preservation is very good; bones are dark brown and little eroded. In contrast the surface of the bones from the upper units, especially the uppermost unit, M, is severely eroded and has begun to exfoliate, and the colour is paler. There is a trend from good to poor preservation from the bottom to the top of the sequence (Table 44), but the correlation is not straightforward. In the lowest unit, G, just over half (56%) of the bones are very well preserved and 41% are well preserved; only 3% are eroded. The bones from the two units above, H and I, are even better preserved; in both, over 80% are very well preserved, and fewer than 3% are eroded. The poorer preservation in unit G can be related to the interpretation of the deposits; the bones are from soil layers and features associated with structures which preceded the rich refuse marked by units H-I. The very good preservation of the surviving bone from both H and I suggests that any reworked material was at no time exposed for any significant period near the surface where it would have been subject to weathering; rather it suggests that it was reworked from protected deposits nearby. The upper units show a steady trend upwards towards erosion of the bone surface, with only 6% of bones from unit J eroded but over 35% in unit M. The proportion of bones with very good preservation diminishes sharply, from 47% in unit J and 23% in unit K to 3% and 6% in units L and M. The proportion of identified bones overall is 24%, but declines from the bottom to the top of the sequence. Material in sediments closer to the ground surface inevitably suffers relatively greater damage from rootlets, soil fauna and water percolation than does material in deeper deposits. In addition, at Runnymede the uppermost units have suffered gross disturbance.

Table 44: LBA bone surface preservation. Surface preservation (%) based on bones identified to anatomical element, excluding teeth.

UNIT	G	H	I	J	K	L	M
VERY GOOD	55.9	86.5	83.8	46.9	23.0	3.0	6.3
GOOD	40.9	13.3	14.0	47.6	59.7	71.5	58.6
ERODED	3.2	0.2	2.2	5.5	17.3	25.5	35.1
n	93	570	271	595	794	365	174

The degree of fragmentation, analysed in the interim study (Serjeantson 1991, Fig. 7), shows a trend towards greater fragmentation of the limb bones in the upper units. This is also found with the teeth. In the lower units teeth are either still in the jaw, or are isolated but unbroken, whereas in unit K 5% of the teeth, and in L and M up to 40% are broken fragments (Fig. 104).

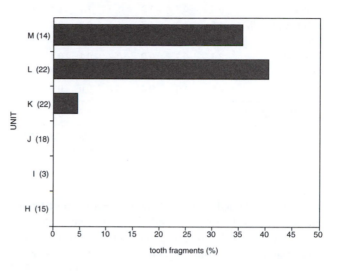

Fig. 104 *Late Bronze Age cattle teeth: tooth fragments as a percentage of all teeth.*

Gnawing (Table 45) causes fragmentation of bones including mandibles, but individual teeth remain in one piece until attacked by chemical and mechanical degradation, which eventually causes both teeth and bones to erode, crack and fragment in the ground. At this stage it is no longer possible to separate the effects of the different agencies of destruction. The upper units have suffered from a combination of the destructive agencies described, as well as trampling and disturbance by humans, dogs and possibly pigs. Between 5% and 11% of the bones collected by hand are burnt, most charred or calcined. The proportion is higher in the sieved samples, being nearly one-third.

Table 45: LBA gnawed bones (%). Percentage of total, of identified bones and of identified bones excluding teeth.

UNIT	G	H	I	J	K	L	M
% GNAWED							
of total	3.1	8.3	8.1	8.8	5.9	1.6	0.9
of identified	13.6	13.5	15.1	19.9	15.2	4.8	4.9
of identified less teeth	13.6	13.9	16.1	23.0	18.2	5.9	6.9
n	129	895	471	1109	1928	1408	632
n identified	22	341	179	292	414	251	81
n identified less teeth	22	330	168	252	347	203	58

Table 46: LBA burnt bones. Percentage of unit assemblages. See text for explanation of colours.

UNIT	G	H	I	J	K	L	M
WHITE	0.8	0.4	0.8	1.4	1.0	0.6	1.4
BLACK & WHITE	0.0	1.0	1.9	2.0	1.1	0.9	2.1
BLACK	0.0	0.3	1.9	1.4	1.1	1.4	2.2
BLACK & BROWN	1.6	1.2	4.7	1.4	0.9	0.9	1.4
BROWN	0.0	0.6	0.0	0.3	0.3	0.9	1.4
GREY/PINK	3.1	0.3	0.0	0.2	0.1	0.1	0.3
PARTLY	0.0	0.9	1.1	0.2	0.4	0.3	0.2
PROBABLY	0.0	1.3	0.4	0.4	0.0	0.1	0.0
OVERALL% BURNT	5.4	6.1	10.8	7.3	4.8	5.1	9.0
n	129	895	471	1109	1928	1408	632

Unit G

This unit contained only 129 bone fragments, most from the soil layers 16.896/908 and the rest from features. They are less well preserved than those in the layers immediately above and contain fewer identified bones (17%). Only three of the identified bones are recognisably chewed and few are burnt (Table 46). Bones of all three main domestic species were present, including calf and lamb bones as well as those from adult animals; despite its small size, the sub-assemblage includes bones from at least four different animals. All parts of the skeleton of sheep were found, including mandibles, horn cores and other skull fragments (Table 47), but these elements were lacking for cattle (Table 48) and pig (Table 49), an effect which is the reverse of what would be expected if resistance to decay alone was conditioning survival. The number of fragmentary undiagnostic limb bone splinters is high, as are fragmented vertebrae and ribs (Table 43). These bones did not suffer the post-occupation damage of those in the upper layers.

The fragmentation that is not the result of butchery is therefore interpreted as being the result of trampling or sediment compaction. The assemblage is a typical mix of species and anatomical elements discarded close to the origin of food consumption, including rib and vertebra fragments.

Units H and I

Nearly 900 bones were excavated from unit H and just over half that number from I. The surface preservation of the bones from both is similar. In both units 38% of the bones could be identified to species, the highest proportion in the Area 16 East sequence, and notably higher than the average for the LBA which is 24%. Proportions of gnawed bones are also similar: 14% of identified bones in unit H and 16% in I as a proportion

of identified bones, and *c*.8% of all bones (Table 45). Radiocarbon dates suggest that some bone material in unit I may be earlier than the formation of unit H (Chapter 5).

Finds of articulated bones and unfused bones found with epiphyses are few in the LBA deposits, but most of those found were in units H and I. In 16.872 four immature pig long bones and two of lamb were found with epiphyses, and a further lamb tibia with epiphyses was found in 16.897. Several pieces of skull from the same context, not closely associated in the ground, appear to be from the same immature sheep. In 16.890 articulating lumbar vertebrae of pig were found, and tarsal bones in 16.876. A row of three thoracic vertebrae of a mature sheep was found in 16.886. No articulated cattle bones were seen.

In unit I, context 16.873 yielded some associated bones of immature sheep, some or all of which may belong to the same animal. A fusing pelvis and unfused femur and tibia were found in articulation (Fig. 21), and close by was an incomplete skull broken into several pieces and two maxillae with M^3 erupting through the bone. In the same context was an astragalus, an unfused calcaneum and navicular-cuboid which belong together, and a pair of fusing humeri with one scapula and six vertebrae. The skull has a chop mark made with a metal tool close to the mid-line, and the scapula has filletting cuts at the origin of the spine. None are gnawed. The developmental stage of these would allow for all to be from the same lamb, but apart from the back leg and some of the vertebrae they were not articulated. The back leg at least may be an in situ group, only slightly modified by turbation and micro-fauna. In the same context were three articulating lumbar vertebrae from an older sheep, as well as an unfused radius with distal epiphysis and the associated ulna of a calf.

Dating suggests that some redeposited material was incorporated in 16.868, but this deposit also contained some associated bones, a pair of tibias, one of which was with the astragalus and calcaneum. A dense concentration of bones in unit H, 16.897, contained many ribs of sheep and sheep/pig-size limb bone splinters, typical of food waste and perhaps from a stewing pot.

The percentage of burnt bone in unit I is 11%, greater than in other units. Nearly 5% of all bones in I are burnt black and brown, i.e. not calcined but having been exposed to fire and partly charred. There are hearth bases or spreads of burnt material in contexts 16.875 and 16.889, but the burnt bones in unit I do not correlate closely with these.

Very few bones other than from the main food species were found in H and I. There is only a single red deer metatarsal in I, and the first phalanx of a goose, too small to be considered as domestic, in H. All parts of the skeleton of the main domestic animals were present

Table 47: LBA sheep bones: summary of anatomical distribution, NISP and MNE (MNI). The final row shows the overall MNI for each unit

UNIT	G NISP	G MNE	H NISP	H MNE	I NISP	I MNE	J NISP	J MNE	K NISP	K MNE	L NISP	L MNE	M NISP	M MNE
MANDIBLE	2	2	3	2	2	2	3	2	7	10	4	3		
MANDIBLE FRAG			4		3		1		10		2		1	
LOWER TOOTH			1		2		6		18		7		2	1
MAXILLA			3	4	2	1	4	4	3	5	1	2		
UPPER TOOTH			1				6		17		5		2	1
TOOTH FRAG									4		4		3	
HYOID			1		1	1			1	1				
PARIETAL					2	1								
TEMPORAL			2				1							
PREMAXILLA			5	3			2	1	3	1				
OCCIPITAL			1											
FRONTAL							2		1					
HORN CORE	2	2	2	1	5	2	1	1	6	2				
ZYGOMATIC			1		1		3							
SCAPULA			18	7	5	3	5	2	3	1				
HUMERUS	4	2	9	5	5	3	6	3	4	2	3	2	1	1
RADIUS			7	4	2	1	15	8	8	7	3	1	3	1
ULNA			5	3	1	1	2	2	5	2	2	1		
CARPALS							1				1			
PELVIS	2	1	3	2	11	5	6	2	3	1	1	1	1	1
FEMUR	1	1	5	2	6	3	6	3	10	4	1	1		
TIBIA			9	4	6	3	9	4	10	5	6	3	1	1
LAT. MALLEOLUS			2											
PATELLA					2		1				1		1	
ASTRAGALUS			1	1	4	4	4	3	2	1	1	1		
CALCANEUM	1	1	5	2	1	1			2	2	2	1		
TARSALS					1		3				1			
METACARPAL			2	1	2	1	11	5	7	2	7	2	1	1
METATARSAL			7	2	8	4	13	4	15	4	6	2	4	1
METAPODIAL					3				2		2			
PHALANX 1			3	1	2	1	2	1	7	2	1	1	1	1
PHALANX 2			1	1	1	1	2	1	3	2	1		1	1
PHALANX 3			1		1				2		2		3	
ATLAS	1	1	2	2	1	1					1	1		
AXIS			2	2									1	1
CERVICAL			5	1	5	1	2	1	1	1				
THORACIC	1	1	19	2			1	1						
LUMBAR			5	2	3	1								
SACRUM			1	1			2	1						
CAUDAL									1	1				
RIB	1	1	14		10	1	8	1						
total	15		150		97		128		155		65		26	
Overall MNI		2		7		5		8		10		3		1

Table 48: LBA cattle bones: summary of anatomical distribution, NISP and MNE (as Table 47)

UNIT	G		H		I		J		K		L		M	
	NISP	MNE	NISP	MNE	NISP	MNE	NISP	MNE	NISP	MNE	NISP	MNE	NISP	MNE
MANDIBLE			8	3	1	1	7	5	7	3	8	4	2	2
LOWER TOOTH			4		2		7		5		2		4	
MAXILLA			1				1		9		3		3	
UPPER TOOTH			2				3							
TOOTH FRAGMENT									1		9		5	
FRONTAL					1				1				1	
HORN CORE					1		5		3		5		2	
PREMAXILLA									1					
NASAL							1							
PALATINE									1					
TEMPORAL			1				2		2		1			
ZYGOMATIC							2		4		1			
OCCIPITAL									2	1				
HYOID			2											
SCAPULA	1	1	6	2	3	1	5	4	4	2	1	1	1	1
HUMERUS			4	1	1	1	4	2	2	1	2	1		
RADIUS			1	1	4	2			2	1	2	1		
ULNA	1	1	2	1	3	2			4	2	3	2		
CARPALS			1		2		1		5		2		1	
PELVIS	1	1	7	2	2	2	2	1	4	1	1	1		
FEMUR			6	2	3	2	4	2	10	2				
TIBIA			2	1	1	1	2	2	3	2	2	1	1	1
PATELLA					1		1							
ASTRAGALUS	1	1	2	2			1	1	3	2	4	4	2	2
CALCANEUM							1	1	2	1	5	2	1	1
TARSALS			1		1		2		1		1			
METACARPAL					1	1	2	2	6	2	4	3	1	1
METATARSAL	1	1	1	1	1	1			5	1			2	1
METAPODIAL									3				1	1
LAT. METAPODIAL											2			
PHALANX 1					3	2	3	1	5	2	5	1		
PHALANX 2			5	2	3	2			3	1	3	1		
PHALANX 3			1				2		1		3			
SESAMOID			1						1				1	
ATLAS			2	2	1	1	2	1	2	2				
AXIS			3	2										
CERVICAL			4	1	1	1								
THORACIC			7	2	2	1			1	1				
LUMBAR			8	2	2	1	2	1	2	1				
SACRUM			3	1	1	1								
CAUDAL			3	1	1	1								
RIB			13		7		10		5	1				
total	5		101		49		72		110		69		28	
Overall MNI		1		3		2		5		3		4		2

Table 49: LBA pig bones: summary of anatomical distribution, NISP and MNE (as Table 47)

UNIT	G NISP	G MNE	H NISP	H MNE	I NISP	I MNE	J NISP	J MNE	K NISP	K MNE	L NISP	L MNE	M NISP	M MNE
MANDIBLE			2	1	1	1	4	3	8	2	2	3		
MANDIBLE FRAG			3						3		1			
LOWER TOOTH					7		5		14		9			
MAXILLA			5	3			4	3	6	3	2	2	1	1
UPPER TOOTH			2				8		5		3		1	
TOOTH FRAG									1		9		4	
PARIETAL			1											
TEMPORAL			1						1					
NASAL			1											
OCCIPITAL			1	1	1	1	2	2	2	1	1	1		
FRONTAL					1		2		2					
LACHRYMAL									1					
ZYGOMATIC					1		2							
SCAPULA	1	1	1	1			2	1	5	2	3	1	2	2
HUMERUS			5	2			5	2	6	2	1	1		
RADIUS			1	1			3	2	3	2	4	2		
ULNA			1	1			1	1	8	4	3	1	1	1
CARPALS					1				5		5			
PELVIS	1	1	1	1	1	1	1	1	2	1				
FEMUR			5	3			2	1	8	2	1	1		
TIBIA			3	1	1	1	4	2	6	3	4	1	1	1
FIBULA			2	1			5	2	4	1	2	1		
PATELLA			2				2		1					
ASTRAGALUS			1	1					2	1	2	2		
CALCANEUM			3	3	1	1	1	1	2	2	3	1		
TARSALS			4	1			3		2		3		1	
METACARPAL			3	2	2	1	1	1	5	1	3	1	2	1
METATARSAL			3	1	2	1			1	1				
MED. METAPODIAL							4	1	1	1	4	1	2	1
LAT. METAPODIAL			1		2		2	1	1		7			
PHALANX 1			5	1			5	1	9	1	5	1	1	1
PHALANX 2			3	1			6	1	6	1	6	1		
PHALANX 3			1				3		5		8		2	
LAT. PHALANGES					3				6		5			
ATLAS			1	1					1	1				
AXIS											2	2		
CERVICAL			1	1	1	1					1	1		
THORACIC			7	1	1	1	3	1	3	1				
LUMBAR			7	1	2	1								
SACRUM			1	1	1	1					1	1		
CAUDAL									1	1				
RIB			9	1	1		4	1	3	1				
total	2		87		31		84		139		100		18	
Overall MNI		1		3		1		3		4		3		2

(Tables 47–9); but the MNE from mandibles is lower than that from some of the main long bones. This is the opposite of the finding expected when survival is dependent on bone density. As bone is well preserved, this must reflect the composition of material originally entering in the deposits: the trunk and limbs, including metapodials, predominate over skull, but fragments of the latter from lambs and pigs were also found.

The preservation and the occurrence of associated bones show that the cycle of refuse disposal was not a long one before these were protected from damage. Not all carcasses were fully disarticulated at the time when the meat was consumed: some bones, particularly of sheep, have not been disarticulated for stewing or smashed to obtain the bone marrow. Although some have not been fed to the dogs, a significant proportion were. The original point of meat consumption is likely to have been close in time and perhaps space. Interpretation of the sub-assemblage in H and I is clearer than that of unit G below or those higher up.

Unit J

The bones from unit J have some of the characteristics of those from H and I. Few of the bones are very eroded, but in contrast with H and I, only half of the remainder have very good surface preservation. Isolated teeth were present but none was broken in the ground. The proportion of identified bones is 26%, slightly above the mean for the Late Bronze Age. The unit is rather more disturbed and the assemblage more mixed than those below: there is an absence of articulating bones or bones with epiphyses still present, but two sheep metapodials appear to be a pair.

A small proportion (7%) of the bone is burnt, most calcined or charred. Gnawing was seen on a greater proportion than for other units, 20% of identified bones and 9% of all bones. This would suggest that there was a slower accumulation of refuse at this stage, which allowed dogs and possibly pigs to root around before the material became buried. Two mammal bones have the characteristic narrow parallel striations of rodent gnawing, and rodent remains were recovered from this unit. Rodents will gnaw old bone as well as the more nutritious fresh bone, so the rodent activity was not necessarily contemporary with deposit formation.

A wider variety of species was found in this unit. As well as sheep, cattle and pig, there were a horse tooth, a dog metatarsal and two badger limb bones. Two thin-walled bone splinters are probably bird. All parts of the carcass of the main food species are present, with mandibles most common for cattle and pig, but limb bones more common for sheep (Tables 47–9). The unit differs from those below in that the bones have suffered apparently greater disturbance and mixing before and during deposition.

Unit K

In this largest sub-assemblage, comprising nearly 2,000 bones, the surface preservation is mixed: one-quarter are very well preserved, but nearly 20% are heavily eroded. More than one-third were unidentified. Some tooth fragments were found as well as jaws and isolated teeth, but the percentage (5%) is low. The proportion of bones on which gnawing was clearly visible is lower than in unit J. The proportion of burnt bone is low. One rodent bone was recovered.

Table 50: LBA unit K pig bones: anatomical distribution, NISP, MNE and MNI. Most frequent zones also shown. (Other tables of anatomical distribution in archive.)

	NISP	MNE L	ZONE	MNE R	ZONE	MNE M	ZONE
MANDIBLE	8	2		2			
MANDIBLE FRAG	3						
LOWER TOOTH	14						
MAXILLA	6						
UPPER TOOTH	5						
TOOTH FRAG	1						
OCCIPITAL	2					2	Z1
TEMPORAL	1						
FRONTAL	2						
LACHRYMAL	1						
SCAPULA	5	2	Z3,5	1	Z3–4		
HUMERUS	6	2	Z6	2	Z8		
RADIUS	3	2	Z8				
ULNA	8	2	Z4	4	Z4		
CARPALS	5						
PELVIS	2			1	Z4,5,7		
FEMUR	8	1	Z1–4	2	Z7		
TIBIA	6	1	Z1,4,5	3	Z3		
FIBULA	4	1	Z5,6	1	Z5–8		
PATELLA	1						
ASTRAGALUS	2	1	Z1–8	1	Z1–8		
CALCANEUM	2			2	Z2–6		
TARSALS	2						
METACARPAL	5					4	Z2
METATARSAL	1					1	Z1–2
MED. METAPODIAL	1						
LAT. METAPODIAL	1						
PHALANX 1	9					7	Z3–6
PHALANX 2	6					6	Z6
PHALANX 3	5					5	Z1–6
LAT. PHALANGES	6						
ATLAS	1					1	Z2,6,8
THORACIC	3						
CAUDAL	1						
RIB	3						
total	139						

Overall MNI = 4

The proportion of pig bones is rather above the mean for the sequence, and that of sheep is lower. All parts of the carcass of cattle, pig and sheep were found, with skull fragments better represented in cattle (Table 48) and sheep (Table 47), but not in pig (Table 50) and phalanges of the three main species common. The high proportion of fragments of cattle- and sheep-size vertebrae and rib (Table 43) is in part a reflection of greater fragmentation of these elements than in the lower deposits. The anatomical distribution of cattle and the estimation of MNI shows that parts of at least three animals contributed to the deposits. Furthermore, although there were no mandibles sufficiently complete to provide age data, two isolated teeth as well as the fusion evidence show that these included both adult and immature cattle. Elements from all parts of the body are represented, including horn cores, which are otherwise rare in the Runnymede deposits.

The group is more heterogeneous than those from units below: there is a greater mix of skeletal elements, bones are more fragmented and articulated bones are lacking. The material probably derives from a wider range of activities and appears to have accumulated over a greater length of time. It is closer to what might be expected in a typical settlement assemblage.

Unit L

The percentage of eroded bones (25%) is higher than in unit K, and the percentage unidentified (65%) is notably greater. The proportion of fragmented teeth (41%) is much higher than in K and compares with unit M above. Rodent bones were found in a sieved sample. The proportion of burnt bone is 5%, which includes both charred and calcined bone and also less heavily burnt fragments. The proportion of gnawed bones recorded is 2%, or 5% of identified bones, less than in unit K but more than in M.

The most common part of the skeleton for all the main species is the mandible. All ribs, and all but one vertebra were too fragmented to identify to species, although fragments of both elements of sheep size and cattle size were common. The relative abundance of parts of the skeleton in this unit follows the relative robustness of the skeleton. The proportion of pig is highest in unit L, from both NISP and MNI (Table 49). Analysis of bones from other sites has often found that post-cranial bones of pig survive relatively less well than do those of cattle and also of sheep, and there are usually fewer fragments of pig than of sheep per MNI, so the high proportion of pig remains in this unit seems likely to reflect a real increase.

Unit M

The sediments in unit M have been transformed by natural agencies, particularly flood-reworking, and this is reflected in the preservation of the bone. Only 6% is very well preserved, and 35% is eroded. The fragmentation can be judged from the fact that 64% of the bones were unidentified, the same proportion as for unit L. A high proportion of teeth (36%) were broken in the ground. The proportion of burnt bone in this unit is the second highest after unit I; nearly all of these are charred and/or calcined. Burnt bone survives chemical attack better than unburnt bone, and as the top of the sequence will have been more exposed to the slight acidity of percolating ground water, burnt bone will have survived relatively better than unburnt bone. On the other hand burnt bone, being more brittle, is less resistant to mechanical damage from trampling and reworking. While the relatively high proportion of burnt bones may suggest a higher contribution from domestic fires, it is more likely that relative preservation has influenced the proportions. The percentage of bones on which gnawing was noted is only 5% of identified bones, and 1% of all bones, the lowest proportion in the sequence. As discussed, this reflects survival of the evidence, rather than a lower proportion of gnawing.

The identified bones include horse, red deer and a carpo-metacarpus of a tawny owl *Strix aluco*. In view of the fact that this unit is reworked, we need to keep an open mind about whether this is necessarily anthropogenic in origin, and whether it or indeed other bones have been imported by flood action.

The anatomical distribution is biased towards the denser elements of the skeleton and to the larger species. This is the only unit in which cattle, with an MNI of two, are relatively more numerous than sheep for which there is an MNI of one. The most frequent elements of cattle are isolated teeth and the astragalus, elements best able to withstand reworking and chemical damage. No ribs or vertebrae survived in a condition sufficiently complete to be identified to species, though fragments of both were present.

On balance, most of the distinctions between this unit and units L and K seem to be a consequence of bone survival, and thus cannot be used to argue for any change in the activities which generated the rubbish.

Discussion

Samples of ageable jaws and teeth and of bones with fusion evidence surviving is small, so here the LBA assemblage is discussed as a whole, despite the date range involved and the evidence that the assemblage was moulded by a variety of activities.

CATTLE

Approximately 28% of identified bones are from cattle; the MNIs suggest broadly similar proportions between cattle, pig and sheep. The proportion of cattle bones is

fairly constant in the lower deposits, but rises in the upper parts, especially in unit M, whether calculated from NISP or MNI (Fig. 105a). As the discussion of the taphonomy has shown, the best explanation for this is that cattle bones and teeth have survived relatively better in the units closer to the modern ground surface, and should not be taken as evidence of an increase in dependence on cattle in the later period of occupation of

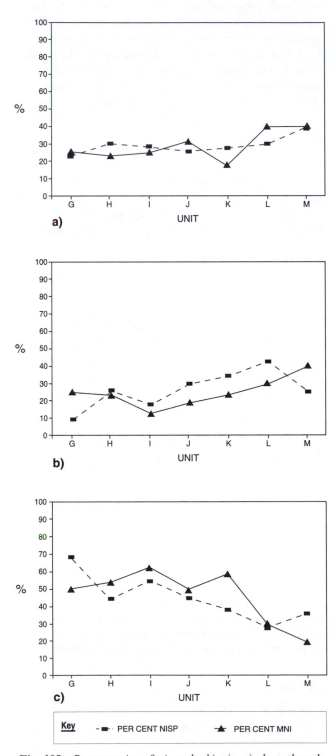

Fig. 105 *Representation of a) cattle, b) pig, c) sheep through the Late Bronze Age sequence, shown as percentages of both NISP (numbers of identified bones) and MNI (minimum number of individuals).*

Table 51: LBA cattle: eruption and wear codes of mandibles and teeth, after Grant (1975). Stages after Legge (1992).

Legge Stage	Unit	Spec. No.		Side	Grant wear code DPM4	M1	M2	M3
1	J	45	MANDIBLE	R	b	C		
1	K	7	TOOTH	R	b			
4	H	104	MANDIBLE	R	h	b	C	
4	J	70	MANDIBLE	R	j	f	E	C
4/5	J	34	TOOTH	R	j			
5	H	560	MANDIBLE	R	m	g	d	
5	H	573	MANDIBLE	R	j	g	e	V
5	H	559	MANDIBLE	L		g	e	E
7	L	642	TOOTH					g
7	J	78	MANDIBLE	L				g
7	L	638	TOOTH	R				g
8	K	757	TOOTH	L				k

Table 52: LBA cattle bone fusion. Key: VJU – porous/very immature; UF – unfused; FG – fusing; FUS – fused; % UF – VJU, UF and FG together as a percent of total.

	VJU	UF	FG	FUS	%UF
GLENOID	3			4	
ACETABULUM	1		1	7	
P. RADIUS	2			3	
PHALANX 2	7			6	
D. HUMERUS	1			3	
Early fusing subtotal	14	0	1	23	39.5
PHALANX 1	4	1		7	
D. TIBIA		1		3	
D. METACARPAL		1		5	
D. METATARSAL	2			1	
Mid fusing subtotal	6	3	0	16	36.0
CALCANEUM	1	1			
P. FEMUR		3		2	
P. ULNA	4	2		1	
P. HUMERUS		2			
P. TIBIA	1	1			
D. RADIUS	1	1		1	
D. FEMUR				3	
Late fusing subtotal	7	10	0	7	70.8

the settlement. The dental (Table 51) and fusion data (Table 52) show that both adults and calves are present. The jaws and teeth include some animals in the first year, a few in the second and third year, with the remainder adult.

The bones include a higher proportion from young calves than do the jaws and teeth, with nearly 40% of the early fusing bones unfused. Fusion stages used are from Silver (1969). The age of fusion is likely to have been delayed with more primitive stock raised in a less intensive husbandry regime than with the recent stock used to compile Silver's tables. It is unusual to find more evidence for juvenile bones than for teeth, as here. It emphasises the good preservation of most of the material in the assemblage.

PIG

Relative proportions of pig bones range from less than 20% in unit I to 40% in unit L (Fig. 105b), with an overall proportion of nearly 30%. MNIs suggest slightly lower proportions of animals represented except in unit M. These are unusually high for a British site of the first millennium BC. The ageable jaws (Table 53) and the bones with fusion evidence (Table 54) are more numerous for pig than for cattle.

SHEEP

Sheep are 40% of identified bones overall. The proportion is 68% in G, a small and probably anomalous sample, and lowest in L, 26%. MNIs suggest a rather higher proportion (Fig. 105c). Of the eighteen jaws and teeth which could be assigned to a stage of eruption and wear, over half are from lambs dead by the end of the first year, stage C of Payne (Payne 1973) (Table 55). The immaturity of the sample is confirmed by the fusion evidence (Table 56); over 50% of the bones which would have fused within about six months or not much later are unfused. Only two of the jaws and teeth are from sheep over approximately four years, and the fusion evidence of the latest fusing bones confirms this. The proportion of young animals is greater than that for pigs, which is unusual.

There is surprisingly good correlation between NISP and MNIs, despite the small numbers from each unit, and some differences between the parts of the body most frequent in each unit. Overall, as would be expected on a site of the first millennium BC, the proportion of sheep is considerably higher than in the Neolithic. The increase is almost entirely at the expense of cattle. In units H to K, sheep are the most common species whichever method of calculation is used; cattle and pig are more common in units L and M, but as discussed, differential survival has affected bone in the upper units more than in the lower units. Nevertheless, it has been possible to argue that the increase in representation of pig in units K and L reflects a real trend.

Table 53: LBA pig: eruption and wear codes of mandibles and teeth, after Grant (1975)

Unit	Spec. No.		Side	DP4	P4	M1	M2	M3
K	15	MANDIBLE	L	h				
K	738	TOOTH	L	m				
I	547	TOOTH	L			b		
K	750	MANDIBLE	L			e		
L	618	TOOTH	L				E	
J	55	MANDIBLE	L		E	h	a	V
K	724	MANDIBLE	R		E		b	V
L	656	MANDIBLE	R		b	h	d	a
H	570	MANDIBLE	R		d	j	d	b
K	37	TOOTH	L			j		
I	552	TOOTH	R				d	
I	540	MANDIBLE	L				e	b
J	52	MANDIBLE	L				e	
J	2	MANDIBLE	R				e	b
L	617	TOOTH	L					g

Table 54: LBA pig bone fusion (as Table 52)

	VJU	UF	FG	FUS	% UF
ACETABULUM	1		1	3	
D. HUMERUS		2	1	4	
P. RADIUS	1	1			
GLENOID				3	
Early fusing subtotal	2	3	2	10	41.2
1ST PHALANX		11	1	9	
D. TIBIA		2	2	1	
M. METAPODIALS		12		4	
L. METAPODIALS		7		1	
Mid fusing subtotal	0	32	3	15	70.0
CALCANEUM		10			
P. ULNA	1	1	1	1	
P. FEMUR	1	4			
P. HUMERUS		3			
P. TIBIA	1	2	1	2	
D. RADIUS	1	1		1	
D. ULNA	1	1		1	
D. FEMUR	1	7			
Late fusing subtotal	6	29	2	5	88.1

Table 55: LBA sheep: eruption and wear of mandibles and teeth, after Grant (1975). Stages after Payne (1973).

Unit	Stage	Spec. No.		Side	DP4	P4	M1	M2	M3
J	A	22	MANDIBLE	R	a		C		
I	B	546	MANDIBLE	L	c		E		
J	B	61	MANDIBLE	L	e		E		
I	C	567	TOOTH	L			b		
K	C	14	TOOTH	R			b		
H	C	103	MANDIBLE	R	h		c	E	
K	C	767	TOOTH	L	f				
K	C	725	TOOTH	L	f				
K	C	733	MANDIBLE	L	h				
K	C	707	TOOTH	L	h				
L	C	637	TOOTH	L	h				
K	D	1	MANDIBLE	R				b	V
K	D	715	MANDIBLE	L	g		g	c	
H	E	558	MANDIBLE	R		c	g	f	b
K	E	716	MANDIBLE	L		g	h	g	
L	E	625	MANDIBLE	R					b
K	G	717	TOOTH	L					g
K	I	12	TOOTH	R					h

Table 56: LBA sheep bone fusion (as Table 52)

	VJU	UF	FG	FUS	% UF
D. HUMERUS	3	8	6	8	
P. RADIUS	5			6	
ACETABULUM			1	10	
GLENOID	5	2	2	8	
Early fusing subtotal	13	10	9	32	50.0
1ST PHALANX		8	5	4	
D. TIBIA	5	9		5	
D. METACARPAL	3	6		3	
D. METATARSAL	5	14		4	
Mid fusing subtotal	13	37	5	16	77.5
CALCANEUM	1	8			
P. ULNA	3	5			
P. FEMUR	6	9	1	1	
P. HUMERUS	1	8	1	2	
P. TIBIA	6	7		3	
D. RADIUS	4	7		2	
D. FEMUR	6	9			
Late fusing subtotal	27	53	2	8	91.1

OTHER DOMESTIC ANIMALS

Evidence for horse is rare, and more common in the upper than the lower deposits. All but three finds are

teeth: a molar in J, two mandible fragments in K, two molars in L and two tooth fragments in M. The bones are a carpal, a distal metatarsal and a tibia fragment. At 53.8 mm the crown height of the complete molar in unit L suggests an animal of about 7–8 years (Levine 1982). Despite the abundant evidence for gnawing, the only remains of dog bone is a broken fourth metatarsal.

WILD ANIMALS

There is surprisingly little evidence for wild animals. There are eight red deer bones and thirteen fragments of antler; one of the bones is worked into a spatula (Cat. No. B19) made on a metatarsal and three antler pieces are worked (Table 18). The finds other than antler are:

Unit	I	metacarpal shaft fragment
	K	femur, astragalus
	L	distal tibia, lower molar
	M	two tooth fragments

The astragalus has cut marks.

Other bones from wild species are the humerus and radius of badger, a radius of otter and a tibia shaft of a cat. This cannot be distinguished between wild and domestic cat but for this period it would be expected to be wild. Although only the badger humerus has cut marks from skinning, it is likely that these are from animals caught for their fur.

BIRDS

The goose first phalanx is from a grey goose *Anser* sp., which cannot be identified more closely. A broken scapula is from duck, *Anas* sp., of mallard size. These species are far from unexpected on a settlement beside a river. The tawny owl find is from the end of the wing bone; a distal wing with feathers, selected for ornament or decoration, could for example explain the introduction of this bone if it was brought in by the occupants of the settlement rather than flood action (as mentioned above). No other definite bird bones were identifiable, but eleven further probable fragments were found. The very small number of bird bones in the Neolithic as well as the LBA might be considered surprising in view of the riverside location, the careful collection of bone fragments and the good preservation in all units other than L and M. It is however typical of inland sites in prehistoric Britain. In lowland Britain the only inland sites where bird bones are at all common are settlements in the Fenlands (Evans and Serjeantson 1988) and the Somerset Levels, some of which have evidence for substantial exploitation of swans, pelicans, ducks and other waterfowl. In prehistoric times the Thames, with its braided course and meanders will undoubtedly have supported a rich bird population, including mute swans and many of the ducks, though perhaps not the pelicans which require large undisturbed water bodies on which to breed. It appears that little attempt was made by the Runnymede population to exploit the waterfowl or other birds.

OVERALL COMPARISONS

Some interesting points of comparison may be made between the LBA assemblage from Area 16 East and those from the rescue excavations of 1976 and 1978, which struck different parts of the settlement complex. The bones from the river channel deposits in Area 6 are very well preserved and less fragmented than those from Area 16 East (Serjeantson 1991, Fig. 7). The relative proportions of the main species (Table 57) show that proportions in Area 6 (Done 1991, Table 52) are very similar to those from Area 16 East. However, in Area 2 (Done 1980, Table 2), sheep are much more common than pigs.

Table 57: LBA percentages of cattle, pig and sheep (%NISP) from other Areas at Runnymede

	Cattle	Sheep/Goat	Pig	n
A2	58.1	27.6	14.2	2724
A6 A-B	53.7	22.1	24.2	95
A6 C-D	36.7	34.4	28.8	215
A6 Occupation	32.5	27.3	40.1	618
A6 Pit F6	41.4	24.7	33.8	263
A6 E-G	35.1	26.8	38.1	467
A6 H-J	20.0	34.2	45.8	445
A6 Total	33.0	28.8	38.2	2103

It is more difficult to make comparisons with other animal bone assemblages of the Late Bronze Age. No others of any size have been published from the south of England at the time of writing, though one, Potterne, is in preparation (Locker pers. comm.). Done has already pointed out that Early Iron Age sites of a few centuries later have fewer pigs than Runnymede, which is also the case in the Middle Bronze Age middens at Grimes Graves (Legge 1981a; Legge 1992). As in the Neolithic, pig is unusually common for a British site. Proportions are more typical of Iron Age sites in France and elsewhere in continental Europe (Meniel 1987).

The role of pigs

It has been shown that in both the Neolithic and Late Bronze Age deposits pig remains are more common than on contemporary sites. There is more than one possible reason for this. Pig meat may have been preferred to that from cattle and sheep. They may be more common because the riverine location provided ready forage in the vicinity of the settlement. Pigs may have been the chosen medium through which power, wealth and social control were expressed. Indeed elements of all these may have been involved at different periods. These environmental or cultural 'reasons' are discussed here, and the constraints of the data are explored.

Domestic or wild?

The identification of wild boar among the bones of domestic pigs from archaeological sites has relied on distinctions of size and shape which depend in turn on survival of either a key anatomical element or the presence of a large sample of measurable bones. Even when useable criteria exist for adult pigs they are not applicable to immature pigs, yet it is these which make up the great majority of the Runnymede pig sample in Area 16 East.

The main change in bone shape is that of the skull. The snout is more elongated in wild boar. A shorter snout has been observed as early as the Neolithic in Britain (Grigson 1965) and continental Europe. The bone which shows the distinction most clearly is the lachrymal bone (Clutton-Brock 1981, 72), which is longer in wild pig. However, 'rooting ... markedly affects the development of cranial and lachrymal conformation in growing pigs' (Epstein and Bichard 1984, 149), so the distinction is not absolute. No complete skulls have been found at Runnymede and the single lachrymal bone from Area 16 East, from unit K (LBA), matched the shape of domestic pig.

Wild swine attain a greater size than domestic ones, and absolute size distinctions are often made (e.g. Clason 1967, 61–72; Lasota-Moskalewska *et al* 1987). The conventional view is expressed by the last authors: 'It is generally known that all the bones of a domestic pig are smaller and more delicate than those of a wild pig' (ibid. 56). However, there was an overlap in size, particularly between male domestic swine and female wild, which has been recognised at some sites (e.g. Willburger 1983; Payne and Bull 1988). The numbers of wild pigs on prehistoric sites have probably been underestimated because they cannot always be distinguished from domestic pigs, even amongst the adult population.

A further complication is that interbreeding between wild and domestic swine probably continued during these periods, thus inhibiting any extreme change in size and shape from the wild form.

The third molar is both longer and wider in wild boar (Payne and Bull 1988). Two M3s in wear were recovered from Neolithic contexts, with lengths of 32.4 mm and 35.0 mm, well within the range for the domestic pigs in the large sample from the Heuneburg (Willburger 1983, 87). There the minimum length for wild boar is 40.0 mm.

	range (mm)	n
Runnymede Neolithic	32.4 – 35.0	2
Mesolithic N Europe	39.0 – 58.0	
Heuneburg	24.0 – 48.0	>200

In subsequent recording of the Runnymede pig bones, the width as well as the length of the molar teeth has been measured. This should allow the index of Payne and Bull to be used to offer greater precision in future Runnymede reports.

Size

Some exceptionally large post-cranial bones were considered to be from male wild boars, though none recovered was complete enough to be measured. An ulna shaft from the Neolithic was notably larger than the others.

Late Bronze Age contexts yielded up to eight exceptionally large bone fragments. An enigmatic tablet of bone which has been modified (Chapter 11 B24, sf226) is made from a large mandible which matches pig more closely than cattle, deer or horse. Seven further incomplete bones from LBA contexts compare better in size with a large modern pig. These, if not from wild boar, must be from large male domestic pigs. Three from unit L may be from the same pig: a fused distal humerus fragment, an unfused radius shaft and an axis. The others, one each from units I to M are a pelvis, a frontal bone, a thoracic vertebra and an unfused medial metapodial. Several exceptionally large bones and canine teeth have been found in areas other than Area 16 East.

A further criterion which has been invoked for identifying domestic animals is the presence of a high proportion of juveniles. In the Neolithic assemblage, about 30% of the skeletal elements which fuse before the age of one year are unfused, as are 60% of those which fuse by about two years (Table 37). The calculation is based on all bones for which fusion evidence survives and if anything, underestimates the unfused fraction. Many bones have been gnawed along the fusion line, which raises the strong suspicion that they too were unfused. The fifteen jaws and teeth suggest a greater age at death than the post-cranial bones (Table 39): there are no jaws from piglets, two are from pigs killed within the first year and at least four are from pigs over about two years, with the third permanent molar in wear.

For the LBA material both dental eruption (Table 53) and bone fusion (Table 54) suggest that the number of pigs killed below two years is also very high. As in the Neolithic, there are fewer jaws and teeth than post-cranial bones from very immature pigs. Of the bones which fuse before one year, over 40% are unfused; of those which fuse before two years, nearly 70% are unfused. These figures are closely similar to those for the earlier period.

If a prevalence of immature pigs is an indication of domestic status, then most of those consumed at Runnymede in both the Neolithic and the Late Bronze Age were domestic. This seems likely. However, there are enough fragments of very large pigs to suggest that wild boars were hunted in both periods. The numbers from Area 16 East which were judged to be from exceptionally large pigs and thus potentially wild boar, are approximately the same in the Neolithic as in the LBA as a proportion of the total identified bones (0.42% and 0.45% respectively).

Material considerations

Pigs, unlike cattle, sheep and goats, provide few secondary products, but of all the domestic animals provide the best return when kept for meat (Pimentel and Pimentel 1979). They convert feed to kilocalories more efficiently than cattle and twice as efficiently as sheep. Pig litters are larger and under domestication sows may farrow more than once a year. Pig manure may be a valuable secondary product, but there seem to be no records of communities keeping pigs for this or any other secondary product, such as blood.

Since pigs are omnivorous they can be kept under a wide range of regimes. Even when they still had hairy coats, as they did in Britain until the modern period, they require shelter in winter. In the wild they find shelter in woods and swamps, but under domestication they would presumably be provided with some kind of shelter at night.

Their preferred diet in the wild is roots, plant stems, fungi, acorns, chestnuts, beech mast, grain, insect larvae, worms, eggs, frogs and reptiles (Epstein and Bichard 1984). They will also kill and eat the chicks of ground nesting birds and litters of mammal young. They are very effective scavengers, more so than dogs, as they eat both plant and animal foods. Pigs will eat bones as well as soft parts but unlike carnivores, cannot live on a diet which consists mainly of bones. They also scavenge carrion and human excrement. In the Middle East today this is the reason why pig meat is not eaten, but most societies do not make a taboo of eating pig.

For some foods, such as hazelnuts, the monogastric pig will have been in competition with the human population (Braude 1962, 306). Others however, such as bracken rhizomes and acorns, have only been resorted to by human communities in western Europe in times of hardship and poor harvest.

Regimes of pig keeping

Historically in western Europe pigs have been kept under a variety of regimes. Three historically attested regimes are summarised here as a background to considering more closely how the Runnymede pigs were kept.

MEDIEVAL PIG KEEPING

In the Anglo-Saxon and later Medieval period pig keeping was carried out in an extensive mode. On many estates, herds of pigs were taken daily to feed in woods, to eat acorns and beech mast. The nuts were important in the early autumn, as the immature pigs which were not to be kept for breeding were slaughtered in the late autumn. This picture of pig keeping, familiar from Domesday (Darby 1973; Rackham 1980), only accounts for the larger estate herds and leaves unanswered the question of what was eaten during the remaining months of the year, or indeed in the years in which both acorns and beech mast failed. Presumably in the woods pigs also had access to rhizomes, tubers (including truffles if they were lucky) and other plant and animal foods. Fallen nuts will keep into the following year if they are not all eaten in the autumn. Though most of the references in Domesday are to pannage in woods, it also took place in 'parks, fields, stubble' and in one reference only a 'garden'.

Further clues as to how pigs were husbanded are found in a record from Writtle of 1398 (quoted by Rackham 1980, 155). There, '37 pigs (belonging to eleven owners) were pannaged in the Forest, i.e. Epping Forest, and 41 under oak trees in the warren'. This suggests that the sty pigs (see below) kept by individual villagers were also taken out to feed in the woods.

STY PIGS

From at least the classical period pigs have been reared in sties and fed on waste scraps. Although it is more labour-intensive to bring the food to the pigs rather than vice versa, rearing pigs on this scale was and is easily done on a domestic or household scale. Farmers whose main income was from other products also often kept pigs in small numbers. Pigs kept in these conditions eat a wide variety of foods and their economic value lies in the fact that they live principally on domestic scraps, both plant and animal, thus converting to meat what would otherwise be waste.

COMMERCIAL PIG KEEPING

Commercial pig keeping, like domestic pig keeping, is at least partly based on feeding pigs products surplus to, or unfit for, human consumption. In historical times the surplus tends to be food which in other circumstances would be eaten by the human population. One specialised form is associated with cattle dairying. When this began in the later Middle Ages on a commercial scale to provide towns and cities with milk and cheese, the quantity of whey remaining was greater than could be used or sold, and the surplus was used to fatten pigs for sale (e.g. Marshall 1817, 165). Pigs have also been kept as a complement to the commercial orchards. In the autumn the pigs were fattened on the windfalls. Today pigs are fed surplus grain and potatoes (Braude 1962).

Pig keeping at Runnymede

There is nothing in the material remains from Runnymede to suggest that pig keeping approached the intensive scale described above. It is likely that cattle (Legge 1992) and perhaps also sheep were milked in the prehistoric period, the milk being used to produce butter, cheese and other dairy products, but this is unlikely to have been on a scale which produced whey surplus to the needs of the human population.

There are reasons for considering it unlikely that the pigs were kept in sties for most of the time. When pigs are confined for long periods sties need to have strong walls and floors to prevent them from digging their way out. It is doubtful if the wooden buildings of the first or the fourth millennia BC were strong enough. The pigs may also have been fed some domestic waste, but experiments in which bones have been fed to pigs kept in sties (Greenfield 1988) and to dogs in runs (Payne and Muson 1985) suggest that the bones are more intensively broken up in these conditions than any recovered from the settlement deposits at Runnymede. The large spreads of bone and other rubbish indicate that much was left after both dogs and pigs had scavenged. This is not to say that the pigs would not have been penned at night.

There is no need to look beyond the forage available in the vicinity of the site, supplemented by some domestic waste, as the source of most of the food for the pigs. The pollen and macrofossil evidence suggest that the area was heavily wooded in the Neolithic, with oak, lime and elm as the main components of the forest (Greig 1991, 256). By the Late Bronze Age the composition of the nearby woodland had become more varied, with more secondary woodland (ibid. 261) and larger areas permanently cleared of woodland. Probably just as important for successful pig rearing, since they complemented the acorn crop, were the plants of the river margin and backwater swamps, such as waterlilies which provided rhizomes and roots. It is likely that the pigs were kept in herds, and most of their diet obtained from forage in the woods or by the river. The Runnymede cattle would have been able to graze and browse in the same areas as the pigs; they would not have been in competition with the pigs for food because they have a system which allows digestion of cellulose from leaves, twigs and grass.

There is one major disadvantage to keeping pigs: the damage they cause to fragile soils (Ross 1983). This was quite as fully appreciated in early times as today. The *mucca gentliuchta* ('pigs of magic') described in the Mabinogi of Culhwch and Olwen caused severe damage: 'Round whatever thing they used to go, till the end of seven years neither corn nor grass nor leaf would grow through it' (Ross 1974, 398). In fact pigs are highly destructive of growing crops and must be herded clear of them, but the effect of their rooting would be to clear the ground. 'Seven years' is of course a device of Celtic fiction to represent a fairly long period of time, and is not to be taken literally. Though pigs ring-bark trees, which in the end will kill the tree and might certainly inhibit regrowth for up to seven years, grass would return in a shorter period and corn planted in the ground turned over by rooting pigs would flourish, provided the soil was not then vulnerable to wind or water erosion. The silty clay of the floodplain near the settlement would withstand rooting pigs well. The sandier sediments of the rising ground to the south and west would have been more vulnerable and use of these by pigs could have been a factor in creating the heathland vegetation which they carry today. The boggy river margin vegetation and the oak-dominated forest in the hinterland would have been ideal for grazing pigs, with the added benefit of keeping them off arable soils in the vicinity of the settlement.

Social importance of pigs

As pigs provide little other than meat, keeping pigs in quantity can signal wealth and status in the owner. The ability to provide pigs to be consumed on special occasions gives status to the individual who has control of the herd. The major sources of written evidence for Celtic society are the Irish legends and law tracts from the early first millennium AD. Such written and iconographic evidence as survives does suggest that one of the means by which the Celtic chiefs demonstrated their power and influence over their retainers was to provide pigs and wild boar for consumption at feasts. At these, the pig was impaled on a forked stick and roasted over a fire, and carefully apportioned according to rank (ibid. 403). The antiquity of such practices can only be inferred from archaeological evidence.

However, in Celtic society pigs played a complementary role to cattle. The latter were even more important, at least in Irish society, for expressing the wealth of the chiefs, but they were kept predominantly for milk rather than for eating (Lucas 1958). They were extolled for their numbers, their beauty and their milk yields, but not for providing meat. Cattle were the main medium for social exchange, both peaceable exchange to cement family and tribal alliances, and also raiding.

There are some aspects of the treatment of the carcasses after death that can be used to test the hypothesis that pigs had a role in feasting and, therefore, perhaps bearing on social interactions. Pig bones at Runnymede were butchered little beyond separating the carcass into joints. This suggests that the meat was roasted rather than stewed, although there were no traces of burning or butchery at this site which specifically suggest spit roasting. Few of the pig bones, unlike those of cattle, appear to have been chopped for marrow. In the Neolithic some associated bones from the front leg appear to have been discarded with little modification beyond initial butchery. Finally, in both periods even the smallest groups include bones from several different animals, which suggests consumption on some scale.

Pigs had an important role in Celtic mythology (Ross 1974, 390 and *passim*) and in some societies hunting the wild boar was a past-time of those of higher rank, as indeed it continued to be into the Middle Ages. In Celtic iconography the wild boar is depicted as a fearsome creature with a huge bristling mane. In the legends it comes from the other world to terrorise the hero. Such legends are part of a culture where prowess is shown by hunting and slaying wild boar. As discussed, a small proportion of the remains from both periods are of wild boar. It is clear that the location was well suited to pig husbandry; the question then is whether pigs were at the same time favoured for the status they could bring as well as for the meat which they provided.

Discussion

For the Neolithic the contrast with Staines may be the key to interpreting the role of pigs. At the causewayed enclosure, cattle was the animal most in evidence. The bone remains, if nothing else, suggest that the two sites had different functions. If sacrifice or slaughter of cattle for consumption was appropriate at a causewayed camp, pig consumption may have been appropriate for a settlement, and it may have everything to do with the ease of rearing pigs and nothing to do with ritual or the status of the occupants of the site. If this is so, then we should expect to find other Neolithic sites with high proportions of pigs when other domestic sites (with good bone preservation) are found.

Pigs are routinely found in high proportions on Late Neolithic sites in England, particularly on sites where Grooved Ware pottery was in use. The henge monuments, especially Durrington Walls (Harcourt 1971), are the most notable examples, but several groups of grooved ware pits have now been excavated and studied, with assemblages with similarly high proportions of pig bones, such as those at Barrow Hills, Radley (Levitan and Serjeantson, forthcoming). The henges are the major ritual monuments of the period and pigs here are therefore seen to be associated with ritual, and possibly also with a more ranked society. We may be seeing in these social contexts the ultimate origins of the tradition of pig feasting witnessed in Celtic texts.

By the early first millennium BC the immediate environment of the settlement had become much less wooded and consequently less favourable for pigs than in the Neolithic. Mostly because of the value of wool, sheep had become more common. The human population was presumably greater than two millennia earlier and the area of land under cultivation will also have been greater. Where cultivation is widespread sheep and cattle are of more economic use than pigs because they provide more useful manure for arable fields. A decision to keep pigs in large numbers may have diminished the amount of cereal cultivation which could be carried out and diminished the potential wool crop. Pig keeping in this period could thus have been a greater expression of wealth than it was earlier.

Very few useful comparisons can be made with other sites. At neither Grimes Graves, which is a few centuries earlier, or Danebury a few centuries later, are pigs as common as at Runnymede. Those sites however, are in very different environments; Grimes Graves in sandy breckland, and Danebury on chalk downland. Had pig keeping been regarded as highly desirable at those sites, the cost in terms of labour inputs in providing forage and of damage to local agricultural land would have been more than in an environment such as that found at Runnymede. However, while the high numbers of pigs in this period partly reflect the site environment, they probably also have some association with the high status of the settlement which is suggested by the material culture.

CHAPTER 13

Coprolites and plant remains

Coprolites

SUE WALES

A number of suspected coprolites were recovered from both Neolithic and Late Bronze Age contexts at Runnymede Bridge. These appear to have been preserved by mineralization and are thought to be dog coprolites. The mechanism of preservation by mineralization has not been well studied. A coprolite from Winchester is reported to have been preserved by the replacement of organic material with calcium phosphate (Green 1979). It is also possible that the activity of bacteria might be responsible for the accumulation of metals in coprolites, leading to their preservation.

If coprolites are to be of use to the archaeologist in either the interpretation of the site or, in the case of human coprolites, in reconstructing ancient diet, then it is obviously important to be certain that the samples in question definitely are faecal in origin. Traditionally this has been decided on the basis of visual examination and an assessment of the shape, texture and type of inclusions visible in the sample. This may be adequate for well-preserved samples but for fragmentary samples it is not. In some cases the visual evidence may suggest faecal origin, yet not be conclusive. A reliable, objective method of confirming faecal origin is needed.

Where parasite remains are well preserved they may be useful as indicators of faecal material (Jones 1982). Neither parasite infestation nor their archaeological survival, however, can be assumed. Another method suggested for identifying coprolitic material is based on the colorimetric estimation of the concentration of nitrates. This assumes that coprolites would have significantly high levels of nitrates. In practice, however, there is likely to be interference from soil contaminants and some difficulty in distinguishing coprolites from other biological material.

The use of coprostanol as a faecal indicator

Coprostanol (5β–cholestan-3β–ol) is produced from cholesterol by the gut bacteria and is normally only found in the faeces of mammals and some birds (Hoskin

and Bandler 1987). This has led to its use as an indicator of sewage pollution, its presence being identified by either High Performance Liquid Chromatography (HPLC) or Gas Chromatography/Mass Spectrometry (GC/MS). In 1983 the detection of coprostanol and other faecal steroids was used to identify a sewer at the Roman fort of Bearsden on the Antonine Wall (Knights et al 1983).

The use of coprostanol as a faecal indicator has also been explored by the Food and Drug Administration in the USA. Their concern was to develop a cheap, reliable method of detecting small amounts of faecal contamination in food products. They successfully developed a method of detecting coprostanol by thin-layer chromatography (TLC). This procedure was subjected to rigorous testing to ensure that reliable, repeatable results were produced. They found that they could recover enough coprostanol for firm identification from 0.15 mg dry weight of rat faeces, which has a high proportion of coprostanol. Cow faeces, however, have a much lower proportion of coprostanol and a sample >0.5 mg was required. A sample size of 1 mg was suggested for routine testing (Hoskin 1987; Hoskin and Bandler 1987).

TLC was selected by the Food and Drug Administration because it required simple equipment and was suitable for occasional use. These attributes should make it a suitable method for archaeological use. In order to investigate this a number of samples were investigated following the method of Hoskin and Bandler. These included modern freeze-dried faeces, a sample from the gut of a Chilean mummy, desiccated human coprolites from Texas and possible dung from a medieval ship excavated in Denmark, as well as soil and other control samples where available. This successfully demonstrated the usefulness of this method in attributing faecal origin to possible coprolites (Robinson et al in press; Wales and Evans in press).

Runnymede samples

Eight possible coprolites were recorded from Area 16 East, of which six were investigated along with two soil samples. (See Table 58 and Plate 24).

Table 58: Samples from Area 16 East investigated for the presence of coprostanol

Context	Unit	Grid ref.	sf No.	Sample No.
16.822	16.K	54/13	136	ERB85/03
16.872	16.H	55/12	197	ERB85/07
16.872	16.H	56/12	199	ERB85/32
16.872	16.H	56/13	196	ERB85/31
16.887	16.H	59/12	183	not sampled
16.887	16.H	59/12	184	ERB85/30
16.887	16.H	59/12	198	not sampled
16.953	16.B	57/12	15	ERB86/09
16.872	16.H	57/12	-	ERB85/33 (soil)
16.876	16.H	58/12	-	ERB85/34 (soil)

Table 59: Samples from other Areas investigated for the presence of coprostanol

Context	Date	Grid ref.	sf No.	Sample No.
13.021	LBA	36/28	27	ERB84/01
13.024	LBA	35/31	39	ERB84/02
13.554	LBA	34/43	119	ERB85/10
13.707.2	Neolithic	36/38	195	ERB86/11
18.762	LBA	84/24	80	ERB86/04
19.240	Neolithic	34/13	171	ERB87/08
22.019	LBA	41/36	127	ERB87/05
22.019	LBA	41/36	-	ERB87/06 (soil)
20.765	Neolithic	38/29	-	ERB89/16 (soil)

A further seven coprolite samples from different areas of the excavation were examined along with two further soil samples. (See Table 59).

These samples varied in appearance and some were more convincing as coprolites than others. Initial visual descriptions are given alongside the results in Tables 60 and 61.

METHOD

Samples were extracted with hexane. Two methods of extraction were used. The first involved placing the sample in a closed sample vial for two hours with $10\mu l$ of hexane to 1 mg of sample. This was carried out with samples of 1 mg, 5 mg, 10 mg and 20 mg.

The second method involved extracting larger samples (1 g) in a soxhlet apparatus for 6 hours. The soil samples extracted were 2 g each.

Silica gel TLC plates were dipped in 5% phospho-molybdic acid in 95% ethanol. The reagent was allowed to saturate the gel for 10–15 seconds; the plates were left to air dry for 24 hours. Individual samples were applied to the plates alongside reference standards. The plates were next developed for 10 cm in diethyl ether-heptane

(55 + 45) in a closed TLC tank. The plate was then removed and dried in an oven set at 120 C for 20 mins.

Any spots corresponding to coprostanol or cholesterol were noted. Faecal material was indicated primarily by the presence of coprostanol, although cholesterol was also expected to be present.

RESULTS

A summary of the results is presented in Tables 60 and 61.

Table 60: Results from Area 16 East, showing the relative amount of coprostanol in the samples as indicated by TLC results

Sample No.	Description	Coprostanol
ERB85/03	end fragment, certain	+++
ERB85/07	?squashed coprolite with straw impressions	+
ERB85/30	? greater part of squashed coprolite with impressions	+++
ERB85/32	small fragment ?uncertain	-
ERB85/31	3 joining fragments making end of large-ish ovoid	+++
ERB86/09	bullet-like end, fairly certain	+++
ERB85/33	soil sample	-
ERB85/34	soil sample	(?+)

Table 61: Results from other Areas, showing the relative amount of coprostanol in the samples as indicated by TLC results

Sample No.	Description	Coprostanol
ERB84/01	fragment, but shape certain	+++
ERB84/02	fragment, but shape/texture/bone inclusions confirm	++
ERB85/10	?tufa whorl	++
ERB86/11	?tufa pellet	?
ERB86/04	fragment, but shape good	++
ERB87/08	end fragment, certain	+++
ERB87/05	end fragment, fairly good shape	+++
ERB87/06 (soil)	soil sample from below find spot of coprolite ERB87/05	-
ERB89/16	soil sample	-

The LBA coprolites gave consistent results from all sample sizes. It was not, however, possible to extract enough material from the Neolithic samples using the first extraction procedure and the results given were obtained using the second method.

Organic material is obviously preserved within these part-mineralized coprolites. It is not, however, as well preserved as in some desiccated coprolites previously examined.

Discussion

The results from the non-Area 16 East samples confirm the potential of this procedure. All the coprolite samples, except one, gave positive results. The one exception was the least convincing of the coprolites, and the results here indicate that there is no evidence for supposing that it was faecal in origin. The soil samples all proved negative, including one sample excavated from immediately below a coprolite find spot. This does not, of course, indicate that no coprostanol was present in the soil but rather that the quantity needed to be detected by this means was not present.

The results from the Area 16 East coprolites confirmed the faecal nature of all the coprolites except one small fragment. It may be that this was not a coprolite, or that having broken in the past it has lost more of its organic content than other, more intact samples.

The results from the soil samples are interesting. Whilst one sample was negative, which is consistent with all the other soil samples in this and earlier investigations, the other showed a small positive reaction. This would indicate that the coprostanol level of this soil has been measurably enhanced, which can only occur through the addition of faecal matter. It may be that the deposit (context 16.876) was a recipient of latrine waste from the settlement. Another possibility is that it is the result of contamination of dog faeces from dogs scavenging for food in the dump. The presence of gnawing on many of the bones would appear to support this possibility, as well as the survival of a number of intact coprolites from neighbouring grid squares in surrounding contexts in stratigraphic unit H.

As this area has apparently seen a rapid build-up of a mixed deposit it is possible that there will be good survival of organic compounds. If that is the case it may well repay more detailed chemical analysis.

Charcoal

ROWENA GALE

The Neolithic levels in Area 16 East yielded relatively little charcoal, but the LBA levels were more productive. Although some of the charcoal was very friable, identification was usually possible. The charcoal was prepared and examined using methods described by Gale (1991).

The results have been summarised in Table 62. Fragments arising from stem/twig have been indicated (+). In some instances the minimal size or poor structural condition of the specimen prevented the assessment of maturity.

Species identified:

Angiosperms (broadleaf species):

Acer campestre	field maple
Corylus avellana	hazel
Fraxinus excelsior	ash
Prunus sp.	British species include *P. avium*, wild cherry, *P. padus*, bird cherry, *P. spinosa*, blackthorn. These are anatomically similar.
Quercus sp.	oak
Rosaceae, subfamily Pomoideae	*Crateagus* sp., hawthorn, *Malus* sp., apple, *Pyrus* sp., pear, *Sorbus* sp., rowan, whitebeam and wild service tree. It is not possible to distinguish these genera using anatomical methods.
Salicaceae	*Salix* sp., willow and *Populus* sp., poplar. These closely related genera can not be separated reliably using anatomical methods.
Ulmus sp.	elm

Gymnosperms:

Taxus sp.	yew

Neolithic

UNIT A

The few fragments of charcoal found at the eastern end (16.960) of this unit, in the upper layers of otherwise sterile alluvial silt, were in poor condition with insufficient diagnostic information for identification.

UNIT B

This unit comprised the main cultural bearing level of the Neolithic and included a general scattering of charcoal. Fragments examined from 16.937, 952, 954 and 930 included oak and/or *Prunus*. This would appear to have been a very narrow range at a time when the countryside at Runnymede was moderately rich in woodland species. Pollen analysis (Greig 1991) indicated that the region was fairly densely wooded during the Neolithic period, with a wide range of arboreal species including oak, lime, elm, field maple, ash, birch, alder, yew, willow/poplar, hazel, blackthorn, hawthorn and elder.

UNIT C

Although designated separately from unit B, it may relate closely to the lower level. The charcoal (16.946) was identified as elm.

Late Bronze Age

UNIT G

Unit G represents a layer of shallow soil underlying the main refuse-rich layers. Charcoal fragments identified from contexts 16.896 and 909 were roughly similar in species content to those in the Neolithic and included oak, ash, *Prunus* and, in the latter context, hazel. The fragments from 16.909 were mainly from stem material. Fragments of hazel stem were associated with post hole 16.900.

UNIT H

This level was characterised by dense layers of burnt clay, burnt flints and dark soils. Although the dark colouration of the soil (more marked on the eastern side) has been attributed to an increased charcoal content, relatively few fragments of charcoal of sufficient size for identification were recovered. At the NE corner, oak charcoal (16.894) was associated with a group of animal bones, some burnt, and burnt flint nodules. Charcoal from contexts 16.899.1 and .2, a spread of burnt clay, included elm, *Prunus* and ash. From a spread of burnt flints (context 16.882.2), a single poorly preserved charcoal fragment was recovered and tentatively identified as oak. The association of burnt flint and charcoal was a common factor in these three contexts. Interestingly, only oak appears to have been used in context 16.894, whereas a mixture of species was present in contexts 899.1 and 899.2, including elm which burns slowly and makes a poor fuel.

UNIT I

Unit I comprised further dumping which may have been similar in origin to unit H but was stratigraphically higher. A wedge of soil (16.868) tapering out between 56 and 57 east included several charred fragments of hawthorn/apple/*Sorbus*.

UNIT J

Within the dark earth layers (contexts 16.834, 836, 849 and 865) of this stratum contexts 16.849 and 865 differed not only in colour, but also in the woody species present. The former, of brown-grey/greeny-grey shades, included elm and hawthorn/apple/*Sorbus* whilst the latter of typical dark grey, loamy midden soil, included fragments of oak, ash, *Prunus* and willow/poplar. Contexts 16.834 and 836 included oak and hazel, with the addition of hawthorn/apple/*Sorbus* in 16.836. Above these deposits in one corner of the trench lay a thin layer of clean clay sealing the underlying material. In 16.869 a few fragments of oak and field maple were present.

UNIT K

This unit comprised less concentrated cultural debris than those preceding and is thought to have represented not so much an area of active dumping as one of gradual accumulation of general refuse. Charcoal from 16.829, 824 and 822 included oak (some stem), *Prunus*, hawthorn/apple/*Sorbus* (some stem), field maple (16.829 only, stem) and elm (16.824 only).

UNIT L

A localised deposit of burnt flint separated units K and L. It is thought that unit L includes material from sequential flooding mixed with in situ refuse. Associated charcoal in 16.819 comprised hawthorn/apple/*Sorbus* and in 16.820, ash (stem), *Prunus* and yew.

Discussion

The charcoal finds related predominately to the LBA phase with little from the Neolithic deposits. Charcoal appeared to be abundant but frequently remained only as a dark stain in the soil. The number of fragments identified from each context were relatively few, usually less than 5, and the following conclusions based on this limited quantity of material is offered in a purely speculative manner.

Much of the material retrieved from the LBA deposits was thought to derive from residues of daily domestic life; charcoal fragments may have represented remnants from cooking hearths and the like. The association of charcoal with large quantities of burnt flints and clay (16.882.2, 894, 899.1 and 899.2) suggests that activities in operation close by may have included firing pottery. A supply of good quality firewood (or potential charcoal fuel) was almost certainly available in the locality. The existence of wood coppicing, particularly of oak, was suggested by the waterlogged wood excavated in Area 6 (Gale 1991). Although the maturity of the charred wood from Area 16 East was difficult to assess, a proportion of it was from stems/twigs. Heartwood was not evident but cannot be ruled out since the minimal size and poor condition of some fragments hindered observation. The mixture of wood identified, including elm (which smoulders slowly producing relatively little heat and which is unlikely to have been grown as coppice) and willow/poplar (which are generally light-weight woods and make poor firewood) suggests that wood may have been gathered from various sources (i.e. woodlands, scrub, hedgerows and/or from residual debris from other activities) and used for various purposes. This hypothesis is supported in part by the evidence from pollen analysis (Greig 1991) which showed that by the LBA deforestation had reduced the wooded landscape of the Neolithic to

Table 62: Wood genera identified in relation to stratigraphic unit

Unit	Context	Grid Ref.	Acer	Corylus	Fraxinus	Pomoideae	Prunus	Quercus	Salicaceae	Ulmus	Taxus
Neolithic											
B	16.930	53/12	-	-	-	-	-	X	-	-	-
B	16.937	53/12	-	-	-	-	X	-	-	-	-
B	16.952	56/12	-	-	-	-	?X	-	-	-	-
B	16.954	59/12	-	-	-	-	X	X	-	-	-
C	16.946	55/12	-	-	-	-	-	-	-	X	-
LBA											
G	16.896	55/13	-	-	X	-	X	-	-	-	-
G	16.896	54/13	-	-	X	-	-	-	-	-	-
G	16.896	57/12	-	-	X	-	-	?X	-	-	-
G	16.900	55/12	-	X+	-	-	-	-	-	-	-
G	16.909	58/12	-	X+	X+	-	X	X+	-	-	-
H	16.882.2	56/12	-	-	-	-	-	?X	-	-	-
H	16.894	(897)	-	-	-	-	-	X	-	-	-
H	16.899.1	54/12	-	-	-	-	X	-	-	X	-
H	16.899.2	55/12	-	-	X	-	-	-	-	-	-
I	16.868	57/12	-	-	-	X	-	-	-	-	-
J	16.834	53/12	-	?X	-	-	-	-	-	-	-
J	16.834	54/12	-	-	-	-	-	X	-	-	-
J	16.836	53/12	-	X	-	-	-	-	-	-	-
J	16.836	56/13	-	-	-	-	-	X	-	-	-
J	16.836	59/12	-	X	-	?X	-	X	-	-	-
J	16.849	56/13	-	-	-	X	-	-	-	X	-
J	16.865	55/12	-	-	X	-	-	X	X	-	-
J	16.865	57/13	-	-	-	-	X	X	-	-	-
J	16.869	59/13	X	-	-	-	-	X	-	-	-
K	16.822	54/12	-	-	-	-	X	X+	-	-	-
K	16.822	57/13	-	-	-	X+	-	-	-	-	-
K	16.822	59/13	-	-	-	-	X	X+	-	-	-
K	16.824	55/12	-	-	-	-	X	X+	-	-	-
K	16.824	57/12	-	-	-	-	X+	-	-	-	-
K	16.824	57/13	-	-	-	-	X	X	-	-	-
K	16.824	59/13	-	-	-	X	X	X	-	X	-
K	16.829	56/12	-	-	-	-	X	X	-	-	-
K	16.829	56/13	-	-	-	X	-	X	-	-	-
K	16.829	59/13	X	-	-	-	-	X+	-	-	-
L	16.819	53/13	-	-	-	X+	-	-	-	-	-
L	16.820	53/12	-	-	X+	-	X	-	-	-	X

X = present; + = stem wood

mainly scrub and open grassland – a habitat that would have favoured the colonisation of blackthorn (*Prunus spinosa*); *Prunus* (possibly blackthorn – see below) charcoal occurred consistently throughout the Neolithic and LBA deposits. In such an environment, wood or charcoal fuels of high thermal capacity (i.e. from ash and coppiced oak) may have been reserved for industries that required prolonged high temperatures, e.g. metal-working. By comparison, pottery kilns could have been operated at relatively low temperatures: some types of

clay can be fired in a small bonfire. The use of lower grade fuels for firing pottery at Runnymede may have been offset or boosted by the use of heated flints.

Alternative uses of some woods such as elm and willow/poplar should be considered since their presence amongst apparent fuel residues may be incidental. Despite their poor performance as fuel woods they possess excellent qualities for artefactual purposes. For example, crocks ready for firing may have been contained or transported in baskets made from withies (willow). Tool handles or other small items may also have been made from willow. Poplar timber is tough and slow to ignite and has traditionally been used in areas of high fire-risk (Edlin 1949). In the past it has been used to make the bodywork of carts and wagons and for some construction work. Rods from pollarded poplars have similar uses to willow. Elm is tough, difficult to split and very durable when persistently wet. It has been used for water pipes and hard-wearing items such as cart wheels, pulley blocks and wheels, mallets and tools (Edlin 1949). *Prunus* wood is fairly dense and burns well. Its frequent occurrence in the deposits in Area 16 East indicates that it was readily available in the neighbourhood. As previously discussed, blackthorn would have thrived in the contemporary landscape, particularly in the LBA. Blackthorn is a spiny shrub capable of forming dense thickets and impenetrable hedges or barriers. It is fairly fast growing and regular pruning or hacking back of invasive scrub would have provided handy firewood or kindling. Blackthorn is therefore, perhaps, the more likely origin of the charcoal than either cherry (*P. avium*) or bird cherry (*P. padus*).

Organic material associated with three bronze artefacts

CAROLINE CARTWRIGHT

M20 KNIFE BLADE. PLATE 23.
(See Chapter 11 for context)

Although the object has been coated with consolidant which has obscured some details of the organic material, several areas of different organic materials have been identified. Closest to the metal blade are mineral-replaced strips of willow (*Salix* sp.) which have been bound obliquely around both sides of the knife blade. The binding is irregular and frequently crosses underlying strips at right angles. One side of the blade has an organic patch adhering to it which mostly comprises oak wood fragments, oak charcoal flecks and more mineral-replaced willow strips held together in a matrix of copper alloy corrosion products and what may be decayed leather. A detached organic 'crust' found with the blade also comprises oak wood and charcoal, willow strips and possible leather fragments (obscured by consolidant but appearing to be very brittle and more blackened than those on the blade itself). It is possible

that the oak wood formed a handle for the knife which may have had the blade wrapped in withies and sheathed in leather for safe keeping. However, it is also possible that the withies, the wood and the leather components may have become dislodged on burial and preserved in the burial soil as an organic 'mat' in association with the metal blade but not in their original positions. The presence of the charcoal flecks tends to support the latter suggestion (although small flecks are mobile enough to become incorporated into most deposits).

M24 TWEEZERS. PLATE 23

Examination of the bronze tweezers under the optical microscope revealed a partial binding of willow strips, bark fragments and a thin area of willow wood (*Salix* sp.). Most of the willow strips were in mineral-replaced form although small areas of intact wood cells have survived.

M26 PIN

Examination of the pin's head revealed an organic lump comprising fragments of animal bone (some calcined), mineral replaced areas of Pomoideae wood, *Salix/Populus* wood, *Quercus* sp. (oak) charcoal flecks, copper alloy corrosion products, quartz grains and calcareous pellets. This combination of different materials is very similar to mixed hearth, refuse or midden deposits. The pin may have been lost or discarded into such deposits.

Discussion

Rowena Gale has already reported on the presence of Pomoideae (fruitwood), *Quercus* sp. and Salicaceae charcoal from Area 16 East (above). Most appears to be stem/twig-size material, suitable for hearth fuel. Schweingruber records Pomoideae timber as being suitable for the fabrication of special handles, percussion tools and spoons (Schweingruber 1990) but the presence of Pomoideae charcoal in association with pin M26 (see above) together with *Salix/Populus* (willow/poplar) and *Quercus* sp. (oak) charcoal fragments is more likely to represent bonfire debris.

If the *Quercus* sp. wood associated with the bronze knife M20 is indeed the handle, it matches well with Schweingruber's entry for oak being used for tool handles in Neolithic and Bronze Age Europe (ibid. 1990).

CHAPTER 14

Synthesis and broader implications

The chronology of Area 16 East in relation to Late Bronze Age occupation

STUART NEEDHAM

The chronology of the cultural assemblage in Area 16 East is relatively well defined by radiocarbon, metalwork and pottery evidence and in general terms reinforces the overall picture gained from the previous excavation reports of settlement activity within a full LBA milieu of Ewart Park stage, c.ninth-eighth centuries cal BC. Careful evaluation of dating evidence is now, however, directed at more refined issues, notably on the relative dating of different zonal sequences within the settlement area. The Area 16 East evidence turns out to be important in this regard. Emphasis is placed on the independent evidence of radiocarbon given the inexactitude of metalwork dating within the Ewart Park phase and the complexities of understanding ceramic variation. The evidence would suggest that formation of the dark earth deposits began (unit H) somewhere in the late ninth-early eighth centuries cal BC. This is significantly later, by around a century, than the inception date for the cultural sequence in the Area 6 river channel, viz. close to the turn of the tenth/ninth centuries cal BC (Needham 1991, 352). In order to be sure that the two sets of dates (done in different laboratories) were compatible, three samples from the

Area 6 river channel sequence have been dated by the British Museum laboratory; they gave comparable results to those obtained by Harwell (Table 63; Ambers and Bowman 1994, 98–100: BM-2646, 2647, 2652).

Occupation is believed to have begun around 900 cal BC, yet the base of the dark earth deposit in Area 16 East began to form approximately a century later. This is not entirely surprising given the evidence for a structural history in the area prior to the unit H refuse accumulation (Chapter 3). Indeed, neither is at variance with the situation on the occupied levee in Area 6 where, immediately alongside the river channel, the refuse-rich dark earth is seen to equate with mid-late channel deposits (Needham 1991, 212 Fig. 107, 377 Fig. 138). It is furthermore possible that the Area 2 sequence (Longley 1980, 12) begins relatively late, based on one radiocarbon date from F31 (HAR-1833) and the overall ceramic repertoire, but this assumes that the second radiocarbon date for the same context (HAR-1834) was on a sample of mature timber. It is not being suggested that these dark earth beginnings were necessarily synchronous across the site, but rather that they cannot be expected often to reflect the beginning of activity in that zone or on the site at large. This reinforces the need for careful evaluation of each zonal sequence and careful intercomparison.

It is worth briefly considering whether our understanding of the pottery assemblages can be reconciled with the suggested time difference between Area 16 East

Table 63: Radiocarbon dates for Area 6 additional to those previously published (Needham 1991, 346)

Lab. ref.	Context	Unit	Material	^{14}C Measurement BP	Calibrated date range BC 1σ	2σ	$\delta^{13}C$ (per mil)
BM-2646	F163/2	6.B	Cellulose from branch wood	2680 ± 50	895–875 860–810	930–795	-28.6
BM-2652	F117c	6.D	Cellulose from trunk wood	2730 ± 50	930–830	990–810	-25.2
BM-2647	F164/9	6.F	Cellulose from branch wood	2640 ± 50	895–885 850–790	915–765	-26.1
OxA-3428	F6.5	6.(E)	Bone from horse skeleton (part)	2790 ± 70	1020–845	1135–810	-22.9
OxA-3368	F111	6.G	Bone from dog skeleton	2690 ± 65	900–810	995–790	-26.6

Calibrations after CALIB rev 3.0, rounded to nearest 5 years.

230

and the Area 6 lower channel. It can be suggested that Area 6 units A-D span much of the ninth century cal BC and are therefore the deposits that most obviously precede Area 16 East unit H; for the present they can be used to define an early Runnymede assemblage. Those deposits contain a rather limited range of forms (Longley 1991, Figs 76–82). The fine wares are mainly based on simple, weakly to moderately carinated bowls with slightly hollow necks; decoration is absent with the exception of a single groove (P31), and burnish is frequent regardless of whether thick or thin-walled.

These vessels are often very well made, but have simple profiles with very little 'elaboration', namely some omphalos bases (P44, P49, P73) and internal rim bevels (P35, P64). The latter feature is also present on some jars or coarser wares (P51, P54, P62). The basic carinated bowl form also occurs in coarser or less well-made wares (e.g. P1, P60x) as can other bowl forms (P85). Few jar forms are reconstructible, but high-shouldered vessels with constricted mouths seem to be significant (e.g. P45, P46, P51, P62), P7 being an unusual variant with only a little constriction before the neck flares outwards. Tall flaring necks feature on P13 as well as on a finer 'vase', P61. Some sherds seem likely to belong to handled globular vessels (P68, P75, perhaps P46). There is also a thickened rim on P63, unusual in the Runnymede assemblage. A few coarse-ware vessels carry finger-tip decoration on rim or shoulder, or in one case diagonal rim incisions (P7).

The lowest units of pottery in Area 16 East (H and I) have much in common with the above-defined 'early' assemblage, not unexpectedly, but there may be some differences. Some thin-walled wares have rounded profiles with out-turned rims (P666, P667), a phenomenon seen in mid to late Area 6 channel deposits (e.g. P114, P192). Amongst the burnished carinated bowls there are more elaborate profiles (P654, P692), perhaps a chronological development, and Area 16.H-I also yielded some very thin-walled cups (P653, P688, P689), a type not found in the lower Area 6 channel despite the strong presence of tableware.

The coarse-ware jars in Area 16.H-I are fairly homogeneous with only moderate depth necks, weak to moderate shoulder angles and very little mouth constriction. Although comparable jars may be present as sherds in Area 6.A-D, they do not seem to dominate as in Area 16.H-I. Decoration is, however, equally sparse, but the moulded neck cordon on P683 is thought to be a feature of later rather than earlier PDR assemblages. The flared mouth bucket P679 has already been paralleled to vessels in Area 6.E and upwards (Chapter 8).

It would seem possible then to regard the 16.H-I assemblage as an early development out of a primary site assemblage defined on Area 6.A-D, a development

dating to the late ninth or early eighth centuries cal BC. This unit (16.H-I) also produced the wart-headed pin, a continental type (M26). The currency of the type in northern Europe could span as much as three centuries, within which the Runnymede context would appear to fall fairly late on.

Various changes have been documented in the pottery assemblages following on from 16.H-I and these do not need detailed reiteration (Chapter 8). A further trend towards more varied fine-ware bowls was noted, and indeed seems to mirror a similar process in Area 6. None of the new bowl forms can, on current evidence, suggest an absolute date for the upper dark earth in Area 16 East. However, the addition to the repertoire of sherds belonging to the distinctive beaded biconical bowls (P761, P847; Longley's type 8, Longley 1980, 66 Fig. 43) is thought to show a temporal development with the type becoming abundant in the Petters B pottery group datable perhaps as early as the eighth century cal BC (Needham 1990, 123–6, 140; see also Barrett 1978, 278). A highly decorated bowl from Area 6.E-G (P104) is a variant of this type.

Overall the ceramic changes identified between units 16.H and 16.M give the impression of a duration spanning at minimum a few decades. Some diagnostic sherds might point to a more protracted sequence. For example, the pronounced foot-ring or pedestal in unit L (P842) would traditionally be dated somewhat later, e.g. sixth century at the earliest (Barrett 1978, 286–7); less developed foot-rings occur in Area 6.E-I (P158, P198) and Area 16 East (P742). A similar argument might apply to the internally flanged rim in the same unit (16.L). On this basis the Area 16 East sequence (16.H-16.L) would have spanned two centuries or more. However, unit L is interpreted as a product of conflation thus allowing the possibility that some contained material could be considerably later than that in the in situ deposits immediately below (i.e. unit K). The in situ sequence could then still be of rather shorter duration. The various finger-decorated treatments on coarse wares which increase from 16.J upwards find a good match in the higher Area 6 stratigraphy, 6.E-J. In this respect these later groups can be regarded as belonging to a transitional LBA/EIA assemblage in south-eastern Britain, typified by such well-known sites as West Harling, Staple Howe, Scarborough, and Petters B. Loosely associated metalwork is of Ewark Park and Llyn Fawr types, but dating of this transitional ceramic tradition is not currently very refined, *c*.eighth-sixth centuries BC.

Formation and Late Bronze Age activity in Area 16 East

STUART NEEDHAM, TONY SPENCE,
DALE SERJEANTSON AND
MARIE-LOUISE STIG SØRENSEN

A framework

Through the careful definition of appropriate terminology in Chapter 1 we hope to have provided a useful baseline from which matters of refuse history and deposit function can be discussed. Before embarking on a detailed synthesis of Area 16 East, it is worth presenting some of the systems involved in schematic form. Other researchers have modelled both the flow of objects through their life cycles on settlements and the passage of transformations that assemblages may undergo, and have in this process generated many useful terms and concepts (e.g. Sullivan 1978; Hayden and Cannon 1983; Deal 1985; see also Chapter 1). For our own purposes however, we have found it necessary to offer fresh diagrammatic conceptualisations.

Initially we seek the inevitable passage of all material objects that we recover archaeologically from a settlement site. A flow diagram in Fig. 106 begins with manufacture or procurement and shows the use cycle and refuse cycle as successive or alternating phases of the life cycle of the object or fragment. For such pieces to be capable of archaeological recovery they would need to reach ultimate incorporation state (with possible very rare survivals continuously exposed on the surface on some sites?). Incorporation could have happened on any

number of previous occasions, each followed by gross disturbance so that those earlier burial contexts are effectively irretrievable as archaeological contexts, but may on occasion be inferred.

Our use cycle would embrace both the 'interactive context' and 'depositional context' of Sullivan (1978, 196–7). His point in this distinction, that many objects in use are in fact for a large part of the time merely in latent use, remains important, but choice of the term 'depositional context' for this is unfortunate given the more general connotations of 'deposition' in archaeological usage. We show it instead as 'concealed/stowed' material.

The transition from use cycle to refuse cycle occurs when artefacts are discarded, abandoned or lost, or when structures are dismantled, decay or collapse. (Objects lost/discarded off-site are not considered here). Although objects deliberately concealed, for retrieval or not as the case may be, may not normally enter the refuse cycle, they may do so if later they are unwittingly disturbed and thus made accessible, their previous status no longer being recognised. Broken or disfunctional material can also of course be deliberately buried at any stage; in the extreme case of burial immediately on breakage or disfunction (e.g. in the burial of hazardous broken glass), then its refuse cycle is of negligible duration. Because of the poor demarcation between provisional refuse and abandoned refuse (both physically and conceptually) they are blocked together, but this is not to deny essential differences in the status of materials that happen to remain in visible/accessible contexts.

Obviously the more straightforward life cycles for

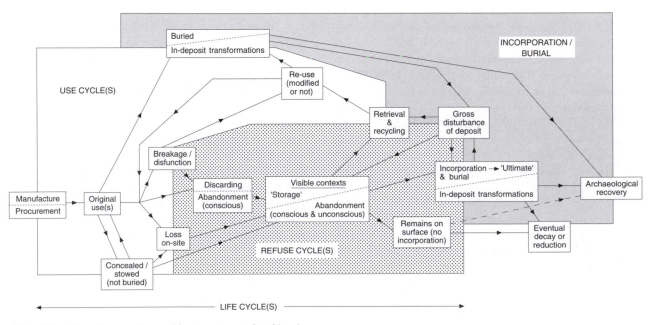

Fig. 106 *Flow diagram for possible stages in artefact histories.*

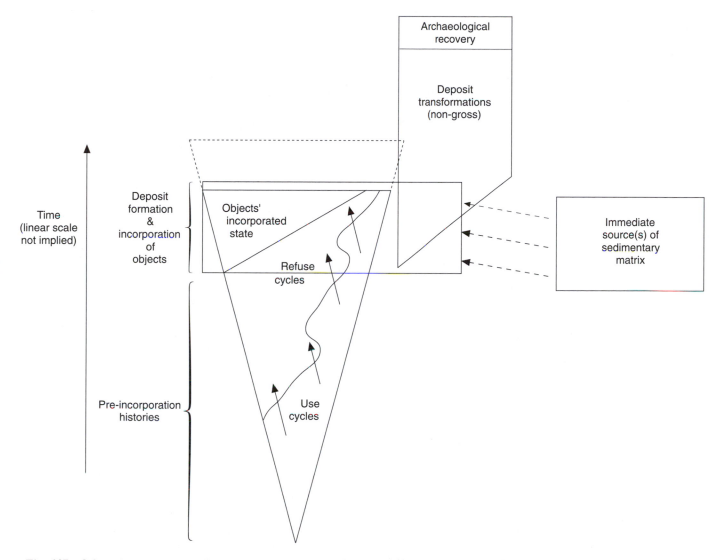

Fig. 107 *Schematic representation of the history of refuse components contributing to the sub-assemblage contained in a particular in situ deposit. The 'shape' of the aggregate histories through time may vary considerably. See text for fuller explanation.*

objects would see their passage from left to right of Fig. 106, but this can be complicated by reverse cycles which occur when:

1. material in visible contexts is retrieved for re-use;
2. buried material (either derived from refuse cycle or direct from use cycle) suffers gross disturbance resulting in reinstatement in visible contexts, or re-use; gross disturbance may be deliberate (based on recollection of buried material), opportunistic (in the expectation of certain materials or categories), or incidental (in the course of human or natural ground disturbance).

Our diagram makes explicit the possibility of artefact (and deposit) alterations once buried/incorporated, but takes for granted that modifications also occur during use and refuse cycles (for trace production see Sullivan 1978, 194ff).

A second diagram (Fig. 107) deals with a refuse sub-assemblage, whether defined on the basis of a single excavated context or a suite of closely related contexts. Here we see the process of deposit formation and the incorporation into it of an assemblage of objects. These may not be simultaneous processes (cf. Matthews 1993, 58), but we are presenting here a relatively straight-forward situation where, once the two came into association, there was no gross transformation to disrupt that association. Thus recovery is of an archaeologically in situ deposit. The constituent objects each have their own history and these can be portrayed schematically as generally diminishing in frequency with time backwards (shown as a triangle) and as having variable use-/refuse-cycle balances. In reality the shape of this composite time trajectory for the given sub-assemblage has scope to vary considerably, and its characterisation is of central interest to formation studies. For example, material of a

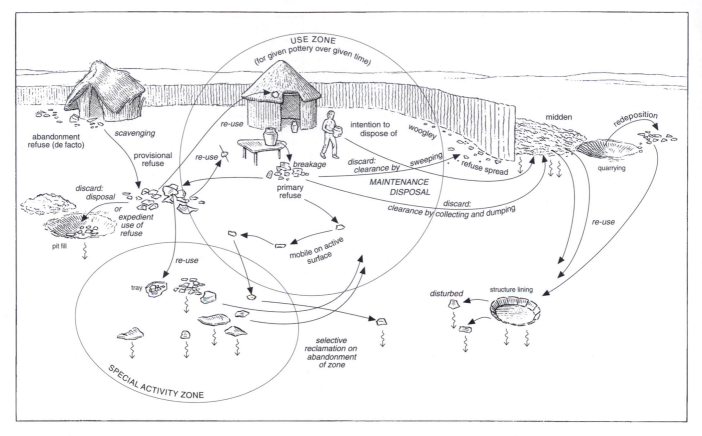

Fig. 108 *Schematic illustration to show diversity in the refuse cycles of broken pottery. It serves to illustrate the terminologies applied.*

much earlier phase might be redeposited *en masse*, thus outweighing contemporary material. In this case, the shape in a schematic representation such as Fig. 107 might instead be an inverted triangle.

The dashed projection of the object time trajectory allows for the possibility that some (even rarely all) object incorporations took place by infiltration from above after deposit formation had ceased. If deposit formation was of long duration relative to the typical life cycles then it may have subsumed most or all of the assemblage time trajectory. The sedimentary matrix engulfing the assemblage could involve material arriving with the objects as part of the same transportation process, or from quite discrete sources, or some combination of both.

To help visualise potential complexities in the histories experienced by a common type of find – pottery – we have hypothesised part of a settlement with its refuse regime in Fig. 108. This is not an attempted reconstruction of the situation at Runnymede or any other site, but instead an illustration of the diversity of refuse cycles that we believe would have commonly existed (cf. Deal 1985). Above all, it gives image to some of the processes and states we have defined. It should be noted that the majority of refuse states shown are still within reach of the systemic sphere and only incor-

poration takes them out of visibility and makes them less accessible. In most of the states depicted incorporation can take place providing that they were left undisturbed for long enough, or are sealed by material placed or accreted on top.

Objectives and potential

The wide range of material evidence in the Area 16 East sequence has allowed investigation of assemblage change using a variety of attributes. The individual studies presented in the foregoing chapters had *perforce* to deal thoroughly with discrete categories of evidence in effective isolation. We now wish to examine the interaction between the different branches and thereby attempt a more holistic characterisation of sub-assemblage composition at each appropriate level. For the most part this is conveniently and appropriately conducted at the level of the defined stratigraphic units, the formulation of which took place after initial studies and thus in part anticipated broad compositional distinctions.

To talk of 'holistic' characterisation does not presuppose single origins or explanations for the given sub-assemblage. On the contrary, consideration of the manifold evidence may show that different branches cannot be reconciled with a single *raison d'être* and that the idea of multiple simultaneous processes needs to be explored.

Any notion that materials within a sub-assemblage should necessarily tell a consistent story would deny the premise that refuse cycles can take enormously varied forms and work differently according to cultural context and coeval natural agencies. There should be some particular situations for which consistent interpretations would be expected. For example, if one material category showed evidence of having been subjected to heavy *in loco* trampling, then there should be appropriate indications of this process on any associated materials. If, however, different interpretations were drawn (despite allowance for intrinsic properties in each material), then something is obviously amiss, be it the choice or quantification of condition attributes, the interpretation drawn (i.e. *in loco* as opposed to deriving from a former locus), or the assumption of association. On the last point, for example, one might envisage differently-composed assemblages becoming incorporated in quick succession and being conflated by soil processes, thus to appear as one 'horizon' or sub-assemblage.

Perhaps it would be possible to explain 'inconsistent' deductions in terms of different balances in the histories experienced by different materials. This is undeniably legitimate as a general principle, but it is important to acknowledge that it potentially precludes recognising when classification of condition is 'poor'. If virtually all permutations are to be regarded as admissible, each having its own specific cultural explanation, then it leaves us with little to check our analytical procedures. For this reason if no other it is crucial that the means of measuring condition should be reproducible, whatever the final interpretation of the distributions found. This of course necessitates clear elucidation of the methods and philosophies employed, and the standards referred to.

The depths of interpretation we are drawing from a small excavation trench may cause some comment and this merits further discussion. We fully recognise that in some matters of interpretation it poses severe constraints (Chapter 1): the problem of not having identifiable structures to correlate with the deposits. No single zone of a site, especially when explored so restrictively, can be taken to be representative of the whole. However, for the kind of study we are engaged in here this is a point of strength, not a drawback. We are not in any way trying to use Area 16 East to typify the Runnymede Bridge site; on the contrary, we are looking to set it apart as having its own particular history and complex interrelationships with other deposits elsewhere on the site. In this respect trench size need not inhibit good understanding of many local features. We are interested to look at the changing status of the particular plot in terms of the temporal and spatial components. At any given point of the occupation span we can envisage a single recipient area, such as Area 16 East, as having a 'catchment' from which the incorporated materials come. In practice that catchment will probably involve a complex multi-dimensional distribution with special emphasis on the spatial distribution of immediate source locations (i.e. the previous loci in the refuse cycles) as well as original sources (i.e. the discard or loss loci) and the associated temporal distributions. The behavioural patterns of the site occupants, human and animal, will lie behind these distributions.

In many respects then a single trench study can stand in its own right, but this is not to say that its comprehension will not benefit from detailed comparisons with other sets of deposits, at Runnymede or elsewhere. That has to be the greater objective.

The questions we have been asking of the material in Area 16 East can be reduced ultimately to a deceptively simple one: what are the various materials doing there? This of course masks a complex array of finer questions such as:

1. what range of activities were responsible for initially generating the refuse, and how confident can we be of these?
2. what range of activities account for the arrival of the materials in Area 16 East?
3. at what remove, spatially and temporally, were these activities from the point of final incorporation?
4. over what timescale were these events taking place and how rapid was the accumulation of the deposits?
5. how fortuitous or how significant are the apparent associations between categories in a particular unit?
6. what conclusions may be drawn on status change for the particular zone?
7. what are the implications for broader site structure and organisation?

These questions essentially focus on cultural issues, but we are of course also concerned with understanding the natural processes at work on the material. Matters such as sediment accumulation or depletion and any natural alterations are central to identifying differential survival and its effects on cultural interpretations.

General features of the LBA deposits

The overall balance between the major finds categories (pottery, bone, burnt flint) does not change radically through the deposits. At a general level one might thus conclude that a broadly similar range of activities is ultimately responsible for these elements of refuse. However, Leese's statistical treatment has highlighted some significant variations between them (Chapter 6).

The first point is that although all three categories are reasonably well correlated, the correlation between the quantities of pottery and animal bone is rather stronger than either category with burnt flint. This could suggest that some, at least, of the burnt flint did not come from the same general activity or activity set as the pottery and bone, or alternatively that there was a divergent regime of re-use and discard. At the risk of pre-empting discussion below, it is necessary to say that some of the lower deposits are interpreted as containing 'industrial' debris and that the industry in question was consuming burnt flint. This explains neatly a further observation by Leese, that burnt flint is relatively less abundant in unit I than elsewhere and it is suggested that it was being preferentially consumed. In this way we can account for both the specific proportional representation of burnt flint, and its apparently different life cycle when compared to bone and pottery in the three-way correlations. We should, nevertheless, stress that much of the burnt flint was probably originally generated during cooking.

Even the suggested linking of pottery and bone refuse (and perhaps some burnt flint) should only be accepted at a rather general level. We may be witnessing nothing more than a common point (or points) of origin, for example a domestic residence, which regularly puts out similar proportions of these refuse types. Generation of the two types is inherently likely to stem from different, if interacting, spheres of household activity, though both could be seen at a general level to relate to food – its storage, preparation and consumption (e.g. Halstead *et al* 1978). Again, their respective refuse cycles would tend to be different in character because of the very different intrinsic properties and utilities of sherds and skeletal remnants. The generality of the linkage is highlighted by the exceptions noted by Leese. The occurrence of three contexts in unit H with higher than usual bone:pot ratios and of three in unit J with lower than usual bone:pot ratios could be an important indication of different mechanisms of accumulation; these deserve fuller exploration in consideration of the relevant sub-assemblages.

In the past a broad distinction has been claimed between an upper and lower zone in the Runnymede deposits (Needham and Sørensen 1988). This distinction has been upheld well by the detailed studies presented here and we feel confident in identifying the transition between in situ deposits and those substantially transformed by later agencies. There is, however, a more important distinction which relates to contemporary (LBA) activity. All the major lines of taphonomic study – on pottery, fired clay, stone and bone, supported by the statistical evaluations of gross bulk finds data – point to a general upward trend towards more attrition of finds, more mixing and more homogeneity. This trend already makes its mark at the unit J/K interface, somewhat below our interpreted in situ/transformed deposit boundary (unit L). Although we cannot rule out the possibility that unit K material has suffered some

post-abandonment transformations (of a lesser degree than those above), we would argue that its character is primarily the product of original formation during the occupation period. It is thus regarded as in situ material in the broad sense defined in Chapter 1.

Working from the pottery taphonomy, Sørensen in fact sees the possibility of 'background noise' material, in 'pure' form in unit K, and furthermore suggests this is present also in the lower deposits where it is over-whelmed by the superimposition of much early-stage refuse. The highly visible structuring of much refuse in the lower deposits (units H-J) in dumps and spreads argues at most for limited secondary disturbance and perhaps by corollary a relatively rapid accumulation (this matter will be examined in more detail for individual units below). We exclude from 'secondary disturbance' the process of compaction consequent on organic decay which almost certainly was significant soon after accumulation. The processes of accumulation resulted in assemblages which were relatively inhomogeneous with respect to pottery abrasion patterns and average sherd weight. By contrast, bone in the lower deposits focuses heavily on the 'good-very good' end of the condition spectrum and is thus more uniform. This again suggests some fundamental differences in their respective life cycles (as well as their material properties). The lower deposits, however, are categorically not built up uniformly from the life assemblage through a consistent set of processes. If the site's life assemblage remained essentially unchanged through units H-J, then formation processes must have fluctuated to allow differing contributions into the Area 16 East trap.

Again we need to reinforce a point of principle. Many dumps and spreads are interpretable as the direct result of individual acts of dumping. In this sense, they could be termed *primary dumps*, but this does not automatically mean that all the contained material is *primary refuse*, i.e. freshly generated.

Throughout this study we have worked from the premise that there will have been an unspecified amount of reworking and redeposition of earlier material and that we are studying sub-assemblages of *ultimate incorporation*. This is axiomatic nowadays, particularly in settlement studies, and Area 16 East presents two particular kinds of evidence in support of redeposition:

1. the radiocarbon dating of some bone material in unit I which indicates an earlier date than dated bone below in unit H.
2. a number of pot joins dispersed over varying vertical distances (Chapter 4).

The relative amount of redeposition at given levels is never easy to assess, but we can at least show that it was endemic and that in all probability it occurred over varied timescales. Some potsherds were demonstrably redeposited after some interval, as probably was the dated bone in unit I, in order for a significant difference to show in the radiocarbon measurements. The extent and nature of redeposition is of course an important contributory factor in understanding the refuse character at large; this will be returned to.

The detailed LBA sequence

UNIT G

Interpretation of unit G is hampered in some respects by its paucity of finds relative to the overlying dark earth deposits. This gross distinction is of course at the same time crucial evidence for a major change of formation process and, by implication, the activity status of the zone. We cannot rule out the possibility of some truncation of the ground surface at the unit G/H interface. This might seem an attractive proposition because of the abrupt change in finds densities, but the latter could just as easily result from a sudden shift in activity status without any truncation.

The artefact finds in this soil profile can be regarded as generally associated with structures in a use phase prior to unit H. Structural evidence is extremely limited by the trench size and deducing the nature of activity thus depends entirely on the evidence of the refuse and soil matrix. In doing so we must also be aware of the possibility that some artefacts had infiltrated the soil from the early dumps of unit H.

Although unit G is relatively ephemeral compared with the overlying dark earth deposits (units H-K), it could, on dating evidence available for the site at large, represent as much as a century of occupation. Finds were relatively thinly spread through the soil body and no artefact groups were recognised. The pottery shows a relatively high degree of abrasion compared to overlying material and the bone is fairly well broken up, probably from trampling rather than butchery. The average weights of bone and pot fragments were moderate and do not imply that the area was heavily trampled during the lead up to the change associated with unit H. Bone condition, although not as extreme as in units H-I, was still strongly slanted towards good and very good condition. In addition little gnawing or burning has been detected. This suggests a degree of protection to this material, yet there is evidence for trampling and/or surface exposure. It seems likely that this area, or its immediate environs was an active settlement zone, i.e. an occupied surface. The anatomical representation seems, for example, to derive directly from food consumption, perhaps therefore directly from a residential household. If the contemporary post holes belong to a residential building, which is possible, then we might speculate that they were situated towards its perimeter allowing some material to escape collection and removal, but also to escape much heavy trampling.

Although some burnt spreads closely overlie unit G, they are seen as relating to new activities at this locus rather than, say, the burning of the pre-existing structures. Charcoal was thinly scattered through the unit G soil. Although it is clear that some structural members, such as the post in 16.900, had been removed shortly before the use change, we do not need to envisage a sweeping change from standing structures to debris accumulation in a cleared area for there is evidence that some posts were standing during the early accumulation. Whether there was a change in structures at this juncture is difficult to ascertain.

The transition from unit G to H gives the impression of dramatic change from no rubbish accumulation to rubbish accumulation. In the earlier phase the Area 16 East zone could have been free of substantial refuse accumulation or, alternatively, such refuse was already accumulating before H but was being systematically cleared away. Whichever is closer to the actuality does not alter the implication that the status of the zone changed with the advent of unit H.

UNITS H AND I

Although it has been useful for analysis to have two units defined in the lower dark earth deposits, in many respects they can be treated together in this discussion. There are a few differences which need to be brought out, but in general these units trapped similar quantities, types and nature of refuse. These deposits are very rich in phosphates, indicating much organic content; indeed there might be a significant increase in levels associated with unit I (Chapter 3) over those with H.

The evidence of pottery linkages could be taken to support little time difference between H and I. The presence of a reasonable number of cross-links need not in itself be significant in this regard, if one accepts the likelihood of much redeposition. More significant is the fact that no such linkages show greater abrasion in the higher unit I. Furthermore the situation contrasts with declining numbers of linkages between H, I and higher units (J-M); these in fact consistently show some upwards abrasion. Overall then we would suggest a negligible temporal difference between H and I and indeed a rapid accumulation throughout. The latter conclusion seems clear from the overall condition of all major material categories, pottery, bone, stone and clay, all of which show very limited abrasion and relatively little fragmentation. In many cases the fragmentation present would have occurred prior to discard and an even smaller percentage of damage was thus the result of post-discard processes such as trampling. Again, some of the residual breakage of large pot crocks is thought to be due to weight of overburden. This might suggest that the near intact cups were deposited under or within soil or other padding, thereby protecting them from much breakage. All this points to very little traffic across the area per unit time. Yet curiously the area seems to have been well used, at least periodically, for certain activities. The implication is that accumulation was sufficiently rapid for material to be quickly protected by succeeding deposits (but also allowing some pressure and impact fracture).

At the beginning of unit H accumulation took place on gently sloping ground, dipping eastwards (cf. Fig. 13). The ground probably rose again towards a natural levee found in excavations in the riverside zone (Areas 14, 18, 21 and 31; Fig. 4). The deposits may thus lie on the western edge of a broad if slight depression. Superficially the character of the unit H and I deposits, having dumps of rubbish interspersed with in situ structures, could suggest a common activity set. However, the detailed analyses suggest to us that the durable remains contributing to units H and I derived from at least three processes.

Certain components of the material within H and I have been argued to relate to *in loco* pottery production. Such primary debris appears to be unusual at Runnymede, despite its rich in situ deposits. A change of status to an 'industrial zone', perhaps more appropriately called a *specialised production locus*, may explain the change in refuse status of the area or vice versa. There must always be an element of uncertainty in this correlation since any systematic clearance of debris and structures prior to unit H (a notion introduced above) could well have swept away any diagnostic set of evidence relating to, for example, pottery production. Specialised tools and raw materials, unless rendered unusable, might be preferentially curated for continued use. Indeed it could be argued that the very survival of a concentrated set of equipment in Area 16 East in units H and I, much of it still usable, was due to a winding down of the activity responsible and its eventual cessation at this particular locus – a kind of accretive abandonment horizon. On the other hand, if the sterile clay deposit in unit J (16.830/.869) was indeed an abandoned dump of potting clay, this might better mark the cessation of pottery production in the immediate environs, as distinct from the cessation of grit production at Area 16 East itself. We have already noted that the lowest proportion of burnt flint occurs in unit I, and suggested that this was due to its preferential consumption. Only one cache of (probably) fully-prepared flint grit was identified during excavation and most was presumably taken up to be mixed with clay.

On balance then we would argue that the specialised production locus was active during units H and I, even if conceivably in decline; this probably took place over a very short time span, perhaps as short as a few seasons. One should also keep in mind the possibility that pottery production was a seasonal activity and that the remains encountered in Area 16 East represent an end of season abandonment assemblage, in this case the last season before the activity shifted to a new locus. Even so, it seems likely that there would be some scavenging for useful materials or tools and it would be unwise to suppose that the assemblage was in any sense 'complete'.

We would identify fired clay beds 16.899 and probably 16.875 as in situ structures for burning flint and/or firing pottery. A large spread of burnt flint and partially broken-down flint (16.882) lay alongside 16.899, whilst a possible firing test piece was directly associated with 16.875. The enigmatic 'keyed' clay fragments (Cat. Nos. C21–6) confined to units H and I would seem to relate somehow to the pottery production centre, although it should be borne in mind that their fabric (fabric 5) would not survive much attrition and this could account for the absence of the type from some higher deposits in Area 16 East.

To accept that the zone was active as a production locus does not mean that all the materials accumulating at that time relate to the production activity in question. On the contrary, the great majority of associated refuse can be regarded as having more everyday domestic origins. The connection between the different categories might for example be that a changed activity status for the zone led to a relaxation of any rules maintaining refuse clearance. Early refuse accumulation in this scenario thus occurs almost incidentally as a by-product of the new activity status, encouraged perhaps by the hoarding of raw materials on the spot suitable for the production involved. It is hard to regard much, if any, of this household refuse as having been brought along as raw materials for pottery production although this does not preclude it being provisional refuse for other purposes. There was no use of grog in the Area 16 East pottery, indeed it is very rare, if not absent, at Runnymede. None of the structures found utilised pot sherds as linings, although this is a feature of some contemporary structures elsewhere (e.g. Barham, Suffolk – Martin 1993). At least one large piece of broken pot in Area 16 East (16.862; P726) was, however, used as a carrying vessel.

A relatively high incidence of burnt bone has been identified in unit I deposits. However, bone is an inferior fuel to wood and charcoal, and for the most part the degree of burning is not consistent with its use as a fuel. It is more likely that incidental burning was frequent simply because of the amount of pyrotechnic activity going on. It should be noted, however, that the charcoal recovered from units H and I (a mixture of

Ulmus, Fraximus, Prunus and Pomoideae) included some species that do not burn at high temperatures.

We now turn attention to the material that has loosely been called everyday domestic refuse. It is heavily dominated by animal bone (virtually all from domesticates) and pottery, though the balance between them is not constant. Unit I yielded the highest density of pottery in the whole sequence, whilst in unit H a few contexts prove to have an exceptionally high proportion of bone. It has already been suggested in the general section above that the bone and pottery could have come into the deposits by different routes, even if ultimately from the same source. The bone taphonomy evidence in units H and I gives an important insight into its refuse cycle when seen against other evidence.

In isolation the bone evidence might be taken to tell a straightforward story. A very high proportion is in excellent surface condition and fragmentation is rather limited, much perhaps caused during initial preparation, consumption and discard. This pattern gives the impression of material being dumped and sealed in Area 16 East very quickly after discard, often perhaps on initial discard; in other words a very short refuse cycle, or 'primary refuse' in so far as this term can be applied to butchery and food consumption waste. However, a reasonable proportion of bones have been gnawed (15% of identified bones) and this suggests that some bone experienced at least a short history between human disposal and final incorporation. To judge from the structure of the deposits, with intact dumps and little-disturbed structures, there was no significant scavenging of material in loco in Area 16 East. Coprolites, presumably from dogs, were associated especially with unit H, in part perhaps a function of preferential survival. There was also a trace of coprostanol found in the soil of 16.876 58/12 which must also derive from latrine waste (Chapter 12). It is perhaps most likely that defecation actually took place in Area 16 East, although one cannot rule out the possibility that droppings would have been collected up with other refuse from residential areas.

Nevertheless, it seems likely that much of the gnawing was taking place at some intermediate station, probably close to discard in time and space, i.e. around the eating areas. If this material had lain on the surface for any length of time it must have been protected from significant weathering or trampling. It seems possible, however, that some bones incorporated in H and I had become buried at an earlier stage of their refuse cycles only to be retrieved and redeposited. The radiocarbon dated bones from unit I were chosen for dating precisely because they were in very good condition, yet some appear to have been redeposited after an interval of some years or decades. Protection over this length of time is perhaps most likely in a sub-surface context.

The mixture of pottery classes represented, with a good balance between jars and finer bowls supplemented by some cups, again points to material coming from areas of consumption. The condition of the pottery and the number of conjoins would suggest that, like the bone, it experienced for the most part rather short-lived refuse cycles. We would see the source or sources, i.e. areas of consumption, breakage and discard, as lying relatively close by. We would not expect any important timber structures (e.g. houses, granaries) to be immediately adjacent, however, given the fire risk from pottery manufacture. More difficult to evaluate at this stage, in the absence of further detailed analyses for other parts of the site and particularly those with reconstructible building plans, are the status, intra-site location and frequency of the episodes of consumption responsible. It would be unwise at present to presume any higher status of consumption than was general for the site. The balance of meat apparently being consumed (beef, pork and lamb/mutton in descending order) is similar to that reconstructed from earlier studied assemblages (Areas 2 and 6; Done 1980; 1991). Notably absent however is horse, a minor but significant component in those assemblages. The suggested reverence attached to the eating and disposal of horses, argued to have been highly valued in life, could explain their concentration in particular parts of the site (Needham 1991, 380).

Some deposits of bone and pottery might be regarded as more deliberately contrived and specially deposited. These constitute the third main process we interpret. Special deposits of ostensibly mundane artefacts or refuse are clearly difficult to isolate from the spectrum of less overtly structured refuse accumulation, but we would draw attention to some groups that appear atypical for one reason or another. At the base of the H-I units two virtually fully-restored cups sat amongst the early-forming refuse heaps. Although they had sustained a little damage, it is believed that they were deposited intact, perhaps also standing upright. As Sørensen argues (Chapter 4), these appear as a quintessentially distinct phenomenon from the mass of associated pottery. A possible interpretation raised in Chapter 8 is that these functioned as water receptacles for use in pottery manufacture. Alternatively they might be regarded as event-marking deposits, perhaps marking the change of activity at the beginning of unit H. One could speculate for example that they held libations for the success of the pottery production to be engaged in.

Some deposits at a slightly higher stratigraphic level show an interesting disposition, with four small pot groups ranged around a dump of predominantly bone (16.873; Chapter 3). The central deposit contained the articulated hind-leg of a lamb as well as other, disarticulated parts, some from the same animal (Chapter 12). None showed signs of gnawing and a scapula showed filletting marks. At least part of the group would appear thus to represent meal refuse and it is difficult to assess what significance the configuration of pot groups might have, particularly given the small size of the excavated trench. This formation does however, seem distinct from any others encountered in these deposits, even if there was a purely functional reason for it, for example marking out a patch or weighing something down.

Should the refuse-rich deposits in units H-I automatically be regarded as a midden? There is a theory that rubbish attracts rubbish (Arlo-Guthrie trash-magnet effect – Schiffer 1987, 62), although we must be wary of assuming cross-cultural norms here. It is possible, however, that the continued accumulation of refuse of diverse kinds during units H and I signals another transition by which this area progressively became a specific midden. In the mechanistic, structural sense defined in Chapter 1 these are definable as midden deposits; always more difficult to determine is the extent to which the living people saw this as a particular kind of accumulation which was allowed in specific parts of a site and was definable in those functional and spatial terms (irrespective of whether clearly delimited or not). Moreover, was such a process seen entirely in terms of provisional refuse, or was there a distinguishable concept of refuse disposal – a desire to get rid of it from certain other quarters *and* an intention to put it beyond effective recovery?

UNIT J

There are signs of an archaeologically perceptible time interval from unit I to J, though still not of a long duration. Some upwards abrasion was noted amongst the pottery linkages with the underlying units. On the other hand, the weathered peaks of the by now largely buried clay spread 16.899 projected into unit J deposits but had not been severely reduced prior to their sealing. The sterile clay deposit 16.830 and the crock full of burnt flint, 16.861/862 at the base of unit J are taken to represent the termination of pottery production locally.

Two different modes of refuse collection/disposal can be suggested for unit J, one being marked by frequent artefact groups wholly or largely dominated by pot sherds. Conjoins were frequent within individual groups and it appears that large crocks of pottery entered the deposits intact. These groups explain why some contexts were shown to have abnormally low bone:pot ratios compared to the general picture in the Area 16 East sequence. The reason for the sequential accumulation of these pot groups in a limited area is not well understood, but they may have been considered to have high recycling potential, thus be accumulated as 'provisional' refuse (Schiffer 1987, 64–72; Deal 1985, 253).

The physical structure of the pot groups indicates some minor irregularities in the contemporary surface, assuming these were not caused by differential loss of organic refuse. Whatever the cause, the internal formations of the pot groups demonstrate minimal disturbance after deposition. This could mean that, as for units H and I, the deposits had accumulated rapidly ensuring that much material was sealed before there was opportunity for disturbance, or alternatively that this area was now at some remove from everyday production, consumption and traffic, whether human or animal. In this context it is noteworthy that even the one substantial block of fired clay present (16.845) is best interpreted as redeposited (Chapter 10).

If formation was as rapid as in the underlying deposits, there is good evidence nevertheless from certain materials that the refuse cycles of the incorporated material were generally lengthening. The most friable sandstones, for example, decline to about half their representation in units H and I; this seems to be due to taphonomic factors rather than any underlying change in the proportions of the stone in use. More definitively, there is a measurable decline in the condition of the animal bone (a decline which continues through overlying units K, L and M) which, in conjunction with the virtual absence of articulation and epiphyseal unions, argues for significantly longer refuse cycles, involving intermediate buried stations and/or periods of surface exposure. A peak in the incidence of gnawing suggests that longer surface exposure did play an important part in this process. The incidence of burnt bone decreases, perhaps no more than a reflection of a decrease in local pyrotechnic activity.

The greater spatial variability in average pot and bone weights compared to unit I below suggests the collection of debris from more diverse pathways and perhaps more episodic dumping and accumulation. These processes also caught up a greater quantity of domestic tools and accoutrements (Chapter 6). As argued for the lower units, pottery and bone again do not paint similar pictures and suggest arrival via different pathways. For example, localised variation in sherd size within unit J does not correlate well with changes in bone fragment size. The bone evidence includes all parts of the carcass of the major species supplemented by a minor component of species not present lower down. In contrast, the pottery gives the impression of a narrowing functional range relative to the contemporary site repertoire, being concentrated on vessels of modest volume.

Although much of the pottery appears to have been freshly discarded at the time of incorporation, a few instances of downwards-abraded linkages, both within unit J and between J and K, suggest that even some unabraded material was redeposited from protected intermediate loci. Overall, however, the bulk sherds give a growing sense of time differential between discard of vessels and incorporation of their fragments in the Area 16 East deposits.

Sherd linkages found show a strong association with overlying unit K deposits, but they fall off rapidly with higher units. Few further linkages were found between unit K and the lowest units (G-I) giving the impression that the early K deposits effectively sealed not only the immediately underlying deposits, but also their lateral equivalents beyond the trench, thus reducing the prospects of recycling the constituent rubbish.

UNIT K

The importance of the unit J/K transition has already been highlighted above in discussing general trends through the Area 16 East sequence. The material in this unit is characterised by much greater abrasion and fragmentation than encountered below. The average weights of both bone and pottery are reduced from unit J and the overall size of clay fragments also decreases. In more detail there is rapid diminution of fired clay fabric 3 which is particularly friable, thus a sign of longer exposure and reworking. Another feature of the unit is the virtual absence of artefact groups, just one burnt flint cluster at the top (16.822), and this seems to go hand in hand with a more even distribution of finds. At the same time the pottery abrasion pattern shows homogeneity within individual context levels. It is considered that homogenisation was largely created by formation processes during the occupation period with only a minor contribution from post-incorporation transformations.

Although much of the animal bone has suffered from attrition, a large assemblage survives and shows a wide spectrum of conditions. This suggests diverse life cycles with little of the material arriving from sources close by. This might be supported by the higher percentage of head and feet if we assume that primary butchery was taking place away from the residences. There was also less burnt bone than found below, perhaps another indication of the general remove from domestic routines.

As with the bone, the pottery can be regarded as deriving from a broad functional catchment within the settlement. The general functional classes of ware are well represented and this is a point of contrast with unit J below. The broadening of the catchment may in part explain an expansion in the range of bowl forms and the appearance of further decorative techniques. However, the overall conclusion based on the range of pottery attributes is that by this stage the site's ceramic assemblage had developed perceptibly from that contributing to the lowest dark earth deposits.

One somewhat surprising association with this unit and unit L above is the occurrence of the greatest number of wattle-impressed clay fragments. Given the high risk of loss of such impressions from abrasion and breakage it seems likely that the strength of this association is actually under-represented. The fragments are distributed through the vertical sequence rather than concentrated at a particular horizon and it is therefore difficult to see them as resulting from the destruction of a nearby building. Again, no concentrations of charcoal reflecting fire destruction were recognised. The fragments may be from buildings burnt over a period of time, or if from a single building, they imply a gradual dispersal and their progressive incorporation in the upper Area 16 East deposits. This reinforces a sense of moderate distance between the zone and the source building(s).

During the formation of unit K we do not see Area 16 East as particularly close to or accessible from areas of residence, food preparation and eating, or any specialised activity. In this respect it is thus possible to regard the assemblage as refuse of a sort that, we might postulate, will tend to accumulate almost anywhere within an occupied zone, even areas of unspecific and low level use. The rate of accumulation and the overall density and balance of finds may obviously vary according to circumstances, but generally we are talking about relatively slow accumulation of artefacts and perhaps organic material. How this manifests itself in terms of archaeologically recovered density will also depend on duration of the conditions, the relative quantity of simultaneous sediment accretion and any conflation due to organic decay. With these qualifications in mind the high density of material in unit K should not be read as high levels of activity or discard without supporting evidence.

Although unit K is interpreted as an archaeologically in situ occupation deposit and also classified as a dark earth, it seems difficult to regard it as a midden in the same sense as we see units H-J. Given that there are no indications of ploughing or other gross disturbance, it seems reasonable to assume that concentrated dumps were never a feature of this phase and that the practice had ceased in this area. Yet it was still the recipient of large quantities of refuse. These were apparently accumulated over a much longer time-scale than were the deposits of equal volume beneath and this again tends to deny any specific and regular practice of dumping. Indeed deposit volume per unit time may be even more discrepant. We argue that units H-J would have had a substantial component of vegetal refuse, but this seems likely to have fallen substantially by unit K given the rise in later-stage refuse and the decline in phosphate values seen in the columns; later-stage green refuse would have already decayed and deflated and thus unit K soil volumes may never have been much greater than those excavated.

Yet there clearly was persistent accumulation of

material at varied refuse stages and we need to comprehend the mechanisms by which this occurred. To some extent the mixed character of the refuse without very distinctive components might be regarded as *undirected refuse aggregation*, determined above all by the level of activity on the site at large and the status of the plot at the time. Durable refuse not taken (or flood-washed) off the site must by default accumulate on it. The arrival of material and its final incorporation at a particular part of the site would doubtless be due to a variety of processes including kicking, small-scale carrying, throwing, yard sweeping, shovelling, transportation by animal or child and even, where slopes exist (i.e. not at Runnymede), downhill soil movement. It seems fair to assume that an aggregation of many minor and incidental acts of transportation account for such deposits where, firstly, no clear episodic or wholesale dumping took place and, secondly, where much of the material seems to have had a moderately long refuse cycle prior to incorporation. It is difficult to regard such assemblages as either unused provisional refuse (although that does not exclude possible individual retrievals) or as the piecemeal accumulation of fresh discards and/or fresh sweepings from an activity zone. It may be that what we are seeing here is the typical collection of material in a space that has no specified use, is open or accessible and is within or alongside the occupied zone; it is frequented, but not for any particular or tangible purpose. One might imagine an unused part of a compound or a bit of 'waste' ground between residential units or activity areas.

UNITS L AND M

Most characteristics of the finds in these layers can be interpreted in terms of the processes of flood reworking, conflation and further soil processes which are believed to have given rise to these sediments. They are very pale in comparison with those below having lost significant charcoal elements, whilst phosphate levels decline to very low levels through L and M. Finds are of a small average size and their distribution is rather uniform, especially on the horizontal plane, giving the impression of a homogenised body. The abrasion pattern for pot sherds within each spit is also homogenous.

Burnt flint is now by far the predominant category of finds (by weight) and the more concentrated band which characterises unit L is thought to represent differential settling out of the heavier elements during flooding and subsequent conflation due to later worm-sorting. Any downward migration due to the latter process could lead theoretically to the infiltration of flood-reworked objects into the top of an undisturbed profile. The presence within unit L of some rather fresh artefacts and of moderate phosphate levels have led us to the conclusion

that infiltration has indeed taken place and hence that the contained assemblage is a mixture of flood-reworked material and some archaeologically in situ material. This would also explain why most of the reasonable number of pottery linkages between unit L and unit K (mainly upper K) exhibit no greater abrasion in the higher stratigraphic level.

Beyond this crucial point, deductions made from the pottery linkages between units K, L and M and any lower deposits requires some caution because the higher rates of attrition will tend to impede the confident recognition of joining or belonging sherds. Actual joins could obviously suffer preferentially, thereby emphasising the importance of identifying belonging sherds, but those matches depend on diagnostic attribute combinations.

In keeping with the retention of burnt flint, it is also the more durable stone types (Greensand and sandy limestone) which survive preferentially in these upper units. Both friable and medium-hard categories of stone decline in percentage steadily from unit J up to unit M (about 16–0% and 38–22% respectively). These changes are taken to be primarily due to taphonomic factors.

Bone has become a very minor proportion of the assemblage, average fragment size is now small and surface condition is generally poor. The species and anatomical representation must be seen as being heavily dependent on robustness. This probably explains for example the apparent increase in cattle bones in unit M. However, the higher proportion of pig in unit L continuing a trend from K runs counter to expected taphonomic processes and is thought to reflect a real, possibly under-represented, increase in pig. A similar trend was observed in the upper Area 6 sequence (Done 1991, 341), which suggests the possibility of a wider site-level shift in the balance of animals or carcasses brought in to the settlement.

The nature and meaning of midden deposits in the early first millennium BC

STUART NEEDHAM AND TONY SPENCE

If 'midden' is to be an useful concept in settlement studies it needs to be given its own definition which is both capable of archaeological discernment and yet sufficiently flexible to permit various interpretations depending on the specific social context and the state of our enquiries. It may seem preferable to define a midden in terms of its function, or the contemporary meaning attached to its formation and existence. Ethnoarchaeology could certainly approach the problem from this standpoint, but it would surely be prejudicial in archaeological studies. It therefore seems more profitable to start by defining a midden archaeologically as a set of deposits with a particular structure and certain kinds of spatial and temporal interrelationships (at various scales). This already requires considerable interpretation of the excavated data, but it is in large measure a definition of a physical construct without reference to the circumstances by which it came about and what value it had to society. These kinds of issues should indeed be better addressed once we have a fuller semantic framework for different kinds of occupation-generated deposit, allowing us to explore and articulate more readily the workings of the settlement system and its implications for refuse.

In this volume we have taken pains to resist employing the term midden in order simply to denote the existence of refuse-rich deposits. It seems to us that such use is not only superfluous but of no value in promoting the understanding of settlement debris. We have proposed (in Chapter 1) that *occupation deposit* is a suitable generic term to cover all contexts interpreted as relating to settlement, regardless of how rich or poor they are in recovered artefacts. It seems more than probable that it will often not be feasible on the evidence available to go beyond such a vague and unspecific term. Indeed, even at Runnymede with its abundance of different branches of evidence, one hesitates to refine the interpretations of all deposits. To reiterate, it is not considered helpful simply to brand all the refuse-rich, usually dark earth deposits as 'midden' and, although there is no hard and fast boundary, the conclusion we have reached above is that only part of the Area 16 East dark earth sequence might be regarded as a midden. A structure we can call a midden, in our predefined terms, emerges early in the sequence at some unspecified moment during units H and I, and continues through most or all of stratigraphic unit J. On the other hand unit K seems to break with the underlying principles of formation and it has been suggested that it represents a shift towards *undirected refuse aggregation* at this locale. This is certainly a case where wider excavation to reveal contemporary structure plans might help in understanding the functions that give rise to such a pattern.

Runnymede is one of a small group of sites showing the development of extensive refuse-rich deposits early in the first millennium BC. Certain or probable sites are Potterne (Lawson 1994), East Chisenbury (Brown *et al* 1994) and All Cannings Cross (Cunnington 1923) (all in Wiltshire) and Wallingford (Thomas *et al* 1986) (Berkshire). This is a phenomenon that is understandably attracting growing interest and such sites have been referred to as 'midden-sites'. Because of the evident scale of deposition witnessed it seems highly likely that middens in the sense employed here would be an important component of such sites. However, this does

need to be demonstrated, not least because in doing so meaningful internal variation in deposits will be elucidated, thus facilitating reconstruction of site organisation and maintenance routines. If we continue to refer to these as 'midden-sites' (or in some cases 'midden-mounds'), it needs to be understood that this is not a blanket statement to the effect that all refuse-rich deposits on these sites should be regarded as midden.

The problems inherent in treating all refuse concentrations as middens become apparent when considering many more localised instances within site complexes, for example as components of the fill of ditches or pit groups, or as spreads surviving in pockets or otherwise. These contexts are almost inevitable traps for the detritus of proximate human existence, which does not mean to say that a 'midden' will not on occasion be recognisable within them. But we cannot fail to recognise the obvious from our study of past societies: food consumption itself creates debris and, once humans start regularly to produce artefacts and structures, there is a further trend towards refuse accumulation. Re-use and recycling will only vary the *rate* of accumulation, and removal from the particular site would result in its different distribution across the landscape. Thus areas of occupation will always have featured such debris prior to any erosion, except when it was systematically and painstakingly removed from the site. Even extensive plough damage rarely brings about the latter circumstance completely.

To take an example, at the site of Petters Sports Field near Runnymede, the excavator recovered a large group of pottery from the uppermost fills of a large ditch on a site otherwise typically truncated (O'Connell 1986). This deposit had some modest depth and could have been a candidate for sequential dumping in this chosen place, but for the fact that the excavator found pottery joins from top to bottom of the deposit from which he deduced a single episode of dumping. For as long as this deduction stands (and obviously it is not unchallengeable), it seems best to regard this deposit as a *dump*, not a midden, although the material might very well have been drawn from a midden as much as from another refuse-rich source. We might of course debate the purpose of that dump: expedient use of refuse in order finally to level the ditch terminal; material to seal the underlying bronze hoard for cult or functional reasons; or disposal of unwanted material in a convenient depression.

So, refuse accumulation is endemic and so-called midden-sites seem to retain accumulations on a grand scale. Naturally, consideration has to be given to whether in part these reflect preferential preservation of the deposits when compared to the majority of sites which have suffered much erosion. However, it is difficult at present to find ways of evaluating this

243

differential. For the present purposes, discussion will proceed on the basis that preferential survival has at most exaggerated the apparent scale of accumulation.

If we are to accept that 'midden-sites' show refuse generation and then accumulation on a disproportionate scale, then we need to account for this. Larger resident populations could be one obvious reason for large-scale accumulation, but there is a perception (again impossible at present to quantify) that, despite much structural evidence at a site like Runnymede, the population level alone does not adequately account for the discrepancy. Other contributory factors are worth exploring, but first we need to look schematically at the flow of materials,

artefacts and refuse in and out of an individual settlement site. The principal flows likely to affect a prehistoric settlement site are shown in Fig. 109. Not all these flows will necessarily appertain to all situations and the crucial point is to consider which ones may differ for different classes of contemporary settlement site. Five primary categories of flow are outlined, each of which is prone to the conversion of materials and artefacts into refuse on the settlement site itself.

1. *On-site artefact production* will obviously involve the introduction to the site of raw materials, whether fuel, clay, stone etc. These would typically come from

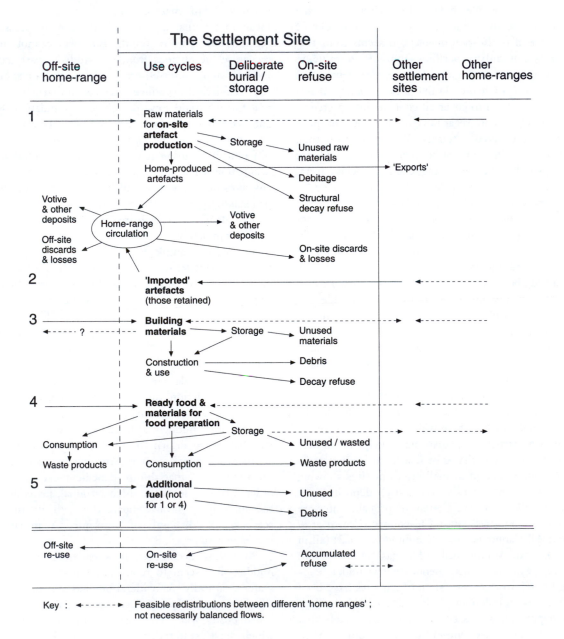

Fig. 109 *Flows of materials and artefacts in and out of settlement sites in relation to on-site storage and conversion to refuse.*

the 'home-range', but some may come from further afield. This material will end up in four main forms as a result of the production stage:

    (a) unused material;

    (b) debitage;

    (c) products (home-produced artefacts);

    (d) structures.

Products are the only component here likely to go systematically into circulation, involving either a sphere, or 'home-range', around the production site or, if 'exported', another home-range. The other portable components are likely instead to join discarded/abandoned products in refuse cycles immediately. Structures may of course remain in use (albeit intermittently) for some time but would perhaps only exceptionally be moved *en masse*. Normally they would face ultimate collapse, decay or dismantling.

2. *Imported artefacts*; objects brought onto the site from other home ranges for various possible reasons, such as:

    (a) personal accoutrements of visitors/temporary residents;

    (b) externally-produced objects for use by the main occupants (whether gifts or exchanges);

    (c) objects brought in for deliberate, permanent deposition – e.g. votive deposits.

Much of 2(a) is likely to exit the site, with the possible exception of items lost or damaged beyond utility during the visit. Objects in category 2(c) would obviously be a net gain to the site assemblage, but would presumably in most circumstances be a very minor component. The impact of 2(b), however, could be very variable depending on the particular socio-economic relations with the occupants from other settlements. In terms of gain or loss to the site, the key factor would be the balance between 2(b) and 'exports' within category 1(c).

3. *Building materials* would normally be supplied from off-site sources, at least in part. It is of course also possible that some materials would be stored on site for later use elsewhere, e.g. timber. Materials used for construction on the site itself would usually not be removed from it prior to the refuse stage; one exception might be the dismantling and transportation of buildings during abandonment.

4. *Ready food and materials for food preparation*; both ready-to-consume food and materials for producing edible food (foodstuffs, fuel, equipment) would in large measure come from off-site. Whether coming from near or afar, one would expect some correlation with the size of the population consuming the food. Temporary boosts to the population would be one factor likely to increase refuse generation, as would

more opulent eating due to, for example, higher status or affluence. Finally, the processing and cooking of food on site would generate more refuse than food introduced ready-to-consume; thus the balance between these contributions is a further important factor.

5. *Additional fuel*; this covers the introduction to the site of fuel for purposes other than items 1 and 4 above, notably for heating. Over time this could make a significant addition to the burnt debris on a site.

In almost all categories there is the possibility of reciprocal flows between different settlement sites, but fundamental to the matter of on-site refuse generation will be the extent to which these are proportional to recipient population levels. In addition we need to bear in mind the likelihood of a steady drain of 'home-range' artefacts and some foodstuffs away from the settlement to become abandoned in the hinterland, not on other occupied settlements. These would partly be items lost, broken and abandoned or consumed during the daily routines of subsistence, but could also include, for example, offerings taken for burial or abandonment at certain sacred, non-occupied places. It is accepted that there might be some differential loss from the latter circumstance according to individual site status, but for present purposes it is taken that these off-site drains were essentially proportional to the given site's material output or population.

Further potential gains and losses on the given site can occur once material is in the form of refuse (see bottom of Fig. 109). Although there need be no hard distinction between flows occurring at this stage or earlier, material as refuse is used for a different range of purposes, giving rise to different reasons for its transportation. Any deliberate transportation of manure, for example, would likely follow a settlement to non-settlement passage. It is certainly conceivable that such practices would not be proportional to site populations for sites of different status or farming economy (e.g. arable/pastoral balance). Cult refuse could be even more complex since if there existed a practice of carting refuse around under the cloak of 'cult' needs, then it could actually be travelling on-site or off-site, or in both directions.

Putting aside these possible disproportionate movements of refuse itself, one can suggest that the major distinctions in refuse generation between different classes of site might arise from the following:

(a) The balance between on-site artefact products going out of the home-range and off-site products coming in; the lower this ratio, then the greater is the relative accumulation of refuse.

(b) The amount of artefact production relative to site population, with particular regard to the generation of debitage and structural refuse. This begs the question, is production activity focused on certain sites?

(c) The quantity of refuse from food consumption per capita; a combination of both food debris itself and resulting utensil breakages/loss is involved. As mentioned in 4 above, this could be greater if the occupants ate and drank more opulently and were less careful with the tableware. Again, the temporary boosting of numbers of consuming individuals could also increase these refuse outputs relative to the site's resident population (assuming, of course that we are not considering hardship conditions with the same amount of food being distributed amongst a greater number of people).

(d) The extent to which the given site was engaged in arable and/or pastoral farming and artefact or raw material production. For example, a site devoted to extractive industries might well not be engaged in farming locally, so that any green refuse would have the potential to accumulate on site rather than being further recycled (assuming that green refuse was being generated).

(e) The concentration of other special activities/roles. For example, a special storage role, e.g. of grain, might well involve additional structures and, ultimately, more refuse. Again, 'market' activities might incidentally produce refuse that gets left behind on the site. The maintenance of horses for riding may involve on-site stabling and hence importation of large quantities of fodder and additional structural timbers, as well as the production of specialised equipment for equitation. In this particular situation, the supplement in terms of durable artefacts may be limited, but there could be a significant increase in horse manure, i.e. 'green' refuse.

It has been argued elsewhere in considering south-eastern Britain that by the early first millennium BC communities were concentrating a range of specialised activities on particular focal sites (Needham 1993, 67). Amongst these activities were craft production, feasting rituals involving the burial of special deposits and perhaps mortuary practices. Material exchanges of various kinds might well accompany some of these activities. From the foregoing it can be seen that any of these had the potential to enhance the generation of refuse per head of population relative to other sites not used in the same ways. Furthermore, evidence from Runnymede suggests the keeping of horses within the settlement limits (Done 1991, 342: Robinson 1991, 325), whilst some deposits at Potterne have also been identified as being rich in horse manure (Lawson pers. comm.). The evidence for developing equitation during the British Late Bronze Age may not be unconnected

with the emergence of 'midden-sites'. Certainly if differential flows of people between sites caused the latter phenomenon, then the means of transportation available will have affected the ease or otherwise with which those flows could take place for the given demographic pattern. If ready access to focal sites was indeed crucial, this could also explain for example, the choice of the river confluence location for the Runnymede settlement so that the communication network benefitted from river transportation as much as possible. Although this returns us to the idea of a primarily 'nodal' siting for the settlement, it has formerly been argued that this nodality was not in terms of some kind of mercantile economic system (Needham 1991, 383), and again we would stress the social background to settlement siting.

It is then possible to understand the quantities of refuse present at the 'midden-sites', providing they are not just a distortion due to preferential preservation, in terms of a set of social engagements specific to the particular cultural context that emerged during Post Deverel-Rimbury times. Any enhanced generation of the dominant refuse – broken pottery, butchered animal bone, perishable organics and burnt flint – could be due to the factors given above in (c) and one very influential circumstance would be the foregathering at the site from time to time of a large number of people who did not normally reside there, for example, kith and kin from settlements dispersed through a wider territory. If these folk regularly assembled at the special site, for whatever reasons – exchanges, religious ceremonies and other festivities – bringing with them materials and foodstuffs much of which was not taken away, then there would clearly be the likelihood of a net gain in refuse.

If there was indeed increasing preoccupation in and centralisation of some of the concerns listed above then it would not be unnatural for the residues, as part of the focal places, to acquire their own special symbolism to the participants. In this way substantial refuse-rich deposits would become a potent marker of a particular kind of site, being the stage for fundamental, ostentatious and cohering community activities. It seems more than likely that this would be a conceptual association that would emerge rather than one determined at the outset, but obviously if such associations gained a wide appreciation, the development of a 'midden' might have become an inescapable corollary of giving a site those certain special functions. Nevertheless, it still may be prudent to view disproportionate refuse accumulations as by-products of particular generative systems caused by certain social practices.

The theoretical discussion above also allowed for possible losses from site and these need to be considered further. If there was disproportionate refuse enhancement through certain activities and that enhancement shows through in the excavated in situ deposits, then it must mean that any depleting effects were not increased in similar measure and hence an overall imbalance in favour of enhancement was maintained. This does not mean that no refuse would have been transported away from the 'midden-sites', but rather that any such removals were more consistent from site to site in a given socio-economic framework, regardless of site status. This suggests that the refuse-rich deposits were not deliberately orchestrated with the intention of producing a resource for off-site use. Some 'green midden' might have been taken as fertiliser but, to judge from phosphate values, much was left on site.

On the basis of this discussion it seems reasonable to hypothesise that the vast quantities of refuse present at Runnymede derive not only from consumption, storage and production on the part of the resident population, but in part also from the regular entry of materials with visitors. One important implication of this hypothetical system is that there is a greater flow of persons engaging in refuse generating activities into the site than out of it. Where such activities were conducted between equals, for example between territorial chieftain bands of acknowledged equal status, it would seem likely that reciprocation would entail roughly equal flows of material in terms of worth into and out of the respective sites. Whether they were necessarily equal in volume needs to be considered. If however, we are right to see Runnymede and similar accumulations as reflecting a net gain over and above autochthonous refuse, then this seems most likely to derive from one-sided relations, most obviously perhaps the ingress onto the site of dependents from a 'hinterland' and any vassal groups.

Regardless of the precise system of social movements, it is clear that the occupants and frequenters of the Runnymede site were often engaged in, *inter alia*, refuse-generating activities, notably food consumption, pottery breakage and craft production. This raises the possibility that at least some production was specifically undertaken in the context of large gatherings and/or in the context of refuse dumps. There may have been practical advantages from both these associations, on the one hand the pooling of labour or the forgathering of a few existing experts, and on the other, the availability of raw materials. These contexts could also have developed particular connotations; for example, production amongst refuse heaps which were seen to symbolise socially-bonding activities could have been thought to assure the success of the venture. This is pure conjecture, but it will be important to see from future research the extent of *in loco* production amongst refuse, whether provisional or otherwise, at Runnymede and other sites.

The large quantities of material allowed to accumulate on the site could of course have been regarded as potential resources for recycling in various ways, as we have made clear throughout this report. It is important to recognise however, that recycling and incidental redeposition do not in their own right significantly alter the gross quantity of durable refuse deposited over time; even if further broken, most refuse will retain essentially the same bulk, albeit in a great quantity of fragments or in altered state, e.g. reheated. Re-used refuse will at some point again be rejected or abandoned, thus entering the site deposits. The crucial distinction appears instead when recycling and redeposition involve the movement of the material off-site – and we have already taken account of that potential factor.

It is difficult to quantify the proportion of refuse abandoned at Runnymede which had at some point in its refuse cycle been re-used in any way. Despite the fact that much material seems to have experienced moderate to long refuse-cycles, it may be suspected that only a minority, perhaps only a small minority of objects saw re-use after initial breakage or discard. There is, however, a problem of visibility here since late-stage refuse will tend to have lost any traces of re-use episodes earlier in its refuse-cycle and, moreover, is also perhaps unlikely to remain in its spatial context of re-use. This problem is exacerbated by deposits featuring material having complex life histories and it seems possible that this will be the typical situation on 'midden-sites'.

Equally difficult to evaluate is the Late Bronze Age attitude towards refuse in terms of its *potential* utility, which is quite a different matter from the actual extent to which it was put to use. It would seem likely that pre-industrial societies would generally consider refuse to be potentially useful for any of a number of purposes: for incorporation in new structures, reworking into new artefacts, use as organic fertiliser or even as cult fertiliser. In this way a high proportion of refuse, i.e. anything not considered to be undesirable or utterly useless according to the etiquette of the time, might be seen as potentially useful. Any accessible refuse accumulations, definable as midden or otherwise, would thus constitute 'provisional' refuse. The fact that some or most may not find subsequent use is immaterial to the contemporary perception of its utility. As we have already said, with more refuse continuously being generated, especially under the social preconditions we have suggested, it is inherently likely that much would never be required for secondary purposes. This may explain why legitimate provisional refuse (in the eyes of the occupants) can nevertheless soon be allowed to be covered and made difficult of access. What we may be witnessing is a perpetual slide in which certain material is at first considered potentially useful, but then the unused portions almost imperceptibly become redundant and abandoned as they are replaced by more recently generated refuse of the same type. This is a classic drift that most of us today will recognise in the context of material in lofts, outbuildings and little-used cupboards or wardrobes.

If we can accept that there is no incompatibility between the fact of progressive refuse accumulation and a widespread valuation of refuse as 'provisional', we nevertheless still need to enquire into their specific articulation. For example, is the midden the place where refuse deemed to be provisional is immediately stashed only to be subsequently, and sometimes quickly, covered by further deposits and thus rendered invisible? Or could we be seeing more conscious acts of abandonment by which provisional refuse, initially stored elsewhere, was at some critical point transferred to a midden with an implicit change in its perceived value?

It may be a mistake to look for too clear-cut a distinction between these hypothetical systems. The pot group concentrations in Area 16 East unit J might however, illustrate an example of the former situation. Like the deposits beneath, those of unit J are considered to have built up fairly rapidly and they also follow the earlier pattern of episodic accretion. Thus we regard it as a developing midden, yet at one specific horizon low in J the midden was favoured as a locus for disposing of or stockpiling pottery-only groups. Although the evidence may not be wholly conclusive on this point, the strong impression gained is that these pot groups were deposited sequentially rather than as a single event. This argues against any wholesale transfer of a former dump of provisional pottery refuse. On the other hand the deposits are consonant with the demarcation of a particular part of a midden at a particular stage of its growth for a particular kind of resource – i.e. sizeable crocks of pottery.

In this final discussion we have touched on some broader issues, some culturally and site specific, others concerning wider questions about the nature of refuse and human perception of it. Yet we have still been drawn back to the minutiae of the Area 16 East evidence, a recognition that this level of detail will ultimately be instrumental in providing a basis for wider social interpretations of these exceptionally formed and/or exceptionally well-preserved 'midden sites'. We have dared to venture some ideas about the social background on the strength of rather one-sided evidence, given the poverty of comparative studies. This is a challenge to all those studying refuse and formation on contemporary sites, of any nature, since the distinctions between 'midden sites' and others (if they stand scrutiny) will be as crucial as the intrinsic evidence from the former sites themselves. The existence of the social system outlined earlier in this discussion would potentially have a range of interesting, even surprising ramifications, some of which should be testable against other evidence, but this goes beyond our objectives in this volume.

References

Aldsworth, F., Kelly, E. and Needham, S. 1981. A Late Bronze Age founder's hoard from Bramber, West Sussex: a preliminary report. Chichester, West Sussex County Council (circulation report).

Ambers, J. and Bowman, S. 1994. British Museum natural radiocarbon measurements XXIII. *Radiocarbon* 36: 95–112.

Ambrosiani, B. and Clarke, H. 1992. *Investigations in the black earth*. Birka Studies Vol. 1, Stockholm.

Audouze, F. and Gaucher, G. 1981. *Typologie des objets de l'Age du Bronze en France, Fascicule VI: Epingles*. Paris, Société Préhistorique Française, Commission du Bronze.

Barrett, J. 1978. The EPRIA prehistoric pottery. In J. Hedges and D. Buckley, Excavations at a Neolithic causewayed enclosure, Orsett, Essex, 1975. *Proceedings of the Prehistoric Society* 44: 268–288.

Barrett, J. 1980. The pottery of the Later Bronze Age in Lowland England. *Proceedings of the Prehistoric Society* 46: 297–319.

Barrett, J., Bradley, R. and Green, M. 1991. *Landscape, Monuments and Society: the prehistory of Cranborne Chase*. Cambridge University Press.

Baudou, E. 1960. *Die regionale und chronologische Einteilung der jüngeren Bronzezeit im Nordischen Kreis*. Acta Universitatis Stockholmiensis, Stockholm.

Binford, L.R. (ed.) 1981. *Bones: Ancient Men and Modern Myths*. New York, Academic Press.

Bowman, S. 1990. *Radiocarbon Dating*. London, British Museum Press.

Bradley, R. and Fulford, M. 1980. Sherd size in the analysis of occupation debris. *Bulletin of the Institute of Archaeology, London* 17: 85–94.

Braude, R. 1962. Some concepts of nutrition of the pig. In J.T. Morgan and D. Lewis (eds) *Nutrition of Pigs and Poultry*: 295–315. London, Butterworth.

Britton, D. 1968. Late Bronze Age finds in the Heathery Burn Cave, Co. Durham. *Inventaria Archaeologica*, GB55. London, British Museum.

Bronk Ramsey, C. 1994. Analysis of Chronological Information and Radiocarbon Calibration: The Program Ox. Cal. *Archaeological Computing Newsletter*, 41: 11–16.

Brown, G., Field, D. and McOmish, D. 1994. East Chisenbury midden complex, Wiltshire. In A.P. Fitzpatrick and E.L. Morris (eds) *The Iron Age in Wessex: recent work*. Salisbury, Wessex Archaeology.

Buck, C.E., Kenworthy, J. B., Litton, C.D. and Smith, A.F.M. 1991. Combining archaeological and radiocarbon information: a Bayesian approach to calibration. *Antiquity* 65: 808–821.

Bullong, C.A. 1994. Analysis of site stratigraphy and formation processes using patterns of pottery sherd dispersion. *Journal of Field Archaeology* 21: 15–28.

Butzer, K.W. 1982. *Archaeology as Human Ecology*. Cambridge Unversity Press.

Celoria, F. 1974. A Late Bronze Age pin from Brentford. *Transactions of the London and Middlesex Archaeological Society* 25: 278–281.

Clarke, D.V. 1978. Excavation and volunteers: a cautionary tale. *World Archaeology* 10 (1): 63–70.

Clason, A.T. 1967. *Animals and Man in Holland's Past, Vol. A.* Groningen, J.B. Wolters.

Clutton-Brock, J. (ed.) 1981. *Domesticated Animals from Early Times*. London, Heineman and British Museum (Natural History).

Clutton-Brock, J. 1984. *Excavations at Grimes Graves, Norfolk 1972–1976, Fascicule 1: Neolithic antler picks from Grimes Graves, Norfolk and Durrington Walls, Wiltshire: a biometrical analysis*. London, British Museum Press.

Coffyn, A., Gomez, J. and Mohen J-P. 1981. *L'apogée du Bronze Atlantique: le dépôt de Vénat*. L'Age du Bronze en France, 1. Paris, Picard.

Cohen, A. and Serjeantson, D. Forthcoming. *A Manual for the Identification of Bird Bones from Archaeological Sites*. Revised edition. London, Archetype Press.

Coles, J.M. and Darrah, J. 1977. Experimental Investigations in Hurdle-making. *Somerset Levels Papers* 3: 32–38. University of Exeter, Department of History and Archaeology.

Coles, J.M., Caseldine, A.E. and Morgan, R.A. 1982. The Eclipse Track 1980. *Somerset Levels Papers* 8: 26–39. University of Exeter, Department of History and Archaeology.

Coles, J.M. and Orme, B. J. 1977. Neolithic hurdles from Walton Heath, Somerset. *Somerset Levels Papers* 3: 6–29. University of Exeter, Department of History and Archaeology.

Courty, M.A., Goldberg, P. and Macphail, R. 1989. *Soils and Micromorphology in Archaeology*. Cambridge University Press.

Cowie, T., O'Connor, B. and Proudfoot, E. 1991. A Late Bronze Age hoard from St. Andrews, Fife, Scotland: a preliminary report. In C. Chevillot and A. Coffyn (eds) *L'Age du Bronze Atlantique: Actes du 1er Colloque du Parc Archéologique de Beynac*: 49–58. Beynac.

Cunnington, M.E. 1923. *The Early Iron Age inhabited site at All Cannings Cross Farm, Wiltshire*. Devizes, George Simpson.

Darby, H.C. 1973. *A New Historical Geography of England.* Cambridge University Press.

Davis, S.J.M. 1992. A rapid method for recording information about mammal bones from archaeological sites. London, Ancient Monuments Laboratory, circulation report 19/92.

Deal, M. 1985. Household pottery disposal in the Maya Highlands: an ethnoarchaeological interpretation. *Journal of Anthropological Archaeology* 4, 243–291.

Dobney, K. and Rielly, K. 1988. A method for recording archaeological animal bones: the use of diagnostic zones. *Circaea* 5 (2): 79–96.

Done, G. 1980. The animal bone. *In* D. Longley 1980: 74–79.

Done, G. 1991. The animal bone. *In* S.P. Needham 1991: 327–342.

Drew, C.P. 1935. A Late Bronze Age Hoard from Lulworth, Dorset. *Antiquaries Journal* 15: 449–451.

Driesch, A.v.d. and Boessneck, J. 1975. Schnittspuren an neolithischen Tierknocken. *Germania* 53: 1–23.

Edlin, H.L. 1949. *Woodland crafts in Britain.* Batsford.

Epstein, H. and Bichard, M. 1984. Pig. In I.L. Mason (ed.) *Evolution of domesticated animals:* 145–162. London, Longman.

Evans, C. and Serjeantson, D. 1988. The backwater economy of a fen-edge community in the Iron Age: the Upper Delphs, Haddenham. *Antiquity* 62: 360–70.

Ewbank, J.M., Phillipson, D.W., Whitehouse, R.D. and Higgs, E.S. 1964. Sheep in the Iron Age: a method of study. *Proceedings of the Prehistoric Society* 30: 423–6.

Farrington, O.S. and Bateman, R.M. 1992. A holistic approach to the analysis of archaeological deposits illustrated using a late Roman urban sequence from Northwest Europe. In P.B. Vandiver, J.R. Druzik, G.S. Wheeler and I.C. Freestone (eds) *Materials Issues in Art and Archaeology III:* 179–192. Pittsburgh: Materials Research Society, Symposium series Volume 267.

Fox, C. 1939. The socketed sickles of the British Isles. *Proceedings of the Prehistoric Society* 4: 222–248.

Freestone, I.C. 1991. The Petrology of the Stone Materials. *In* S.P. Needham 1991: 138–139.

Gale, R. 1991. The identification of wood remains. *In* S.P. Needham 1991: 226–233.

Gaucher, G. 1978. *L'Age du Bronze dans le Bassin Parisien: les ensembles et les groupes culturels du Bronze Moyen et du Bronze Final.* Thèse de l'Université de Paris I.

Gibson, A. and Woods, A. 1990. *Prehistoric pottery for the Archaeologist.* Leicester University Press.

Gilchrist, R. and Mytum, H.C. 1986. Experimental archaeology and burnt animal bone. *Circaea* 4 (1): 29–38.

Gillespie, R. 1989. Fundamentals of bone degradation chemistry: collagen is not the way. *Radiocarbon* 31 (3): 239–246.

Gingell, C. 1992. *The Marlborough Downs: a later Bronze Age landscape and its origins.* Wiltshire Archaeological and Natural History Society, Monograph 1, Devizes.

Gingell, C. and Lawson, A.J. 1983. The Potterne project: excavation and research at a major settlement of the late Bronze Age. *Wiltshire Archaeological and Natural History Magazine* 78: 31–34.

Gingell, C. and Lawson, A.J. 1985. Excavations at Potterne, 1984. *Wiltshire Archaeological and Natural History Magazine* 79: 101–108.

Grant, A. 1975. Appendix B: the use of tooth wear as a guide to the age of domestic animals. In B. Cunliffe (ed.) *Excavations at Porchester Castle, Vol. 1:* 437–450. London, Society of Antiquaries.

Grant, A. 1982. The use of tooth wear as a guide to the age of domestic ungulates. In B. Wilson, C. Grigson and S. Payne (eds) *Ageing and Sexing Animal Bones from Archaeological Sites:* 91–108. Oxford, British Archaeological Reports 109.

Green, F. J. 1979. Phosphatic Mineralization of Seeds from Archaeological Sites. *Journal of Archaeological Science* 6: 279–284.

Greenfield, H.J. 1988. Bone consumption by pigs in a contemporary Serbian village: implications for the interpretation of prehistoric faunal assemblages. *Journal of Field Archaeology* 15: 473–479.

Greig, J. 1991. The botanical remains. *In* S.P. Needham 1991: 243–262.

Grigson, C. 1965. Faunal remains: measurements of bones, horncores, antlers and teeth. In I. Smith (ed.) *Windmill Hill and Avebury: Excavations by Alexander Kieller 1925–1939:* 145–167. Oxford, Clarendon Press.

Grigson, C. 1987. Animal bones. *In* R. Robertson-Mackay 1987: 123–125.

Halstead, P., Hodder, I. and Jones, G. 1978. Behavioural archaeology and refuse patterns: a case study. *Norwegian Archaeological Review* 11 (2): 118–131.

Harcourt, R. 1971. The animal bones. In G. Wainwright and I.H. Longworth, *Durrington Walls: excavations 1966–1968:* 338–350. London, Society of Antiquaries.

Hayden, B. and Cannon, A. 1983. Where the garbage goes: refuse disposal in the Maya Highlands. *Journal of Anthropological Archaeology* 2: 117–163.

Hill, J.D. 1993. Ritual and Rubbish in the Iron Age of Wessex. Unpublished PhD thesis, Cambridge University.

Hoskin, G.P. 1987. Identification of Mammalian Feces by Thin-Layer Chromatography of Coprostanol – Collaborative Study. *Journal of the Association of Official Analytical Chemists* 70 (3): 499–501.

Hoskin, G.P. and Bandler, R. 1987. Identification of Mammalian Feces by Coprostanol Thin-Layer Chromatography – Method Development. *Journal of the Association of Official Analytical Chemists* 70 (3): 496–498.

Jones, A.K.G. 1982. Human parasite remains: prospects for a quantitative approach. In A.R. Hall and H.K. Kenwood (eds) *Environmental archaeology in the urban context*: 66–70. London, Council for British Archaeology Research Report No. 43.

Jones, R.T., Wall, S.M., Locker, A.M., Coy, J. and Maltby, M. Undated. *Computer Based Osteometry: Data Capture User Manual (1)* (3342). London, Ancient Monuments Laboratory.

Kinnes, I. 1991. The Neolithic pottery. *In* S.P. Needham 1991: 157–161.

Kinnes, I., Gibson, A., Ambers, J., Bowman, S., Leese, M. and Boast, R. 1991. Radiocarbon dating and the British Beakers: the British Museum Programme. *Scottish Archaeological Review* 8: 35–68.

Knights, B.A., Dickson, C.A., Dickson, J.H. and Breeze, D.J. 1983. Evidence concerning the Roman military diet at Bearsden, Scotland, in the 2nd century AD. *Journal of Archaeological Science* 10: 139–152.

Kobyliński, Z. and Moszczyński, W.A. 1992. Conjoinable sherds and stratification processes: an example from Wyszogród, Płock Province, Poland. *Archaeologia Polona* 30: 109–126.

Lambrick, G. 1984. Pitfalls and possibilities in Iron Age pottery studies – experiences in the Upper Thames Valley. In B. Cunliffe and D. Miles (eds) *Aspects of the Iron Age in Central Southern Britain:* 162–177. University of Oxford, Committee for Archaeology, Monograph No. 2.

Lasota-Moskalewska, A., Kobryn, H. and Swiezynski, K. 1987. Changes in the size of the domestic and wild pig in the territory of Poland from the Neolithic to the Middle Ages. *Acta Theriologica* 32 (5): 51–81.

Laux, F. 1976. *Die Nadeln in Niedersachsen*. Prähistorische Bronzefunde, XIII.4. Munich.

Lawson, A.J. 1994. Potterne. In A.P. Fitzpatrick and E.L. Morris (eds) *The Iron Age in Wessex: recent work*. Salisbury, Wessex Archaeology.

Legge, A.J. 1981a. The agricultural economy. In R. Mercer, *Grimes Graves, Norfolk: Excavations 1971–72*: 79–103. London, Her Majesty's Stationery Office.

Legge, A.J. 1981b. Aspects of cattle husbandry. In R.J. Mercer (ed.) *Farming Practice in British Prehistory*: 169–181. Edinburgh University Press.

Legge, A.J. 1992. *Excavations at Grimes Graves, Norfolk, 1972–1976, Fascicule 4: Animals, environment and the Bronze Age economy*. London, British Museum Press.

Levine, M. 1982. The use of crown height measurements and eruption-wear sequences to age horse teeth. In B. Wilson, C. Grigson and S. Payne (eds), *Ageing and Sexing Animal bones from Archaeological Sites*: 223–250. Oxford, British Archaeological Reports 109.

Levitan, B. 1990. The non-human vertebrate remains. *In* A. Saville (ed.) *Hazleton North*: 199–214. London, English Heritage Archaeology Report 13.

Levitan, B. and D. Serjeantson. Forthcoming. Animal bone. *In* A. Barclay and C. Halpin (eds) *Excavations at Barrow Hills, Radley, Oxfordshire. Volume 1. The Neolithic and Bronze Age monument complex*. Oxford, Thames Valley Landscape Monograph.

Longley, D. 1980. *Runnymede Bridge 1976: Excavations on the Site of a Late Bronze Age Settlement*. Surrey Archaeological Society Research Volume No. 6, Guildford.

Longley, D. 1991. The Late Bronze Age Pottery. *In* S.P. Needham 1991: 162–212.

Lucas, A.T. 1958. Cattle in ancient and Medieval Irish society. In *O'Connell School Union Record 1937–1958*. Dublin.

Macklin M.G. and Needham, S.P. 1992. Studies in British alluvial archaeology: potential and prospect. In S.P. Needham and M.G. Macklin (eds) *Alluvial Archaeology in Britain*: 9–23. Oxbow Monograph 27, Oxford.

Marshall, W. 1817. *Volume 5: Southern and Peninsular Departments*. London. Reprinted by David & Charles, Newton Abbot.

Martin, E. 1993. *Settlements on hilltops: seven prehistoric sites in Suffolk*. East Anglian Archaeology Report No. 65, Ipswich.

Matthews, K. 1993. A futile occupation? Archaeological meanings and occupation deposits. In J.W. Barber (ed.) *Interpreting Stratigraphy*: 55–62. AOC Scotland Ltd, Edinburgh.

Meniel, P. 1987. *Chasse et élevage chez les Gaulois (450–52 av. J.-C.)*. Collections des Hesperides, Editions Errance.

Millett, M. 1979. How Much Pottery? In M. Millett (ed.) *Pottery and the Archaeologist*: 77–80. University of London, Institute of Archaeology, Occasional Papers No. 4.

Mohen, J-P. and Bailloud, G. 1987. *La vie quotidienne: les fouilles du Fort-Harrouard*. L'Age du Bronze en France, 4. Paris, Picard.

Mook, W.G. 1986. Business meeting: Recommendations/Resolutions adopted by the Twelfth International Radiocarbon Conference. *Radiocarbon* 28: 799.

Needham, S.P. 1980. The bronzes. *In* D. Longley 1980: 13–27.

Needham, S.P. 1990. *The Petters Late Bronze Age metalwork: an analytical study of Thames Valley metalworking in its settlement context*. London, British Museum Occasional Paper No. 70.

Needham, S.P. 1991. *Excavation and Salvage at Runnymede Bridge 1978: The Late Bronze Age Waterfront Site*. London, British Museum Press.

Needham, S.P. 1993. The structure of settlement and ritual in the Late Bronze Age of south-east Britain. In C. Mordant and A. Richard (eds) *L'habitat et l'occupation du sol à l'Age du Bronze en Europe*: 49–69. Paris, Editions du Comité des Travaux historiques et scientifiques, Documents Préhistoriques 4.

Needham, S.P. *et al*. Forthcoming. Runnymede Bridge Research Excavations Vol. 1.

Needham, S.P. and Hook, D.R. 1988. Lead and lead alloys in the Bronze Age: recent finds from Runnymede Bridge. In E.A. Slater and J. Tate (eds) *Science and Archaeology, Glasgow, 1987*: 259–74. Oxford, British Archaeological Reports 196.

Needham, S.P. and Longley, D. 1980. Runnymede Bridge, Egham: a late Bronze Age riverside settlement. In J. Barrett and R. Bradley (eds) *Settlement and society in the British later Bronze Age*: 123–130. Oxford, British Archaeological Reports 83 (2 vols).

Needham, S.P. and Sørensen, M-L.S. 1988. Runnymede Refuse Tip: a Consideration of Midden Deposits and their Formation. In J.C. Barrett and I.A. Kinnes (eds) *The Archaeology of Context in the Neolithic and Bronze Age: Recent Trends*: 113–126. Department of Archaeology and Prehistory, University of Sheffield.

Orton, C. 1975. Quantitative pottery studies: some progress, problems aand prospects. *Science and Archaeology* No. 16: 30–35.

Orton, C. 1993. How many pots make five? – an historical review of pottery quantification. *Archaeometry* 35: 169–184.

O'Connell, M. 1986. *Petters Sports Field, Egham: excavation of a Late Bronze Age/Early Iron Age site*. Guildford, Surrey Archaeological Society Research Volume No.10.

O'Connor, B. 1980. *Cross-Channel relations in the later Bronze Age*. Oxford, British Archaeological Reports, International Series 91 (2 vols).

Payne, S. 1973. Kill-off patterns in sheep and goats: the mandibles from Asvan Kale. *Anatolian Studies* 23: 281–303.

Payne, S. and Bull, G. 1988. Components of variation in measurements of pig bones and teeth, and the use of measurements to distinguish wild from domestic pig remains. *Archaeozoologia* II 1.2: 27–65.

Payne, S. and Muson, J. 1985. Ruby and how many squirrels? The destruction of bones by dogs. In N.R.J. Fieller, D.D. Gilbertson and N.G.A. Ralph (eds) *Palaeobiological Investigations: Research Design, Methods and Data Analysis*: 31–39. Oxford, British Archaeological Reports, International Series 266.

Pearson, G.W., Pilcher, J.R., Baillie, M.G.L., Corbett D.M. and Qua, F. 1986. High-precision ^{14}C measurements of Irish Oaks to show the natural ^{14}C variations from AD 1840–5210 BC. *Radiocarbon* 28(2B): 911–934.

Pearson, G.W. and Stuiver, M. 1986. High-precision calibration of the radiocarbon time scale, 500–2500 BC. *Radiocarbon*, 28(2B): 839–862.

Pimentel, D. and Pimentel, M. 1979. *Food, Energy and Society*. London, Edward Arnold.

Plog, S. 1980. *Stylistic variation of prehistoric ceramics*. Cambridge University Press.

Poole, C. 1984. The Structural Use of Daub, Clay, and Timber. In B. Cunliffe (ed.) *Danebury, An Iron Age Hillfort in Hampshire, Vol. 1, The excavations 1969–1978: the site*: 110–123. London, Council for British Archaeology Research Report No. 52.

Rackham, D.J. 1986. Assessing the relative frequencies of species by the application of a stochastic model to a zooarchaeological database. In L. van Wijngaarden-Bakker (ed.) *Database Management and Zooarchaeology*, Journal of the European Study Group of Physical, Chemical, Biological and Mathematical Techniques Applied to Archaeology, 1986. Research Volume 40: 185–192.

Rackham, O. 1980. *Ancient Woodland: its History, Vegetation and Uses in England*. London, Edward Arnold.

Robertson-Mackay, R. 1987. The Neolithic causewayed enclosure at Staines, Surrey: excavations 1961–63. *Proceedings of the Prehistoric Society* 53: 23–128.

Robinson, D., Aaby, B., Wales, S. and Namsen, P. In press. Botanical, parasitological and chemical analyses of organic material from the Gedesby Ship – a medieval shipwreck from Falster, Denmark. In I. Vuorela (ed.) *Proceedings of the European Workshop on Underwater Archaeology and Archaeometry, Tvärminne, Finland, October 15–18, 1992.*

Robinson, M. 1991. Neolithic and Late Bronze Age insect assemblages. *In* S.P. Needham 1991: 277–326.

Ross, A. 1974. *Pagan Celtic Britain*. London, Sphere.

Ross, E.B. 1983. The Riddle of the Scottish Pig. *BioScience* 33 (2): 99–106.

Rozanski, K., Stichler, W., Gonfiantini, R., Scott, E.M., Beukens, R.P., Kromer, B. and van der Plicht, J. 1992. The IAEA [14]C Intercomparison Exercise 1990. *Radiocarbon* 34: 506–519.

Rychner, V. 1979. *L'Age du Bronze Final à Auvernier, 2: typologie et chronologie des anciennes collections conservées en Suisse*. Cahiers d'archéologie Romande No. 16, Lausanne.

Schiffer, M.B. 1976. *Behavioral archaeology*. New York, Academic Press.

Schiffer, M.B. 1987. *Formation processes of the archaeological record*. Albuquerque, University of New Mexico Press.

Schiffer, M.B. and Skibo, J.M. 1989. A provisional theory of ceramic abrasion. *American Anthropologist* 91 (1): 101–115.

Schweingruber, F.H. 1990. *Microscopic Wood Anatomy*. (3rd edition) Birmensdorf, Swiss Federal Institute for Forest, Snow and Landscape Research.

Serjeantson, D. 1991. 'Rid Grasse of Bones': a taphonomic study of the bones from midden deposits at the Neolithic and Bronze Age site of Runnymede, Surrey, England. *International Journal of Osteoarchaeology* 1: 73–89.

Serjeantson, D. 1995. Antler implements and ox scapulae shovels and Animal bone. *In* R.M.J. Cleal, K.E. Walker and R. Montague (eds), *Stonehenge and its Landscape: Twentieth-Century Excavations*: 414–430, 437–451. London, English Heritage Archaeological Report 10.

Serjeantson, D, Wales, S. and Evans, J. 1994. Fish in later prehistoric Britain. *In* D. Heinrich (ed.) *Archaeo-Ichthyological Studies*. Papers presented at the 6th Meeting of the I.C.A.Z.

Fish Remains Working Group. Sonderdruck Offa 51. 1994: 332–339. Neümunster, Wachholz Verlag.

Shennan, S. 1988. *Quantifying archaeology.* Edinburgh University Press.

Silver, I.A. 1969. The ageing of domestic animals. In D. Brothwell and E.S. Higgs (eds) *Science in Archaeology:* 283–302 (2nd edition). London, Thames & Hudson.

Snedecor, G.W. and Cochran, W.G. 1991. *Statistical Methods.* (8th edition), Iowa State University Press.

Stokes, P. In prep. The Butcher, the Cook and the Archaeologist. In Proceedings of the Annual Conference of the Association for Environmental Archaeology.

Stuiver, M. and Polach, H.J. 1977. Discussion: Reporting of ^{14}C data. *Radiocarbon* 19 (3): 355–363.

Stuiver, M. and Reimer, P.J. 1987. *Users guide to the programs CALIB and DISPLAY, Rev 2.1.* Quaternary Isotope Laboratory, University of Washington.

Sullivan, A.P. 1978. Inference and evidence in archaeology: a discussion of the conceptual problems. In M. B. Schiffer (ed.) *Advances in archaeological method and theory (Vol.1):* 183–222. New York, Academic Press.

Sullivan, A.P. (III) 1989. The technology of ceramic re-use: formation processes and archaeological evidence. *World Archaeology* 21: 101–114.

Talon, M. 1987. Les formes céramiques Bronze final et premier Age du Fer de l'habitat de Choisy-au-Bac (Oise). In J.C. Blanchet (ed.) *Les Relations entre le Continent et les Iles Britanniques à l'Age du Bronze: Actes du Colloque de Lille*, 1984: 255–273. Amiens, Supplément à la Revue Archéologique de Picardie.

Thomas, R., Robinson, M., Barrett, J. and Wilson, B. 1986. A Late Bronze Age Riverside Settlement at Wallingford, Oxfordshire. *Archaeological Journal* 143: 174–200.

Varndell, G. 1991. The Worked Chalk. In I.H. Longworth, A. Herne, G. Varndell and S. Needham, *Excavations at Grimes Graves, Norfolk 1972–76, Fascicule 3: Shaft X; Bronze Age Flint, Chalk and Metalworking*: 94–153. London, British Museum Press.

Wales, S. and Evans, J. In press. The identification of coprolitic material – a chemical method of confirming the faecal origin of suspected coprolites. In J. Szymanski (ed.) *Proceedings of Archaeological Sciences Conference, York, 1991.*

Watson, J.P.N. 1979. The estimation of the relative frequencies of mamalian species: Khirokitia 1972. *Journal of Archaeological Science* 6: 127–137.

Willburger, L. 1983. *Tierknochenfunde von der Heuneburg, einem frühkeltischen Herrensitz bei Hundersingen an der Donau (Grabungen 1966 bis 1979): die Schweine.* Munich.

PLATES

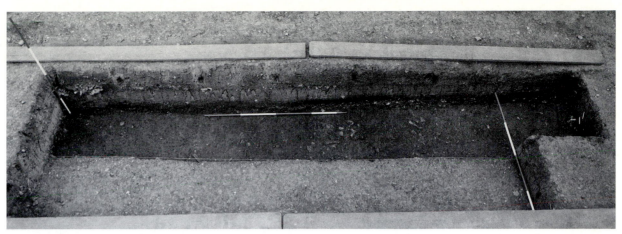

2 *Gravel deposit 16.933 and the adjacent erosion gully, under 16.932 (cf Fig. 11). The cluster of LBA material at the left end (east) of the section includes bone continuing from 16.890 and overlying burnt flint 16.874.*

3 *The surface of the gravel deposits, stratigraphic unit D, and south section of the trench. The sample holes in the upper section are the horizontal transects for phosphate measurement. Also showing is modern over-burden above the walkway.*

1 *The in situ Neolithic soil, stratigraphic unit B, after removal of the gravel deposits (units C and D); some of the unit B finds have already been lifted (cf Fig. 10). Viewed from grid North.*

5 *Cup P651 in refuse cluster 16.891 (cf Fig. 17).*

7 *Spreads of burnt clay 16.899 and burnt flint 16.882 in the western half of the trench on surface 16.896 (cf Fig. 19).*

4 *Early dumps 16.897, 16.898, 16.891, 16.888/889 in surface 16.890 at the eastern end of the trench (cf Figs 16–18). Viewed from grid East.*

6 *Early dumps 16.897 (left) and 16.898 (right); the cup P652 had been removed in 1985 (cf Fig. 18). The arrow on the board points to True North.*

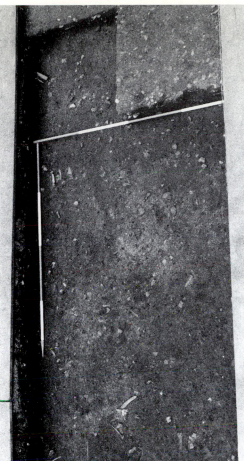

8 Refuse including bone concentration 16.873, pot groups and burnt clay 16.875 on the surface of 16.872/876 in the eastern half of the trench (cf Figs 20 and 21).

9 The surface of context 16.872 in the western half of the trench showing burnt clay patches 16.884 and 16.885 (cf Fig. 20).

ERB 85
AREA 16
CONTEXT 873
GRID 5612
BONE GROUP

11 Bone concentration 16.873 and part of pot group 16.866 (right); (cf Fig. 21).

ERB 86
AREA 16
CONTEXT 900
GRID 5512
PIT

10 Feature 16.900: the top fill has been excavated in the northern half to reveal slumped clods of the flanking burnt clay 16.899 (cf Fig. 14).

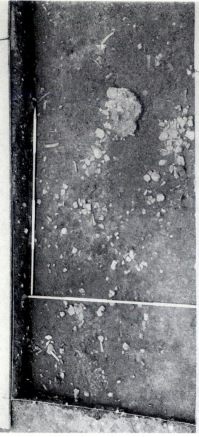

12 *Detail of the south section showing burnt flint cluster 16.874 and large bone material in 16.890 beneath.*

13 *Refuse on surface of 16.849 and 16.865 in the eastern half of the trench (cf Figs. 23 and 24).*

14 *The surface of context 16.836 east with pot groups, burnt clay and sterile clay 16.830 in the bottom left hand corner (cf Fig. 25).*

15 *The surface of context 16.836 west with pot groups and other refuse (cf Figs 24 and 28).*

16 *Pot group 16.862 overlain by burnt flint cluster 16.861 and surrounded by abandoned stone equipment (cf Figs 23 and 24). All on surface 16.849/16.865.*

17 *Burnt clay dump 16.845, pot group 16.852 (left) and pebble pounder (cf Figs 24 and 31).*

18 *The surface of context 16.829 with 16.830 beginning to show in the bottom left corner (cf Fig. 33).*

19 *The two cups from stratigraphic unit H, P651 and P652.*

20 *Equipment used in the preparation of flint temper for pottery production in Area 16 East. Left: pebble pounder S213, lower quernstone S222 and partially crushed flint from 16.868 57/12; top right: pottery 'tray' 16.862 and contained burnt flint 16.861; bottom right: broken pebble pounder S214 and crushed burnt flint cache 16.883.*

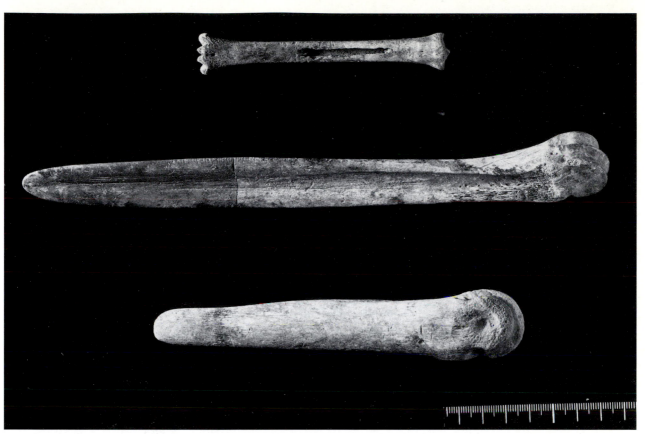

21 *Bone tools probably used for burnishing pottery; from top to bottom: B21, B19 (showing tally marks), B20.*

22 *Antler handle B22 in situ.*

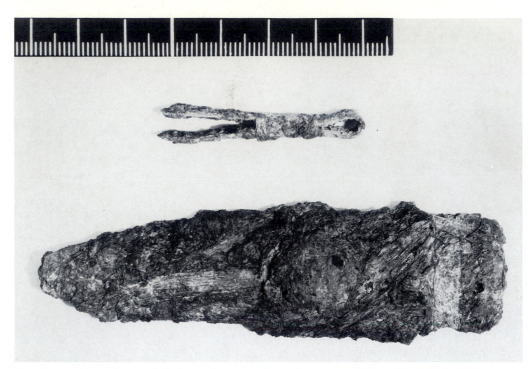

23 *Bronze objects with attached mineral-impregnated organics: tweezers M24 and knife blade M20; organics have been cleaned off a strip towards the broken end.*

24 *Coprolitic material from Area 16 East: top left to bottom right 1985 sf 136, 197, 199, 184, 198, 196.*